Women and Chinese Patriarchy

Submission, Servitude and Escape

But can we ever hear women who live in other worlds – worlds which have been subjected to white imperialist domination – in the voices of Third World women themselves? Of course there can be no pre–given unmediated experience of women in either the Third World or the West. All understandings are filtered through our theoretical positions. There is no easy answer to the dilemma of theoretical imperialism, of the need to avoid imposing our own agendas on other women's experiences (Chilla Bulbeck, p. 88).

Women and Chinese Patriarchy

Submission, Servitude and Escape

Edited by Maria Jaschok and Suzanne Miers

Hong Kong University Press

Zed Books Ltd
London and New Jersey

Women and Chinese Patriarchy was first published in 1994
by:

Hong Kong, China, Taiwan and South-East Asia
Hong Kong University Press, 139 Pokfulam Road, Hong Kong.

Rest of the World
Zed Books Ltd, 7 Cynthia Street, London N1 9JF, UK, and
165 First Avenue, Atlantic Highlands, New Jersey 07716, USA.

Cover designed by Andrew Corbett.
Laserset by Keith Addison, Hong Kong.
Printed and bound in the United Kingdom
by Biddles Ltd, Guildford and King's Lynn.

A catalogue record for this book is
available from the British Library.

US CIP data is available from the Library of Congress.

Hong Kong, China, Taiwan and South-East Asia
ISBN 962 209 361 2 Pb

Rest of the World
ISBN 1 85649 125 0 Hb
ISBN 1 85649 126 9 Pb

Contents

Part I: Introduction

1. Women in the Chinese Patriarchal System: Submission, Servitude, Escape and Collusion

By Maria Jaschok and Suzanne Miers

Part II: The Spectrum of Chinese Female Roles in a Changing World

2. Girls' Houses and Working Women: Expressive Culture in the Pearl River Delta, 1900–41 25

By Rubie S. Watson

Contributors

Claire Chiang has an M.Phil. in Sociology from Hong Kong University. She is currently engaged in research for the Centre of Advanced Studies at the National University of Singapore. Her main research interests are early Chinese female immigrants to Singapore and Chinese entrepreneurship. She is co-authoring *Stepping out: Chinese Entrepreneurs in Singapore*, and *The Role of Religion in Entrepreneurship* and has several articles in progress.

James Hayes served in the Hong Kong civil service from 1956–88. He has a Ph.D. from the University of London and was president of the Hong Kong Branch of the Royal Asiatic Society from 1983–90. He is currently an Honorary Research Fellow at the Centre of Asian Studies, Hong Kong University. He is the author of *The Hong Kong Region 1859–1911: Institutions and Leadership in Town and Countryside*, Hamden, Archon Books 1977; and *The Rural Communities of Hong Kong: Studies and Themes*, Hong Kong, Oxford University Press 1983; and numerous articles. He is now completing a book for Oxford University Press on the Town and District of Tsuen Wan in Hong Kong's New Territories.

Maria Jaschok has an M.A. in Chinese Sociology and Anthropology and a Ph. D. in Modern Chinese History from the School of Oriental and African Studies, University of London, as well as a diploma in Modern Chinese language. From 1981-87 she was a Lecturer in the graduate school at Zhongshan University, Guangzhou. After a period at Hong Kong University and at Long Island University's Hong Kong Centre for Chinese Studies, she is currently Vice-President of the International Institute of Women's Studies, Zhengzhou University, China. She teaches Chinese History and Politics as well as Women's Studies, and is responsible for the university's undergraduate programmes in Taipei, and in Hangzhou. She is the author of *Concubines and Bondservants*, London, Zed Books 1988, and a number of articles. She edited *How History Turns into Nature: A History of the Women of Hong Kong*, proceedings of the 1988 workshop on women's history, Centre of Asian Studies, Hong Kong University, Hong Kong Council of Women publication 1989.

Koh Choo Chin was born in Malaysia and speaks several Chinese dialects. She was appointed a Lady Investigator in the Singapore Social Welfare Department in 1948. Her work included meeting immigrant ships to determine whether incoming Chinese women and girls were coming of their own free will; or, if they were children, whether they were being imported by genuine adoptive parents or other relatives, or whether they were destined to become prostitutes or *mui tsai* (females sold into domestic servitude). In suspicious cases the girls were either put in a home or allowed to live with their importers subject to visits from Mrs Koh and other members of the department. Similarly the department raided brothels to rescue under-age prostitutes. Mrs Koh became Lady Inspector in 1953 and in 1957 she became the first After Care officer in Singapore. She retired in 1966.

Sarah Mason has a Ph.D. from the University of Illinois. She was visiting Professor at Zhongshan University, Guangzhou in 1986–7, and Assistant Professor of History at the University of Minnesota, Morris 1989–90. She is the author of *Training Southeast Asian Refugee Women for Employment: Public Policies and Community Programs, 1975–1985*, Minneapolis: Center for Urban and Regional Affairs, University of Minnesota 1986; and co-author of *The Hmong Resettlement Study*, Washington, D.C., U.S. Department of Health and Human Services, 1984. She has also written a number of articles.

Suzanne Miers has a Ph.D. from the University of London. She is Emeritus Professor of History at Ohio University. She specialised in African history. She also taught cross-cultural interdisciplinary courses on slavery and on women's history. She was Assistant Lecturer at the University of Malaya (now the National University of Singapore) from 1955 to 1958, where she taught Southeast Asian and Indian history. She was Visiting Lecturer in African History at the University of Wisconsin in 1967-68 and 1969-70. She is the author of *Britain and the Ending of the Slave Trade*, Longmans 1975, and numerous articles. She is the co-editor of *Slavery in Africa*, Wisconsin 1977, and *The End of Slavery in Africa*, Wisconsin 1988. She is currently writing a book on the suppression of slavery in the twentieth century. Her chapter is based on interviews with Janet Lim, who published her autobiography, *Sold for Silver*, Collins, in 1958. Janet Lim was sold as a child in China and imported into Singapore as a *mui tsai*. After years of abuse, she escaped and was educated at the Zenana Missionary School in Singapore. She became a nurse. After the Second World War, she became the matron of a children's hospital in Singapore. She married an Australian doctor and now lives in Brisbane.

Elizabeth Sinn has a Ph.D. from Hong Kong University where she has lectured on modern Chinese intellectual history. She is currently Resources Officer and Honorary Lecturer in the Department of History, Hong Kong University. She is the author of *Power and Charity: The Early History of the Tung Wah Hospital, Hong Kong*, Hong Kong, Oxford University Press 1989; and of numerous articles. She is the editor of *Between East and West: Aspects of Social and Political Development in Hong Kong*, Hong Kong, Centre of Asian Studies Hong Kong University 1990. She co-edited *Research Materials for Hong Kong Studies*, Hong Kong, Centre of Asian Studies Hong Kong University 1984, and *Labour Movement in a Changing Society: The Experience of Hong Kong*, Hong Kong, Centre of Asian Studies Hong Kong University 1988. She has been commissioned to write the history of the Bank of East Asia and is engaged in a number of other research projects on Hong Kong history.

Carl Smith was a Lecturer in Theology at Chung Chi College, the Chinese University of Hong Kong, from 1962 to 1983 and Vice President of the Hong Kong Branch of the Royal Asiatic Society. He is the author of *Chinese Christians:*

Elites, Middlemen and the Church in Hong Kong, Hong Kong, Oxford University Press 1986, and co-author of *Hong Kong Going and Gone*, Hong Kong, Royal Asiatic Society Photographic Survey Series no. 1, 1980). He has written some 50 articles and is a well known authority on the history of Hong Kong.

James Warren has a Ph.D. from the Australian National University. He has held teaching appointments at Yale University and the Australian National University. He is currently Associate Professor of Southeast Asian Modern History at Murdoch University, Western Australia. He is the author of a number of books on the social and economic history of Southeast Asia including *The Sulu Zone, 1768–1898: The Dynamics of External Trade, Slavery and Ethnicity in the Transformation of a Southeast Asian Maritime State*, 1981; *Rickshaw Coolie: A People's History of Singapore (1880–1940)*, Singapore: Oxford University Press 1986; and *At the Edge of Southeast Asian History*, Quezon City, New Day Publishers 1987; *Ah Ku and Karayuki-San: Prostitution and Singapore Society, 1870–1940* forthcoming.

Rubie S. Watson has a Ph.D. in Anthropology from the London School of Economics. She studied Cantonese at Yale University and Mandarin at the School of Oriental and African Studies, London University. She now holds a joint appointment as Associate Professor in the Departments of Anthropology and History at the University of Pittsburgh. She was visiting Professor at Zhongshan University in 1985. She was Associate Director of the Asian Studies Program at the University of Pittsburgh 1984–88. She has conducted extensive field research in Hong Kong and Guangdong. She is the author of *Inequality Among Brothers: Class and Kinship in South China*, Cambridge University Press 1985, and of numerous articles. She co-edited *Marriage and Inequality in Chinese Society*, Berkeley, University of California Press 1991.

Preface

The idea of this book took root in 1987 when I went to Hong Kong to do research on the Chinese practice of buying little girls, known as *mui tsai*, as servants.[1] Although this had been denounced as slavery and had been the subject of controversy in Britain in the 1920s and 1930s, as well as of discussion at various League of Nations anti-slavery committees, very little had been published on it. When I discovered that Maria Jaschok had written a doctoral dissertation on *mui tsai* and concubinage in Hong Kong, I went to Guangzhou, where she was teaching at Zhongshan University, to discuss it with her. Sarah Mason, then a visiting professor at the same university, joined us for dinner and, as we talked, the possibility dawned on me that we might publish a book on forms of bondage among Chinese women. They received the suggestion with enthusiasm and Maria Jaschok and I immediately began the long process of defining the scope of the volume and recruiting contributors.

From the start we decided that these should include people with personal experience of the institutions we were analysing as well as scholars. This led me to Brisbane to interview Janet Lim, who had been sold as a child in China and imported into Singapore as a *mui tsai*. She is an outstanding example of a woman who managed against all the odds to change her fate, first by having the initiative to escape while still a young girl, then by the courage which enabled her to survive terrible years as a prisoner-of-war of the Japanese, and finally by the determination with which she pursued her career as a nurse, ending as the matron of a children's hospital in Singapore. She even defied the social stigma that haunts all former *mui tsai* by publishing a book about her experiences. My chapter in this volume is entirely based on her account and could not have been written without her generous collaboration. We have to thank her for being willing to discuss what was a very sad period in her life.

I was also fortunate enough to be put in touch with Koh Choo Chin, who was a government social worker during the two decades when Singapore evolved from a British colony into a prosperous independent nation. She had firsthand experience of the problems facing women and girls at the time and of the implementation of official policies to protect them. The work was testing but she found her vocation rescuing ill-treated *mui tsai* and *san po tsai* (little daughters-in-law), saving women and girls from prostitution, and helping them to solve their problems. We are most grateful to her for her account of her work which is an invaluable addition to our book.

Then began the arduous process of recruiting the scholars whose contributions we wanted. In the process the final shape of the book emerged, bearing the imprint of the diverse personalities and differing scholarly approaches of our contributors, some of whom took part in a panel organised by Maria Jaschok at the 12th conference of the International Association of Historians of Asia, held at Hong Kong University in 1991.

Our academic contributors all have a strong commitment to the subject through personal involvement with China, Hong Kong or Singapore, either through birth and nationality or through living and working in East Asia. We have to thank them for their patience during the six years this book has been in progress.

Inevitably the scope of the volume changed. The focus was broadened to include all forms of submission and servitude rather than just *mui tsai* and prostitution – the two types of exploitation which most nearly approached slavery in the Western sense. This has enabled us to put these more extreme forms into the context of the status of Chinese women as a whole. We could not recruit authors who had done research in parts of China other than Guangdong and Yunnan, and most of our studies deal with Chinese communities outside the country. Nevertheless, we have been able to cover a wide variety of institutions, and, we believe, present a picture of the lives of poorer Chinese women from the early 19th to the middle of the 20th century. We hope other studies will fill the inevitable gaps in this one.

I owe a great debt to Professor Mary Turnbull, who gave me invaluable help in Hong Kong, and to Dr Elizabeth Sinn who introduced me to Maria Jaschok and aided me in many other ways. Mrs Yoke-Lan Wicks of the National Library, Singapore, not only gave me generous hospitality in Singapore, but she and her staff traced Janet Lim and put me in touch with Miss Malini Menon, then Assistant Director of the Residential Care and Aftercare Section of the Children and Youth Services of the Ministry of Community Development. Miss Menon led me to Mrs Koh Choo Chin, and also produced valuable primary sources. Miss Lilly Tan and her staff at the National Archives of Singapore gave me advice and help in tracking down documents. I also received useful suggestions from Dr Paul Kratoska of the Department of History, National University of Singapore, and Mrs P. Lim Pui Huen of the Institute of Southeast Asian Studies, Singapore.

Maria Jaschok is grateful for the assistance provided by the staff of the Basel Mission Society, the Rhodes Library, Oxford, to whom I am also indebted, and the Marburg Mission. In Marburg in particular she received the kindest and most hospitable treatment from Herr Reinhold Abraham and the Marburg Mission sisters. Herr Abraham proved an invaluable go-between for encounters with the former missionary Pfarrer Dietrich, a most knowledgeable and erudite man, and with Sister Liu and other members of the Protestant community in Yunnan. Sisterly support came from Tessa Stewart and Annegret Jaschok-Kroth. Finally, Frau Hildegard Jaschok, intrigued by her daughter's research in German missionary work in China, proved herself an expert on the deciphering of handwritten German gothic script.

Suzanne Miers
Ohio University

Notes

1. This was for a book on slavery in the 20th century now in progress.

Glossary

(c.)	Cantonese	
(h.)	Hakka	
(m.)	Mandarin (pinyin)	
(mal.)	Malay	

ah ku (c.)	阿姑	traditional form of address used for prostitutes in Singapore society
ah so (c.)	阿嫂	form of address for elder brother's wife
Amah Jie (c.)	阿媽姐	lit., Elder Sister Amah, familiar form of address used with older servants
bao juan (m.)	寶卷	religious literature which contains 'precious' core tenets of a religious society
bao liang ju (m.)	保良局	Society for the Protection of the Innocent (known as the Society for the Protection of Women and Children) in Hong Kong
buluojia (m.)	不落家	a practice popular in South China whereby married women delayed residence in their husband's home for a number of years (length of delay varied from village to village)
cai tang (m.)	菜堂	vegetarian halls which offered a home to many zi shu nu, sworn spinsters
cha gwo (c.)	茶果	Hakka-style cakes
da po (m.) daaih pouh (c.)	大婆	senior wife
dan jia (m.)	蛋家	Tanka, a marginalised boat people which could be found in the Southern provinces of China
faan ngoi ka (c.)	返外家	visiting one's mother's family, usually on special occasions

fung shui (c.)	風水	lit., wind water, the principles of the science of fung shui require that an all-pervasive spirit, ch'i, must be allowed to animate, without obstruction by natural or artificial objects, nature and all of its elements
ga chong (c.)	嫁妝	dowry
ga po (c.)	家婆	mother-in-law
gai shiu yan (c.)	介紹人	go-between
guaiyou (m.)	拐誘	'kidnap' by enticement
guan di (m.)	關帝	martial god, god of war
gupowu (m.)	姑婆屋	houses where those women lived who had vowed life-long spinsterhood (the zi shu nu)
gum shan (c.) jin shan (m.)	金山	lit., Gold Mountain (San Francisco and the gold fields of Western USA), emigrants' fantasies of riches awaiting them in the New World
haam sui mui (c.)	咸水妹	lit., Salt Water Girls, women plying their trade on the waters, a name under which prostitutes serving Westerners became known
hsien (m.)	縣	county
hunyinfa yundong (m.)	婚姻法運動	a series of campaigns to implement the Marriage Law, 1951 to 1953
jimui (c.)	姊妹	sworn sisters
jia zhang (m.)	嫁妝	Mandarin equivalent for ga chong
jiaoshi (m.)	教士	missionary
ka kung ka po, tak tsui [nan zi de] lo po	家公家婆 得罪男子 家老婆	words attributed to a bird's song in Cantonese folklore, denoting the bad treatment commonly accorded by parents-in-law to their son's wife

kai (c.)	髻	hair worn in a bun
kam kai (c.)	金髻	gold hairpin used in sheung tau ceremony
kapala (mal.)	工頭	lit., the head, here refers to the head or chief contractor
kongchu (amaksan) (c.)	公豬	a sold prostitute with no rights over the disposal of her own person
Kuan Yin (m.)	觀音	the Goddess of Mercy
kwai po (c.)	龜婆	a female brothel-keeper (Singapore)
Lai Di (m.)	來弟	lit., come younger brother, the name of Lai Di was commonly given to a girl adopted to 'bring in' a long-awaited son
lai kam (c.)	禮金	the bride price, handed over by the bridegroom's family upon entry into her new family
lai see (c.)	利是	so-called 'lucky money' contained in a red envelope given to children and the unmarried on festive occasions
lao renjia (m.)	老人家	form of address conveying a respectful but loving familiarity
li jin (m.)	禮金	Mandarin equivalent for lai kam
lo kui chai (c.)	老舉寨	whore house – derived from lo kui, meaning 'whore' (Singapore)
matze (c.)	媽姐	so-called 'black and white amahs' — in reference to the typical amah's dress
mai menkou (m.)	買門口	lit., to buy a threshold, a practice whereby wage-earning and far-sighted single women bought access to ancestral worship, and independence, through the purchase of a surrogate bride for their intended but rejected husbands-to-be

mei zi (m.) mui tsai/jai (c.)	妹仔	a young girl owned by a family not her kin worked as a domestic drudge until the owners disposed of her in marriage or in any other way they saw fit
ming mai, ming mai (m.)	明買明賣	legitimate and open purchase and sale (of persons)
Nan Yang (Nanyang) (m.)	南洋	an old name for southeast Asia
nei ren (m.)	內人	women whose identity is derived from their confinement to the domestic sphere, who are 'inside persons'
ng ka p'ei (c.)	五加皮	a popular Cantonese wine
pau chai (c.)	炮寨	working-class brothels offering on-demand sex (Singapore)
pau po (c.)	炮婆	prostitutes working in the pau chai, rudimentary brothels, catering to labourers
ping chai (c.)	平寨	equality in status between a husband's two wives
ping kam (c.)	聘金	betrothal money paid out by the bridegroom's family
pipa (m.)	琵琶	a traditional Chinese plucked string instrument
pipa tsai (c.)	琵琶仔	a female musician, owned often by an elderly woman or a pimp, who also provided sexual services
Po Leung Kuk (c.)	保良局	see bao liang ju
pongnin (c.)	擋年	lit., assist for a term of years, women pawned or hired to a brothel (Singapore)
qie (m.)	妾	a concubine, or minor wife
sai pouh (c.)	細婆	Cantonese equivalent of qie

san chu pai (c.)	神主牌	an ancestral tablet
san cong (m.)	三從	a woman's Three Obediences: owed to her father, her husband, her son
san gu (m.)	三姑	Third Paternal Aunt
san ka (c.)	身價	lit., body money which is handed over to the natal family of the san po tsai upon her transfer to the future husband's household, mostly used in adult marriage
san po tsai (c.) sim pu tsai (h.)	新抱仔	a daughter-in-law raised in the family of her future husband from a tender age, when of age she would assume the official status of a daughter-in-law with the sheung tau ceremony
Shen (m.)	神	a god
sheung tau (c.)	上頭	a ritual in which a decorated hat was placed on the head of the san po tsai , denoting her change in status to that of a married woman
shu qi/shu ti (m.)	梳起	a ceremonial combing up of a woman's hair, marking her new status as a sworn spinster called zi shu nu
shang jie bai (m.)	上契拜	the vow of life-long, all-defying solidarity with a sworn sister
sifang qian (m.)	私房錢	a married woman's private fund, in large part derived from her dowry
sik fu (c.)	媳婦	a daughter-in-law
sin pui (c.)	先配	this term refers to the intended wife (commonly used in genealogies) who died before marriage
singkeh/sin-ke (c.)	新客	lit., new guests, meaning depends on context, here refers to newly-arrived migrant workers

sui (m.)	歲	Chinese custom of reckoning age whereby the day of birth is counted as a first birthday
ta pau (m.)	大炮	a client, such as a labour, sailor or soldier who patronised pau chai
Ta Pe Gong (m.)	大伯公	Earth-God
tai kam (c.)	大妗（姐）	the traditional profession of a bride attendant
tai pang po (c.)	大幫婆	brothel servants (Singapore)
tanggung (mal.)	擔光	to guarantee someone
tap tang (c.)	搭燈	lit., sharing the lamp, a voluntary prostitute with no debt to pay off (Singapore)
tau shik (c.)	頭飾	the bridal headdress worn in the sheung tau ceremony
Tien (m.)	天	Heaven
tong (c.)	（私會）黨	secret society or triad: the union of heaven, earth and man, the philosophical concept that underlies the Chinese secret societies and brotherhood
tong-yang-xi (m.)	童養媳	literary version of more colloquial san po tsai (c.), an infant or child daughter-in-law
ximin (m.)	細民	hereditary slaves
xian shui mei (m.)	咸水妹	see haam sui mui
xiao (m.)	孝	filial piety owed to parents and parents-in-law
xiao po (m.)	小婆	Mandarin equivalent of sai pouh; also equivalent to qie
xiao xi (m.)	小喜	lit., Little Happiness, reference here is to a girl taken into a family destined to become a san po tsai

xin ke (m.)	新客	see singkeh
yan yat (c.)	人日	the second birthday celebration on the 7th day of the first month of the lunar year following the year of birth
yatou (m.)	丫頭	a slave girl, often used interchangeably with mui tsai
Yu Jie (m.)	玉姐	Elder Sister Jade
yuen pui (c.)	元配	replacement wife in cases where first wife (sin pui) died
zi shu nu (m.)	自梳女	lit., a woman who combs up her own hair in the ceremony of shu qi, a sworn spinster

Maps

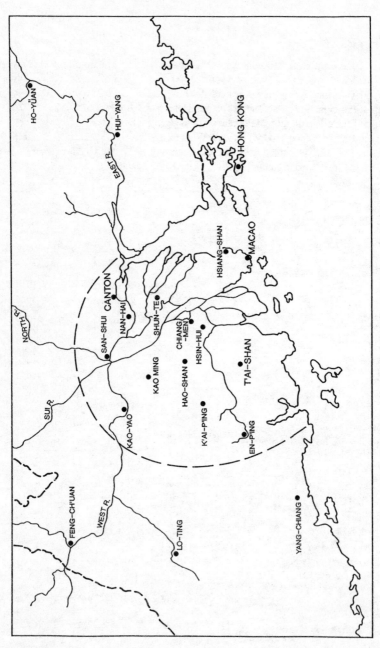

The Cantonese emigrant area of China

The Ah Ku in Southeast Asia c. 1900

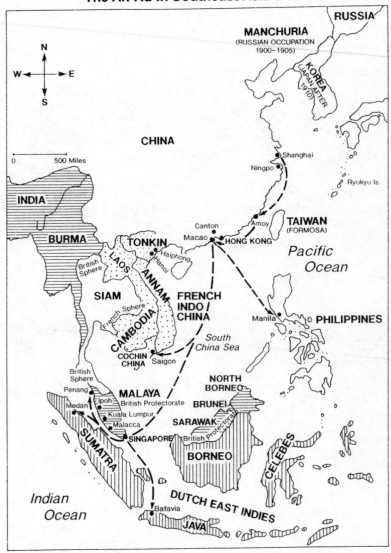

•   *major ports and cities where Ah Ku resided in Southeast Asia*

--   *pattern of traffic in Cantonese women and girls*

▤   *British colonial territory*

▥   *Dutch colonial territory*

░   *French colonial territory*

Part I: Introduction

1. Women in the Chinese Patriarchal System: Submission, Servitude, Escape and Collusion

By Maria Jaschok and Suzanne Miers

Introduction

The two accounts which follow have been chosen for the light they throw on the position of women in a patriarchal Chinese household in the late 19th and early 20th centuries.

The Account of Poon Choi-kun

(Interviewed by Maria Jaschok, Hong Kong 1989)

Poon Choi-kun thinks she may be around 70. She must have been born in Guangdong Province not too far from Hong Kong, where she was sent by her kidnappers to be sold for about a hundred Hong Kong dollars.

'When I was little, I was bought for working' – this is how she begins the story of her life.

My friend Mrs Anna Lee (pseudonym) employs her from time to time as a gardener. She has taken pity on Poon Choi-kun, who supports herself and her sickly husband by selling aluminium cans and empty bottles collected from garbage pits. Mrs Lee gives Poon a generous wage and treats her kindly. But what induces her to talk about herself is the knowledge that Anna Lee is herself the descendant of a woman sold as a child – a background which overshadows her life as much as it has overshadowed Poon's. Anna Lee's grandmother was re-sold by her first owner into a wealthy household. She became the concubine of an old but still powerful man and was thus able to acquire for herself and her descendants riches far beyond her natal family's station. Poon's life story, however, is one of unrelieved drudgery, and is thus perhaps more representative of the fate which befell the majority of *mui tsai* (girls sold into slavery).

Poon Choi-kun arrived at Anna Lee's home for the interview at the agreed time, wearing her best clothes. Her feet bare, she sat opposite us in the large sitting room with its imposing rosewood furniture and oil paintings of the ancestor who changed the fortune of the family and came to occupy a position of power and influence in Hong Kong society. Poon's plastic sandals sat on the step outside the servants' entrance at the back of the house as she began her tale.

1

The mistress who bought her for $100 from a go-between had told her she was an only child. She must have been four or five when she was kidnapped from her home village, where she had lived with her father.

She was old enough to work. She cleaned the master's house, and did the shopping and laundry. The work was hard and never-ending as there was no other *mui tsai* or servant in the family. She remembers being tired all the time, always exhausted and slightly ill.

She also served the master's No. 2 concubine as a personal maid. This was the youngest of the master's wives and it was she who had bought Poon, and who ran the household. She had herself been a *mui tsai*. She was strict but fair, and made sure the child had enough to eat. The master was a small trader in firewood. He died soon after Poon was bought and she does not remember much about him.

Poon never thought of running away. Where would she have gone? She had no relatives. She did not really know anyone outside the family she served. She had heard about the Po Leung Kuk (an orphanage for girls) but never wanted to go there. She did not know any other *mui tsai*. She simply worked, and was fairly content. At least she was not hungry: her owners allowed her to eat with them. Once a year she was given a set of new clothing, and sometimes the mistress would give her a cast-off garment.

She worked as a *mui tsai* for about 15 years. During this time she never heard of any law in Hong Kong forbidding transactions in *mui tsai*. Only now, in 1989, did she hear of the compulsory registration of *mui tsai* (in terms of a 1929 ordinance), of a mandatory wage for *mui tsai* and of prohibitions on the purchase of new *mui tsai*. Nor had she ever heard of inspectors employed by the Secretary for Chinese Affairs to oversee the implementation of the 1929 ordinance, let alone ever seen one.[1] Poon's mistress died, and soon afterwards the mistress's daughter married Poon off to a man much older than herself. It was arranged through a go-between employed by the bridegroom, a tailor whose trade had taken him to the household of Poon's owners, to whom he paid about HK$200 as a bride price. Poon received no dowry – the daughter merely gave her a set of clothing when she left the house. Poon thinks this was a better deal for her husband than he would have got from the Po Leung Kuk, where many a man wanting a young and hardworking wife went to select his spouse.

Poon's views were not asked, and the marriage was unhappy. Her owners had at least fed her adequately, but her husband was mean. She had to work hard for him and toil in the fields, which she had not had to do before. Later she worked as a carrier coolie on building sites. Her husband was always ailing, always needing more money for opium than he could make. So her drudgery continued.

It was also an unlucky marriage, as Poon could not have children. They adopted a son, and Poon shouldered the burden of supporting the family. Her husband comes from a Hakka background, which, according to Poon, means that the women have a particularly harsh lot to bear, working harder than the men.

Now she is old, and still working from morning to night. She and her husband live in a small hut near Aberdeen on Hong Kong Island. They have lived there for many years among people equally impoverished, equally disadvantaged. But Poon Choi-kun has never told anyone the story of her life. She doesn't want them to know. They would look down upon her for never having known her parents and for having been sold like a beast of burden. She would have no face left were people to find out about her past.

The Account of Edith Wong Moon-ho
(Interviewed by Maria Jaschok, Hong Kong 1989)

Edith Wong[2] and I have a superficial acquaintance from sitting together in seminars or conferences. But she trusted me enough to give me her views and the history of her family, who have owned *mui tsai* for many generations, and taken many generations of concubines from their ranks.

She comes from an extended Chinese family of scholars and successful merchants, with many households. When she was a child, in the 1920s, her mother, the No. 2 concubine, and her stepmothers,[3] concubines No. 3 and No. 4, lived in the same house in Hong Kong. Her father's first wife, the *daaih pouh*, lived in the ancestral village on the West River, not far from Guangzhou (Canton), where she had many *mui tsai* helping her. Apart from household tasks, they worked in the fields, sowing, planting and harvesting.

Although her earliest personal recollections are of the 1920s, Edith Wong has listened to family tales all her life, and her grandparents' generation seems as familiar to her as if she had herself lived in the household of her eldest grandmother.

Edith's grandfather was born in the 1870s. His wife had borne him only a daughter, but he was initially reluctant to take a *sai pouh* (a concubine) – perhaps he hoped sons would be still be born. But his wife insisted on it as it was her duty to ensure that there were sons to continue her husband's family line, and she felt it would give her face to initiate the action. At the same time she looked out for her own interests. She chose a *mui tsai* from a poor family, a particularly plain girl who would produce an heir but pose no threat to her control over the household. Wives preferred *mui tsai* they had themselves moulded into submissiveness by years of servitude. This *sai pouh* produced the eldest son of the family, Edith Wong's father. However, once her grandfather got used to having a concubine, even an ugly one, he had no hesitation in taking more. Finally he had one wife and five concubines, and some of the later ones were really good-looking.

The grandfather spent time in Shanghai managing the family business, while the *daaih pouh* looked after the estate and cared for her parents-in-law. But she did not know how to read and write and her business associates cheated her, so the first daughter-in-law had to be educated. Thus when Edith's father married, his wife stayed with her mother-in-law to help manage the estate, while he went on business to Shanghai and elsewhere, wherever grandfather sent him. Eldest grandmother engaged a village tutor, an old man, to teach first daughter-in-law to read and write. It was very rare for a woman of her generation to be literate. But she too produced only a daughter, Edith's eldest (half) sister.

Her father's No. 1 concubine was again a former *mui tsai* from a poor family who, in line with family custom, lived with his wife to help her run the estate. It is said that the wife bought her to lure the absent husband back to the village. But she died soon after the birth of her only child, again a girl, Edith's second (half) sister, who was brought up by the No. 2 concubine, Edith's mother.

Edith's mother, also a former *mui tsai*, was bought from a Cantonese family in Shanghai where she had attended to the needs of the *daaih pouh*. She was bought because Edith's father needed someone to comfort him on his travels, and to keep him company in Shanghai and Harbin, where he did business for some years.

It was she who chose the No. 3 concubine. She bought a *mui tsai* when visiting relatives in Macau, because Edith's father was by then spending so many nights away from the family that her mother decided he needed a younger concubine to keep him at home. But, like the senior wife before her, Edith's mother discovered that the ruse did not work – he did not return to the household. Soon afterwards he decided to move to Hong Kong because of violence on the mainland.[4] He thought the British colony would be a safer abode for the family.

He bought several properties in Hong Kong. When the family moved there, they discovered he had a hitherto unknown concubine he had taken without bothering to consult his *daaih pouh* and the other concubines. But there were by then already so many concubines that it hardly mattered.

This latest addition moved into Edith's mother's household, but first she had to perform the tea ceremony to admit her officially into the family. The *daaih pouh* was visiting Hong Kong. She and the concubines sat in a row and the new concubine, to express her submission, handed each of them a bowl of tea, presented with both hands. In families where the wife was particularly kind, she might not sit down for this ceremony. This was up to her. A wife had great power over a concubine and could humble her in many ways, making her go through humiliating rituals or assigning her a 'cheap' name.

As the most senior concubine, Edith's mother was the housekeeper and generally in charge. Yet she was naturally timid; only by virtue of her many years as the husband's favourite did she enjoy a position of authority. Also, the eldest mother, the *daaih pouh*, lived on the country estate, and was generous. Even on her annual visits of a few weeks, she let Edith's mother carry on and did not seek to interfere.

Concubines who had once been *mui tsai* were treated differently from those who came from poor backgrounds but had not been sold before becoming concubines. The latter had more standing. Also, the status of a former *mui tsai*-turned-concubine in a family depended on the status of her former owner. If she had been sold into a wealthy and well-respected family, she would be seen as having acquired the sort of education that marks a respectable woman. If her previous owner was of low standing, this would reinforce her treatment as a base creature. If any concubine, even one who had once been a *mui tsai*, bore a son, her standing in the family became more secure. She need no longer fear being sold at the slightest whim of the family's senior members.

The Wong family led a rather relaxed life. Of course, not every household was as liberal. Yet Edith's father was a traditional Chinese scholar who would have nothing to do with domestic life. He lived in a different sphere, isolated from the rest of the family. He did not know it was a parent's duty to get to know his children. Instead, servants were entrusted with their care. They saw him only twice a day, when they went to bid him good morning, and when they had to report to him on their return from school in the afternoon. He had nothing whatever to do with matters such as the buying of *mui tsai*. They were entirely the concern of the women of the house.

Mui tsai were acquired in different ways. Sometimes they had been abandoned, and knew of no parents. Sometimes their parents had died. Some poor families just wanted one less mouth to feed, and gained some money by selling their daughters. Edith's stepmother and mother each had a *mui tsai*, as a personal maid.

When Edith was a child the family went to their house in Tai Po (Hong Kong, New Territories) for holidays, and if there had been a flood or a drought, a number of weeping women would come to the house wanting to sell their little daughters. If the girls were around eight or nine years old, they would usually be left in the household. At that age they could work, running messages, dusting, and so on.

Mui tsai were brought into Edith's family mostly through servants who were in touch with their home villages. They would have relatives or know of people in financial difficulties. And people knew of the Wong family's wealth and charitable deeds and felt encouraged to approach them for help.

There was no fixed price. Each time a *mui tsai* was acquired the price was negotiated. Edith's mother might suggest a price based on the age of the girl and her work experience. The agreed sum would be handed over in a red packet. Always there was this formality. The girl would be given to the servants to be trained: to the cook, the parlour maid or the washerwoman, depending on the family's needs.

Never was a deed of sale drawn up, a verbal agreement sufficed. In the same way, Chinese merchants of the time did not draw up written contracts.

There were people who traded in children, and parents might be so desperate as to sell their children to these traders. But in Edith's family the purchase was handled as a private matter where parents approached the family either directly or through a family servant. The family was always in touch with the ancestral estate and was well known in the countryside. They also had many contacts in the New Territories where they kept a summer house, only returning to their town house on Hong Kong Island for school terms.

A *mui tsai* would have no money at all – no wages – until she was about 14, when Edith's mother would pay her some pocket money. Once she earned a wage, it increased with her age, and twice a year she would be given new clothes.

The *mui tsai* stayed with the family until she was 18, when Edith's mother or stepmother would ask her what she would like to do. Usually she would want to get married, and a go-between would be hired to find her a husband. *Mui tsai* always married as *daaih pouh*. The family's *mui tsai* were never married off as concubines. (See R. Watson 1991b for a discussion of Chinese forms of marriage).

It was Edith's mother who decided on the future of their *mui tsai*. As a concubine herself, she knew what women in her position had to suffer. She would look for an honest labourer who wanted a wife. As the wife of a labourer, the *mui tsai* would at least have her own household, and be her own mistress. No money was ever exchanged, and the mothers saw to it that there was a proper marriage ceremony, and that the couple were introduced to each other before the marriage – and that they liked each other. Even *mui tsai* who had been bought for domestic work were married to someone they liked. They would always be consulted beforehand. One, about 15 years old, had the habit of standing all night at the window watching the doings of the cats, and the family thought she was a bit unbalanced. It was discovered that she wanted to get married, so she was married off much earlier than the others. A servant's friend who lived in Kowloon was the go-between and introduced the girl to a confectioner's assistant. The *mui tsai* liked him, and they married. But he set up his own business and constantly lost money. Edith Wong was not sure what became of her.

Another *mui tsai* was married to a man in Tai Po. She had been Edith's mother's personal maid and the family stayed in touch with her after the marriage. Her husband was a Hakka, and Cantonese looked down on Hakkas, so her mother had not quite approved of the marriage. But the *mui tsai* was happy. This husband was much luckier in his job and was able to send his daughters abroad, not to study but to marry restaurant owners and waiters in Germany, where they lived for many years. They are quite well off, and she herself is comfortable.

One *mui tsai* did not want to get married, and she stayed on as a paid servant. Her face was pockmarked and she felt she could never get a husband, no one would be interested in her.

Edith's mother kept in touch with former *mui tsai* as a matter of principle. On New Year's Day they would visit the Wong household to pay their respects and bring presents. Edith's mother gave them red packets containing money. So there was some concern for the fate of former *mui tsai*, and the *mui tsai* all liked to stay in touch – they had no other family.

Mui tsai did not usually resent their parents for having sold them. Chinese are realistic people, and a *mui tsai* would know that her parents must have been very poor. It would have been a choice between selling her or letting the whole family starve. Chinese do not resent such things, they understand the difficulties of life.

Edith's family's *mui tsai* were lucky. For most *mui tsai* life was hard. Some families were cruel, their behaviour showing their ill-breeding and lack of education. The sort of home education Chinese valued had to come from the women. Men had nothing to do with such things.

Edith Wong's mother's relationship with the other concubines was cordial. Unlike most of the noisy Cantonese families around them, the household was quiet and harmonious under her influence. It was a large household, with three concubines, each with a personal *mui tsai*, plus the nine children and the servants.

Each *mui tsai* was very loyal to her own mistress. No one in the family believed in being hostile to anyone. Everyone was careful not to cause resentment. Nobody ever raised their voice or made any noise. The children had to take their slippers off in the house to avoid disturbing anyone. Edith's mother had been a *mui tsai* in a good, educated, Cantonese family, and in her father's family there were always men preparing for imperial examinations, so a tranquil way of life was part of the family tradition.

Edith's mother never talked about her past. One does not talk much about inner feelings in Chinese families, and so much remains unknown. What is known comes from other people. It was a hard life for women: illiterate, confined to the house, they could only concern themselves with children and servants. Thankfully, this life is in the past, but it is important to learn more about it.

The Aim of This Book

The two accounts above show how Chinese women from very different backgrounds coped with their allotted roles in life.

Poon Choi-kun suffered the fate of many girls from poor families. She was bought by a family of relatively low status and limited means. Her mistress, while not cruel, was indifferent. After years of faithful service, her reward was to be sold like a commodity to a man old enough to have saved the money her owners demanded. She was not consulted and she gained nothing from the marriage but years of grinding poverty. She produced no son – a disgrace, though a son was adopted. She was but one of a vast pool of girls disposed of by parents or guardians unable or unwilling to spend their resources on mere females. They were bought as servants and were often later sold into marriage or concubinage by owners extracting the last ounce of value from them.

By contrast, Edith Wong's grandmother was born into a well-to-do, conservative family, and in the closing years of the 19th century became the *daaih pouh* of a successful merchant. She bore one child, a daughter. In the patriarchal scheme of things, this should have sealed her fate. A daughter had no place in the patriline, no access to ancestral worship, no right of succession or inheritance. She had thus failed in her principal duty – to bear a male heir. Yet her husband, the head of the family, seemed impervious to ancestral displeasure and was reluctant to take action. It was she who took the initiative by bringing in a pliant and submissive concubine – a *mui tsai* from a poor family, who would not undermine her position but who would safeguard the continuity of her husband's family by bearing the son she could not produce. She thus secured her senior status in the domestic hierarchy since she became the boy's rightful mother, and ensured that she had a son to look after her in her old age. Later, when the son married, she had her daughter-in-law educated, to increase her own efficiency in running the estate. In the next generation, it was Edith's mother, herself a concubine and former *mui tsai*, who took charge of the extended household and her husband's numerous concubines, most of whom she chose in the hope of curtailing his extra-marital affairs and keeping him under her control.

We see in the strategies resorted to by Edith's mother and grandmother what Margery Wolf (1972) calls the imperative to protect the 'uterine family' (a womb-centred one-generation family unit), as opposed to the multi-generation patriline. These strategies, however, depended on the exploitation of a ready supply of women. Concubines acquired for the sexual gratification of the husband were also tools in the hands of these dominant women, who fortified their domestic positions at the expense of females more vulnerable than themselves, from whose ranks came the concubines and *mui tsai*.

However, when her *mui tsai* came of age, Edith's mother broke the accepted pattern by refusing to support concubinage, the very institution which had given her identity, economic security and a high degree of domestic power. Her *mui tsai* were not only consulted about the men they were to marry, they became *daaih pouh*, not concubines. They were given face by the employment of a go-between and the arrangement of a wedding ceremony.

This No. 2 concubine, whose authority over domestic affairs was not disputed even by the *daaih pouh*, who did not hesitate to replenish her husband's supply of sex objects to suit her own needs, brought about a change which promised her former *mui tsai* what she had never enjoyed, a family life without the tension suffered by women in hierarchical polygynous households. This may have been a way of maintaining harmony in the household by keeping up the morale of her remaining *mui tsai*, and of ensuring that desperate parents around the family estates would continue to sell her their daughters. Alternatively her actions may indicate a smouldering resentment at her own situation and a determination, when the opportunity presented itself, not to condemn others to the same fate.

Edith Wong's narrative of three generations of women in her family illustrates their subservient position in the patriarchal order, but it also highlights the wisdom, pragmatism, ruthlessness and compassion, acquiescence and resource-fulness, which allowed them to exert some control over the patriarchal institutions to which they were subjected. Over one hundred years have passed since Edith's grandmother overcame her failure to produce a son by buying a concubine. The change in the lifestyles of grandmother and granddaughter is remarkable. But equally remarkable are the changes brought about by women, like her mother and others who appear in this volume, who were ready to break with tradition and thus alter the pattern of life for themselves and those around them.

However, Edith Wong's account must be treated with caution. Remarkable as is the voice she gives her grandmother and mother, her story is notable for the silence of the concubines and *mui tsai* subordinated to their interests. Empathising with her forebears, she touches only lightly on the women whose meekness and ignorance left them with no control over their destinies. For all the richness of her account, we must consider the position of the narrator in this nexus of relationships – a position which creates its own emphases and omissions.

These two accounts express many of the preoccupations of our book. We seek to show the constraints which grounded Chinese women, outlining their functions and responsibilities while simultaneously presenting life histories of women who challenged their allotted role, on their own initiative or with the aid of outside agencies, or because they were caught up in the social and political changes of their day. The once ubiquitous stereotype of the long-suffering, meek, submissive Chinese woman as simply a victim of family interests, a vision of compliance and self-sacrifice, stands thus revealed for what it is – a stereotype in need of reappraisal and an empirical context.

This book thus contributes to the academic debate of recent years on the accuracy of long-held perceptions of the subordination of the Chinese woman. This debate is itself part of a wider trend which rejects as simplistic and Orientalist earlier constructs of Asian women (for a general debate, see *Inscriptions*, 1988).

Since we are investigating social change, we have focused not only on women trying to change their lives at the grass-roots level but also on the agents involved in changing the position of women. These include Western governments and non-government organisations, such as missionary societies, and individual reformers and feminists, as well as Chinese philanthropic bodies and the Chinese Communist Party (Jaschok; Koh; Mason; Miers; Sinn; Warren; Epilogue). We examine the context of their intervention as well as their motives, perceptions and strategies, which were sometimes rooted in a deep concern for women's welfare but were more often tied to vested political, patriarchal, commercial or ideological interests, which we seek to identify. Moreover, the attention some of our contributors have paid to the personal dynamics of social change has led us to explore the impact these agents of change had on the subsequent fate of the women they sought to help, and to ask how these women now view those who spoke and acted on their behalf (see particularly Jaschok).

The years under discussion were years of rapid political, social and economic change (see *Historical Background*, below), during which the private and public roles of women, and their very perceptions of themselves, were reshaped in complex ways. Careful empirical investigation is needed to determine the extent to which their lives continued to be shaped by Chinese traditional values, and to identify those socio-economic forces which supported, and those which undermined, patriarchal responsibilities, as well as the new opportunities for profit in China's large market in females. Our studies of women as domestic drudges, sex objects and child-bearers (Hayes; Jaschok; Koh; Miers; Sinn; Watson) illustrate the continuing use of women in age-old ways, showing the transmutation and politicisation of these uses in the colonial societies of Hong Kong and Singapore, and in San Francisco, where the emergence of modern commercial opportunities also created new forms of exploitation, most notably the use of women for the sexual servicing of coolies and other immigrants (Koh; Mason; Warren) and of Western and other foreign men far from home (Smith).

Where possible we have included Chinese women's personal accounts of their experiences (Account of Poon Choi-kun, Account of Edith Wong Moon-ho, above; Koh; Lim). We are aware that each person's life is unique, and that there is a delicate balance between contextual analysis and individual narrative. In this respect, it is important to point out that although each chapter is a separate study, they complement each other. Thus Watson's description of women's contribution to the fertile material and spiritual culture of southern China's Pearl River delta region provides the background to Chiang's account of how women migrant workers from that region successfully exploited economic opportunities in Singapore. Sinn's chapter on Chinese patriarchal conceptions of the protection of women as exemplified by the establishment of the Po Leung Kuk (the Chinese home for women in need of protection) is important for an understanding of the comments on the institution in other chapters (Koh; Miers). Koh, Mason and Warren throw light on different aspects of the lives of Chinese prostitutes. Jaschok, Miers and Koh add to our information on *mui tsai*; while Hayes' discussion of early marriage and childhood betrothal may be read in conjunction with Watson's study of Chinese marriage customs. A number of chapters deal with how the various agents of change worked to protect the most vulnerable women (Jaschok; Koh; Sinn). Several show how women themselves were able to change their lives (Chiang; Miers; Smith; Watson).

This volume, therefore, brings together case studies illustrating changes in the position of women in the last 150 years or so. Although limited to South China, Hong Kong, Singapore and San Francisco, they cover a wide variety of women's roles and show women's responses to the changing world in which they lived.

In this also lies our contribution to the historiography of Chinese women. Recent studies have given increasing attention to redressing the 'invisibility' of socially disadvantaged women. The problem is how to bring them 'to voice' – to enable them to speak for themselves in the ongoing process of social continuity and disruption (e.g. Sheridan & Salaff 1984). The impact on women of industriali-sation, modernisation and sexual commoditisation, previously rarely investigated by scholars, has been the subject of only a few publications (e.g. Gronewold 1982; Hershatter 1986, 1991; Honig 1982; R. Watson 1991b). Here we present studies of the lives of some of the most invisible women – the *mui tsai* and prostitutes, on whom the literature is particularly sparse (see Gronewold 1982; Hershatter 1991; Jaschok 1988; Lim 1958; Meijer 1979; Miners 1990; J.L. Watson 1980), and the women migrant workers who left China in their thousands to seek their fortunes overseas, about whom we have almost no information. However, these studies are merely a beginning. We hope they will encourage further research in these little explored fields.

Many of the institutions analysed here still exist, some of them in new and even more oppressive and virulent forms (see Epilogue), not only in China but in much of the Asian region and in other areas of the world. This volume thus sets at least some modern forms of exploitation in their historical context.

Forms of Exploitation

San Po Tsai

Our contributors analyse Chinese forms of marriage and other forms of institu-tionalised servitude. James Hayes discusses early betrothal, focusing on the *san po tsai* in the rural communities of Hong Kong's New Territories. These were little girls transferred from their natal families to the households of future husbands often as young as, or even younger than, themselves. The wedding did not take place until they were able to consummate the union. This 'minor marriage' provided a wife for a son of the receiving family without the normal costly gifts to the bride's family. Hence it was a despised form of marriage found in poor areas where the girl's parents were glad to be relieved of the expenses of rearing her, and the boy's parents gained both a cheap bride and an extra pair of hands. Clearly these children were powerless to influence their fate, and could be trained to be submissive daughters-in-law. Abuses were not uncommon (see Koh). In the normal course of events, however, a *san po tsai*, should she be fortunate enough to produce a son, could expect in her turn to become a mother-in-law, often wielding considerable influence in the family and authority over its female members, although her powers were limited to the domestic sphere. The roots of the institution lay in rural poverty, and it died in the 1960s because the villagers were becoming more prosperous as traditional farming gave way to urbanisation; at the same time, girls (and presumably boys) were better educated, more mobile and increasingly able to take advantage of growing job opportunities and were less willing to submit to arranged marriages.

Mui Tsai

Several chapters deal with *mui tsai*, raising the controversial issue of how we should see this institution. Was it child slavery, as depicted by Western missionaries in China (Jaschok) and the League of Nations slavery committees in the 1930s, and as it is graphically described in this volume by two of its victims, Janet Lim (Miers) and Poon Choi-kun (above)? Or was it a charitable system, enabling poor families to assure the welfare of their daughters by selling them to rich households, who would provide for them while they were young and find them suitable husbands when they grew up? This was how it was viewed by the owners, by the Chinese establishment and by the British authorities in Singapore and Hong Kong (Account of Edith Wong Moon-ho, above; Sinn; Miners 1987 ch. 8), and how it is viewed by the descendants of owners today. Theoretically, the girls were adopted by the recipients, who paid the parents often very small sums. In practice, the girls were often treated not as adopted children but as household drudges. Some suffered unbelievable cruelty, including sexual abuse (Jaschok; Koh; Miers). Moreover, some were sold to dealers and changed hands more than once. They also suffered an indelible social stigma because their families had made money out of them, and this was worse than if they had been abandoned (Miers). They were left with no kin and hence no 'face' in a society where only family ascribes identity. The shame is so great that even now, 60 years after they were sold, most are unwilling to reveal the fact (Account of Poon Choi-kun, above; Koh; Miers).

This institution was widespread in China, where the impoverishment of the peasantry, wars and natural disasters produced a steady supply of girls for sale by destitute or sometimes even greedy parents. It has been suggested that in villages where parents sold their children to local people and could keep an eye on their treatment, the institution may well have worked as the owners depict it and not have been too exploitative (Lebra 1983 p. 14). However, the experiences of Western missionaries who established a home for former *mui tsai* in Yunnan in the 1930s would appear to belie this view (Jaschok). There is certainly plenty of evidence that girls sold far afield often fell into unscrupulous hands.

The sale of *mui tsai* continued in China until the Communist government stamped it out in the 1950s during the campaigns to implement the Marriage Law (1950). However, private information indicates that the practice continued beyond that time, if under a different label. In Hong Kong it was still practised in the New Territories up to the late 1950s (J.L. Watson 1980; Jaschok 1988), as well as in Singapore (Koh), where children were either traded locally or, until the supply dried up, smuggled in from China.

Pipa Tsai (girls sold as entertainers)

Many of the features which characterised the practice of *mui tsai* also applied to *pipa tsai*. Poverty or greed which compelled the family to sell their daughter, sometimes in ignorance of what might befall her in a distant city, coupled with demands in urban Singapore for entertainment, created the *pipa tsai* – girls who played the *pipa*, a traditional musical instrument. Often a matter of luck and a modicum of musical talent brought a girl into this world of entertainment. Perhaps good looks were decisive. In theory a *pipa tsai* was only an entertainer, but Koh suggests that opportunities for hiring such girls out to spend the night with clients were eagerly sought by their owners. The owners were often single women from Guangdong Province, providing an interesting twist to the story of women's search for independence, which was often achieved at the expense of other women. An owner might use a *pipa tsai* both as a source of income and as an adopted daughter who would care for her soul tablet after her death. The boundaries here between outright exploitation, emotional dependence, servitude, and filial submission are especially fluid.

Prostitution

Perhaps the most exploitative form of servitude was – and is – prostitution, often called 'white slavery'. As has been noted, the gender imbalance among Chinese overseas communities led to an extensive traffic in women and even quite young girls. At first this was facilitated by the governments of Singapore and Hong Kong, driven by the need to keep a large coolie population of single males, crucial to the development of the colonies, pacified by the growth of a large sex and entertainment sector (Hoe, n.d.; Miners 1987; Warren). Until the 1930s they selected areas for brothels, registered and licensed them and medically inspected the prostitutes in order to check the spread of venereal disease (Warren; Hoe, n.d.; Miners 1987). Their main interest was in protecting British servicemen rather than Chinese men. James Warren reconstructs the life of prostitutes and examines the organisation of the traffic and of brothels. Poverty and the patriarchal system in China, British labour recruitment practices, the indifference of both the Chinese and British governments, and the lucrative nature of the traffic all conspired to turn prostitutes into marketable commodities. An equally lucrative traffic developed in San Francisco, although the importation of women for 'immoral purposes' was outlawed in 1870 and laws were passed against the employment of minors in brothels in the 1880s (Mason).

A minority of Chinese prostitutes emigrated of their own free will to earn money for their families in China, but most were sold by poverty-stricken parents, kidnapped or lured away by trickery. Many were originally *mui tsai*. They ended up in various forms of bondage. Those sold by their parents often felt bound by filial duty to work off their purchase price (Warren; Lebra 1983 p. 13). By various means brothel owners kept them indebted, trading them off as they grew older (Warren). They usually lived drab lives in miserable conditions with little chance of escape and every chance of contracting disease, a personal tragedy that might lead to their being thrown out on the streets to live out the rest of their short lives as best they could (Jaschok 1981, see particularly p. 139; Hoe, n.d.; Warren).

Ironically, while the use of prostitutes abroad was acceptable in China, as it did not disturb the marriages of male emigrants if and when they returned home, maintaining the purity of marriageable Chinese women both in China and overseas was the subject of draconian patriarchal control (Mason). Prostitution also infringed British concepts of morality, but for many years the colonial governments, fearful of losing the goodwill of their Chinese male subjects, simply sacrificed these women in the economic interests of their territories (Hoe, n.d.; Warren).

Women's Avenues of Escape

Our contributors identify a number of ways in which women sought to better their lot. Some women, like Edith Wong's mother and grandmother, operated within the patriarchal family structure, while others found ways to escape its control and shape their own destinies. At this point, however, we simply know too little about the social dynamics of society in the latter half of the 19th and the first half of the 20th centuries to state with certainty whether they made their own choices or their lives were shaped more by traditional morality in an era of rapid social and economic change.

Zi Shu Nu (non-marrying women, lit. self-combing women)

Rubie Watson, in analysing marriage practices and women's contributions and responses to the economic development of the Pearl River delta of Guangdong, shows how some women were able to marry and thus acquire the status of an ancestress worthy of worship, ensuring themselves a peaceful afterlife, without actually fulfilling their conjugal duties. In this 'compensation marriage' they bought girls, often *mui tsai*, to take their place in the bedroom and the kitchen. In other cases, wage-earning brides delayed going to live with their husbands. Still other women eschewed marriage altogether. In their case the various support groups women developed were particularly important since unmarried women sought security in organisations such as vegetarian halls, Buddhist nunneries, or the houses of sworn sisters.

Haam Sui Mui (protected women)

In the geographical margin of the Pearl River delta, but also in its social and cultural margin, lived the *haam sui mui*, whose gutsy determination to negotiate a better livelihood for themselves led them to live with Western males. This was a risky but sometimes successful strategy for escaping from patriarchal domination (Smith). The economic independence they could gain as a reward for their services enabled some of them to become property owners in Hong Kong, achieving a financial security otherwise unattainable. The cost was social ostracism by both the Chinese and European communities for themselves and their children, who founded some of the Eurasian families in Hong Kong. The risk was that their Western male partners might simply abandon them and their children, in which case they were likely to die in penury, rejected by both their own people and Western society.

Female Migrant Workers

The women Chiang describes in her study of migrant workers in Singapore came from the Pearl River delta. Without depending on men, they found work, places to live, companionship with women like themselves, and an inner resourcefulness which did not require the guidance of fathers or husbands. Their 'strategies for coping' embraced cultivating sisterhoods, acquiring a monopoly over certain types of work, and making social time for talking, reminiscing and exchanging confidences. These women supported themselves, and often their families back in the home villages. In a society where other Chinese women endured exploitation and abuse, they carved out a vital space for themselves in Singapore's social history. Neither victims nor exploiters of others, the work they found on the building sites of Singapore was hard and back-breaking, but they gained self-esteem. The contrast between them and the successful 'protected' women (Smith) provides material for thought. Where the latter gained economic security in a social climate of contempt, the migrant women laboured painfully for a livelihood, but in the process achieved dignity and independence.

Collusion: Women as Exploiters of Other Women

In considering *mui tsai*, *pipa tsai*, prostitutes, perhaps to a lesser extent *san po tsai*, as well some *zi shu nu*, it is essential to note that the primary beneficiaries from their exploitation were usually other women. The *mui tsai* relieved the owning family women of household chores and agricultural labour. Even where the work was light and the treatment humane, female owners depended on *mui tsai* for personal service, as allies in family disputes, or for emotional support. The lot of each girl depended largely on how her mistress treated her.

Christian missionaries in Yunnan noted that even well-to-do Christian Chinese women opposed steps against the sale of *mui tsai* since they themselves owned *mui tsai* (Jaschok). The dealers in these slave girls were often women (Miers). Women procurers and brothel owners took a prominent part in the exploitation of prostitutes, while ageing prostitutes bought young girls to live off their earnings.

Compensation marriage depended upon a ready supply of girls who could be bought to replace the reluctant bride. It was such a girl who fulfilled the bride's domestic and sexual duties, squatting humbly beside the door when the bride paid her rare visits and took the seat of honour.

San po tsai, indeed all young daughters-in-law, were vulnerable to bullying by their mothers-in-law (Hayes). Concubines were under the domination of the first wife and were sometimes chosen by them. Thus in all cases we have the spectre of women playing a part in the exploitation of other women. The trade in females, while victimising some women, created opportunities for others to make an independent living or to live a life free of manual labour or sexual services (Koh; Warren).

Western Imperialism and Asian Women

The Feminist Discourse

In the context of changes in women's lives, the discussion of the motives of the agencies, both institutions and individuals, campaigning against inequities and providing rescue and shelter, as well as of their long-term legacies, has become especially controversial.

In the heyday of Western imperialism, once a social problem in an Asian society was identified, Westerners assumed responsibility for 'indigenous' people and prescribed remedies. Today, any attempt on the part of Western observers, including feminists, to impose ethnocentric notions of a 'superior' understanding or a better moral solution is increasingly rebuffed by Asian feminists, academics and activists, who are battling not only their indigenous patriarchal institutions, but also the universalist assumptions of Western scholars claiming to represent women outside their own cultures.

At issue is not only the abuse of women as a historical reality, but, equally important, the universality of moral constructs based on Western culture, and the legitimacy of intervention by Western agencies or individuals in Asian social practices.

The crucial debate among feminist scholars today centres on the Western feminist claim that women share a common experience of oppression. Within the framework of Edward Said's analysis (1985) it can be argued that colonial power structures inspired and sustained a body of knowledge, the 'Oriental', predicated on the monopoly of power held by Western voices. When, in the wake of Said's seminal study (*Orientalism*, 1978), a critical dismantling of the scholarly legacies of colonialism laid bare the assumptions Western traditions imposed on non-Western cultures, the works of feminist scholars were not spared.

For a few of our contributors – those who see themselves as feminist historians – the imperialism with which white women are charged is a matter of special poignancy (in particular see Jaschok; Mason), a legacy to confront. Critical voices abound. The historian Astrid Albrecht-Heide (1988) argues that women were as vital as their fathers and husbands in the creation of a colonial civilisation. According to Elise Boulding (1988 p. 228), they helped to develop the social infrastructure that provided 'the health, education and human services required for [colonial] society not to fall apart'. Moreover, the situation of 'native women' was by far the most popular cause for white women to espouse; it was not rare for them to establish charitable institutions, providing a 'civilising' impulse for colonial society. As Lata Mani put it, 'a dominant story about colonialism and the question of woman is: "we came, we saw, we were horrified, we intervened" (Mani 1990 p. 35).

Susanna Hoe, a historian whose research focuses on Western women in colonial contexts (1991), takes issue with this depiction of all white women as unthinking tools of colonialism. In her study of British women's activism in 20th-century Hong Kong (n.d.), she shows how women like Stella Benson pushed against colonial inequities and actually earned the hostility of the colonial authorities by attacking British policies on Chinese prostitution and *mui tsai*. However, it has become a focal point for anti-colonial criticism that white women took on the suffering of their Asian counterparts from a vantage point of privilege, which ultimately subsumed the victims' voices under the dominant voice of the one representing them (Bulbeck 1991; Mani 1990; Ong 1988). We feel that this criticism must not deflect from the courageous stance taken by a number of women who took on colonial and other vested interests when they campaigned against the exploitation of Chinese women.

The role of Western women and their work in China is treated by Jaschok, who explores the impact German missionary sisters have had on the lives of the Chinese girls and women with whom they worked in early 20th-century Yunnan. Her depiction of the relationships they developed with their wards (former *mui tsai*) and co-workers suggests the need to move away from static conceptions of the missionary as simply a 'cultural imperialist' moulding passive recipients of their religious and social work into their own perfect mirror image. While it is important to grasp the forces which brought together 'rescuers' and 'victims', the intimacy of interaction, often over long periods of time, left no one, Western missionary or Chinese ward, unchanged. 'Pitiable slave-girls' who were saved by German missionary sisters became fellow-preachers and adopted daughters (Jaschok).

The participation of white women in the reform of sexual mores and their efforts to meet the perceived needs of Asian women in distress is also addressed in Sarah Mason's chapter. Again fired by feminist convictions that women's suffering everywhere needed remedying, whether at home or in distant Asian countries, reform-minded Presbyterian women in late 19th-century San Francisco turned their energies to establishing a shelter for Chinese prostitutes which became a house of rehabilitation. As in the case of the German missionary sisters and their charges, relationships between the women who ran Cameron House, the name by which the shelter was eventually known, and the Chinese inmates could lead to the former prostitutes aspiring to lives that had been unthinkable in their mothers' generation. At its best the Cameron House community evolved into a surrogate family from which the Chinese women could derive support, group identity and important new role models. Many of the descendants of the first groups of women who entered the home still feel an attachment to its memory and its great women activists which is not unlike the traditional kinship ties binding people to their families and ancestors.

Mason's study suggests that American women activists did not regard Chinese prostitutes as 'fallen women' but as innocent victims of exploitation by their own society, to whom universally applicable human rights standards applied which transcended class and race. One may speculate that Asian prostitutes were more likely to invite compassion than their white counterparts, because they were more readily perceived as helpless victims, their helplessness compounded by the generalised image of helpless Asian peoples.

Jaschok's and Mason's writing raises the question of how far socially conscious women could ameliorate the oppression of women more vulnerable than themselves. They also raise the more fundamental question of the extent to which the most well-intentioned activism could indeed ever penetrate the barriers of cultural difference, which Trinh Min-hwa calls 'apartheid difference' – a difference too deep for the most socially-aware person to overcome, because it is conditioned by the intellectual and philosophical milieu of the time. Mason's study portrays activists who were separated from the women around them by a strength of moral conviction and an intellectual penetration of issues that led them to question ethnic and political prejudices accepted by their more complacent compatriots. This must at least cause us to qualify, if not to question, current assumptions about women's share in the colonial enterprise (see also Hoe 1991).

Women's Voices

Instead of the construction of what Chandra Mohanty calls the Woman as a cultural and ideological composite Other (p. 63), the call now is for writing which gives women voices from within their native milieu, from within the tension, the harmonies and dissonances which shape individuals as tradition and modernity impinge on each other. In this context Koh Choo Chin's personal account of her work for the Singapore Social Welfare Department between 1948 and 1966 helps us to understand what motivated educated women from a colonised society to work under a colonial administration in order to alleviate the lot of abused girls. This is also the value of Janet Lim's story, the story of a woman who was the victim of the most traditionalist manifestations of Chinese patriarchal culture when she was sold as a *mui tsai*, and who benefited from a change in colonial policy in Singapore which enabled her to escape her bondage and gave her educational opportunities rare even for free Chinese women at the time. She entered a successful career which brought her self-affirmation and economic independence, but, although she escaped from overt oppression, the legacy of her servitude is with her to this day.

Chinese and Western Concepts of Women's Rights and Individual Freedom

In her study of the origins of the Po Leung Kuk, Elizabeth Sinn identifies the culture-specific notions of individual freedom and bondage that led the British to condemn all transactions in persons for profit as slaving, while the Chinese considered sales by parents or legal guardians to be legitimate. To the Chinese the transfer of females was an integral part of the legitimate sphere of patriarchal privilege: the right to dispose of a daughter as dictated by her family's needs. Thus the Po Leung Kuk founders sought merely to prevent kidnapping and sale by persons with no rights over their victims rather than to end all selling of women and children.

They also sought to retain and demonstrate Chinese (male) control of their own affairs and to ensure the continuance of what Lau Siu-Kai calls 'the doctrine of laissez-faire and social non-interventionism' of the colonial government, which enabled the Chinese to safeguard their patriarchal familial culture (1990). By taking the initiative efficiently and quickly, members of the Chinese establishment demonstrated to the satisfaction of the administration their capacity to dispose of problems of conflicting morality in an elegant and face-saving manner, neutralising potentially embarrassing and divisive issues.

Sinn's identification of distinct culture-specific notions of individual freedom and bondage help us to understand the conflict between British proponents of legal and social change and the Chinese supporters of the indigenous case for action. However, neither she nor our other contributors deals directly with the women's own concept of freedom. From the point of view of those who were traded, we need to know whether the delineation between 'legitimate' transfer by legal guardians was more acceptable than 'illegitimate' transfer by kidnappers. Several of our authors point out that in cases of 'legitimate' transfer, deeply ingrained feelings of filial duty and an understanding of the reality of poverty led both prostitutes and *mui tsai* to accept their fate (Warren; Account of Edith Wong Moon-ho, above), and James Hayes makes it clear that his informants did not consider the transfer of a *san po tsai* to be an infringement of her rights. One may speculate that freedom to most Chinese woman before the mid-20th century may well have meant to be a *daaih pouh*, and it is worth noting that this was the position sought not just by Edith Wong's mother for her *mui tsai*, but also for the wards of the Anglican convent in Singapore, where Janet Lim was educated after her escape from bondage (Miers). However, against this we set the marriage resisters described by Watson and the migrant workers discussed by Chiang, who rejected marriage altogether or found ways to modify it.

Historical Background

China, Singapore, Hong Kong and San Francisco

To set our studies in historical perspective we turn to a brief history of the geographical regions we cover, including recent changes in the laws affecting women. The particular institutions and events described in each of our chapters must be seen against the rapidly changing conditions of the last century.

China: An increasingly weak and irresolute Manchu dynasty allowed the British to establish themselves in Hong Kong in 1841, and suffered a series of humiliating defeats in wars with foreign powers, to which China was forced to grant unrestricted access to trade, extra-territorial rights, control over foreign residential areas of the main cities, and leases over certain territories, including, in 1897, the New Territories of Hong Kong. These events brought foreign troops and warships to China and eroded the sovereignty of its government. Added to these military and commercial pressures came the cultural imperialism of Western missionaries, penetrating to the heart of China, preaching Christianity, running schools, hospitals and other philanthropic enterprises, and spreading Western political and social ideas.

At the same time rebellion and natural disasters took their toll of peasant lives, eroded rural prosperity and further weakened the central government. Between the 1840s and the 1890s millions of Chinese, mostly men, emigrated to Southeast Asia, the Americas and Africa, driven out by famine, landlessness, oppressive landlords and overpopulation, and attracted by the prospect of making a better living elsewhere. The emigration of women was illegal until 1911. This, combined with family attitudes and the fact that many male migrants intended to return and so did not take their wives with them, led to an excess of women in parts of China and an even greater excess of males among overseas Chinese. While the wives of these emigrants were closely watched in China to ensure they remained faithful (Mason), thousands of unfortunate women and girls were exported, usually against their will, to become prostitutes serving male migrants (Koh; Warren). Others were exported as *mui tsai*.

Rising nationalism and a growing reformist movement spearheaded by the emerging Western-educated Chinese intelligentsia led to the overthrow of the imperial system and the establishment of the Chinese republic in 1911. In the early 1920s there emerged two starkly contrasting parties, the Nationalists (Guomindang) and the Communists, each determined to restore full Chinese sovereignty but each offering their own political agenda to a deeply divided nation. Factions within these parties struggled for power, while local warlords established control over large areas of the country. Japan seized Manchuria in the early 1930s, bringing a temporary truce between the Communists and the Nationalists, who controlled the central government. But in 1937 the outbreak of war with Japan, which merged with World War II, brought years of defeat, devastation and heavy losses as large areas came under Japanese occupation. As soon as Japan, defeated in the war, pulled out of China the conflict between the Nationalist and Communist parties revived.

As the economy deteriorated and fighting escalated, the lot of both rural and urban women worsened. Thousands were sold or driven to migrate to work in factories and towns under appalling conditions. Strikes and resistance movements resulted. Pioneer organisations were set up by educated women interested primarily in promoting nationalism and women's rights, but it was the Communist Party which systematically mobilised women at the grass-roots level, promising them marriage reform and education, together with the land reform and other radical changes wanted by both sexes (Siu 1982 pp. 120 ff.). In 1949, supported by a popular revolution, the Communists drove the Nationalists from the mainland, established themselves in power and soon introduced sweeping reforms in all spheres of Chinese life.

In 1950 a new Marriage Law was followed by a nationwide campaign to eradicate the subordination and sale of women. Attempts were made to remove the stigma suffered by *mui tsai* and prostitutes, who were informed that they were the victims of feudalism, imperialism and capitalism, which were to be stamped out in the new People's Republic of China. Further upheavals came with the Cultural Revolution (1966–76), which was designed to ensure an ongoing radical Communist revolution.

Despite enduring resistance to the far-reaching changes in gender relations, and despite the subordination by Communist Party leaders of women's rights issues to competing concerns requiring 'mass line' support (see Wolf 1985), the irrevocable politicisation of the cultural and familial spheres brought women undeniable legal and political gains. However, the diversity and cultural richness which had in the past granted women an array of choices (see Watson) was no longer possible under Communist insistence on uniform modes of liberation and life-styles for women. Those women to whom the Party's prescription for proper socialist womanhood was unpalatable, whether because of sexual, religious, or other proclivities, paid a heavy price for their liberation (Jaschok).

In recent years China has turned in another direction. While still Communist, it has taken steps to encourage private enterprise and the progressive dismantling of structures stemming from a command economy, with a return to the renewed emphasis on the family as a major unit of production. Establishment of a market economy in the so-called Special Economic Zones to attract foreign investment has been accompanied by social developments which include the resurgence of some of the old forms of exploitation and oppression of women (see Epilogue). Official acknowledgement of this came in the Anti-Six Evil campaign begun in late 1989, which targets, among other sexual inequities, prostitution and trading in women.

Singapore and Hong Kong: Thousands of Chinese emigrated to Singapore after it came under British rule in 1821, and to Hong Kong after it became a British colony two decades later. Both had an ever-increasing, predominantly Chinese population under a British ruling class with its typical colonial social hierarchy and co-opted local elites. Both owed their prosperity to their position as entrepôts on the lucrative east Asian trade routes. Free-market enterprise and the influx of a hard-working Chinese population gave rise to rapid economic growth, only briefly checked by the Japanese occupation during World War II and accelerating rapidly in the following decades, with new investment and an expanding manufacturing industry. Politically, Singapore became fully independent in 1965. Hong Kong, still a colony, is due to be returned to China in 1997. In recent years it has benefited from the opening of parts of China, particularly areas of neighbouring Guangdong, to a free-market economy.

Although from the start the Chinese family in Singapore, which was mainly urban, was somewhat different from that of China, polygyny, female subordination and customary forms of marriage continued under British rule (Turnbull 1977; Lebra 1983). Brothels were legal until 1930 and little was done to check the inflow of prostitutes (Lai 1986; Warren); there was also no serious attempt to prevent the import or use of *mui tsai* (Miers).

After 1930, and particularly after World War II, more stringent efforts were made to stop both abuses (Koh). Moreover, because women were scarcer, urban life the norm and patriarchal controls weaker, proportionately more women entered the workforce than in China and they achieved more economic independence: neither infanticide nor the sale of girls developed locally in Singapore (Lebra 1983). The 1930s saw an influx of female immigrants from China after taxes were imposed on male migrants, and the sexual imbalance began to decline. In the 1950s the supply of women from China was cut off by local legislation as well as by the Communist government of the People's Republic. By this time Chinese girls in Singapore were going to school in larger numbers and many women were working for themselves. In 1957, as Singapore moved towards independence, women were given the vote. In 1961 a revolutionary step was taken with the promulgation of the Women's Charter, introducing monogamous marriage and women's rights to property and to divorce (Lebra 1983).[5]

In Hong Kong, the ratio of Chinese men to women was seven to two in 1872. It began to drop as whole families came in from southern China from the 1850s and the settled community in the colony increased, until by 1931 the ratio was only four to three. From the start, the British announced that the Chinese would be governed according to their own laws and customs, except for the use of torture. This policy of non-intervention as long as British political interests or capitalist development were not threatened served the interests of both the colonial administration and the Chinese elite. In this symbiotic relationship of colonialism and patriarchy women had no voice: their lives continued to be governed by the cultural strictures and economic vicissitudes of old.

Rapid urban development, coupled with a demand for females, caused many women to be torn from their rural homes and forced into servitude in families or in brothels. Smuggling people in was particularly easy as the population of Hong Kong moved with astonishing fluidity backwards and forwards across the Chinese border, and the harbour was always full of small boats plying the China coast. In this flux of urban culture, traditional sources of communal support withered. In China, fear of losing 'face' or of public opinion could often protect women from the worst abuses, but in the anonymity of urban Hong Kong amid the competitive struggle for a livelihood the abuse of vulnerable women as a financial asset and a traders' commodity became too common to merit notice.

Eventually, the kidnapping and illegitimate sale of women were attacked both by the Chinese establishment, trying to deflect the impact of British laws for the protection of women and children through pre-emptive action of its own (Sinn), and by a reluctant colonial government, forced to act by a British government facing parliamentary criticism and a campaign by English women attacking what they saw as intolerable abuses (Hoe, n.d.). As in Singapore, laws against trafficking in females for *mui tsai* or for prostitution were not seriously enforced until the 1930s, and abuses certainly continued into the 1950s (Jaschok 1988; Miners 1987, 1990).

It took until 1970 to introduce monogamy laws in Hong Kong. A study has yet to be written of the consequences for the countless concubines who lost the security and comfort of what had been their rightful homes.

In the rural villages of the New Territories traditional agriculture and patriarchal practices continued virtually unchanged until overtaken by rapid urbanisation in the 1960s and 1970s (Hayes; J.L. Watson 1980). Even now in 1993 women in the New Territories cannot inherit lineage property.

San Francisco: Thousands of Chinese flocked to join the California gold rush, which began in 1849. Twenty thousand came in 1852 alone, and by 1900 more than 200,000 Chinese were settled in the state (Mason). In the 1860s many Chinese were employed in San Francisco, in industry and in service jobs. As elsewhere the immigrants were mainly men, and a flourishing traffic in Chinese women soon developed, providing prostitutes and *mui tsai*. This only ended in the 1930s (Mason). Many Chinese immigrants imported 'mail-order' brides from China, sometimes as secondary wives, or as concubines.

Today there is an area of San Francisco that is predominantly Chinese. Unlike Singapore and Hong Kong, however, the Chinese are a small minority of the population. They have shared in the general growth of American prosperity and Chinese women were gradually brought under American laws enforcing mono-gamy, allowing divorce, outlawing prostitution, child labour and the sale of women, and protecting their right to property. More recently they have benefited from the women's rights movement, as a result of which discrimination against women in all fields has been outlawed.

Everywhere these Chinese emigrants went they brought with them their culture, customs, traditions and religions, a dedication to hard work and considerable business skills, and their clan, village, or district associations, which in many cases served as support groups overseas. Many retained their links with China; the men returned to get married or sent home for brides. Many conducted business both in China and in their host countries. Workers of both sexes often remitted substantial sums of money to their relations. Some returned home to die. The fate of the emigrants varied according to their abilities and fortune: some became immensely wealthy, while others eked out a living as coolies.

Conclusion: Social Patterns and Women's Choices

It is now necessary to reconsider the position of Chinese women in traditional society, and to decide whether the stereotype of the submissive victim described above needs revision in the light of our contributions. These have shown the various initiatives taken by women to escape patriarchal domination and the more extreme forms of servitude. Rubie Watson asks whether, because 'women created and maintained affinal networks, labour exchanges, festival associations, temple groups, girls' houses, and religious movements', while some became independent wage earners and marriage resisters, we should discard the notion of the stereotypical cowed wife and frightened *mui tsai* – and, we may add, that of the exploited prostitute.

Her conclusion is that the axiom remains true for the vast majority of Chinese women in our studies. Only a small number were able to take advantage of the various avenues of escape opening up in the late 19th and early 20th centuries. They showed great ingenuity in forming support groups and making their own way against great odds. The vast majority remained firmly enmeshed in the patriarchal system. While many became respected matrons, countless numbers ended their lives as 'desperately poor widows, harried concubines, or childless marginals'. However, in the finer tracings of individual lives, as in Edith Wong's account, we uncover subtle shifts and readjustments. While these may not have provided escape routes, they do suggest how inroads into patriarchal mores were made by some women who managed to better their lot and to affect the lives of those around them.

As pointed out earlier, non-Western women have criticised Western feminist assertions of 'universal sisterhood' and have urged research into specific mechanisms of subordination, giving due recognition to the diversity of women's experiences of sexual inequality. Our authors have sought to explore the legacy of the institutionalised subordination of Chinese women in the hope that their studies will contribute to the contemporary discourse on women's placement and valorisation in specific cultural and socio-economic formations. We have also sought to enhance our understanding of the way women place themselves. In the process, our awareness has grown of the multifarious constituents of complex historical processes and how they were sanctioned through traditions, customs, and laws. But our awareness has also grown of the wide range of responses by which women negotiated, adapted, and sometimes reworked the texture of their lives, whether through internalisation of approved role models and a stoic submission to a seemingly inexorable fate, through enterprising exploitation of commercial opportunities in the lucrative market in females, through solitary fortitude or through a mutually-inspired participation in a collective social identity which challenged the ways of their mothers. Not all the women in our book escaped patriarchal subordination, but very few left the structures of subordination unchallenged and unchanged.

Notes

1. The main provisions of the Female Domestic Service Ordinance No. 1 promulgated in 1923 prohibited the acquisition of new *mui tsai* and the transfer of existing *mui tsai* (except with official permission). It required that all *mui tsai* be registered, that those over 10 be paid wages, that those over 18 be allowed to leave if they wished and that all under 18 be returned to their parents on demand without compensation. It also forbade the employment of any domestic female under 10. However, the crucial clauses requiring the registration of *mui tsai* and the payment of wages were not put into force and the ordinance remained largely a dead letter (see Miners 1987 ch. 8). The 1929 Ordinance to Amend the Female Domestic Service Ordinance required the registration and remuneration of all *mui tsai* and forbade their import into Hong Kong. Orders were given that the laws were to be enforced and regular reports were to be sent to the Colonial Office on the subject (Miners ch. 9).

2. Edith Wong Moon-ho is a pseudonym as the information given is considered too sensitive by Mrs Wong to allow the use of her real name.

3. Edith Wong Moon-ho used the English term 'stepmother' to refer to all of her father's concubines. The father's first wife was referred to as 'eldest mother'. This was the senior wife, or *daaih pouh* (*da po* in Mandarin) as opposed to *sai pouh* (*xiao po* in Mandarin), the junior wife.

4. During the early 1920s in Guangdong Province Communist-led workers' strikes were violently suppressed by Chinese government and Western allied forces. During this time, Guangdong also saw the formation of the United Front (consisting of the Guomindang and the Communist Party) to organise nationwide resistance to warlord dominance. After the breakup of the United Front in 1927, the border province proved an ideal base for Communist activists from which to subvert Nationalist rule.

5. The rights of Muslim women are not governed by the Women's Charter but by the Administration of Muslim Law and are more limited than those of other women.

2. Girls' Houses and Working Women: Expressive Culture in the Pearl River Delta, 1900–41

By Rubie S. Watson

Many of the women discussed in this volume were born and raised in the villages of the Pearl River delta. Our understanding of the choices they made, or were forced to make, and the frames of reference they used in making those choices depends, at least in part, upon our knowledge of delta culture and society. The following is an effort to describe the lives of delta women during the early decades of the 20th century. The discussion relies on a variety of secondary sources as well as my own field research in two Cantonese villages.[1]

Unfortunately, because histories of rural China have neglected women, our appreciation of their contributions to village society and culture, to agricultural and wage labour, and to handicraft production before the Maoist revolution is limited.[2] In study after study one encounters general statements that southern women were more active in agricultural production than their northern counterparts, that Hakka women worked longer hours in the fields than their Cantonese neighbours, that women in the southeast made greater contributions to household livelihoods than women in the northern heartland, but supporting evidence for these generalisations is rare.[3] Although many scholars assume connections between women's work on the one hand and such factors as household organisation, marriage payments, post-marital residence, marriage forms, infanticide, and footbinding[4] on the other (see e.g. Buck 1937 p. 292; Davin 1976; Topley 1975 p. 70), these connections have yet to be examined in any detail.

The following discussion sketches out what we know about women's labour and culture in the Pearl River delta during the first half of the 20th century. Special attention is paid to the region's 'silk district' because, thanks to the work of scholars like Topley (1975), Eng (1986), So (1986) and Stockard (1989), we have a solid foundation from which to analyse patterns of women's work and cultural production. Fortunately for our purposes, this is also the region that produced many of the women described in this volume.

In writing about delta women it is easy to see them as subordinated victims – as 'inside persons' (*neiren*) – without influence in or knowledge of the world beyond the family compound. These characterisations are not without merit. There is no doubt that delta women suffered serious inequities and that many led highly restricted lives. Men, supported by androcentric laws and ideologies, exerted considerable control over their daughters and wives. Until 1949, delta women, like their counterparts in other areas of China, suffered legal restrictions, especially in the area of property rights and family law which were based on the primacy of patrilineal descent and patriarchal authority. Daughters and wives could be sold or indentured; Gates contends that women in traditional China were expendable, providing a kind of ballast that could be jettisoned when family circumstances required (1989 p. 814).

This is, however, not the whole story. The Pearl River delta was also famous for its girls' houses, marriage resisters, and a complicated, and some might argue highly un-Confucian, range of marital and residential choices, including the option not to marry or to maintain a separate residence from the husband. In many cases the same 'inside persons' discussed above created – sometimes in conjunction with and sometimes separately from their brothers and husbands – a richly varied set of social and cultural forms. From one generation to the next, women contributed to, nurtured and transmitted an expressive culture of songs, domestic arts, stories, ritual knowledge and religious practices that we are only beginning to appreciate. As daughters and wives they made valuable contributions to household livelihoods: the delta, it should be noted, was famous for its women farmers, silk producers, domestic servants and factory workers.

Do the images of the resourceful marriage resister and influential matron require that we relinquish or amend our views of delta women? Is our image of women as subordinated victims wrong? That delta women have been portrayed as mute yet capable of projecting powerful alternative visions of society presents a fascinating challenge to scholars working on Chinese gender inequality.

Rural Society in the Pearl River Delta

The Pearl River delta was marked by great variety. Busy markets grew up amid well-tended rice paddies, mansions stood next to the mud huts of slaves, and inch by inch new fields were created as reclamation workers pushed the polders of their overlords farther and farther into the estuaries, bays and rivers for which the delta is famous. Long-established and highly stratified villages of rice farmers and leisured gentlemen bordered new and transitory settlements of reclamation workers. Flimsy shacks clung to the edges of the delta's canals and waterways as temporary communities of boat people, marsh dwellers and oyster workers appeared and disappeared with considerable rapidity. It is not surprising that in the midst of all this variety we should also find a diversity of ethnic and occupational groups, local organisations, political alliances and livelihood strategies.

During the late 19th and early 20th centuries the physical environment of the

Pearl River delta supported a series of complex ecosystems: agriculture, sericulture and aquaculture coexisted in an elaborate set of symbiotic relationships. The region was both agricultural and industrial – in fact, unlike many 'developed' areas of China, rural factories, some of them employing hundreds of workers, were a common sight in the countryside. Out-migration was extensive and many villagers had themselves lived abroad or had kin who worked in the tin mines of Malaya, the sweatshops of San Francisco or the small trading companies of the Philippines (see e.g. T. Chen 1939; Davis 1964; H. Siu 1989 pp. 25–35, 1990; So 1986 pp. 76–9, 107; Stockard 1989 pp. 135–41; J.L. Watson 1975b).

Most delta inhabitants spoke subdialects of Cantonese, although a significant minority were Hakka (see Aijmer 1967; Cohen 1968; E.L. Johnson 1976). In this chapter I am concerned primarily with the rural Cantonese population. In most communities, ties to kin were strong and corporate interests were pervasive. Men took precedence over women, elders over juniors, married over unmarried. The landscape of the delta was peppered with tightly nucleated villages[5] in which people depended upon neighbours and kin (often neighbours were also kin) for their social and physical welfare. People living in the countryside managed their own schools, markets, water resources, pathways, rubbish collection and security forces. State authorities were physically and conceptually remote from village life (for further discussion see e.g. Faure 1986; Hayes 1977; W. Hsieh 1974; H. Siu 1989; Wakeman 1966; J.L. Watson 1975b, 1977, 1991; R. Watson 1985).

Stratification in the delta involved a series of interlocking relationships. Inequalities based on class, gender, education, occupation and tied labour were the major points of cleavage. For men, positions in these hierarchies tended to be mutually reinforcing: a wealthy landlord, for example, was likely to be more highly educated than his landless tenant. However, the situation for the landlord's wife and daughters was more complex. They might indeed lead lives of considerable luxury, but they shared with their poor female neighbours a high rate of illiteracy and a second-class legal status.

In China, as in most societies, gender is related to other forms of inequality in extremely complex ways. As I have argued elsewhere (1991a), women in China were never just women. They were also members of classes and elites, but their membership in these groups was conditioned by the prevailing gender hierarchy. Women as women shared certain vulnerabilities. They could be divorced, although it was nearly impossible for them to divorce; they had no rights to family property, yet they could be pawned or sold. They could not take the imperial exams and were barred from holding office. Their legal status was rather like that of a jural minor; even as adults they remained under the authority of a husband, or if he was dead, a son. If a woman remarried or was divorced, she was likely to lose control of, and even access to, her children. The list of limitations and disabilities could be extended, but it is sufficient to demonstrate that in China prior to 1949, gender stratification was not subsumed by the structure of class relations (on the legal position of women in the Qing and Republican periods, see Ocko 1991; Buxbaum 1978; Ch'u 1961; Ng 1987).

Class, gender, and education do not exhaust the categories of stratification in the delta. Pariah-like occupational groups and servile or indentured forms of labour also played an important role. Fisherpeople living on boats, marsh dwellers who harvested reeds and shellfish, reclamation workers, *mui tsai* (or indentured maidservants), concubines, prostitutes, musicians, funeral specialists all suffered discrimination and fell outside the boundaries of 'proper' society. Although slavery was outlawed when the Republic was established in 1912, many forms of unfree labour continued to exist well into the 20th century. In fact, concubinage, debt bondage, indenture and the outright sale (albeit illegal) of girls and women were features of Chinese society until the late 1940s and in Hong Kong many of these practices continued into the 1950s and 1960s (see e.g. Hayes 1990; Jaschok 1988; Smith 1981; J.L. Watson 1976, 1980; R. Watson 1991b).

During the period under discussion, the larger villages and towns in the Pearl River complex included members of the national elite, locally prominent landlords and merchants, tenant farmers, wage labourers, various forms of tied labour, and, at the margins of these communities, pariah-like occupational specialists. Agricultural land tended to be concentrated in the hands of private landlords and corporate ancestral estates. Many farmers were landless or owned small amounts of land and so were forced to rent fields from others. Chen H.S. calculates, according to a survey in the 1930s, that 'nearly half of the peasant families [in Guangdong] are entirely landless' (1936 p. viii). Chen reports that 'public land' (by this I take him to mean male-focused ancestral estates) made up about 35 per cent of the total cultivated acreage (1936 pp. 34–5). This 'public land', it should be noted, was often under the control of managers who were themselves members of the local elite or their agents (see R. Watson 1990b).

It was not uncommon for delta residents to exploit a variety of ecological niches, including high-quality rice paddies, upland or coastal fields of sweet potatoes, brackish paddies devoted to red rice (used in wine and medicine) as well as fish ponds, mulberry shrubs and plots of citrus trees, pineapple, peanuts, and sugar cane (see e.g. Davis 1964; H. Siu 1989, 1990; J.L. Watson 1975b; R. Watson 1985). Coastal areas provided shellfish and materials for mats and fans. In many rural households wage labour and handicraft production supplemented or, in some cases, provided the bulk of family income. Migration within the region and overseas to Southeast Asia and the United States became increasingly important in the period discussed here, making some communities heavily dependent on remittances (see e.g. T. Chen 1939; J.L. Watson 1975b).

Agricultural labour was performed by men and women. Although reliable figures on women's labour force participation in agriculture are few, farm surveys conducted in the 1920s and 1930s provide some indication. In a 1929–33 survey of nearly 17,000 farms in 22 provinces, Buck and his colleagues found that 24 per cent of the women in the study were engaged in farm work; the figures for men were 60 per cent and for children 16 per cent (1937 p. 290). According to this survey, a larger percentage of farm work was performed by women (38 per cent) in the Double Cropping Rice Area (which includes the Pearl River delta) than in any other region of China (1937 p. 292). Buck writes: 'The largest proportion of [farm] labour done by women is in the Double Cropping Rice Area and the smallest (5 per cent) in the Rice-tea and the Winter Wheat-millet Areas' (1937 pp. 292–3). According to Buck, this difference was 'partly associated with the extent to which [women's] feet are bound'. Buck assumes a lower rate, or perhaps a less severe form (see Gamble 1943), of footbinding in Guangdong and the extreme south than in the north. However, it should be noted that Buck does not argue that footbinding totally precluded work in the fields. In the Spring Wheat Area, Buck reports, 'where footbinding is very prevalent and where it is so tight as to compel women to do the field work on their knees, 14 per cent of the [farm] labour is done by women' (Buck 1937 p. 292).

Returning to the Pearl River delta, data collected by Chen H.S. in 10 Panyu villages during the 1930s show that in most of the surveyed communities men and women worked together in agriculture (1936 p. 107). Surprisingly perhaps, Chen found that throughout Guangdong 'women outnumber men among the day-labourers in agriculture' (1936 p. 104). Chen points out that women labourers consistently received lower wages than men; in Panyu villages women earned about three-fifths of what men earned (1936 pp. 104, 105). In Chen's view the 'feminisation' of local agriculture was one of the major reasons for the downward spiral of poor productivity and inefficiency that he believed was forcing the population of rural China into deeper and deeper poverty (1936 pp. 103–4, 107). Although male out-migration certainly contributed to the large numbers of women engaged in agricultural work, especially in day-labour, this was by no means the only cause for such high rates of female labour participation (for out-migration figures see Chen H.S. 1936 pp. 109–11; T. Chen 1939).

In many rural households non-farm employment was an important source of livelihood. Chen reports that half the peasant families living in his Panyu villages had at least one member working in non-agricultural labour (1936 p. 108). Although it is difficult to know whether women were as likely to be involved in non-agricultural work as men, there is no doubt that women were well represented in both the agricultural and the non-agricultural labour force. Based on my knowledge of Hong Kong's New Territories, women were engaged in a variety of productive activities, including handicraft production, wage labour, petty trading,[6] herb and shellfish collecting and livestock tending. They were transport workers and textile producers; they processed food and made clothes for the household and, of course, they cared for the young and aged. As outlined below, women's household and factory labour was extremely important in the delta's silk district.

The complexity of the delta's ecology and economy was matched by a complicated web of kin relations and organisations. Southeastern China, and perhaps particularly the Pearl River delta, was known for its powerful and wealthy patrilineages. In many villages a single lineage numbering as many as 2,000 or 3,000 males plus their wives and daughters made up the population. The women living in these communities may well have experienced special pressures and restrictions. In dominant lineages, divorce and widow remarriage were deplored and existing evidence suggests they were rare. Uxorilocal marriage was not acceptable, adoption of non-agnates was seriously discouraged, and 'little daughter-in-law' or minor marriage (see below) was practically unknown.[7] Codes of sexual conduct for women were often harsh. These restrictions, supported by physical threats if necessary, had important implications for women's lives.

Although the delta is characterised as a 'lineage area' (see Freedman 1958, 1966), it is important to remember that not all villages consisted of patrilineal descent groups. Powerful lineage communities were often surrounded by smaller villages of tenant farmers who were the economic and political dependants of their dominant neighbours (J.L. Watson 1977). While matrilateral ties and bonds of affinity linked many households in these neighbouring communities, dependants and superiors rarely shared a common patrilineal ancestor. Characteristically, dependent villages had small populations of 500 or fewer residents divided into two or more lineages or surname groups. Many delta settlements, because of location or other factors, existed outside or on the margins of the area's wealthy lineages. These communities have been well described in the literature (see e.g. Faure 1986; Hayes 1977; Strauch 1983).

Beyond the confines of the region's dominant lineages, widow remarriage, divorce, uxorilocal and minor marriage, and more open adoption arrangements, while not the norm, were certainly in evidence. However, nearly all women in the delta, whether they lived in powerful lineage communities or not, were excluded from full membership in the family estate or what Gates (1989) labels the patricorporation. Because of this, women lacked the capacity to own or manage family and lineage property. Delta women, however, were not completely alienated from all productive resources or from economic decision making, although the goods they could claim by customary practice were nearly always less significant than those that their brothers and husbands controlled.

A study of marriage that takes into account practices throughout the delta has yet to be written. Nevertheless, some general patterns can be discerned. It was certainly customary, for example, for local brides, like their counterparts in other areas of China, to enter their husbands' households with some dowry goods. They might bring with them little more than a few pieces of jewellery, some clothes, and a small chest, but these dowry items (*jia zhang*)[8] were their own and established them as wives rather than concubines or mistresses. The money used to purchase *jia zhang* may have originated in the groom's family as bridewealth (*lijin*), and/or the bride's family, depending largely on the class and status aspirations of the intermarrying families (see R. Watson 1981, 1991b). However, once married, women retained certain rights over their dowries and jealously guarded their reserve of *sifang qian* or 'private room money'. *Sifang qian* is married women's property and has been reported in one form or another in many parts of China (see e.g. Cohen 1976 p. 178; Gallin & Gallin 1982; R. Gallin 1984; Ocko 1991; Stockard 1989 p. 21; R. Watson 1991a, 1991b; M. Wolf 1975 p. 135). According to Ocko, this private fund includes the trousseau (or jewellery and household goods brought by the bride at the time of the marriage), gifts she received before marriage, and income earned from her own labour (1991). It is unclear whether women remained in permanent control of this fund throughout their lives. There is some evidence that they relinquished these funds at the time of household division, when their *sifang qian* was combined with their husbands' resources to establish a newly independent household.

In the delta, concubines did not have the same status as wives. Wives had a publicly recognised role both inside and outside the family, they had the status of legitimate kin and therefore could create affinal and matrilateral ties for their husbands and offspring, they commanded dowries, and after death they could command a place on their husband's or son's ancestral altar. Concubines might wield considerable personal influence and they might live in great luxury, but in certain fundamental respects they were non-persons.[9]

While there was certainly more diversity in the 'practice' of patriliny than is usually discussed in the anthropological literature of China, there was even greater diversity in the realm of marriage. Prior to 1949 certain practices were common: for example, surname and village exogamy was widespread, marriage payments tended to involve some betrothal gifts plus either direct or indirect dowry (*jia zhang*) or some combination of the two. The ideal marriage arrangement (sometimes referred to as major marriage) involved the union of two adults, although minor marriage was certainly practised. Minor marriage refers to the union of a young man and a young woman when the bride had been adopted by the groom's family in her infancy with a view toward her eventual marriage to one of the family's sons (see Hayes; Wolf & Huang 1980). There is evidence that minor marriage was practised in many parts of China, although the exact distribution is unclear. Minor marriage was often celebrated by little more than a special family meal; elaborate marriage payments were dispensed with. Because marriage payments and feasting were minimal and dowry processions were absent, minor marriage tended to have a lower status, at least in the delta, than the major form.

In the delta region people married in both the major and minor fashion, although as I note above minor marriages were rare in dominant lineage communities. Generalisations about post-marital residence are, however, far more difficult to make. As demonstrated below, the Pearl River delta exhibited a variety of residence forms including, of course, the patri-virilocal and uxorilocal varieties found in other parts of China (for discussion of uxorilocal residence see e.g. Pasternak 1983; Wolf & Huang 1980). To these well-studied forms a third and perhaps a fourth must be added. In the silk-producing region of the delta and in neighbouring districts post-marital residence involving the delayed transfer of the bride was prominent (see Stockard 1989 pp. 3–4). It is also clear that some delta women eschewed residence with their husbands altogether, preferring to engage in what has been called 'compensation marriage'.[10]

Sericulture and Silk Reeling

Prior to the 1930s the Pearl River delta was one of China's major silk-producing regions. In 1925 more than two million people were employed in sericulture and silk reeling in Xunde, Nanhai, Zhongshan and Panyu counties. Xunde, with 1,440,000, had the largest number (see Howard & Buswell 1925 pp. 15–25; So 1986 pp. 77–9; Stockard 1989 pp. 135n). Howard & Buswell, who conducted a survey of the silk industry in southern China in 1923–4, reported that about 70 per cent of Xunde's land and over 75 per cent of its population were devoted to sericulture (1925 p. 15). In Nanhai, half the population worked in sericulture and 30 per cent of the land was used for mulberry growing. In Zhongshan, Howard & Buswell calculated that 70 per cent of the population was engaged in some aspect of sericulture; considerably lower rates (under 10 per cent) prevailed in Xinhui, Sanshui and Panyu counties (1925 pp. 15–27; see also Topley 1975 p. 70).

Sericulture in this area was characterised by the 'four-water-six-land' system. Stockard describes the system in this way: 'Delta lands were systematically diked and raised with earth from the excavation of fish ponds, resulting in a water-to-land ratio of four to six' (1989 p. 135). Mulberry bushes were cultivated on the raised land while fish, and sometimes ducks, occupied the ponds. Leaves from the mulberry bushes were fed to the silkworms and silkworm waste and duck droppings produced food for the fish. At the end of the year the fish were sold, the ponds were drained, and the resulting mixture of fish waste and silt was applied as fertiliser to the mulberry bushes (see also So 1986 pp. 84–5; Topley 1975 pp. 69–70; for further details see Howard & Buswell 1925 pp. 48–61). So dates this particular ecosystem from the 1860s (1986 p. 85), although silk production in the delta certainly predated the mid-19th century (see L.M. Li 1981 p. 113).

Over time the 'four-six' system and the tropical climate produced a particularly labour intensive and productive regime (see e.g. So 1986 pp. 84–5; Stockard 1989 p. 139). In the major silk-producing counties the sexual division of labour was elaborate. Women were involved in silkworm rearing, mulberry leaf harvesting and silk reeling, while men cultivated the mulberry bushes and marketed the eggs, leaves and cocoons. Men tended the fish ponds and any paddy or vegetable fields the family exploited, although these were by no means exclusively male domains. Stockard writes: 'The task of mulberry leaf harvesting was usually assumed by women, assisted by children, [while] men were typically employed in performing the heavier aspects of worm rearing as well as in the transport and marketing of mulberry leaves' (1989 p. 142). The division of labour in sericulture also varied depending on marital status, with young unmarried women or married women who continued to reside in their natal families (natolocal residence) employed in silk reeling, while patri-virilocally resident wives (usually older) assisted their husbands in raising silkworms (Stockard 1989 p. 142).

As factories and mechanisation were introduced,[11] women supplied nearly all the workers in the filatures. 'In the Canton Delta, in both the pre- and post-mechanisation eras ... silk reeling was the exclusive domain of women,' Stockard writes (1989 p. 148). She goes on to comment that 'women of all ages could reel silk', although the most skilful reelers were teenagers and young women whose smooth, nimble hands and good eyesight made them preferred workers (1989 p. 148). 'Childlessness', Stockard adds, 'was another factor favouring the labour of young women' (1989 p. 149; on division of labour in silk-production areas see also Topley 1975 pp. 70–3). Silk weaving was done by men and was an important income-earner for many delta households. However, as export-oriented filatures rapidly expanded in number and productive capacity, local handicraft weaving declined (see Eng 1990).[12]

The growth of steam-powered reeling in the Pearl River delta was extraordinarily rapid. Eng reports that from the 1910s, Guangdong filatures (mostly concentrated in the Xunde and Nanhai countryside) 'had a total production capacity several times that of Shanghai, and a larger average plant size' (1986 p. 50; see also Howard & Buswell 1925 pp. 121–45). From 1880 to 1929 the number of Guangdong filatures and workers increased dramatically.[13]

In the 1930s, however, there was a significant decline in the silk industry and large numbers of women were thrown out of work (see Eng 1986 pp. 157–62, 1990; So 1986 pp. 135–52; Topley 1975 pp. 84–6; L.M. Li 1981 pp. 5–9, 163–206). The decline was due to many factors, including lack of technological innovation, undercapitalisation, collapse of world silk prices, reduced prices for cocoons, and of course the general effects of the world depression. According to So, in 1932 there were only 58 filatures operating in Guangdong, compared with 200 or more in 1926. By 1935 there had been a further fall with only 21 factories operating (So 1986 p. 137). In Xunde, as a consequence of the slump, nearly a third of the land devoted to mulberry cultivation was abandoned (see Eng 1986 p. 159). More than 36,000 filature workers, So reports, were thrown out of work during this period. Many of these unemployed women became the domestics, mail-order brides, day labourers, and indentured workers who migrated to Hong Kong and Southeast Asia in the decade before the Japanese occupation (see Chiang).

Silk, Work, Marriage and Anti-Marriage

The silk-producing area of the Pearl River delta provides fascinating case material on women's work, marriage and culture. As noted above, marriage arrangements in the delta and especially in its silk-producing areas were highly variable and in some cases extravagantly unconventional. In 1975 Topley wrote an essay on marriage resistance in Guangdong's sericultural region[14] arguing that in the 19th and early 20th centuries many young silk workers had the economic wherewithal to refuse to marry altogether.[15] In some cases those women who chose the life of a spinster swore oaths of chastity and formally renounced marriage (on marriage renunciation rituals see Jaschok 1984 pp. 45, 48; Sankar 1984 p. 58). As these so-called *zi shu nu* grew older many moved from their natal homes[16] into filature dormitories, vegetarian halls (*cai tang*) or spinsters' houses (sometimes called 'old aunt houses' or *gupowu*) (see Topley 1975 pp. 74, 83).

In local society the presence of an adult daughter was inappropriate, inauspicious, even dangerous. The death of an unmarried daughter who was still living in her natal household caused great fear; such a death, it was believed, produced an extremely unsettled and dangerous ghost. Because the soul tablet of an unmarried daughter could not be placed on her father's domestic altar, unmarried women had to find their final resting place in the delta's Buddhist nunneries, vegetarian halls, or in the houses of spirit mediums or sworn sisters (see e.g. Potter 1974; Stockard 1989 pp. 82–9; Topley 1954 p. 60).

There were, according to Topley, two forms of marriage resistance, one in which women (*zi shu nu*) renounced marriage altogether, and another in which married women refused to cohabit with their husbands (sometimes called *buluojia*). According to Topley, some of the women in the latter category eventually returned to their husbands (1975 p. 67). 'Some girls', she writes, 'followed the custom of staying away three years, which gave them time to get to know their husbands … and very young husbands time to mature' (1975 p. 82). This last comment suggests a local practice in which women were married to younger grooms. Unfortunately, we do not know whether such arrangements were common. Of course, given that a non-resident wife might contribute part of her earnings to her husband's household (see Topley 1975 p. 82), this type of union must have made excellent economic sense, especially if the husband's family had no working daughters of their own.

Although both Topley and Stockard agree that the Pearl River delta exhibited some unusual living arrangements for women, Stockard's analysis differs from Topley's in important respects (see Stockard 1989 pp. 3–5, 188–9). First, Stockard takes issue with Topley's classification system,[17] preferring to reserve the term marriage resistance for a narrower range of behaviour. Stockard argues that Topley mistakenly considered local practices that deviated from major marriage to be evidence of marital resistance. (Major marriage is a form of marriage in which an adult bride and groom marry and take up patri-virilocal residence at the time of the marriage.) Stockard writes: 'My research shows that … delayed transfer marriage was not a form of marriage resistance, but rather [was] the customary marriage pattern for an extensive area in the Canton Delta' (1989 p. 4). Brides in the delayed transfer area, she argues, expected to live apart from their husbands (usually remaining with their natal families) 'for the first three years of their marriage'. During this period a bride visited her husband and his family but resided natolocally. If she earned no wages herself, she would expect to receive economic support from her parents until she took up residence in her husband's household. Wage-earning bride-daughters on the other hand contributed cash to their natal families and, if circumstances allowed, kept some money for themselves (Stockard 1989 pp. 19–22). Stockard argues that until a bride-daughter took up patri-virilocal residence, neither her husband nor his family could make claims on her earnings (1989 p. 20). Topley, however, reports that husbands' families sometimes did receive income from a bride-daughter (see above and 1975 p. 82). Although bride-daughters may not have expected as a matter of course to make regular contributions to their husband's households, it appears that such negotiated arrangements were possible. A pregnancy, Stockard explains, often initiated patri-virilocal residence (1989 p. 5).

In her book, Stockard chronicles delayed transfer marriage from the 1860s to the 1930s but argues that the practice predates that period. Although it became functionally linked to sericulture, she maintains it did not originate in response to labour demands within the industry (1989 p. 167) since it not only predated the silk industry, but was also practised beyond the boundaries of what she calls the sericultural heartland (see 1989 pp. 8–12, 136; H. Siu 1990 pp. 36–7), citing cases of bride-daughters living in both rice- and citrus-producing villages (1989 pp. 16, 19, 25, 61). Stockard demarcates a delayed transfer marriage 'core area' which includes all of Xunde and parts of Panyu, Nanhai, Zhongshan, Sanshui, and Heshan counties (Stockard 1989 p. 9; see also Siu 1990). According to Stockard, informants from Taishan, Xinhui, and Hong Kong's New Territories 'reported that delayed transfer marriage was not practised in those areas' (1989 p. 9). To my knowledge there were no cases of delayed transfer marriage in the two New Territories communities (San Tin and Ha Tsuen) where I have conducted field research. In fact, I was often told by women in these two communities that brides should not make regular visits to their natal families during the first year or so of marriage and overnight visits were not allowed except in special circumstances. Village matrons considered it very bad form indeed for young daughters-in-law to make more than occasional visits to their parents' homes. (However, see Hayes.)

A form of resistance that Stockard describes as a radical variant of the delayed transfer system is compensation marriage, which she views as 'a result of an anti-marital bias' coupled with 'economic opportunities for bride-daughters' (1989 p. 18). Jaschok, in a biographical account of a marriage resister, or *zi shu nu*, uses the Cantonese phrase 'buying a threshold' (c. *mai menkou*) to refer to this arrangement. According to Jaschok, 'buying a threshold' is understood to mean that the bride does not cross the threshold of the bridal chamber. In effect, the bride has bought herself out of the bed chamber and sexual contact with the groom (Jaschok 1984 p. 46).

As a form of resistance, compensation marriage occurred when a bride refused to consummate her marriage, negotiating instead to pay the groom's family a sum of money which was used to acquire a concubine for the groom. These concubines were usually *mui tsai* (young maidservants bound to their masters through ties of indenture or debt bondage).[18] 'Compensating bride-daughters', Stockard writes, 'returned to their husbands' home only at old age or death' (1989 p. 48). In this arrangement the bride-daughter reserved for herself the position of wife and mother of her husband's offspring while the groom's side assumed the obligation to care for the bride-daughter's spirit in the afterlife. As noted above, the care of one's soul tablet was a matter of great importance for any Chinese woman who, through choice or misfortune, did not assume the prescribed role of wife and mother. Topley remarks that a woman who initiated compensation marriage had to make financial contributions to her husband's household. Quoting from a study of Cantonese domestic workers in Singapore, Topley reports that women who maintained their chastity and yet supported a husband and his children were admired and respected for their actions (see Topley 1975 p. 82).

Compensation marriage, as a popular alternative to patrilocal residence, Stockard argues, arose at the end of the 19th century, although, as she points out, it is very likely related to an earlier, local practice of renegotiating marriage agreements (1989 pp. 123–6). 'Compensation marriage is perhaps best viewed', Stockard writes, 'as the efflorescence and specialisation of a traditional and general means of renegotiating marriages' (1989 p. 126).

A variety of reasons have been suggested for the rise of a marriage resistance movement in the Pearl River delta. For Eng (1986 pp. 143–5, 155; 1990) and So (1986 pp. 125–9) factors such as male out-migration, filature development, year-round employment in the silk industry and relatively high wages are important. So argues that the rural setting of the filatures, the fact that workers remained part of their village communities, and the strength of patriarchal control in the silk district were also important contributing factors (1986 pp. 127–9; cf. Eng 1990). Given some economic independence, So contends, delta women challenged not their employers but a structure of male authority embedded in the family. In his view marriage resisters thus turned what might have been a workers' struggle into a gender struggle (for discussion of this point see So 1986 pp. 131–4).

While both Topley and Stockard link marriage resistance to the importance of women's labour in the silk industry, neither accepts an unreservedly economic explanation. Although Topley and Stockard agree more than they disagree, they do emphasise slightly different factors. For Stockard, local institutions and cultural practices (particularly girls' houses, unmarried women's festival associations, the custom of marriage at night, and strong bonds among 'village daughters') predated women's wage labour in the delta's silk-producing region. Stockard suggests that these forms and the delayed transfer marriage system itself (1989 pp. 167–75) may in fact be part of 'an older non-Chinese cultural complex, one that fused with Chinese culture to produce the distinctive version of Chinese society found in the Canton Delta' (1989 p. 31). In Stockard's view marriage resistance cannot be attributed to one thing or another. Rather, it was formed in an environment in which longstanding cultural practices combined with changes in local silk production.

Siu also argues for non-Han influences on local marriage practices (1990 pp. 42–51). In her view delta marital and residence arrangements should be seen in broad historical perspective and understood in the context not just of silk production but of the many political economies that developed in the delta. Siu argues that 'resistance' is something of a misnomer because natolocal residence and the outright refusal to marry were 'sustained by the complicity of women's households which stood to gain from [a bride-daughter's or *zi shu nu's*] earnings' (1990 p. 33). Siu prefers to think of the delta's marrying and non-marrying options as well as its residential arrangements as 'a complex of local customs and beliefs' created in an ethnically mixed environment. In this reading delayed transfer marriage and refusals to marry become means through which regional culture is both celebrated and yet encapsulated within an encroaching Han polity (1990 pp. 32–5, 41–51).

While Topley, perhaps wisely, does not concern herself with origins, she too emphasises cultural forms and practices as well as economic changes in understanding why marriage resistance developed as it did. Topley, like Stockard, points to the importance of girls' houses, but places more stress than Stockard on the area's heterodox religious cults (see also So 1986 p. 124). The Pearl River delta, Topley argues, was a haven for semi-secret sects. These sects, which stressed sexual equality and placed a high value on chastity, had a messianic and millennial orientation. By the mid-19th century cult members were distributing their religious literature (*bao juan* or 'precious volumes') and establishing religious centres in Guangdong (1975 p. 74). For Topley, marriage resistance grew out of the interplay of these elements in combination with a particular set of ecological and economic conditions (male out-migration, stable wage labour for women) that made it possible for women to remain unwed (see 1975 p. 89).

Differences in emphasis and perspective distinguish these arguments. Siu is at pains to place delayed transfer and compensation marriages in a broad historical perspective, while Topley utilises a case-study approach detailing how these practices operated in a specific time and place. Stockard stands somewhere between the two, arguing for a long-term perspective yet providing a specific historical context to examine why delta women made the choices they did. All three studies enrich our understanding of delta society by emphasising the cultural milieu within which rural women operated. They also indicate the dangers of proposing a simple causal relationship that automatically privileges productive activities.

Women and Community in the Pearl River Delta

Many scholars of Chinese society and culture have assigned to men the roles of public actors, institution builders and religious innovators. Men are said to have been protectors of the public good and credited with creating the networks that linked households, communities and regions, making society itself possible. Women were the 'silent bridges' through whom men formed alliances. They were the 'inside persons' whose responsibilities stopped at the gates of the domestic compound, although even inside the gates their control is thought to have been limited by the male head (*jia zhang*) who had ultimate authority in both the public and private spheres. Since the 1970s this dichotomy between public men and domestic women has been challenged by anthropologists like Wolf (1972), Topley (1975), Stockard (1989), and Judd (1989).

That delta women produced social networks as well as children, ritual as well as rice, public order as well as silk is still something of a minority view in Chinese studies. Nevertheless, a more complex picture of women's lives in the Pearl River delta is emerging. In the Hong Kong New Territories villages with which I am familiar, women created and sustained affinal relations, they exchanged labour and food, and they maintained elaborate gift-giving networks (R. Watson 1981 pp. 609–12). Sometimes they acted on behalf of their husbands, sometimes they acted in their own right. The village women I knew managed to construct and nurture a set of ties that were vital to their own interests as well as those of their households. Women from different households, neighbourhoods and villages were united, not into formal groups, but into highly interactive, interdependent webs of relatedness based on affinity, residence, friendship, girlhood ties, religious affiliations and many other associations. Compared to their brothers and husbands, the connections among delta women were not highly systematised. Both Wolf (1972 p. 37) and Judd (1989 pp. 537–9) have made this point about rural women in other parts of China. The uterine family (a mother-focused 'family within a family'), Wolf writes, 'has no ideology, no formal structure, and no public existence [but] is built out of sentiments and loyalties that die with its members'. Wolf goes on to conclude that rural Taiwanese women do not live their lives in the walled courtyards of their husbands' domestic compounds. 'If they did,' she argues, 'they might be as powerless as their stereotype' (1972 p. 37). Structured or not, the women that Wolf, Judd, and I describe are a far cry from the 'inside persons' we have been conditioned to expect.

Ties between and among women were created and sustained within a richly elaborate expressive culture. Women's expressive forms in China (narrative traditions, songs, rituals, domestic arts, pilgrimage circuits) have not been well described, although work in the Pearl River delta (see e.g. Topley 1975; Stockard 1989; Blake 1978; E.L. Johnson 1988; Yung 1987; R. Watson 1981) and more recently in Hunan (see Silber 1992) suggests that these expressive genres were widely distributed.[19] In the delta, girls' houses were very important in sustaining many of the social forms and beliefs discussed in this chapter. To my knowledge these houses were not a feature of women's communities outside the delta.

As we learn more about the lives of rural women, we can expect to find considerable regional variation – more than among men perhaps. Because most women were illiterate and had less physical mobility than men, women's knowledge was likely to be local knowledge *par excellence*. Considering the delta's special agricultural and industrial patterns, women's work routines and kin ideologies and practices, it would not be surprising to find that local women's culture(s) was both similar to and yet unlike women's traditions in other parts of China. Whether non-Han influences, land reclamation, irrigation of rice paddy, silk production, rural industry, dominating lineages or some combination of these variables 'explains' women's expressive culture in the delta remains an open question.

Village daughters entered a local girls' house at the age of 10 or 11. For the next six to 12 years they continued to eat with their families and work in their fathers' fields, but they spent most of their leisure time in the close company of their peers, chaperoned by a village widow or two. In the girls' house young women became intimately involved in a set of expressive forms that, in an important sense, created and celebrated the differences that separated them from men. In these houses, which, to my knowledge, were found in Cantonese communities of any appreciable size,[20] girls learned 'how to be a good wife'; they memorised bridal laments, funeral dirges and embroidery styles (C.P. Chang 1969; R. Watson 1990a; for Hakka laments see Blake 1978; E.L. Johnson 1976, 1988). They learned how to mourn and how to cope with a mother-in-law. Girls' houses were not, however, a Cantonese version of a Swiss finishing school, for it was also in these houses that village girls heard stories and sang songs chronicling the hard life of women and extolling the virtues of the chaste goddesses, Tianhou and Guanyin (see e.g. Eberhard 1972; Leung 1978; Yung 1987). Sometimes they even learned to read (see Sankar 1978 pp. 104–5; Topley 1975 p. 75). Young delta women formed festival associations (see Stockard 1989 pp. 41–7) and went on pilgrimages with their sisters, aunts, and mothers (Topley 1975 p. 74). Girls living in these houses considered themselves sisters (c. *jimui*) and some formalised these bonds with pledges and banquets (see Stockard 1989 p. 40; cf. Silber 1992; see Chiang for an account of life in a girls' house). On occasion sworn sisters (*shang jie bai*) threatened collective suicide to protect one of their number from an unwanted marriage. There is evidence that these threats were sometimes carried out (see Stockard 1989 pp. 118–22).

As Stockard argues, the Festival of Double Seven (held on the seventh day of the seventh lunar month) pulls together many of the threads in the lives of delta women. Double Seven was an occasion for celebrating the world of women, their community and their achievements. Stockard's informants described this celebration, which they called the Festival of the Seven Sisters, as the highlight of the calendar year. In many regions of China the festival was an occasion for celebrating women's domestic arts, and marked the annual meeting of a celestial weaving maid and her cowherd husband who had been separated by the maid's father. In a delta version reported by Stockard both the tone and the protagonist have been changed. The father has been replaced by the maid's seven sisters (inhabitants of seven stars), and it is the sisters, not the father, who separate and unite the heavenly couple. Quoting from this version, Stockard relates: 'It is said that one of these sisters made a clandestine marriage with a cowherd occupying a planet on the other side of the Milky Way; and once a year the wife is permitted by her sisters who were greatly incensed at her marriage to cross the Milky Way to meet her husband' (Stockard 1989 pp. 42–3). In this delta version, a community of 'sisters' is threatened by the marriage of one of their number, and it is they, not the usual male authority figure, who are disturbed by and yet allow the conjugal meetings.

In the delta the Festival of the Seven Sisters was organised by associations of unmarried girls from one or more girls' houses, but the audience, according to Stockard, was the total village community (see Stockard 1989 p. 43). Preparations, including the manufacture of furniture and clothing as offerings for the Seven Sisters, took place in girls' houses and were started months in advance of the actual ceremony (see Stockard 1989 p. 43). When an association member left her girls' house to join her husband's household, a banquet was held, paid for by the husband's family. Thereafter, Stockard writes, a woman celebrated the Seven Sisters only as a member of the audience (1989 p. 44; see also Chiang).

Some young women opted out of the cycle of reproduction, remaining in their girls' houses until they took the vows of a *zi shu nu*, at which point they moved to spinster houses or vegetarian halls, or rented rooms shared with others. For the majority who did marry and eventually took up residence with their husbands, the passage from young wife to mother and finally to village matron implied new responsibilities as they assumed important roles in the ritual life of their families and communities (see R. Watson 1990a). As village matrons they were respons-ible for managing the marriages of their own children and those of their neighbours, assisting with the disposal of the community's dead, and overseeing the village's annual rites of purification (c. *pa ting gei*). It was 'old wives' who created fertile brides and guarded the community against mystical attack. In rural Guangdong, women kept hungry ghosts at bay and often became the spirit mediums who soothed both the living and the dead (see e.g. Potter 1974).

In arguing that women from sericultural as well as rice producing villages created and maintained affinal networks, labour exchanges, festival associations, temple groups, girls' houses and religious movements it is tempting to discard altogether the images of the frightened *mui tsai*, the pawned daughter and the cowed wife. In my view this would be a mistake. The expressive culture I have just described does not exhaust women's experience in the delta. There was also a dark side in which girls and women were bought and sold, bartered and pawned. Many women, because of poverty, enslavement, and indenture, did not experience the sustaining networks of village women, the camaraderie of the girls' house, the excitement of a pilgrimage, or the sense of achievement that came from organising a Double Seven festival. It is also well to remember that confident matrons were not always and everywhere mistresses of their own fates.

There are many reasons why the images of the self-sufficient marriage resister and powerful village matron must be qualified. For one thing, there is the question of numbers. Marriage resisters made up only a tiny proportion of delta society, and many women ended their lives not as respected matrons but as desperately poor widows, harried concubines or childless marginals. Furthermore, many delta women who were members of stigmatised occupational groups like the boat people, reclamation workers, prostitutes or *mui tsai* did not grow up in girls' houses or have access to jobs in the region's filatures. Finally, it would be romantic folly to disregard the institutions, structures, behaviour and ideologies of male dominance that conditioned the options available to rural women. It is important to remember that women were both actors and reactors, but the environment in which they lived was often hostile. In such an environment independence and resistance are indeed relative phenomena.

Gates contends that daughters and wives could be jettisoned when the survival of the patricorporation was at stake (1989). Data on female infanticide and the market in girls and women provide evidence for this assertion. In an earlier publication I argue that in the patrilineal/patriarchal world of delta society, men are more clearly defined than women. There is no doubt that the ideology of patriliny is particularly strong in the Pearl River delta, and further, that clear and rigid boundaries between agnates and non-agnates restricted access to crucial resources. Rights to landed estates, political brokers and protection in a violent environment were often linked to lineage membership. In a society where women did not inherit family property and were considered to be of little political consequence, it is not altogether surprising to find that the boundaries that separated servile men from free men were more rigidly drawn than those that delineated servile women from free women.[21] Whether we can argue therefore that male servitude was harsher than female servitude requires further analysis. What is clear is that the Pearl River delta was an area in which gender inequality significantly affected patterns of servitude (see R. Watson 1991b).

In reviewing the roles and options available to delta women, we should not forget that many women had few or no choices. From early childhood *mui tsai* as well as many concubines and indentured labourers were controlled by dealers, masters and overseers. There can be no doubt that some of the delta's marriage resisters obtained their independence by purchasing rights over other women. Who were these women? Did the indentured, pawned, and enslaved women we find in the delta during this period come from poor areas in the sericultural core, from rice-growing areas at the fringe of the silk district, or perhaps from communities that were peripheral to the delta altogether? Were they the daughters of slaves (*ximin*), boat people, reclamation workers, or impoverished peasants? Given that many of these women, especially *mui tsai*, left their home villages at age seven or eight to take up duties in their masters' households, their youthful experiences were of a very different order from those of their better-off 'sisters'. Because many concubines had previously served as *mui tsai* (see e.g. Stockard 1989 p. 29, 66; R. Watson 1991b), they too had been denied the conviviality of the girls' house and festival association.

Whatever their background, delta women who left their rural homes and migrated to urban Hong Kong and Southeast Asia took with them certain institutions, beliefs and patterns of behaviour. These included both girls' houses and the fear of bondage, festival celebrations and the insecurities bred of poverty, poetic laments and illiteracy. In an excellent biographical sketch, Sankar (1984) details the life of a Xunde marriage resister who, as employment opportunities in the filatures declined, was forced to work as a domestic servant, first in Guangzhou and finally in Hong Kong. It is fascinating to see the ways in which elements of rural life were adapted and transformed in these new urban settings. Writing about the bonds formed among marriage resisters, Sankar argues that women migrants were aided in the difficult transition from industrial worker to domestic servant by transforming their rural sisterhoods into part-guild, part-family associations (1984 pp. 51–2). 'Organisation and meaning have varied from place to place and changed over time,' Sankar writes, 'but the basic structure of the sisterhood survived when it was transplanted outside the original culture area that had nurtured it' (1984 p. 52). We must not lose sight of the fact, however, that many delta women were totally unprepared for the new urban environments in which they had to make their way.

In the chapters that follow contributors examine how the various attitudes and practices that women brought with them from their homes in the delta mixed with new ideas, new circumstances and new environments. In the 1930s, women migrants (both voluntary and involuntary) to Hong Kong, Singapore, and British Malaya were engaged in delayed transfer and compensation marriages. In the case of the latter they may have assumed the role of wife or of concubine (i.e. 'the compensation'). They lived in their own homes, in the homes of their masters, in vegetarian halls, crowded rooming houses, or brothels. They adopted *mui tsai* as daughters or were themselves 'adopted'. In some cases women, who had themselves been involuntary migrants, indentured or bought other women. In other instances they were the rescuers of fleeing concubines, indigent prostitutes, and runaway *mui tsai*. They formed cults, transplanted their festivals, preserved and adapted ritual forms, songs and stories as they made their way in what were often extremely hostile surroundings (for examples, see Sankar 1984; Topley 1952, 1954, 1959, 1975; Chiang).

Those whose origins stretch to the Pearl River delta were both sustained and constrained by its richly elaborate culture, its complex interlocking hierarchies of inequality, and its highly public and deeply androcentric dogmas. That this world should have produced women culture-builders as well as women victims is not surprising. The delta was indeed a society of extremes.

Notes

1. I have conducted field research from 1969 in the village of San Tin and from 1977 in the village of Ha Tsuen. Both are in Hong Kong's New Territories.
2. There is excellent work on rural women after 1949; see e.g. Croll 1981; K.A. Johnson 1983; Judd 1989; Stacey 1983; M. Wolf 1972, 1985.
3. For a useful comparison of women's labour contributions in North China and the Yangtse delta see Huang 1990 pp. 49–57; see also Davin 1976 and work cited below.
4. Given the number of historical studies of rural Chinese society, the lack of detailed studies of footbinding and infanticide in Late Imperial and Republican China is particularly depressing.
5. It should be noted that some delta residents lived not in villages but in dispersed households. This residential pattern was most prevalent in the sericulture area (see e.g. Topley 1975 p. 71).
6. For an example of women long-distance traders and 'guides' in the Pearl River delta see Sankar 1984 p. 60.
7. For examples and discussion of these points see Baker 1968 pp. 48–50; J.L. Watson 1975a, 1975b; R. Watson 1985; for areas outside the delta see Hu 1948; Liu 1959. The control that agnatic kin exercised over the adoption of successors is indicative of the kind of constraints 'lineage women' experienced (see J.L. Watson 1975a). When an heirless lineage member died, his widow might expect

to have little say over the choice of a successor. Because an adopted son was central to the widow's own future wellbeing, her lack of control was especially serious. At the death of a spouse a widow was not simply operating under the shadow of her husband's brother(s) or father but under the eyes of the entire lineage establishment as succession, property management and inheritance decisions were made.

8. In a recent essay Siu notes that in Zhongshan gentry women received substantial dowries in the late 19th and early 20th centuries (1990 pp. 36, 38, 40). Siu also refers to dowries of land among wealthy landlord families (1990 pp. 40–1).

9. For more discussion of concubines and wives see R. Watson 1991b pp. 246–50.

10. Delayed-transfer marriage and compensation marriage were found in dominant lineage communities as well as in non-lineage villages. At first this may be surprising considering the restrictions on uxorilocal residence, widow remarriage, minor marriage, and divorce. Although such forms, by the standards of the national elite, may have been judged un-Confucian, these unions did not risk alienating agnatic property from the patriline, nor did they divide the loyalties and affiliations of male offspring who grew up in their fathers' communities and households. In other words such unions did not directly threaten lineage resources or integrity.

11. For further discussion see So 1986 pp. 101–53; Eng 1986 pp. 47–58, 1990.

12. In a recent essay, Eng traces the relationship between Guangdong's weaving and reeling sectors. Although weavers initially encountered difficulties in securing an affordable supply of the hand-reeled silk required for use on their traditional looms, local weaving did not disappear. In time a non-filature based reeling technology was developed (Eng 1990 p. 67). This technology, powered by foot-treadle rather than steam, could be accommodated in the homes and small workshops of delta residents (Eng 1990 p. 72). In effect, two reeling sectors operated in rural Guangdong: one (steam filature) was devoted to exports and the other (treadle-powered reeling) supplied the needs of local weavers.

13. For example, in Xunde county there was only one filature in 1874 but by 1926 there were 154. By 1881 Nanhai had 11 filatures employing 4,000 women, but in 1926 the number of filatures had increased to 45 (Eng 1986 pp. 48–50). Stockard estimates that the number of filature reelers in the sericultural area varied from 63,000–87,000 in 1925 to as many as 136,860 in 1928 (1989 p. 161; see also So 1986 p. 120).

14. Topley includes in this region 'Shun-te *hsien* [county], particularly the eastern part; a small part of Nan-hai *hsien*, adjoining northern Shen-te and including the Hsi-ch'iao foothills; and a small part of P'an-yu, to the east of Shun-te' (1975 p. 68).

15. So reports that silk workers were the highest paid among all occupations in the sericultural region. A woman silk worker, he notes, could earn enough in a year to provide the annual subsistence for a peasant family of five (see So 1986 p. 126; see also Stockard 1989 pp. 156–7).

16. In fact, they often resided in maiden houses in their natal villages (see below).

17. See also Jaschok for terminology used in Xunde for categories of non-marrying women (1984 pp. 45–7).

18. See e.g. Siu 1990 p. 38; Stockard 1989 pp. 29, 66; Topley 1975 p. 77.
19. For accounts of women's communities and expressive culture among the elite during the Qing, see e.g. Ko 1989. It is also interesting to note that Judd (1989) reports residential arrangements in rural Shandong in the 1980s that, while apparently less systematised than Stockard's delayed transfer marriage, are very similar. Clearly, we have much to learn not only about women's expressive culture but also women's networks and relations to their natal families (including whether their contacts involve prolonged post-marital stays in their parental households).
20. I was told by informants living in Ha Tsuen where I have conducted fieldwork since 1977 that there were no maiden houses in the small villages (with populations of fewer than 300 or so) neighbouring Ha Tsuen. However, Sankar describes non-residential 'girls' houses' or groups in small villages (1984 p. 54).
21. I do not argue that distinctions between free and servile women were not drawn, but rather that such distinctions were less clearly marked (both legally and ritually) than those between free and servile men (R. Watson 1991b pp. 249–50). For comparisons with literature on servile women in Africa see Robertson & Klein 1983; Meillassoux 1983 p. 56; J.L. Watson 1980 p. 249; Wright 1983 p. 249; Kopytoff & Miers 1977.

3. San Po Tsai (Little Daughters-in-Law) and Child Betrothals in the New Territories of Hong Kong from the 1890s to the 1960s

By James Hayes

It is perhaps superfluous to state that … a girl is really, even at a very early age, a marketable commodity (Giles 1911 p. 98).

… early betrothals and early marriages are common … especially among the Hakkas, who have, moreover, the custom of sending the betrothed, as soon as she is able to walk, say when three or four years old, to the family of her future husband, where she remains until her marriage … (Eitel Report 1879 p. 54).

This is the most economical, most looked down upon type of marriage arrangement … (Hsieh K. 1962 p. 255).

Why don't they wait another two or three years and carry you through their gate formally, in the red embroidered sedan chair and with the horns blowing and the gongs beating? Then our family also could add something at least to your trousseau. It'd be better for our reputation. Zhongyao [her betrothed] has many younger brothers, and a formal wedding would give you more standing among your sisters-in-law (Wang 1989 p. 148).

Introduction

In the 1950s, when I first served in the District Administration, New Territories, the villagers of the Hong Kong region were still leading a traditional rural existence based on agriculture. The two rice crops a year were still of major importance to most settlements, and the market towns catered largely to the village populations and their agricultural pursuits. Indeed, in most places the position had scarcely changed since prewar times (see Hayes 1977 pp. 32–46). In this very conservative and old-fashioned society, it was still usual to find various traditional kinds of betrothal and transfers of children. There were *san po tsai* staying with their future husbands' families. There were little girls already betrothed but still living with their own parents. There were young, recently betrothed female adults, and there were newly married women who had come into the village from nearby settlements. In practically all cases, the traditional patterns of bride-finding, betrothal and marriage had been observed.

In the practice of what was styled 'major marriage', the employment of 'go-betweens', specialists in fate and letter writers versed in the various forms of

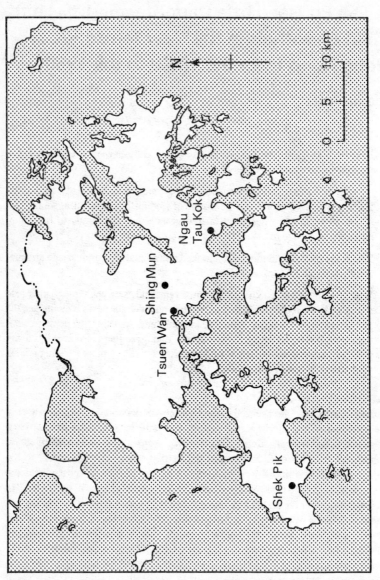

The Hong Kong Region around 1900

Shing Mun

Tsuen Wan

Ngau Tau Kok

Shek Pik

N

0 5 10 km.

documentation needed on such occasions was still *de rigeur*. Bride-price, dowry and presents were obligatory. Use of the red sedan bridal chair to take the weeping bride to her new home was still quite common in the 1950s, and in outlying places it persisted into the 1960s. The traditional bridal laments could also be heard on these occasions (Blake 1978 pp. 13–33; E.L. Johnson 1984 p. 90).

It has not been easy to collect firsthand information on 'minor marriage', the conditions of life, and the rituals associated with *san po tsai* in the Hong Kong region. There are only a small number of persons alive today who were either former *san po tsai* or knew much about them. Also, when compared with betrothal and major marriage, there was much less ceremony attached to the *san po tsai* transfer and its later marriage. Outside the basic ritual essentials, what *was* done to celebrate these occasions seems to have varied from family to family. Even in cases of adult marriage, according to some informants, brides knew little of the details since the arrangements were made by their parents, so former *san po tsai*, transferred as small children, were even less likely to know about them.

The basic information and the personal histories in this chapter come from three areas of Hong Kong: the Cantonese-speaking farming and fishing village of Shek Pik on Lantau Island and the former Hakka stonecutters' settlement of Ngau Tau Kok in East Kowloon, where I collected them in the late 1950s and mid-1960s,[1] and the Hakka settlements of the Shing Mun and Tsuen Wan areas of the mainland New Territories, collected in the last few years.[2]

Infant and Child Betrothal in Chinese Marriage

On the subject of marriage and betrothal, Archdeacon Gray noted in 1878 that around Canton the age of betrothal was between seven and 14, except among the Hakka, whose children were 'affianced in infancy' (p. 189). One of the early District Officers in the New Territories reported in 1912 that the average age of marriage was about 19 for husbands and 17 for wives, but infant betrothal was common among the poorer Hakka population. He added: 'The girl in such case [sic] is regarded as belonging to her destined husband's family, but continues to reside with her parents, until she is of an age to cohabit with her husband: unless her parents die first, when she enters the house of her future husband as an 'expectant' wife' (G.N. Orme 1912 *HKSP* p. 15, para. 93).

It will be noted how in this and other accounts it is always the Hakka who are singled out for notice, yet early betrothal seems to have been a universal practice in 19th- and early 20th-century China. One authority with a keen interest and much firsthand experience, writing at the close of the Qing (1910) about Shandong but with general reference, goes so far as to state that 'the majority of marriages are the outcome of longstanding betrothals' (R.F. Johnston 1910 p. 203). This is affirmed by another impeccable source, the later editions of the Qing Code used by Father Gui Boulais in his Manuel du Code Chinois, in which it is stated, '*Les pères de famille ont l'habitude de fiancer de très bonne heure leurs enfants; ils n'attendent même pas toujours qu'ils aient atteint l'âge de raison*' (1966 p. 258).

Father Boulais adds that betrothals *before* birth were also made: '... *quelque-fois même ils les unissent hypothètiquement avant leurs naissance, pendent qu'ils sont encore dans le sein de leur mère*' (*ibid*.). In this connection, it would appear that these were also to be found in Guangdong. My wife's mother, born in Foshan near Guangzhou in 1907, has told me that such betrothals in the womb were a feature of family life in some well-to-do households there in her youth.

Chang Chun-ch'ien notes another form of betrothal in southeast China:

> There are also some superstitious women, who, being afraid that they may not be able to conceive, take in a young girl child to rear and then wait for a son to be born. When this happens, there will already be a wife ready for the son when he comes of age. They think that once this kind of girl is in the household – known as 'a girl who waits for a son' or the 'girl waiting to be the brother's wife' – there will be more chance of having sons. In this kind of marriage the female is always older than the male (1960 p. 26–7).

In Hong Kong's New Territories, Rubie Watson mentions children 'matched' when they were eight or nine years old in the 1940s (1985 p. 120). By the late 1950s, early betrothals were almost certainly less usual than in the recent past, but I came across a few cases in Shek Pik of couples who had been betrothed in childhood but were only married as adults. I never heard of any betrothals in the womb or 'of girls who wait for a son', although these practices may have existed.

San Po Tsai in Chinese Marriage

A *san po tsai* is a child transferred from her natal family in a particular form of early betrothal. The term is Cantonese for a little daughter-in-law. In Hakka, the other longstanding local language of the Hong Kong region, she is known as a *sim pu tsai* (same characters). In the written language, she was more often referred to as a *tong-yang-xi*.[3]

The *san po tsai* held a special and intermediate position in the household, of lesser status than a bride or a regularly betrothed girl, but not to be confused with the *mui tsai* – the female sold, pledged or leased into domestic service or worse, who was a servant by status and was married outside the household (see Jaschok 1988 and below; Jaschok and Miers; Miers; Koh). She was part of the taking-in family, brought in with the specific intention that she should marry one of its sons when she was old enough.

This traditional institution – for such it may be called – was not merely a phenomenon of the New Territories of Hong Kong, but was known in many other parts of China. Olga Lang states that it was well known in old China, and was even mentioned in the legal code of the Yuan dynasty (1946 p. 127, fn. 16).[4]It is clear that it was common in 19th- and 20th-century Fujian, as stated by Christian missionaries (Maclay 1861, addendum), and reaffirmed more recently by Lin Yue-hua (1947 pp. 16–8) and Lena Johnston (1922 p. 39), as well as in Taiwan (see *inter alia* Chang C.C. 1960 pp. 17, 26–7). Such marriage transfers seem also to have been plentiful in the Shin Hua district of Hunan (Hsieh P.Y. 1943 p. 39). In Central China these children were known as *xiao xi*, and doubtless they were known elsewhere by other names (Levy 1968 p. 91; Fei & Chang 1939 pp. 53–5; Fei 1949 p. 260; Wu 1989 p. 100). In Guangdong itself, the transfer of young children was common[5] and was apparently not a custom of recent origin.

The San Po Tsai Condition and its Associated Rituals

The essentials of the *san po tsai* condition in Guangdong and Guangxi are brought out very clearly by the following extract from the collected papers of Hsieh K'ang, born in central Guangxi in one of the poorer areas of south China in 1901:

> The Little Daughter-in-Law is the most economical and least respected form of marriage, and only to be found among poor people. The girl can be a few years old up to the age of 10 when she enters her future husband's family as a 'not yet married wife'. Upon entry, she and her husband-to-be will be about the same age. She will help with the household duties, and the two will be wed when they are old enough. The boy's father will then ask for the consent of the girl's father, and a celebratory feast will be held, after which they will be considered man and wife (1962 p. 254).

Lou Tzu-k'uang, writing in 1968 about Hakka marriage customs on Taiwan, says:

> When a boy is young, his parents purchase a little girl to be a Little Daughter in Law. When the two are of age, they will be given new clothes and ornaments, and the marriage will take place on the eve of the new year. But before the marriage, the families on each side must secure the other's consent, and the girl must be willing. This type of marriage, though still to be found, is seldom encountered nowadays. The reason is that girls are unwilling to marry in this way (1968 p. 17).

A similar statement also comes from Taiwan, couched in much the same vein, but emphasising the difference between major and minor marriage:

> '*tong-yang-xi*': A proper marriage involves betrothal money, and much expenditure on guests, feasts, wine, and the like, to a not small amount. Therefore in a number of poorer families, in order that out of poverty their sons do not lose the chance to be married, the parents assist them by taking other people's young daughters into the family as *tong-yang-xi* (a child reared as the son's future wife), so that in due course they may be married to their own sons (Chang C.C. 1960 p. 17).

As practised in the Hakka villages of the New Territories of Hong Kong, the *san po tsai* institution appears to have been characterised by the following features and 'conditions'. There had to be a middleman or 'go-between', as for a major wedding. There was also a transfer paper which was given to the taking-in family. My informants said that it was most usual to send away a girl-child 'one hundred days' after birth. I suspect this is a way of saying 'early in life' rather than an exact length of time. Whilst transfer in infancy was stated to be common in the early part of this century, it will be seen from the cases cited here that it was just as common for the transfer to be made later, especially if it was dictated by the death of a parent. The transfer was to be accompanied by a suit of clothing, as a token of the girl's or infant's 'not needing her own mother's milk'. In some cases, a small sum of money and other auspicious small gifts were sent with her, to get her off to a good start. The two families would henceforth regard themselves as relatives.

When the transition from *san po tsai* to the married state was decided, the girl would receive a hat decorated with flowers, as implied by the description used to indicate the marriage of a *san po tsai*. This was styled *sheung tau* or 'Placing [the decorated hat] on the Head'. The hat in question had 'flowers' stuck in it, but it seems from descriptions given that these were made of gold or silver wire rather than being real flowers. In preparation for the *sheung tau* ceremony, the girl, who had hitherto worn her hair in a pigtail, would put up her hair in the *kam kai* style which was used in conjunction with the flowered headdress. The hairstyle was called *tau shik*.

The marriage would be signified by the couple going to worship before the husband's family's ancestral tablets. In the case of *san po tsai* marriages, this would usually be done on the last day of the old year, or eight days before it, at the Winter Solstice. Other than this and performing the *sheung tau* ritual, no other celebration was required; though if money was available and if the family felt so inclined and well-disposed, some little show might be attempted and there might be a dinner for family on the male side.

The Mother-in-Law

Towering over the *san po tsai* even more than in the case of an adult bride was the awesome figure of the mother-in-law. Discussion of the status and condition of the child 'bride-to-be' would not be complete without taking into consideration the practically unfettered authority of the mother-in-law. Her power over the *san po tsai* was that much greater than over older female members of the household, though some women were able to exert their personalities and vent their temper on all regardless of whether they were adults or children. Her authority aside, the nature of the mother-in-law, whether she was kindly or cruel and vicious, was everything to the incoming girl and was not tempered by the blood tie as with a natural daughter.

The prevailing attitude and expectation of older women in traditional rural life was that the advent of a younger woman in the household would free her from menial duties in and around the home and improve her life in other ways. I recall asking one old village woman when she had stopped cutting grass and firewood on the hills and received the prompt answer: 'When I got a daughter-in-law.' It was also traditional for a mother-in-law (and sometimes a father-in-law) to bully a son's wife.[6]

The petty tyranny of a mother-in-law (*ga po* in Cantonese) was of course well known and probably expected. In Hong Kong, and no doubt elsewhere, it was embodied in local folklore. Thus the irritating cries of a bird on Lantau Island are likened to the words '*Ka-kung Ka-po, tak-tsui [nan zi de] Lo-po*' ('Father-in-law,

Mother-in-law, always finding fault with their Son's Wife') and linked to a story about a young wife whose husband went abroad and whose mother-in-law mistreated her so badly that she died or committed suicide.[7]

It seems plain that the harshness often exhibited towards daughters-in-law was extended to 'little daughters-in-law'. Ill-treatment and tears are encountered in a wide variety of literature. Hsieh Ping-yang, for instance, mentions a 'tea garden', seemingly more of a plantation, where she was sent to pick tea leaves along with other girls, most of whom were 'child daughters-in-law'. Their lives at the hands of the mothers-in-law who had sent them out to work to bring money into the family were hard. 'Rarely did they have a good meal ... they were as thin as skeletons ...' and they cried a great deal about their sad lot (1943 p. 39). Lena Johnston's little daughter-in-law was only three at the time of her transfer, yet her mother-in-law 'kept telling her she must be of use', and she received slaps and beatings if she was clumsy or slow, even though her father sometimes came to see that she was not ill and to say that she must 'not be beaten too heavily' (L.E. Johnston 1922 pp. 24–6; see also Wang 1989).

Some accounts in Christian missionary works also make sad reading (see e.g. Guinness 1894 Vol. II pp. 284–5). The Catholic Vicar Apostolic of Zhejiang noted that one little baptised daughter-in-law was 'afraid of going to heaven, for fear she should find her mother-in-law there ... but we succeeded in convincing her that in heaven her mother-in-law could never ill-treat her again' (Reynaud 1897 p. 95). The woes of the little daughter-in-law were also celebrated in folklore (see e.g. Hensman 1971 pp. 17–21). The break for older children who had to leave their own homes must have been traumatic for some girls, and for their mothers. Adele Fielde's 'Aunt Luck' from Swatow was sent from her mother at seven years old. Though not harshly treated, she had to work very hard at spinning from daylight to dark and so missed her own family that she 'kept crying more or less for years' and 'never really stopped crying' until she had her own children (1884 pp. 157–61).

Interestingly, however, I have not had a strong impression of the unkindness of mothers-in-law from my many female informants over the years, though they often mention the hardness of their early lives. They were probably among the luckier children, or perhaps their memories of 'hardness' encapsulated any severities experienced at the mother-in-law's hands, for in those days it was the general practice to be authoritarian in the home and to beat children for real or imagined transgressions.

Cases of San Po Tsai and Other Betrothals in Childhood from the Rural Areas of the New Territories of Hong Kong

The Shek Pik Villages on Lantau Island

The Shek Pik valley is located at the southwestern end of Lantau Island, within the New Territories of Hong Kong. In the 1950s it contained several villages and hamlets. The main village, Shek Pik Wai, had 363 inhabitants at the Colony

Census of 1911, but numbers had shrunk to just over 200 by 1957. The smaller settlement of Fan Pui had exactly 59 residents at each count. Elders said that the population had been much larger in their grandfathers' time, but had been greatly reduced by disease. The villages were farming and fishing communities, settled since the mid-Ming period in the one case and the second half of the 17th century in the other. The larger settlement was multi-lineage, whereas Fan Pui was a single lineage village (see Hayes 1977 ch. 4).

The villagers were Cantonese-speaking, in the particular patois that K.M.A. Barnett called 'Nam Tau Punti' (1974 p. 136). However, the marriages listed in genealogical records or ascertained by enquiry for the hundred years before the removal of the villagers to make way for a reservoir in the late 1950s and mid-1960s, show Hakka- as well as Punti-speaking brides and a complex speech situation.[8]

These settlements were remote. Lantau Island, though much larger than Hong Kong and located closer to Canton and Macau, had not been developed by the 1950s. Save at Silver Mine Bay with its regular ferries from and to Hong Kong, which had attracted immigrant vegetable cultivators, its villages had remained intact and undiluted by outsiders. Life followed pretty much the same patterns as it had done for centuries. This particularly applied to the women, some of whom, up to the time of their resettlement in Tsuen Wan, had never left the island in their lives. Perhaps it should be recorded that the women did most of the farm work as well as the domestic work. This was not uncommon in the region, especially among the Hakka communities whose menfolk had gone abroad in search of less unpredictable means of livelihood than farming.

In my enquiries, I found three *san po tsai* living with their future husbands' families. One was six, the second was 10, and the third, taken in during the removal negotiations, was also six. Their prospective husbands were 12, nine and 11 *sui* respectively.[9] The first two girls came from clans in the village. In the third case, surely the last of its kind in the long history of this old village, the girl of six was the daughter of an immigrant farmer in nearby upper Keung Shan, whose father had come there to settle in 1934. There were three other daughters in the family. The girl's father was paid $600, there were 'all the usual papers', and the boy's family gave a celebration dinner in the big village [Shek Pik], attended by 'all the relatives, clan elders and the village head'. These relatives came only from the boy's side.

Looking for prewar cases, I found another family in which the wife, now 33, had come into her husband's family in 1934 when she was five. Conceivably, there may have been a few more of these former *san po tsai* among the village wives, especially among the older women.

Ngau Tau Kok Village and Neighbourhood, East Kowloon

Ngau Tau Kok village and its residents, together with the neighbourhood to which they belonged, differed greatly from the long-settled, chiefly agricultural settlements at Shek Pik. The East Kowloon sub-district included rice and vegetable farmers, duck breeders, fishermen and the like, often from home areas in eastern Guangdong, but the Ngau Tau Kok stone quarries are of particular interest. These were part of a larger group of quarries in East Kowloon known as the 'Four Stone Hills'.[10] In the early years of this century there were said to be more than 10 quarries in the Ngau Tau Kok section of the 'Four Hills' alone, each employing 20 to 30 persons, all Hakkas from the Tung Kong or East River area of northeastern Guangdong. The quarries engaged stone cutters and polishers, together with the blacksmiths who supplied and repaired the tools of the trade. Ancillary workers, comprising locally recruited casual labour and women and girls from the quarrymen's families, broke the cut stone into aggregate and carried it to junks at the shore. The more prosperous quarrymasters also owned junks which took the cut blocks and broken stone to their clients.

Both male and female recruitment was very selective. The quarry workmen were mainly recruited from the home area in China. They served as apprentices at Ngau Tau Kok, and when trained went back to their home villages to be married, after which they returned to work in East Kowloon. In the case of quarry workers whose families were already settled in the village, their wives might have been living with their parents from the time they were small, having been brought into the household as *san po tsai* from the home area, or in some cases locally, when they themselves were still boys. It was this clear preference for women and girls from the home areas instead of from the local Hakka villages which differentiated the stonecutters' settlements from the farming villages around them.

The greater emphasis laid on bringing in *san po tsai* seems to have been connected with the fact that most of the Ngau Tau Kok quarries of the time were small family concerns. There was a continual need for labour in and around the home and quarry.

My most striking female informant had a clear memory of her childhood, perhaps because it had been so dramatic. She was born in a hamlet at Hang Mei, To Kwa Wan, Kowloon, about 1888. Her father died when she was very small. Her mother, a Poon from the village of Ha Kwai Chung, Tsuen Wan, died when the daughter was in her 20s. However, the girl had been sent to Ngau Tau Kok as a *san po tsai* when she was seven years old, and thereafter lived with her husband-to-be's family there. The boy was two years her senior.

As she grew in size and strength her duties in her new family were to feed pigs, and cut grass and firewood for the family stoves. She also helped to grow vegetables, and had to struggle with the essential regular watering of the plots using two buckets on a carrying pole. For the first few years, being little, she did not go out of the house, which was located beside the family quarry, but later went with a sister-in-law to the village shop. In her 20s she carried cut firewood to market at Kowloon City, a two-hour walk along the shore or over the hill.

Her father-in-law died only two years after her arrival, but her mother-in-law, who, she said, 'had been brought up at the quarries and knew all about the work', ran the business in her husband's place. But soon after the mother-in-law and her partner began cutting stone at a well known *fung shui* spot, in the face of warnings that it would bring misfortune, four of her husband's seven brothers died, after being ill for only a few days. This momentous event, occurring when my informant was still young, left a number of widowed sisters-in-law at home, who told her mother-in-law of her doings, real or imagined. She was not well treated by her mother-in-law and included the presence of the sisters-in-law among her catalogue of the 'disasters' suffered by the family!

Another female informant, also a *san po tsai*, was born in 1892 at Ngau Tau Kok, the daughter of a duck farmer. Her father died when she was small, and so did her only brother. She was then transferred as a *san po tsai* to a Lau family in Hang Hau town, Junk Bay, when she was eight. However, her first husband died, and at the age of 24 she re-married, to a man living at Sai Wan Ho, Shaukeiwan, on Hong Kong Island. Her tale is of interest because she often visited her own mother, both from her new family at Hang Hau, and later from Shaukeiwan. The visits were mainly at festival times.

Another elderly woman, again a *san po tsai*, was born at Pak Mong Fa near Tam Shui, Wai Yeung, about 1894. She had been orphaned when very small and was brought up by a relative, and sent with an uncle to Ngau Tau Kok at the age of seven. The uncle had come to join kinsmen in the quarries, but later returned to the country. She was sent to a Lin family as a *san po tsai* soon after her arrival at Ngau Tau Kok.

Yet another elderly lady, born in 1903, had come to Ngau Tau Kok in her early teens to be a *san po tsai* in the Ko family. She was from Tong Mei village near Tam Shui, and an uncle had brought her from there, and then returned. The Ko family came from a village near to her native place, and were known to her own people there. Her husband-to-be was 10 years her senior.

The Purchase of Children for Adoption

The stonecutters' community also bought in children who were neither *mui tsai* nor *san po tsai*. This included girls as well as boys. One old lady had bought a granddaughter – the child of a stranger, one of the quarrymen employed at Hung Hom, To Kwa Wan, Kowloon. She had bought the girl from the parents when she was a baby in the 1930s. She had met them one day when buying rice at Hung Hom, and upon becoming better acquainted had learned that they wished to dispose of the girl.

Another of the Ngau Tau Kok families had bought a girl and three small boys in the few years prior to the Japanese attack on Hong Kong in December 1941. They were intended as grandchildren after the only son of the family had died without issue. They were bought from 'human traffickers' in Hong Kong.[11]

Shing Mun and Other Villages of Tsuen Wan

The Shing Mun valley, above the former market town of Tsuen Wan in the western New Territories, was formerly home to eight villages and hamlets. These had been built in scattered locations in and above the main valley. The great majority of the villagers belonged to one lineage which was represented in most of the settlements, including the largest, Tai Wai. There were several other, smaller lineages. All the villagers were Hakkas, and the main lineage, the Chengs, had been settled there since the mid-17th century (Hayes 1983 pp. 210–2). At the time of the repossession of the land by the Hong Kong Government for a reservoir project in 1928, the population was recorded as 855 persons (Hayes in *JHKBRAS* 17, 1977 pp. 193–7).

The Shing Mun families were all farmers, growing rice and pineapples. Pineapple growing provided many households with an extra cash crop to supplement the produce of their fields and the sale of grass and firewood in the local market towns, and later in urban Kowloon. This was necessary since many of their fields were on small upland terraces and yields were poor.

By the late 19th century, despite a bitter three-year 'war' with their fellow Hakkas in the Tsuen Wan villages in the 1860s, the families at Shing Mun were again finding wives and little daughters-in-law from Tsuen Wan. At the same time, their women and female children were being married-out to the villages of the sub-district. Their numbers 'in' and 'out' represented a considerable percentage of all such marriages. This was probably due to proximity, and also to the fact that much of their marketing, especially of a heavy export crop like pineapples, had to be done in or through Tsuen Wan with its cargo junks, which encouraged social intercourse and facilitated marriage transfers.

Here I found one woman who had been a *san po tsai*. She was born a Chan of Kwan Mun Hau village, Tsuen Wan, in 1920, the youngest of four sisters, and had two younger brothers. Her mother, who died in 1983, was also a Tsuen Wan native, a Lau of Yi Pei Chun village. Her father died at about the time she was sent at the age of five to a family of Chengs at Fu Yung Shan, Shing Mun, and this could well have been the reason for the transfer. There was a *san ka*, or 'body money' as she described it, of 99 silver dollars; this number whose sound is homonymous with the Cantonese for 'long, long' [*scil*. life] being, as she said, very auspicious. Her husband, who was the eldest son of the family and about five or six years older than herself, had two younger brothers and three sisters. The mother-in-law was another Tsuen Wan person, a Tsang from Hoi Pa, as was her husband's grandmother, a Lau from Wo Yi Hap village just below Shing Mun. Both had been adult brides, not *san po tsai* like 'Little Chan'.

She began to work from the start, looking after the family's cow and calves, cutting grass and firewood, helping with the pigs, and with housework. She was kept very busy. Every day was the same, and life was hard for all. Being fed and kept fully occupied, she didn't have the time or any reason to think much about her own home, she said. Her parents-in-law seem to have been generally kind, calling her 'Chan Tsai' or 'Little Chan', and she addressed them as a daughter would her own parents. Her husband's next younger brother, who was still alive and in fact sitting in on my interview with her and joining interestedly in the conversation, said he had addressed her as 'Ah So', the term for elder brother's wife, right from the start, showing that the married state of both parties was recognised in the family from the time of her entry.

The *sheung tau* ritual was carried out on the 13th day of the 10th lunar month in her case. Her husband wore the clothing that would be worn at a major marriage ceremony: a long gown with black riding jacket and a sash, and an old-style 'gold' hat. The couple bowed to the ancestors in the ancestral hall. There was a feast the night before the ceremony, and the husband's relatives (not hers) were invited.[12] Music was played and her husband's family slaughtered their own pigs and chickens.

Whilst a *san po tsai* she was taken to visit her own family in Kwan Mun Hau for several nights over the Lunar New Year period while she was in Shing Mun, and after the move to the new village in 1928. Visits at other times were fewer, she said.

This was the only former *san po tsai* I found in these villages, although the mothers of some of my informants had been *san po tsai*. It would seem, therefore, that there were very few of them.

However, there were cases of childhood betrothals. One was a Tang of Lo Wai, born in 1909. Her mother was a Cheng, the main lineage at Shing Mun, from Pei Tau To in that area. She had been betrothed soon after birth through a female go-between named Tang from her own clan in Lo Wai to a Yeung of Yeung Uk, Tsuen Wan. The betrothal money was $2. She was married at 13, and went in a bridal chair to her husband's village. He was two years older than she was. Her elder sister, also betrothed in infancy, had been married to a Lau of Yee Pei Chun below Lo Wai when she was 17 or 18.

Another old lady was a Yau of Kwan Mun Hau, Tsuen Wan, born about 1902, who had been betrothed when she was about four to a Cheung of Ho Lek Pui, who was a year younger. The usual two dollars was paid – she called it *lai see* (lucky money) – and her bride price on marriage was $160. The horoscope papers had been exchanged and compared before the betrothal, she thought. It had come about because one of the Cheung wives at Ho Lek Pui was a Yau and knew of her. This 'go-between' had arranged everything. The marriage had been 'blind', and she had not seen her husband until the bridal chair arrived in Shing Mun.

San Po Tsai from Other Parts of the New Territories [13]

I came across a few other *san po tsai* cases among elderly residents of the former villages of Northwest Kowloon when making enquiries there in the early 1960s. An old lady who entered her future husband's family in 1898 at the age of six – he was then 11 – recalled that her (in effect) 'bride price' had consisted of 100 pieces of silver, two chickens, two slices of pork, nine eggs, nine salted fish and two bottles of a fine medicinal wine called *ng ka p'ei*, sent over to her parents by her new family. Her future mother-in-law had treated her harshly, and she was kept very busy helping with pig rearing and cooking the pig food, cutting grass and firewood, carrying vegetables and the like. It seems that all the women in this small Hakka village of Cheng Uk worked in the fields, growing vegetables for the urban market.

Another lady, born in 1892, had lived with her parents in an old house in Law

Uk village, Sham Shui Po. They were casual workers on building sites in the area, and had come from the country before she was born to find work in Hong Kong, because her father, a compulsive gambler, had lost all his property at home. At the age of three, she was sent to a farming family in the nearby village of Sheung Li Uk. She led the usual life of a young village girl, helping to rear the pigs and chickens, cutting grass and firewood and assisting in the rice and vegetable fields. Because her village was close to the sea, she also collected seaweed from the shore in the winter months and prepared and cooked it for the pigs, to eke out the swill obtained from food shops and stalls near the market to which the villagers took vegetables and livestock to sell.

One of the most curious cases that has come to my attention concerned a *san po tsai* in one of the Tuen Mun villages. She had been taken into another family when small, but in 1940 when the time came for her to marry, the husband-to-be wished to marry another girl. The *san po tsai* must have been strong-willed, or else the husband and his parents were unusual. Perhaps both – but the outcome was that he married both of them. Both ceremonies took place on the same day and at the same time, and the two wives were accorded equal status thereafter as *ping chai*.[14]

It is also of some interest that Mr To Tim-fuk of the large and very long-established To lineage of Tuen Mun recounted that his teacher, a Pat Heung (New Territories) man from an area of long-settled mixed Hakka-Punti settlement, had told him that Hakka girls made the best *san po tsai* as they were more likely to settle down sensibly and happily, as well as to flourish and have children.

San Po Tsai in Shenzhen

Finally, to complement the information given by former *san po tsai* from the Shing Mun village, there was the story told to me on 1 July 1990 by a splendidly cheerful and robust elderly village woman at Kwor Yuen Sai Kui, Po On County, near Shenzhen. She was 76, born a Lok in the village of Mong Ngau Kong about 1913–4, and sent as a *san po tsai* at the age of four. She had been carried on the back of one of the women from her own village who, from her description, appeared to be the equivalent of a *tai kam* or mistress of ceremonies, a person well-versed in marriage rituals and customs. The journey to her new family's village had taken half an hour, and she had been accompanied on the way by her own close relatives. The husband-to-be was the second of three brothers. He was two years her senior. All three brothers had *san po tsai* brought into the family for them and there were more than 10 persons in the household. Her husband's family had sent over the following gifts to mark the taking-in: 10 catties of pork, 10 catties of beancurd, two catties of bean vermicelli, two chickens, two fish, four catties of rice and two jars of rice wine, but small ones and more like bottles – not unlike those mentioned in one of the cases from Northwest Kowloon.

When I mentioned the *sheung tau* or putting on the floral headdress to mark the transition to married woman, her face lit up. She motioned to her head and indicated having worn a flowered or decorated hat. She said there had been bowing to the ancestors and to earth and heaven, in the prescribed way, but the ceremony had taken place at the beginning of the year, not at year-end as mentioned in other accounts.

When asked about her childhood, she mentioned being scolded by her father- and mother-in-law to be, and being beaten and denied food on occasion; but it was impossible to tell from her cheerful manner whether this had been the normal childhood experience or an individual bias. With two other *san po tsai* in the family, it may have been the former.

San Po Tsai in Cities

I have little or no information about *san po tsai* in cities. Given that the basic reasons for taking them into households must have been much the same in town or country, there is no reason why they should not appear in accounts of urban as well as rural life. Indeed, Olga Lang cites the case of a Shanghai worker who told her co-researchers: 'We had no daughter so we decided to buy a little girl in order to marry her later to our son. A little girl is cheaper than the grown-up one and we sent her to work in the factory meantime' (Lang 1946 p. 127). However, in an early postwar survey of 516 households in an urban location on Hong Kong Island, whose results are now being examined by Maria Jaschok, not one *san po tsai* came to light, though the survey questionnaire specifically included a question on this topic. The question remains unanswered. Clearly, we need more information on the subject.

The Social Aspects of San Po Tsai

It is clear that *san po tsai* was a minor, muted form of marriage, with the glory and colour removed along with the expense.

A *san po tsai* lived alongside the brothers and sisters of her intended husband. Her position was worsened if her mother-in-law favoured her own children and treated her with open discrimination or even with harshness, or if older members of her own generation took a dislike to her. The position would obviously have varied from person to person, and family to family.

In regard to status, it is of particular interest that there seems to have been no discrimination against the *san po tsai* in the mode of address used within the family. In the local Hakka families the *san po tsai* was treated and addressed as a daughter, no different from those of her future in-laws. As one old lady described it to me, 'before marriage, she was addressed [by the parents] as a daughter: and after marriage, as a bride'. We have also noted how a prospective brother-in-law used the married form of address for his child sister-in-law to be. Though this evidence is slight, it is likely to be accurate. It is also significant that none of my informants over many years, whether speaking of themselves, their mothers, or other relatives who had been *san po tsai*, showed any reluctance to state this fact. One may deduce from this that the *san po tsai* status was for them just one of the traditional forms of local marriage – 'minor' maybe, but to be accepted by all concerned as a feature of family life.

However, there was a great difference in how minor and major marriage was celebrated. In 'major' marriage, the betrothal could take place in infancy or childhood, as well as in the months or year prior to the wedding, and it appears that the age of betrothal made no difference to the customary ceremonies. For the *san po tsai* there was seemingly no exchange of horoscopes or even choosing of a lucky day for the little daughter-in-law to enter her future husband's home, nor was there a dowry or present-giving.[15] The 'lucky money' or token gifts given on the occasion of the *san po tsai*'s transfer as an auspicious gesture normally sufficed for both her transfer and later marriage. And whereas an adult marriage could take place on any auspicious day throughout the year, the *san po tsai* marriage was said usually to have taken place at a fixed time. This was at year-end, on either the evening of the Winter Solstice or the last day of the Old Year, these being the customary times for the *sheung tau* ceremony that converted a *san po tsai* and her husband to man and wife.

In Chinese traditional society these differences in the ceremonies of betrothal and marriage were truly significant, and directly reflected the low-income and financial stringencies always associated with the practice of giving and taking in *san po tsai*. This difference was also underlined by the fact that in an age when infant and child betrothals were common in the local villages and poverty was general, many girls were not sent as *san po tsai*, despite the fact that it would save the cost of the girl's upbringing. The implication is that the sending-away family had to be poorer than most, tying in the *san po tsai* status to inferior financial and, therefore, low social status in her native village. Yet the *san po tsai* did not suffer the stigma that was generally attached to *mui tsai*.

However, whether or not the *san po tsai*'s position was intrinsically inferior because of these differences, and whether or not she held an inferior position in some households, I was assured by some informants that her situation and status improved on marriage.[16] After the *sheung tau* ceremony, she was an acknowledged wife, with the same status as other daughters-in-law, in the same way as her husband was his brothers' equal.

My enquiries into situations in which either the *san po tsai* or her husband-to-be died before the marriage ceremony reveal some important facts about *san po tsai* status. First, in the context of death, both parties were regarded as having been married. Second, where the prospective husband died before the *sheung tau* ceremony had taken place and another marriage was arranged for the girl, she was still not entitled to any of the formalities of 'major' marriage on her entry to her new home upon what was considered her 'remarriage'. In such cases it was usual for the girl to return to her natal family on the death of her prospective husband: but if this was not possible or desired, the taking-in family would find her another husband. However, there was no obligation on either side and the outcome would depend on circumstances. Third, if the *san po tsai* herself died during childhood or girlhood, her funeral arrangements were the responsibility of the boy's family, and burial would take place in his village area. The *san po tsai*'s family would be informed and invited to the funeral.

It is of parallel interest that a betrothed girl, however young when death occurred, would for ritual purposes also be regarded as married. A girl who lived in a village on Tsing Yi Island had been betrothed to an informant's father (born about 1890) when a babe in arms. Sadly, she had died when still young, and another young girl was found in her place. However, in circumstances of this kind, it was the local practice that before a new betrothal could take place, a *san chu pai* or ancestral (spirit) tablet had to be prepared for the deceased girl and brought into the boy's home and placed on the family altar. The children of the replacement partner in the marriage would be brought up to reverence her along with the other ancestors of the clan, in accordance with the general custom.[17]

Logically, the same formalities should have been followed for a deceased *san po tsai* when her husband-to-be married someone else, but I have no information on this point.

The Financial Aspects of San Po Tsai

The difficulties of obtaining reliable information about the financial aspects of *san po tsai* transfer are obvious, especially in the near total absence in my enquiries so far of any supporting documentary evidence (see Appendix). However, my informants' recalled or received statements about payments made to the taking-in family or sent with the girl are probably sufficient to show that the amounts were usually token in nature. They comprised a small sum and sundry items which, within the specific context of future marriage and the village culture, were widely regarded as conferring auspicious aids to the *san po tsai*'s future good fortune.

They appear to have been similar in kind and amount to the level of payments and the accompanying gifts made in village circles to the girl's family when betrothal took place in infancy or early childhood and there was a long wait before the marriage transfer took place. However, as already stated, in cases of 'major' marriage, the celebrations at the time of the marriage ceremony were very different from the simple, unobtrusive *sheung tau* ritual.

The difference in the financial approach to 'major' and 'minor' marriage is made clear in another way. In the ordinary betrothals for 'major' marriage, whether made in infancy or childhood, payments were made (and expected) at the two ends of the long progression from child betrothal to actual marriage. This contrasted with the absence of a 'bride price' when the *san po tsai* was married. A few examples will indicate the position.

One of my oldest female informants, born in 1880 and interviewed in 1969, had been betrothed when not more than a babe in arms. She came from the Punti-speaking village of Ho Chung in the Sai Kung sub-district of the New Territories, and was married into another Cantonese family living in Chuk Yuen, one of the old villages of Kowloon. She was carried there in the traditional bridal chair when 16 years of age. The dowry (*ga chong*) upon marriage was $70, but she had been told that $2 and some *cha gwo* cakes had been given to her own family at the time of the betrothal. In my more recent enquiries, I have found other, later, instances of the same kind in the Tsuen Wan sub-district. The survivor of two sisters born at Lo Wai c. 1905–9 told me they had been betrothed in infancy to boys a few years older than themselves, and were married into their (local) villages when they were 13 years old in the one case and probably a little older in the other. The betrothal money had also been about $2, but the *lai kam* or bride price paid upon marriage had been over $100. Another informant, born in Kwan Mun Hau village, Tsuen Wan, about 1902, who had also been betrothed when small to the younger son of a family at Ho Lek Pui village in the Shing Mun valley above Tsuen Wan, reported the betrothal money as the same $2. However, she described it as *lai see* or 'lucky money' which it probably was. In her case, the bride price upon marriage at 16 had been $160, around 1918–20.

It thus seems likely that these token levels of payment to the girls' families upon early betrothal, followed by a larger 'bride price' sum upon marriage, were the norm among peasant families in the region, and grounded in the realities of life. The emphasis placed on the financial aspects of traditional Chinese marriages reported by leading authorities, together with the severely practical view of these transactions taken by the families concerned, indicate that the customary payments to be made at the different stages of the progression would be fixed at sums considered to be appropriate to the ages of the children. In the case of infant betrothal, the time that must elapse before the betrothal could be replaced by marriage, and the possibility that death might intervene, would be taken into account (Hayes 1977 pp. 41–4). This would explain the obviously token nature of the financial exchange, and its characterisation as 'lucky money', marking a happy event and hoping for the best.

Logically enough, the existence of the *san po tsai* type of marriage arrangement had the effect of keeping the bride price in major marriages at a high level. In this regard, though without reference to the *san po tsai* institution, the experienced and knowledgeable American missionary John L. Nevius wrote at an earlier time:

> Parents of the lower and middle classes, whose daughters live with them till they are married, feel that they are entitled to some remuneration from the parents of the husband for all their expense and trouble in bringing her up. For this reason, when a girl is betrothed with the expectation of her remaining in her own family, her parents expect a considerable amount of money; so that the transaction has very much the appearance of a matter of buying and selling.

This, in turn, had a dampening effect on the marriage prospects of some men, for, Nevius continued: 'many men are doomed to a life of celibacy because they are too poor to buy and support a wife' (1882 p. 253).

Gender Inequality as Seen in Attitudes to Traditional Marriage Arrangements and the Subordination of Females

No discussion of the various aspects of Chinese marriage in traditional society can avoid touching on the subject of gender inequality. The more reading and interviewing one does on the subject of marriage arrangements among a conservative-minded rural population, the more one comes across immensely deep-rooted attitudes which conditioned the individual according to his or her gender. These attitudes were not rooted only in community values and tradition, but were equally grounded in the prevailing economic system and the uncertain life expectancy. Together, these dictated the continuance of social institutions like infant and child betrothals for both sexes, as well as the 'little daughter-in-law' practice, the buying and selling of women and girls, and much else that affected the female sex adversely. Just as importantly, they ensured the women's continued acceptance of these subordinating and demeaning traditions.

Dr Hu King Eng, graduate of the Woman's Medical College at Philadelphia and a regular medical missionary of the Woman's Foreign Missionary Society from 1895, wrote of the first female student graduation from Woolston Memorial Hospital, Foochow in 1902: 'Seeing a Chinese young woman receiving her diploma made many Chinese parents regret that their daughters were engaged, or married, or drowned' (Headland 1912 pp. 198–9). Her words indicate the extent of early betrothals and the enormous burden placed by traditional social practices upon the wives and daughters of her day, at all levels of society. In some ways these were worst for the better-off women who mostly stayed at home, inhibited by custom and by their bound feet from venturing abroad or receiving other than women guests in their houses (see Fagg n.d. pp. 62–3; Gordon-Cumming 1900 ch. XI–XII).

During one of my discussions with an old lady of 87 from Yau Kam Tau, Tsuen Wan, conducted with the help of three men in their 60s from her late husband's lineage, we discussed *ping kam* and *lai kam*, the sums paid to the girl's family at betrothal and marriage. Running through the conversation like a brightly coloured thread on a plain ground was the clear indication that, for the menfolk of the villages, these transactions amounted to sales. As one of them explained to me: 'A man takes a wife but a girl is sold out.' Indeed, they said, the common term in ordinary use in the villages of the Tsuen Wan sub-district to describe a girl leaving the family on becoming a bride, *was* that she was being sold out. Groping for comparisons, in a flash of inspiration, one of the men said that betrothal money was like putting down a deposit on a new house!

Notes of my conversations with village elders at Shek Pik nearly 30 years ago show equally illuminating glimpses of how men there regarded the marriage market. Searching for a meaningful comparison for bride prices recalled for his father's generation, the village head (born in 1899) noted that they were 'about three or four times the selling price of pigs at that time'. Talking about the purchase of village land during the late Qing, he mentioned that the prevailing price of farm land had then been 'several tens of dollars', adding gratuitously that 'a wife could be had for the same sum at the time'.

Thus from these and similar discussions I was obliged, like Reginald Johnston (1910 ch. 9, 10, p. 208) in Wei Hai Wei 80 years ago and D.H. Kulp (1925 pp. 166–86) in the Swatow region of Guangdong in the 1920s, to conclude that these were *clearly* money matters. In recording hagglings over the financial aspects of betrothal and marriage, Kulp commented: 'Such tactics sometimes cause the monetary aspects to become pure purchase of a bride. Cases have been known where purchase was effected as coldly as that of any chattel in the market place' (*ibid*. p. 174). George Jamieson, British Consul-General at Shanghai 1897–9, also emphasised the monetary side of the 'marriage presents':

> This is an essential part of every engagement, and the amount is not left to the goodwill of the parties as the term 'present' would suggest but is exactly stipulated by the negotiators of the marriage. Though the Chinese will not hear of its being called 'price', it is exactly tantamount to the purchase money in a contract of sale, and is no doubt a survival of the time when the transaction was one of ordinary bargain. Actual money always constitutes a substantial part of the 'presents' and of course is paid by the bridegroom's family to the bride's' (1921 fn. p. 33).

In places, it appears that these practices could be taken to extremes. For example, custom in Fujian even allowed for the outright 'buying' of wives, and for a wife to be sold to another person by her husband.[18] There is an echo of this in a case from Tsuen Wan township in the New Territories, recalled by one of my elderly female informants from one of the local villages. In the 1930s, a man from the mainland, who was an opium addict, had sold his wife to another man, whereupon his daughter commented that her mother 'had disappeared into the mouth of the opium pipe'.

As far as my female informants were concerned, they seemed all to have accepted the monetary aspects of their betrothal and marriage as part of their lot in life, along with other aspects of the traditional forms of marriage and betrothal.

Male attitudes towards women and girls 30 years ago in Shek Pik were clearly stated by the elders, who said that a man renting part of his fields to others 'might find himself with a new daughter-in-law and have to take back the land for her to work'. The relative status of men and women was also revealed when the village head recalled that when he was a boy, his family had a new daughter-in-law and had to give a large dinner. 'But,' he added, 'women were excluded on that occasion because of the expense.' At the same discussion, the elders had laughed when, rather naively, I had enquired about bound feet among the women of their fathers' and grandfathers' generations. They said that 60 years before, not one woman in the village had bound feet 'because they had to cut grass and firewood, carry them to market along with other things to sell, and cultivate the fields'. They also emphasised that women took no part in the management of village affairs 'as they did not know how to write or keep accounts' since none went to school.

Gender Inequality: The Lack of Education for Females

The traditional Chinese discrimination against women in regard to the provision of educational opportunities is well known. It was still very much in evidence in postwar rural communities in the Hong Kong region. Here a number of reasons prevented children from attending school, including lack of schools, the difficulty for small children of walking over rough terrain to get to school, and most important, the poverty of the parents at a time when schools were not free. After becoming District Officer in 1957, my visits to villages showed that although a good many boys were not going to school, many more girls were not attending. In one of the Tung Chung villages on Lantau, I recorded that only four children of school age were studying – three boys and one girl. In 1961 at Yuen Tun, one of the outlying hill villages of the District with a hundred inhabitants of all ages, the Census Commissioner reported that 13 children (two boys and 11 girls) were not attending school, compared with six boys and four girls who were. Of the 56 who had passed school age (here defined as over 14), only 18 had at some time been to school (17 males and one female). Of the 38 who had not attended, 12 were male and 26 female.[19]

This difference of treatment had a long history. The 1911 Census of Hong Kong showed that in the Southern District of the New Territories, 231 females were 'able to read and write' compared with 7,760 who were illiterate. In the Northern District only 235 out of 25,664 were literate. I doubt whether these figures are comprehensive (*HKSP* 1911 p. 103 (46)). The greater discrimination in the Northern New Territories where the big lineages were is corroborated in Hugh Baker's study of the large Cantonese-speaking lineage villages of Sheung Shui, where he says:

> … it may be said with certainty that very few [daughters of the Liao lineage] received any education prior to 1932 [when a new-style school was opened in an ancestral hall] while no daughter of school age born after 1945 has gone without education (1968 p. 77).

The Relationship of San Po Tsai and Married Women with Their Natal Families

In older accounts of Chinese society it was usual to paint a uniformly dark picture of women's lives after marriage and the fact that they were cut off from their own families was reported as a particular hardship. However, my local enquiries indicate that it was, in fact, quite usual for village women to make regular visits to their home villages and to maintain ties with their natal families.

In one case that seems to illustrate the situation nicely, I learned that three girls from a village in the Lam Tsuen valley married into the Shing Mun villages above Tsuen Wan had all returned to their own families several times a year, taking their children with them. Such occasions had included the major festivals, including the Lunar New Year (the fourth day was the customary date) and also the marriages of their own relatives on their mothers' side. In this instance and many others of the kind, the villages in question were quite distant. Elderly men from Shing Mun had also all been with their mothers when small to visit the mothers' natal families. It was usual to visit at the main family festivals (New Year, the fifth and eighth moon festivals, and the Winter Solstice) and to go whenever their mothers were invited to wedding celebrations among their own kinsfolk. Such visits were called *faan ngoi ka*. Both men and women said this phrase meant 'visiting one's own people, something we treasure in Chinese village life'.

Furthermore, Frances Lee's account of the lives of the women of her family over the past three generations shows that contrary to anthropological literature which treats married women as members of their husbands' and not their own natal families, the women members of her family included daughters as well as daughters-in-law. She states that:

> Firstly, a difference must be drawn between the women's feelings and commitments to the family of their birth and their customary obligations to the family of their marriage. Moreover, many regular activities were maintained with the village of their origin, such as visiting the parents' family at New Year, and social visits paid to one another. One result of the social network that grew out of these activities was that some women could act as marriage go-betweens ... (1986 p. 52)

These links, and the good feeling that clearly existed in different areas between village families related on the female side, are worth remembering, for they have a bearing on the condition of the *san po tsai*. They were not all cut off from their parents by the transfer at a tender age, partly because of the social network of ties and visits. Some even made extended visits to their own families. Thus Adele Fielde notes that an informant in Swatow, having been transferred as a *san po tsai* at the age of seven, returned to her father's house for four months of every year between the ages of 11 and 14 – when she was married (1884 p. 158). Moreover, the absence from many Hong Kong villages of many men abroad or working on ships further strengthened ties in such communities between women, children and old people.

Avenues of Escape

However, even if they were often not completely cut off from their natal families, it can be seen how the transfer of *san po tsai*, early betrothal and marriage, and female disposability without consultation or consent, meshed with hard work, the lack of an education, narrow confines, and an inferior status. All had to be accepted as the long-established way of life for women in rural life. As my mother-in-law has observed on a number of occasions: 'Patience was an essential part of being a woman in the old society.'

Patience was the more necessary as there were few avenues of escape from unhappiness at home for married women and girls. In extreme cases some were driven to suicide (see for instance Hong Kong Administrative Reports, 1938: District Officer North p. J2; M. Wolf 1975 pp. 111–41). Another alternative was to run away. But this was a last resort since the likely result was that the girl would be shunned by society and all right-thinking people, possibly including her natal family, and then how was she to maintain a livelihood? Even if her own family supported her, the two families would become involved in wrangles and recriminations that could lead to worse troubles. Only the very strong-minded might rise above their situation and effect a measure of change by staying and resisting. A notable case was reported by G.L. Bendelack, who was principal of the Church Missionary Society's St Hilda's Girls Middle School in Guangzhou in the 1910s. Among her pupils was a Christian girl who declined to marry the 'wealthy heathen' chosen for her by her grandmother (her father being dead and her only brother at school in England). Her only escape was to 'put up her hair as a married woman does, have a great feast in her home similar to a wedding one, and announce her decision to all the family and friends assembled there'. This she did, and the author was invited to attend, at the mother's invitation, 'the decided unmarriage of her daughter Wing Yi at 6 p.m. on May 25, at the home of the bride', and did so (1921 pp. 60–1).

Such cases, of course, were rare; but although Chinese women usually accepted their inferior lot in life, they were well aware of it. Thus an American missionary in Ningpo reported finding two or three thousand women all reciting prayers to Buddha, praying that they might be born into the world as men 'so unhappy, as well as inferior, are they taught to consider their present condition' (W.A.P. Martin 1896 p. 82). Funeral laments of women in one of the Tsuen Wan villages are equally revealing (E.L. Johnson 1988 pp. 135–66).

Reasons for the Persistence of San Po Tsai in the Hong Kong Region

Why were *san po tsai* marriages prevalent in the Hong Kong region until several decades ago? The direct, and obviously over-simplistic answer must be that this was a traditional form of marriage and that the area was itself cast in a traditional mould for longer than might otherwise have been the case owing to its having passed under colonial rule. However, this is only part of the story.

Poverty

With regard to the institution itself, most writers on the subject indicate that it was only to be found in poor families. This is also the view expressed to me by village representatives and other local leaders. There were, in truth, many poor families in the villages of the Hong Kong region. Whether in a farming village or one with specialised employment, life was hard for most people. For persons dependent on the farm, the weather was uncertain, crops were subject to disease, natural disasters were not uncommon, and sickness and early death were among the normal expectations of people living in country places. In many village households, cash was usually in short supply, and economy had to be practised most of the time. In particular, all means to reduce the obligatory and normally heavy expenses of marriage had to be considered, out of common prudence.[20]

However, poverty had been accentuated and prolonged by local conditions. From a number of sources, it would appear that from around the 1850s, many villages in the Hong Kong region were afflicted with stagnation and decay. Owing most probably, in the final analysis, to overpopulation – the result of two centuries of peace – the production of staple foods became inadequate in many places. Malnutrition may have set in, creating a greater susceptibility to disease, which was often followed by death. Individual and collective vitality and enterprise dipped, and material prosperity was reduced in proportion.[21] Many signs point to a continuation of this downturn into the early decades of this century. The connection between this and *san po tsai* is made clear by Michael Palmer who states that elderly men of the Liao lineage of Sheung Shui in the northern New Territories, one of the former 'Five Great Clans', told him that 'the 1930s were times when the local standard of living was so depressed that many villagers had to eat sweet potatoes instead of the orthodox staple food of rice *and were driven to marry their children by means of the low-status mechanism of a minor marriage*'(1991 p. 82 n. 26, my italics).

Thus continuing poverty as well as custom explain the continuation of the institution of *san po tsai*, adoptions, infant and child betrothals and the still recent purchases, sales and presentations of children, especially of girls, that were evident to me in the villages of the region in the 1950s.

The Exodus of Males

Another factor that encouraged the continuation of traditional transfer and marriage practices was the absence of many men from the villages, before and after the British takeover of the New Territories in 1898–9. Some worked as cooks and waiters, and others as stokers and seamen, on ocean-going ships of many nationalities from the 1840s onward. Others left to seek work and it was hoped riches, in many countries of the world.[22] Whilst their absence was often balanced by the receipt of remittances by their families, it also resulted in the whole burden of maintaining a livelihood at home falling mainly on the womenfolk. The 1917 Report of the London Missionary Society's 'Hong Kong and New Territories Evangelisation Society' contains a striking testimony to the resulting situation in one such area, the Lam Tsuen valley in the present Tai Po District: 'Over considerable areas the women and girls do, practically, all the field work, heavy and light, including the plowing [sic] of the soil.' Such telling phrases as 'the struggle for existence is keen', 'poverty-stricken folk' and 'the great majority of persons at [church] services are women and girls' appear in this section of the report.

Clearly, the hard-pressed women, and the men who remained because they preferred their fields to going overseas, could use additional help; and since the *san po tsai* institution brought an extra pair of hands into the depleted family, it surely had its practical side.

Female Isolation and Ignorance

Yet another reason why *san po tsai* transfers, child betrothals and even the sale of children were still to be encountered in the postwar New Territories was the restricted horizon of the women, especially in the remoter districts like Shek Pik, where some of the older females, born and married on Lantau, had never left the island. Until the reservoir construction work brought a road and vehicles to its rural solitudes, they had never actually seen a motor car. Limitations on female movement were apparently the norm in the China of their day. When telling me about women's work at home, a male informant born in 1877 in a large single lineage village in Hoi Ping County, Guangdong, said with great finality that 'women were too busy to go outside the village'. In his home area, it was usual for women to have bound feet. Though his own father was only a poor tenant farmer of the lineage, the boy was married at 18 to a girl from an adjoining village complex, whose feet were bound (interview 1963).

Even though bound feet were not common in the Hong Kong region, women were constrained by the narrow village concepts of what was proper for females, especially unmarried ones. I have been told by many persons, male and female alike, that in the earlier part of this century, more distant marketing was usually done by men. Thus, women were confined to the village and its environs, only marketing locally produce from farm and hillside and returning as soon as all was sold.

Added to this was the innate conservatism of country people. Women were often consulted about important family decisions, such as land transactions, but they seem to have accepted traditional institutions uncritically.[23] Commenting on infant betrothals, the *san po tsai* institution and other features of Chinese traditional marriage and family life that now seem so far removed from present-day life, my mother-in-law has reminded me that there was no effort of will, no conscious decision, to be made in settling these matters. They were the norm because they had formed the pattern of behaviour for so long. Thus none of the Shing Mun or Tsuen Wan informants in the last few years ever lamented their 'blind marriages', and indeed, in some cases they chuckled over them. Clearly they were still inclined to regard the whole thing as perfectly normal, as indeed it was at the time. An old lady from Yau Kam Tau explained that she had not seen her husband before her wedding day but as was usual she knew something about his family from the go-between (*gai shiu yan*) who was her neighbour and came from her prospective husband's village and whom she trusted. The *tai kam tse* or knowledgeable woman who guided her through the ceremonies was also from her husband's village. She had felt comfortable about the event, therefore, and it had never crossed her mind to be frightened, although she had to go in a closed bridal chair to a place and family completely unknown to her. It was an old custom and that was that.

So long as economic conditions in the villages remained unchanged, custom and tradition would persist.

Changes in Recent Decades

Whilst the overall economic position of the New Territories may have gradually improved to some extent in the two decades before the outbreak of the Pacific War in 1941, through increased commercial activity in those areas around the market towns, it was not uniform, since the remoter parts experienced little amelioration in their condition from prewar days. The privations and shortages of the Japanese Occupation (1941–5) were keenly felt in most places and starvation was widespread in the final year.[24] In some places both the people and the economy took a long time to recover from the war years. In short, poverty was still widespread, and helped to perpetuate traditional practices that had for centuries been grounded in the old harsh realities of life.

Though the subject of women's life in urban Hong Kong has not been treated here, in fact the country was far behind the city by the 1950s. In many country places there was no significant degree of modernisation or development until recent decades, and women and girls in the villages led very different lives from those in the city until well after World War II. These differences in status and opportunity remained until the end of traditional farming in the early 1970s, its demise hastened by the spread of education among females and the new opportunities for women and girls to gain a living outside the home without any stigma, or interference from the men of their families. Followed by the widespread urbanisation and modernisation of the whole territory of Hong Kong in the later postwar period, such changes in the economic and social life of the community intensified, leading to the disappearance of the old customary marriage arrangements and practices from the villages.[25]

The Frequency of San Po Tsai Transfer in the Hong Kong Region

In the Hong Kong region, the *san po tsai* practice has been specially linked to the Hakka population, and was reported to be 'prevalent' in 1921 (Eitel Report 1882 p. 54; G. N. Orme *HKSP* 1912 p. 15 para. 93; *HKSP* 1921 para. 6 pp. 160–1). However, neither fact is entirely borne out by my enquiries, which covered the several decades before and after 1921. The number of cases I have encountered directly or by report has not been large. As we have seen, the elderly ladies with whom I have spoken on the subject did not think there were many *san po tsai* in their home or married-in villages. It is significant that all the older headmen and elders consulted about it have given similar replies. Also, the majority of marriages reported by my many other female informants, in their own and reported cases, suggest that, though still fairly common, *san po tsai* were certainly the exception rather than the rule during the long period under review. Moreover, they were to be found in Punti- as well as Hakka-speaking villages.

The Validity of the Evidence

In determining the incidence of *san po tsai*, one has to decide whether all the facts have been disclosed. The scarcity of documents on 'minor marriage' led me to consider whether concealment was likely. Was there any reluctance to reveal 'minor marriage' among my female informants, either for themselves or for their mothers and aunts, grandmothers and great-aunts on both sides of their families, because it might carry a social stigma?

Generally speaking, I think not. From long experience of interviewing, I believe that women who came into a household as *san po tsai* would always mention it when asked about the age of marriage. Conversely, it may be assumed with confidence that women who reported an adult marriage had not been *san po tsai*. Moreover, the elderly men who answered my questions on this topic would have had less reason to 'fudge', and in any case, over the years, I have formed a particularly favourable impression of the reliability of information given by most village representatives in view of their extensive knowledge of village affairs acquired over long periods in the post. It also seems that *san po tsai* status was accepted as a fact of life – an established part of old village customs.

The most likely explanation for the received notion that *san po tsai* transfers were common is that they had been more numerous in the 19th century, and declined as the 20th century drew on. It does seem that just before World War II there were not a great many of them, and that by the early postwar years there were fewer still. There is clear support for this in the figures recorded at the Hong Kong Censuses of 1931 and 1961. In the 1931 census no less than 1,365 persons under 15 were reported as married or widowed, including 284 under the age of 10. The 1961 census shows only 14 persons under 15 (three boys and 11 girls) as having reported themselves as married.[26] Of these five were Hakka from farming families, five were Tanka boat dwellers, one was a Cantonese village girl in Sheung Shui district, and three were from the fringes of New Kowloon. All but one were born in Hong Kong. There were also a few married women who, though over 15 at the time of the census, had clearly been married before that age. These were all Hakka farming women or Tanka boat women.[27] The Census Commissioner noted: 'It would appear that though the practice of child marriage, once so prevalent in these two communities, has not entirely disappeared, it is almost a thing of the past' (*Hong Kong Report on the 1961 Census* Vol. II pp. LXIV–LXV).

However, he was probably over-sanguine as it seems unlikely that there were *quite* so few *san po tsai* left in 1961, given that I had found three in one village alone only a few years before.

Conclusion

Whilst the general pattern of *san po tsai* transfer, infant and child betrothal, and the sale of children, especially girls, is generally well known, little has been written on the subject for this part of Guangdong, especially as regards the former rural area of Hong Kong that lay undeveloped on the city's doorstep for so long. Therein lies the main justification for this chapter. The firsthand information it provides can also be set alongside other recently published accounts of life in urban Hong Kong for those girls who came there for domestic service, or worse, at the dictates of others.[28]

However, this chapter is merely a first look into a subject that deserves a deeper and wider treatment. Apart from conducting other interviews with elderly informants like those appearing in these pages, it would be possible to gain more information from the hundreds of handwritten genealogical records from the New Territories which are now available through the efforts of David Faure and the Hong Kong History Project. Displaying considerable variety in format and content, these provide an opportunity to glean useful information on *san po tsai* transfer, infant and child betrothals, and the other family-related practices of the region.

There is also the matter of documentation, discussed further in the Appendix. It will be clear from its contents that there is scope for a lot more work on the documentary side of 'minor marriage', as well as on the rituals and formalities of infant and child betrothals, bride price and the like, whereby our understanding of the parameters of life for women and girls in the rural parts of the Hong Kong region up to the recent past may be enhanced.

Finally, this chapter sets out to be more descriptive than analytical, in the belief that there is a pressing need for more information on the customary family practices and domestic strategies of the region. When this is available, it will be possible to consider them with more confidence within the wider geographical and theoretical contexts provided by other scholars.[29]

Appendix: Documentation for Child Betrothals, San Po Tsai and the Sale, Pledge, 'Presentation' and Adoption of Children

The Hong Kong History Project and Documentary Evidence

Documentation was a striking feature of Chinese social life and was practised at all levels, down to the ordinary strata of Chinese society, however poor.[30] I have found printed Guides and Handbooks on Domestic Rituals, Letter Writing, Forms and Documents and the like in bookshops and second-hand stalls in the central districts of Hong Kong Island. These all came from Guangdong, although some had been published in Shanghai. A few handwritten guides of a similar kind are also available. At my suggestion, scholars at the Chinese University of Hong Kong searched the mainland New Territories for such printed and handwritten documentation, utilising the then-ongoing Hong Kong Oral History and Historical Inscriptions project, conducted in the early 1980s with student help, to widen the search.[31] An impressive amount of documentation was recovered from the villages, copied and bound into 130 volumes (at the last count) and placed in various libraries in Hong Kong and overseas.[32] The Project proved that the handwritten books giving detailed guidance on the forms to be used in correspondence and the documentation connected with the family and its various concerns, as well as some of the printed ones, were indeed commonplace in the New Territories villages.

Documentation for San Po Tsai Transfer

Despite the wealth of documentation available in the many guides I have seen, dating from the 18th century to the early Chinese Republic, the only document encountered which deals with *san po tsai* transfer, actual or in specimen format, came from Shek Pik. My notes indicate that some 'taking-in' papers were reported for the three Shek Pik cases. However, I was only able to obtain the one for the

1959 transfer, and then only the text rather than a copy of the actual paper. A translation is provided below. It covers the main aspects of the transfer, which is specifically stated to be the transfer of a 'little daughter-in-law' (here described as *sik fu*).

A recent search for documents in the Tsuen Wan District was unsuccessful. However, my informants stated that, as for betrothal and marriage, documentation was the rule for *san po tsai* transfers. They said that the transfer document would record *inter alia* the parents' names, the name and birth details of the girl (year, month, day, hour), the go-between's name, the taking-in household head's name, and the price paid upon transfer. The paper would be drawn up for the boy's family and was handed to the girl's grandfather, father or paternal uncle, whichever of them was the surviving senior member of the household. This tallies with the contents of the paper from Shek Pik which, given the time and place it was written, is more than likely to be in the traditional format.

Documentation of Infant and Child Betrothals

The absence of *san po tsai* formats from the printed and manuscript handbooks seems to have a parallel in the lack of specimen documentation for betrothals effected in childhood. After enquiry among some of my elderly informants, my tentative conclusion is that there was no special form of documentation for them. The customary set of procedures governing betrothal and marriage known as the 'Three Documents and Six Ceremonies' were followed whether the future bride was one year old or 20 years of age. However, we may be reasonably sure that, as in the cases listed above, the financial arrangements of the betrothal, especially the *ping kam*, were adjusted to match the age of the children concerned, and also reflected the economic standing of the families involved in the arrangements.

Opportunities for Further Documentary Research

Finally, it must be made clear that I have confined my search for written formats and documents on *san po tsai* and infant and child betrothals to those areas in which I have conducted research and have detailed knowledge. I have not yet examined the 130 volumes of the Hong Kong History Project's documentation nor have I been able to extend my research to other areas of China or to Taiwan where there are extensive collections of documents. These would be rewarding fields for research, as would a survey of novels on the family.[33]

Translation of a Transfer Document for a San Po Tsai, Shek Pik, Lantau

Everlasting Good Fortune Presentation Card

The person drawing up this deed of presentation of a girl [name], with his wife, agrees to send her to [name] of Shek Pik Village. He is willing to accept her, and to rear and bring her up as the future wife of his son [*sik fu* or Daughter-in-Law].

Both sides have discussed and are clear on the giving of a decorated cloth and a *lai kam* [bride price] of 600 Hong Kong dollars. [name] received it in person and returned home with it. The girl was sent forthwith to [name] to be reared as a [Little] 'Daughter-in-Law'.

Henceforth there can be no regrets. This [transaction] has been agreed by both families, and was not done in connection with debts or any other similar situation. May Heaven bless [it].

Lest verbal agreement be insufficient, this document is provided as evidence of the transaction.

Dated the 30th March 1959; that is the 22nd day of the Second Month of the *chi hai* year of the Chinese Republic.

The true signature of the person presenting the girl [name].

Notes

1. The material is based on interviews conducted when I was arranging the removal and rehousing of families in these areas, to make way for the construction of a reservoir at Shek Pik, and for the expansion of Kowloon.

2. I interviewed the elderly former inhabitants of the Shing Mun valley, who had been resettled elsewhere in 1928 to make room for a reservoir, and their relatives from the Tsuen Wan villages in the last four years. I am greatly indebted to my friend Yeung Pak-shing, Village Representative of Yau Kam Tau village, Tsuen Wan, for his help with these interviews.

3. Throughout the chapter romanisation is generally given in a Cantonese form. Where Mandarin terms are used, Pinyin is adopted. See Glossary.

4. In the more recent Codes, the best statement I have come across is the section dealing with *tong-yang-xi* at pp. 76–8 of Marc Van Der Valk's *An Outline of Modern Chinese Family Law* (1939). Cases from a number of provinces, including Jiangxi, Fujian and Sichuan, can be found at pp. 101, 167 and 204 of Van Der Valk, *Interpretations of the Supreme Court at Peking, Years 1915 and 1916* (1949).

5. One must always be prepared to find the exception from time to time, such is the diversity of the Chinese countryside. In Guangdong itself, while the transfer of young children was widespread, it was strikingly absent in a few places, as reported by anthropologists. Villagers in the Chashan district of Donguan county belonging to Zengbu brigade – a cluster of three natural villages and two hamlets, with a population of about 5,000 – have stated that marriages based on the adoption of a child daughter-in-law never occur, and have never been known to occur in the past. They could not believe that such a practice could be Chinese (S.H. Potter and J.M. Potter 1990 p. 207). In her research into traditional marriage in the Delta, Janice E. Stockard, whilst noting with reservations that the Customs sections of local gazetteers provided little information on minor marriage, added that it was not reported from the home areas of her informants. See her *Daughters of the Canton Delta*, 1989.

6. Little daughters-in-law very definitely thought along the same lines! See the 'Song about a small daughter-in-law' (E.L. Johnson 1984 p. 91; and note 16 below).

7. From Mr Wan On of Pui O, Lantau. Chang-tai Hung, *Going to the People: Chinese Intellectuals and Folk Literature 1918–1937* (Cambridge Massachusetts, Harvard University Press, 1985) has a section on child brides (pp. 69–72) stating that the agony of a child bride is a common theme in the songs.

8. See Hayes 1977 pp. 29–30 for a discussion of the mixed settlement of the Hong Kong region, and conversions of Hakka to Punti speech and vice versa.

9. Throughout this paper, save in quotations from other works or government reports, I have used the Chinese reckoning for age. This makes a person one year old at birth, and two on the seventh day of the first month of the following lunar year, a date known as *Yan Yat* or 'Everybody's Birthday'. For convenience, age will be stated in the text without the *sui* from this point on.

10. For an account of the village of Ngau Tau Kok, together with the 'Four Stone Hills' and their organisation, see Hayes 1977 Chapter 6 pp. 151–62 with notes pp. 233–4. Some of the men were also itinerant masons.

11. I did not encounter any cases of this kind at Shek Pik, though there were a number of 'bought-in' sons. This does not mean there were no 'bought-in' girls, but simply that none had come to my notice. See R. Watson 1985 for adoption practices in dominant lineages.

12. In the case reported by Lena Johnston, some little show was also attempted. 'When she was 16 she was married. The mother-in-law did not want much expense, but, still, there was a feast, and Care had some new clothes, and for three days did not need to work' (1922 p. 26).

13. For more information on *san po tsai* in the New Territories see Elizabeth L. Johnson 1976 pp. 169–74 – a study of the women and girls of Kwan Mun Hau. Frances Lee also cites a case of *san po tsai* in the New Territories (1986 Vol. 1 China pp. 551–60). B.D. Wilson gives a general account at pp. 49–50 of his 'Notes on Some Chinese Customs in the New Territories' in *JHKBRAS* 23 1983 pp. 41–61.

14. Elizabeth L. Johnson (1984 p. 253) reports a similar case from Kwan Mun Hau village, Tsuen Wan, also apparently prewar.

15. It is still unclear whether or not horoscopes were exchanged for *san po tsai*, though they probably always were for child betrothal with a view to major marriage.

16. Such a transformation was noted in Zhejiang in the case of girls 'purchased for a dollar out of a heathen orphanage as future daughters-in-law. But if the girl grows up well in spite of the inhuman usage, she is married to the son for whom she has been purchased and instantly is treated with consideration in the household, and in due time her own turn arrives to have a daughter-in-law to maltreat in precisely the same manner' (Reynaud 1897 p. 95).

17. Confirmed by my wife's mother, for the Guangzhou-Foshan area also. Documentary evidence of the recognition given in the male family to deceased betrothed girls is provided by an entry in the genealogy of the Fung clan of Fan Pui, Shek Pik. A betrothed girl who died at the age of six in 1903 is entered together with the intended husband and his replacement wife. The girl is categorised as a *sin pui* and the wife, as usual in these records, as a *yuen pui*. This custom is mentioned in an early Protestant missionary work on China (see Kidd 1841 pp. 179–80).

18. Maurice Freedman cites Van Der Valk on the 1930 compilation of customs published by the Chinese government in connection with legal reform (unfortunately Guangdong is not covered in the survey) in regard to the 'outright buying' of wives in some districts, especially in Fujian. He reports of Nan-an in Fujian that the husband, having 'paid' for his wife, was entitled by custom to 'sell' her to another person, her own family having no right to interfere (1958 p. 32).

19. Letter to District Commissioner, New Territories, Ref. Cen[sus] E/6, 17 August 1961. In the wider context, the Census Commissioner had commented: 'So far, this is the lowest percentage of school attendance of any I have come across in the course of checking the schedules.'

20. For an account of marriage expenses in Guangdong and the Hong Kong region see references to works by John L. Buck and D.T. Lin in Hayes 1983 p. 227.

21. This is part surmise and part based on the received history of many old settlements like Shek Pik and other places on Lantau where the elders have described the resulting depopulation in graphic terms. I have gone into some of the physical evidence for depopulation in the second half of the 19th century in a long note in Hayes 1977 pp. 105–8, 213–4.

22. They were part of the huge numbers of men taking ships to foreign parts from Hong Kong and other ports in the later 19th and early 20th centuries. In 1913, 142,759 left via Hong Kong; in 1924, 129,859; and in 1927 an astonishing 285,593. The majority of these men went to the Straits Settlements. See the *China Year Book*, 1926–7 (Tientsin, The Tientsin Press Ltd) p. 591, and *ibid.* 1931 p. 54.

23. Wives, mothers and grandmothers were consulted over the sale and mortgage of land, and in some cases their names and fingerprints appear among the persons witnessing 19th-century deeds that have survived from Shek Pik. Mothers were often actual parties to the transactions, along with their sons.

24. For an account of the occupation as it affected the villagers in the old Southern District of the New Territories and in New Kowloon see Hayes 1967.

25. For a description of the transformation of the postwar New Territories, see Hayes 1991.

26. The entries for married or widowed persons under 15 years of age by Western reckoning, which produced these figures on 'child marriage' for census purposes, by then included married *and* unmarried *san po tsai* living with the boy's parents. (Conversation with Mr Benjamin N.H. Mok, ISO JP, Commissioner for Census and Statistics, 27 June 1990).

27. I have made no attempt to establish the position among the boat population.

28. See Maria Jaschok 1988; Sinn below; Janice E. Stockard 1989; Hayes 1990 pp. 33–47.

29. Principally, the authoritative work of Arthur Wolf and Chieh-shan Huang which has a chapter on minor marriage (1980 pp. 82–93) and Arthur Wolf (1975 pp. 89–110). There is also Margery Wolf's work on women within the Chinese family on Taiwan (1968 ch. 6–10 and 1972). Myron L. Cohen, whose published work on the Chinese family on Taiwan is now being extended following recent fieldwork in various regions of the mainland, has provided a useful summary of the current scholarly position in regard to the family in his new article (1992

pp. 357–77). Minor marriage is included (pp. 358–9) and is relevant to my account.

30. See my article 'Specialists and Written Materials in the Village World' (Hayes 1985). There are, in addition, a number of my articles on these subjects, and on books from the popular culture, including guides to letter writing, forms and documents, in the *Hong Kong Library Association Journal*, from No. 7 (1983) onwards.

31. Information on the Hong Kong History Project can be found in *JHKBRAS* 27 (1987) pp. 254–77. See also the essay in English by David Faure, Bernard H.K. Luk and Alice Ngai-ha Lun Ng, 'The Hong Kong Region According to Historical Inscriptions' in David Faure, James Hayes, Alan Birch, editors, *From Village to City, Studies in the Traditional Roots of Hong Kong Society* (1984).

32. See Peter Yeung's 'Bibliography of New Territories Historical Literature' pp. 192–206 *JHKBRAS* 25 (1985). This is described as 'a partial bibliography of historical documents collected by the Oral History Project at the Centre for East Asian Studies, Chinese University of Hong Kong, between 1980 and 1982 ...' (p. 192 fn.).

33. Some have been translated into English. See for instance Wang Ying 1989; Xiang Hong 1988; Wu Zuxiang 1989.

4. Chinese Prostitution in Singapore: Recruitment and Brothel Organisation

By James Francis Warren

Introduction
Ah Ku: Prostitutes, Singapore Society and the Historian

A new-found interest in social history, recent developments in historical thought and methodology and a fresh awareness of the importance of gender-specific experience have led historians to question the 'ordinary woman's place' in Singapore's past (Oliver Zunz 1985; Warren 1986 p. 218, 1993 p.3). In the historiography of Singapore, there is a need to bring to the foreground the critical importance of the *ah ku* (prostitutes) in the sex, politics and society of the city, stressing not only alterations in their life and circumstance, but also variations in the role of the colonial government, and changes in the ideology of sex and social policy (Warren 1987 pp. 148–64). The history of Chinese prostitution in Singapore is a subject which not only raises the issues of women's work and status but links these with the much less tractable questions of sex, race and colonialism, as well as male sexuality and women's exploitation of other women. Prostitution, in the period from 1880 to 1940, was determined by complex social and economic forces in Singapore and China. This chapter examines how prostitution was organised and regulated in a period of fundamental change, a historical era which witnessed the emergence of Singapore as the hub of an imperial system in Southeast Asia, and as a coolie town where tens of thousands of Chinese immigrants were becoming part of a large urban society – a Chinese city outside China (*ibid*. pp. 73–81).

The literature on the development of Singapore under colonialism is ample, but little has been written about the history of prostitution. Scholars have usually shied away from it, despite the facts, first, that the problem of institutionalisation and repression from the 1880s to the 1930s was a perennial one, and second, that a detailed study of changes in colonial policy and practice towards prostitution illuminates the life of the urban poor – enabling us to relive the past of Chinese women.[1]

This chapter concentrates on the Chinese prostitutes in Singapore over a relatively short span of time, 60 years. It describes and analyses aspects of the lives of the women themselves and places brothel prostitution and the traffic in women and children in a broader context. First it emphasises the macro-social forces and cultural values which shaped the character of prostitution. It examines the patriarchal system of society and government responsible for the selling of women and young girls abroad. The record of prostitution in Singapore is part of the history of international trafficking and procuring in China where women were oppressed by the dual yoke of sex and class.[2] Second, the social hierarchy within the profession, as well as the exploitation and the economic factors are considered as part of a new interpretive framework.

Chinese women were not all 'total victims'. Some found prostitution to be in their interests, but many, as 'outsiders', simply had no other choice. Their domination by a patriarchal system must be considered as the starting point in examining the process of historical change which determined women's lives in China and Singapore. This perspective of the prostitutes' experience, observed not from the tip but from the base of the iceberg 'which lies sunken, leaden and remote in the depths below' (Tomoko 1975 p. 52),[3] challenges some of the most established dogma about the history of Singapore.

Demography is the vital clue to the importance of prostitution in the history of Singapore. The development and expansion of the city was the direct result of a vast immigration of Chinese labourers that continued steadily from the 1880s. The population quadrupled in 40 years. This massive influx altered the character of Singapore. The labour market could absorb them, but such an unprecedented increase created serious problems, as nearly all the immigrants were single men. These coolies crowded into working-class tenements in Chinatown and the density rates soared. As more and more *singkeh* (newcomers) moved in, the need for prostitutes' services climbed proportionately.

Ordinary Chinese were swept up by Singapore's 'economic miracle' and pushed out of China by uneven development and by the patriarchal family system. China, in this paradoxical century of economic growth and rural deprivation, tended to export labour. Chinese migrated to work overseas, mostly to the *Nanyang* (Southeast Asia), and especially to Singapore, which was commonly referred to as a 'borrowed place' (Quahe 1986 p. 1).

During the second half of the 19th century China had one of the largest population movements in history. Between the opening of the Treaty ports in the 1840s and changes in the Qing Government's non-protection policy towards the overseas Chinese in the 1890s, millions left the provinces of Fujian and Guangdong in southeast China. These peasants were driven out by periodic poor harvests and flood-caused famines, by the price of rice, by overpopulation and by the policies of landlords. But not all emigrated because of wretched conditions. Some were lured away by new economic developments in Southeast Asia and the Pacific, and by the discovery of gold in California, Australia and South Africa. Contract labourers were prepared to risk imperial wrath and emigrate, for instance, to mine tin in Perak and gold in Bendigo, to open up tobacco plantations in North Sumatra, to pioneer railroad construction in the American west, to prop up the flagging sugar industry in Cuba and develop the fertiliser industry in Peru, and to pull rickshaws in Singapore (see Irick 1982; Yen 1985; Warren 1987 pp. 14–9; Ee 1961 pp. 33–51; R.N. Jackson 1961; T. Chen 1940; Campbell 1923).

This phase in Singapore's history is rarely described from the prostitutes' perspective. The extraordinary importation of poverty-stricken peasants from China to build roads and government buildings, to load and unload cargo and supplies and to work in godowns and factories gave rise to a dynamic urban life in which prostitutes were indispensable. The character of Singapore, both as a Chinese city outside China and as a coolie town under British rule, shaped the careers of the *ah ku*. The need for cheap labour, the demand for these women's services, a colonial policy of controlling brothel prostitution through registration and medical inspection, the stigmatising of Victorian racism and patriarchy provide the historical context and social setting which determined the lives and choices of Singapore's Chinese prostitutes.

Poverty and Patriarchy in China and Economic Development in Singapore

Prostitution in Singapore was inextricably linked to economic factors in rural China. Poverty, weak family economies and rising economic expectations created a vast source of supply of Chinese women and young girls for international trafficking (*CETWCE* 1933 p. 132 *passim*; Niccol-Jones 1941 p. 23; Yen 1986 p. 250; Hane 1982 p. 6; Tomoko 1975 pp. 56–7). Life in China was exceptionally difficult in the second half of the 19th century. Although the country had much wealth, most people lived a hand-to-mouth existence in overpopulated rural areas. Poverty in the villages and outlying districts of southeastern China, where many agrarian families lived on the edge of starvation, not only drove women and girls out of the countryside into the ports but acted as a lever on parents already bowed under financial strain. Privation was a handicap which struck hardest at the daughters of peasants and rural labourers. Unable to feed the many mouths for which they were responsible and suffering from chronic economic insecurity, parents sold their daughters to 'benefactors', totally unaware of the fate in store for so many of those who were taken to Singapore. Poverty and desperate hunger in China thus fuelled brothel prostitution in Singapore at the end of the 19th century.

The most important lesson to be learnt from the experience of the young women forced to migrate or sold by their parents into prostitution is how little value a peasant family placed on a female child in an overpopulated region. Chinese agriculture was back-breakingly labour-intensive and in difficult times the production of every bowl of rice was a struggle. For rural farmers and fishermen survival was a primary social and individual goal. Thus, for peasant families devoid of natural resources and with a profound, historical sense of vulnerability, the exchange of a daughter, who was regarded, anyway, as an object to be invested in or sold, was the only guarantee of a future (Gronewold 1982 p. 37).

Patriarchy in traditional Chinese culture was responsible for the exploitation of women financially, physically, sexually and emotionally (Gronewold 1982 p. 37–8; Yen 1986 p. 250). Prostitution in Singapore was directly linked to economic, social and personal problems in traditional family life because of a 'male' ideology that asserted that there could be no equality for women. The family system of China was organised around the kinship and lineage of men. The patrilineal principle, the worship of the male ancestral line in a lineage hall, was instrumental in controlling women, their social roles and sexuality. The subordination of women to men in family and society was justified in Confucian ideology by the importance of filial piety. In a male-centred, patriarchal society the cultural ideal was for a man to produce as many sons as possible for his father's lineage.

Implicit in the traditional status of women in the patriarchal family system was that their position, because of cultural and religious beliefs, was comparable to that of an 'outsider'. Family interest might thus dictate and justify the sacrifice of a female member, including her disposal in a commercial transaction, to ensure the survival of the patriline. Therefore, patriarchy as much as agrarian poverty was a basic cause of prostitution in Singapore, and of the status and condition of Chinese women as migrants and prostitutes. The history of the *ah ku* in this context, which is deeply embedded in the moral and legal framework of traditional patriarchal families (Gronewold 1982 p. 26), is in reality also the history of Chinese men – of their attitudes, schemes, and manipulations.

In many cases an *ah ku* entered prostitution mainly to obtain much-needed financial assistance for parents or kin. The appeal to an ill-fed daughter's filial devotion, by starving or irresponsible parents during periods of pestilence or famine, often resulted in her going abroad to take up a life of prostitution in a brothel in Singapore, in return for payment to her parents (*CETWCE* 1933 p. 41). Ironically, in a case where parents received money upon a daughter's entry to a Singapore brothel, unselfish filial loyalty often compelled the young *ah ku* to honour the debt. Parents took full advantage of this ideology to raise money on the saleable value of their daughters just as they would on any negotiable property (Pruitt 1979 p. 103). The traditional conception of filial piety placed the female child at a severe disadvantage. If a Chinese family had to part with a child because of poverty, it was naturally to the girls that the parents first turned. Female children of 11 or under were often sold by despairing parents to procurers to save the rest of the family. In such circumstances it was not unusual for parents who could not take care of their daughter to consent to the unconditional transfer of the child to anyone who claimed to be in a position to feed and clothe her (*CETWCE* 1933 p. 41). Thus the Chinese patriarchal system constantly produced women and young girls for prostitution abroad, who were sold or pawned by their own fathers or sometimes their brothers to complete strangers who, in turn, after having paid the usual indemnity money, had the right to transfer the child again against the same kind of indemnity to a brothel-keeper in Singapore.

Prostitution was a flourishing business in Singapore at the end of the 19th century. It had become a multi-million dollar network linking remote villages in rural China with ports like Xiamen (Amoy) and Guangzhou (Canton) to the dockside in Hong Kong and the brothels in Singapore. The flood of coolies

Table 1
Chinese Migrants to Singapore Between the 1870s and the 1900s

Years	Total Chinese Migrants to Singapore
1871–74	76,657
1881–84	233,357
1891–94	424,970
1901–04	653,077

Source: Lee P.P. 1978 p. 86.

arriving to work in Singapore had created gender imbalance, and the demand for prostitutes by migrant labourers was responsible for an extensive organised traffic in young women and girls (Warren 1987 pp. 14–9, 161–5, 249; Ee 1961 p. 37; Hirata 1979 pp. 5–7). Brothels were a boom industry by the mid-1890s in Singapore, where the streets were thronged with tens of thousands of Chinese labourers and sailors from the navies and merchant marines of most nations, especially Britain, Germany and Japan.

The economic development and expansion of Singapore required a disciplined workforce to build roads, buildings, wharfs and godowns, and to work on the docks and in the factories. Peasant migrant labour was recruited for these new forms of employment from the densely populated, famine-prone regions of South China. Farmers were regularly separated from their land in the final three decades of upheaval at the end of the 19th century as the 'sleeping giant' of Imperial China painfully struggled to enter the modern world. Disenfranchised, they became part of a sea – multitudes of impoverished, panic-stricken men surging away from the irrevocable collapse of their livelihood, and of traditional China, flowing towards new wealth, work and a future in colonial Singapore. Few could afford to bring their women with them and patriarchal custom and law in China precluded the emigration of married females as both socially unacceptable and illegal. To British administrators, the untiring labour of these poor, unskilled Chinese migrants was the key, the 'bone and sinew', to the economic growth of Singapore. However, the rapid development of the city fashioned the unusual demographic character of its population by the end of the 19th century. Notice the extraordinary difference in the number of migrants between the 1870s and the 1890s in Table 1.

The colonial authorities and *towkays* (businessmen) bent on seeking Chinese labourers from rural villages to work in their factories and godowns brought a major social problem into being. They had put literally thousands of single young migrant men in a place where there were very few women, married couples or older people to provide social balance. The coolies lived together in large sub-standard tenement houses concentrated in the heart of the city where there was the best chance of getting work. Lonely and bored, they sought the companionship and sexual favours of the *ah ku*.

As a committee reported in 1923:

The Chinese population to a very preponderate extent consists of the poorer working class male, mainly from Fuhkien, the two 'Kwang' provinces, and Hainan island. These men emigrate in order to gain a living; few of their womenfolk accompany them; and they live for the most part herded in cubicle lodging-houses, rickshaw-puller 'Kongsi' houses, and coolie lines erected close to the factories. These people are literally packed together at night, and sleep in quarters which contain the minimum amount of air space allowed by municipal regulation. For food, they either 'mess' all together on the ground floor of these dwellings, or eat at one of the many hundreds of open-air street or hawker stalls which line the thoroughfares. In these circumstances ... cut off from any of his own womenfolk, and with no inducement to stay inside his cramped sleeping quarters, the Chinese workman and coolie is inevitably driven to the brothels to seek not only gratification of his most powerful natural instinct, but also the single change possible from the drab circle of his everyday life.[4]

Thus, the economic development of Singapore favoured prostitution as the male population of the city greatly outnumbered the females: the gap was 1 female to 14 males in 1860 and this gender imbalance continued for the next 70 years. Prostitution in Singapore was carried on by *ah ku* in public brothels registered under the Contagious Diseases Ordinance in two parts of the city which were recognised as brothel areas; in public brothels outside these two areas; in private brothels, unregistered and not recognised by the Chinese Protectorate, known as 'sly' brothels; by *ah ku* who did not live in brothels; and by Chinese women and young girls who were not professional prostitutes, but who occasionally prostituted themselves in lodging houses.

International Traffic and Brothel Prostitution

Traffic in women and children from China and licensed brothel prostitution in Singapore were inextricably linked. Both flourished by the early 20th century. The primary incentive for this trade, that made Singapore a major destination for women and young girls, were the organised houses of prostitution. They brought in big money catering to a predominantly Chinese immigrant labour force.[5] Notwithstanding the existence of brothel prostitution in China, this international traffic was promoted primarily by a network of brothels in Singapore and other seaports in Southeast Asia. Since social conditions surrounding Singapore's rapid commercial development in the last decades of the 19th century made the brothels a virtual necessity (*CETWCE* 1933 pp. 21–2, 51, 96; *Nanyo no Gojunen Shingaporu o Chusin ni Doho Kotsuyaku* Nanyo oyobi Nippon jinsha, Tokyo, 1937, p. 160), the houses in the Malay Street and Smith Street areas became major targets for procurers and traffickers – 'flesh traders'. The trade in *ah ku* was extremely lucrative. The demand for Chinese women throughout the region was so great at the turn of the century that it could not be fully met, and large sums of money changed hands in the process of buying and selling.

Late 19th-century *kwai po* (female brothel-keepers) knew that a prostitute could profitably work in a brothel for about four years, and the price placed on her transfer usually rose during that period. *Ah ku*, who had few rights, then usually changed hands at exorbitant prices. Traffickers moved them on, often under duress, from a house in Singapore to one in another colony or country in Asia. The largest group of women supplied by traffickers to brothel-keepers were Chinese, as Singapore was a predominantly Chinese city. Numerically, the Japanese were next in importance followed by a far smaller number of European, Malay and Thai women.

Inter-port trading for brothel prostitution went on in China between Xiamen, Shantou (Swatow), Shanghai and Guangzhou and the colonies of Hong Kong and Macao (*CETWCE* 1933 p. 95). Both colonies were key transit ports for the traffic in Chinese girls going from China to Singapore. Licensed brothels in both colonies, especially Hong Kong, through which most ships bound from China to Singapore had to pass, served as clearing houses where traffickers separated the business of procuring girls from their families from the stage of shipping them to various destinations in Southeast Asia. Victims of this international traffic were detained in the brothels until ready for export, since a young woman could be housed at little or no expense, and even earn money, pending a decision over her ultimate disposal. These establishments were important centres of business for traffickers, who moved girls from one place to another along the China coast before sending them to an assured market in Singapore (*ibid.*).

Singapore, which offered unlimited possibilities to traffickers, was the hub for the movement of women intended for prostitution in Southeast Asia. The port city was the distributing centre for traders who wished to place Chinese girls not only in Johore and the Federated Malay States, but also in Siam, Borneo and the Netherlands Indies (*ibid*. pp. 50–1). The scenario was similar to that in Hong Kong except that Singapore was the key place of transit and the number of destinations multiplied a hundredfold, as the region lay at the city's doorstep. The trade in Chinese women and girls always constituted the largest and most difficult part of the trafficking problem in Singapore. Most were Cantonese from Guangdong province, arriving by junk and steamer from Shantou and Hong Kong; a considerable number were Hokkien coming from Shanghai (*ibid*. pp. 94, 277). Purchased in China, they were forced to work hard for several months in brothels on the southern side of the Singapore river in Chinatown. If they proved satisfactory while making their initial return on an investment as *ah ku*, they were kept and assigned a permanent place in the brothel by the *kwai po*. However, constant demand for Chinese women throughout the region ensured that a fair proportion were sent to brothels in the Federated Malay States in frontier towns like Ipoh, Klang, Kuala Lumpur and Taiping, and to places like east Sumatra, Rhio and Bali in the Netherlands Indies.

The legal codes of the Chinese empire were not concerned unduly with prostitution, brothels and procurers. Most of the special codes or statutes to protect women and girls against international traffic were enacted by local governments (*CETWCE* 1933 p. 131; Gronewold 1982 p. 29). Because Chinese were free to enter and leave the leased territories of Guangdong and Hong Kong without any kind of legal or administrative control over their movements or any identity checks, unrestricted opportunities were created for the supply of Chinese women to Singapore at the end of the 19th century. The traffic ensured flesh traders a quick return on their investment through the disposal of the women to numerous licensed houses that catered to labourers and tradesmen. The profits of these traffickers were made even more secure by the demand from the wealthy *towkays* and well-to-do artisans who frequented the Smith Street brothels. Some traders would have hesitated otherwise to risk investing money in transporting girls merely to satisfy the sexual needs of poorly-paid coolies.

An examination of the movement of Chinese women joining and leaving public brothels in Singapore provides eloquent proof that *ah ku* were found in reasonable numbers throughout Southeast Asia (Statistics of the Registration Office, Contagious Diseases Ordinance, 1887–1894, CO 275/33). The fact that brothels were recognised in Singapore facilitated export traffic, but the scope and rate at which this trade in women developed also depended on whether there was a network of licensed houses in the country of destination. The mobility of women between ports, and between brothels in Singapore, was phenomenal. Traffickers kept most of the women moving at regular intervals, primarily at the behest of brothel-keepers, for economic reasons. According to official statistics, the number of *ah ku* known to have left brothels in Singapore for other destinations in the region in 1891 included: 30 sent to the Federated Malay States; 344 to Johore; 103 to Borneo and the Netherlands Indies; and 101 were sent back to China by traffickers (*ibid.*). In the same year 511 women and girls were transported to Singapore from China as part of the process of becoming *ah ku*; 240 were imported from Johore, and 97 were brought from the Dutch possessions (*ibid.*). Movements to and from China and Hong Kong were commonplace.

The traffic between different ports, cities and regions in Asia gave the populations of Singapore's Chinese brothels a fluid character: the houses were being repopulated on an annual basis. This widespread organisation for the purchase of women for prostitution also ensured that the supply of *ah ku* exported from Singapore was readily replenished by a steady stream of girls from the impoverished interior of China. Some were bought from their parents by women or men who made the rounds locally and took them straight to depots or brothels in either Hong Kong or Singapore. Other girls drifted into towns looking for work as maids, in which case it was common for them to be kidnapped, seduced or raped by importers who brought them to Singapore.

As population densities built up in late 19th-century Singapore, and as patterns of life suited to the spread of infectious diseases developed, certain diseases assumed greater importance, especially syphilis. The coming of prostitutes and coolies in their thousands in the 1880s led to the accentuation of venereal disease. To prevent the spread of sexually transmitted diseases, the 1870 Contagious Diseases Ordinance imposed a strict registration system, rules for the conduct of brothels, and stringent health controls. These were developed in the early 1880s under the supervision of a single government authority, the Chinese Protectorate.

Table 2
Prostitutes Entering or Leaving Brothels in Singapore, 1887–94

Leaving for:		Entering from:	
Johore	1,740	China	2,650
China	693	Hong Kong	1,946
Borneo & Netherlands Indies	594	Johore	1,302
Federated Malay States	397	Borneo and Netherlands Indies	544
Straits Settlements	312	Straits Settlements	381
Hong Kong	127	Federated Malay States	329
Japan	28	Japan	305
Total for 8 years	**3,891**	**Total for 8 years**	**7,457**
Annual Mean Average	486	Annual Mean Average	932

Source: Compiled from statistics of the Registration Office, Contagious Diseases Ordinance, 1887–1894, CO 275/33.

Table 2 shows a marked difference in traffic in women entering and leaving registered brothels in Singapore between 1887 and 1894 for destinations in Northeast and Southeast Asia. Over that seven-year period, when brothel registration was in force, 3,891 women left Singapore, averaging 556 per year, with the largest number being moved to Johore between 1889 and 1891; 693 women were sent back to China over the whole period while the Netherlands Indies accounted for 594. Hong Kong's importance as a redistributive depot at the China end of the traffic is highlighted by the fact that far fewer women were shipped back to the colony during those years – just 127 – while the women and girls who were sent to Singapore from there numbered 1,946. This total was only exceeded by those women entering brothels from China – 2,650, nearly four times more than the number leaving Singapore for China by 1894. By then the average number of Chinese women entering the city's brothels annually was more than 900; this figure would almost double in the first decade of the 20th century (*ibid.*). The results of colonial efforts at the end of the 19th century to suppress the flesh trade and enforce the Women and Girls Protection Ordinances, through inspection of incoming ships and visits to the brothels by officials of the Chinese Protectorate, met with only limited success.

The traffickers were usually middle-aged or elderly Cantonese women (*CETWCE* 1933 pp. 59–62; Niccol-Jones 1941 p. 8). Female traffickers buying girls who were eventually brought to Singapore and resold to proprietors of brothels and lodging houses can be distinguished from those procuring girls in order to live off their earnings as prostitutes (see Koh below). In either case the traffickers were generally ex-prostitutes or *tai pang po* (brothel servants), who intended either to bring the adolescent up in the trade as a 'daughter', depending on the physical and intellectual qualities she possessed, or sell her for a lump sum into an established house. In such transactions the girl was usually bought from the parents on speculation, like a piece of merchandise, by women who professed to be seamstresses, hairdressers, maidservants or, perhaps, a 'travelling trader', but who, in fact, were ex-*ah ku*, *tai pang po* or *kwai po* (*CETWCE* 1933 p. 171).

Other types of females were also prominent in procurement traffic from China to Singapore. They were connected with employers or syndicates who rented boarding houses for purposes of sly prostitution outside the public zones. These women, whose occupations included passage brokers, moneylenders, jade dealers and vegetable sellers, lived in private houses, generally in Upper Chin Chew and Nankin Streets, or in the Banda Street area (Niccol-Jones 1941 p. 8). At the China end many women in Donguan district, Guangdong, were alleged to be involved in selling young girls to the brothels in Singapore in the 1890s (Yen 1986 pp. 248–9).

The social status of these traffickers was low and the funds at their disposal limited as many of them were working on commission, as agents. However, some *tai pang po* in Singapore, who had saved two or three hundred dollars, would borrow several hundred more, and go to China to buy girls. On the way back from China the young maidens were taught what to say about who they were and where they were going, but in spite of this coaching they occasionally made a slip of the tongue and were detained by the Chinese Protectorate (Statement of McBreen, 11 May 1898, in Swettenham to Chamberlain, 5 August 1898, CO 882/6, p. 79). It was only then, usually when an error had been made at the point of entry, that information was disclosed about the procurer's continual transactions. Brothel servants were known to make two or three journeys a year to China, deriving almost all their income from participation in the Singapore traffic. For some *ah ku* too, as they grew older and lost their looks and health, their chief interest in life became the procurement and training of Chinese girls for brothels, girls who, in their own lifetime, when prostitution had finished with them, would do the same in turn, thus perpetuating the ironic, oppressive role of older women preying upon younger women in a vicious circle of traffic and procurement. In the last few decades of the 19th century thousands of female children were either sold annually by their parents to organised traffickers or abducted to supply the brothels of Singapore and other major colonial cities and port towns throughout Southeast Asia.

Female traffickers employed stock-in-trade lures and dirty tricks to deceive destitute rural parents who were reluctant to sell their child, as well as kidnapping young girls with impunity. By almost every steamer from Hong Kong, young girls were brought down by an 'aunt', 'adopted mother' or some other ersatz relation, ostensibly to find them paid work as servants, nurses or hairdressers, or possibly a husband or an education (Koh below, *CETWCE* 1933 p. 171; Gronewold 1982 pp. 71–72; Yen 1986 p. 251; Hirata 1979 p. 9). Besides these hopeful promises and baits, there were other methods of recruitment. The standard one was outright purchase from an irresponsible father who drank or gambled and disposed of his daughter to anyone who wished to buy her. The wife was rarely consulted about such transactions and was left to mourn her daughter's loss, alone (Niccol-Jones 1941 p. 88). Parents or guardians also allowed their female children or wards to be brought to Singapore under pretence of adoption or marriage (Weld to Derby, 27 August 1882, CO 273/121, No. 2476).

Girls purchased by procurers or *kwai po* in China became the absolute property of their owners, chiefly older women whom they called 'mother', who on arrival in Singapore either placed them in their own brothels, or sold them to other keepers. In the case of sale, the *kwai po* accepted the price paid for her 'daughter' from the trafficker, and the young girl signed a promissory note for the amount with heavy interest. The trafficker then returned to China, leaving the unfortunate girl bound to serve the brothel-keeper (*ibid.*). Such sales were very common. These girls, with their promissory notes, were passed from one hand to another in sale, or as pledges for loans, as noted by a Protectorate official in 1882:

> ... in one brothel I found two Teo-chew girls who had, on arrival in Singapore from China six years previous, signed a note for some $300 each, of which every cent had been received and taken back to China by the person who had disposed of them. During the six years, they had been the property of two or three successive owners ... with the original promissory note hanging over them, though the sum had been paid over and over again. On my insisting on accounts being produced by the brothel-keeper, I discovered that, for three years, the girls had each been earning from $20 to $30 [US] per month ... (*ibid.*).

The prices traffickers paid for women varied according to the individual and with circumstances, from several dollars up to four hundred for an exceptionally beautiful virgin or a stunning woman who had been a prostitute before (Evidence of Rogers in Swettenham to Chamberlain, 5 August 1898, CO 882/6, No. 227; Gronewold 1982 pp. 72–3). Women for whom such large sums were paid were obtained for the better class of brothel in Singapore. In some of the worst affected areas of Northern China during periods of severe drought, prices ranged from as little as US$1.50 to $75.00 for a woman or child (Mallory 1926 p. 3). The initial outlay also included the trafficker's expenses associated with passage and importation which could add a hundred dollars to the cost of a woman's delivery in Singapore.

The prices of imported women for brothel prostitution soared at the end of the 19th century. In the 1880s an ordinary young girl who sold for $45 in Hong Kong fetched up to $350 in Singapore, while girls purchased for $50 in Guangzhou were being resold to houses in San Francisco for between $1,000 and $3,000 (Yen 1986 p. 250; Hirata 1979 pp. 12, 16; Mason below). Despite increasing efforts by the Singapore authorities to curb the traffic in women and children from the late 1880s onward, which resulted in higher importation costs, the system proved impossible to curtail, because it was lucrative and the demand was so great.

The authorities in China and Hong Kong were equally helpless to suppress the smuggling of women and girls out of China for brothel prostitution. Female traffickers were assisted by males in bringing out their human cargoes undetected. The men involved were usually Cantonese or Hokkien, whose ages varied considerably. They were either connected with lodging houses in the port cities of China, or acted as passage brokers, or were employed on board the ships which carried the women to Singapore, as compradors or sailors. The following extract from the correspondence of a trafficker engaged in taking girls from China to Singapore throws light on the important role these men played in the importation of women.

My dear Mother,

... Someone in Singapore has asked me to buy for him five or six girls of 14 to 15 years of age. I am anxious that you should get these for me. If you have any already, bring them with you to Singapore. If you are short of money, borrow some and let me know by cable so that I can remit it for you. Do not accept any ugly girls; they should not be less, and if possible, should be more, beautiful than Shun Yau and Sam Mui. When you buy the girls, send them by steamer of which Li is a comprador. And when you send them, tell some of them to say that they are your younger sisters, and the others to say that they are your nieces. But don't tell Li about this ... If you are short of money, ask Li to give you credit as far as Singapore; and send me a cable when they are coming, so that I can meet them (*CETWCE* 1933 pp. 64–5).

Trans-oceanic traffickers who had experience in dealing 'illegally' with local authorities organised the clandestine passage and often accompanied the girls on the entire journey. Junks from Xiamen, Shantou, Guangzhou and Hong Kong which were used for the immigration of Chinese males were at the same time often employed by these traffickers to bring in women and girls (*ibid.*, pp. 277–8; Yen 1986 p. 249). Some, rarely detected by marine police, were smuggled over a foreign steamer's side into small boats in Singapore's roadstead, right under the nose of the authorities (*CETWCE* 1933 pp. 64–5). Traffickers often evaded examination of women and girls coming by junk from China on their arrival at Singapore, declaring that the girls were their relatives in transit for one of the Dutch islands in the Rhio archipelago, where immigration restrictions were lax. From there the traffickers would come back to Singapore without fear of examination, as Dutch vessels from the Netherlands Indies were rarely boarded for inspection. Chinese junks sometimes deliberately by-passed Singapore and sailed directly to Rhio with cargoes of girls subsequently trans-shipped to Singapore. Sometimes they were also taken by traffickers from these islands to the plantation frontier on the east coast of Sumatra to break them in before shipping them back to Singapore.

Many of the women who arrived in Singapore from China after 1882 were brought to the Chinese Protectorate for examination, and in suspicious cases personal guarantees had to be given that the girls would not be sold or otherwise disposed of for prostitution against their will. However, despite all the officials could do, it was difficult to protect a young Chinese girl once she landed in Singapore. She often believed that she had to fulfil the promise made to the trafficker to whom she had been sold and felt compelled to be an *ah ku* to carry out her filial obligation, and she would agree to any coaching, fraud or false declaration to pass the examination of the Secretary for Chinese Affairs (Weld to Derby, 27 August 1883, CO 273/121, No. 247).

Since incoming traffic in unregistered women and children was illegal it is difficult to delineate short- and long-term trends in the number of women who passed through the port to become inmates of brothels. On the other hand, it is reasonable to assume that increases in the supply of fresh prostitutes from China and the progressive opening of registered brothels were linked almost exclusively to demand and the development and growth of the traffic. The Registrar-General, who in an *ex officio* capacity had control of the Contagious Diseases Ordinance, declared in 1876 that the total number of *ah ku* receiving Chinese clients was 1,156 (Evidence of A.V. Cousins in Anson to Carnarvon, 21 April 1877, CO 273/91, No. 132). On the basis of figures given six years later in 1882, when Singapore had a population of 60,065 Chinese men and 6,601 women between the ages of 15 and 60, W.A. Pickering, the Chinese Protector, estimated that at least 2,000 women were prostitutes, almost all Cantonese and some *Teochiu* (Weld to Derby, 27 August 1883, CO 273/121, No. 247; Turnbull 1977 p. 87).

One of the most striking features of the traffic and the character of Singapore's Chinese prostitutes late last century was this lack of diversity of sub-communal origins (Anson to Carnarvon, 21 April 1877, CO 273/91, No. 132; Weld to Derby, 27 August 1883, CO 273/121, No. 274). As there was no way China could prevent the smuggling of women or their emigration, chiefly as prostitutes, the number who were brought steadily rose between 1876 and 1887. On 1 January 1887, there were 1,608 'strictly Chinese' *ah ku* on the Contagious Diseases Ordinance (CDO) Register. A total of 17,444 Chinese women were seen at 12 monthly examinations, an average of 1,453 per inspection.[6] As the number of women from China registered as prostitutes in Singapore rose, so did the monthly average of *ah ku* listed under the CDO. The following year the Annual Report of the Chinese Protectorate showed a markedly different monthly average registered in brothels – 2,124; this sharp rise reflected a steady increase in the traffic in women and girls. But growth in demand gained real momentum with the abolition of brothel registration in 1894, resulting in a dramatic increase in the number of brothels. From 1894 to 1905, many organisations with links to secret societies in Hong Kong and Singapore were founded in Guangzhou and elsewhere for processing women and girls for brothel prostitution. By 1897 there were over 3,000 identifiable prostitutes in Singapore, the rise again reflecting the growth of traffic. About three-quarters of these women were China-born, the rest were mainly Japanese (Straits Settlement Association to the CO, 8 November 1897, CO 882/6, p. 46).

This is probably an underestimate. There was a great deal of sly prostitution in private lodgings and boarding houses where women lived and carried on business on their own account. In the early 1900s it was estimated that there could have been as many as 4,000 *ah ku* in the metropolitan area. Protectorate officials also knew that during this period there were houses in Singapore operating as 'baby farms' where infants and young girls were brought up and kept. *Kwai po* from public houses went to these places to make offers for girls just old enough, at the age of 12 or 13, to become inmates of brothels. The numbers supplied from these establishments helped to augment the total of Chinese women and girls imported, as traffic increased (Statement of McBreen, 11 May 1898, in Swettenham to Chamberlain, 5 August 1898, CO 882/6, No. 227 p. 79). Of the women who registered as prostitutes in Singapore before 1894, it was impossible for the authorities to state how many did so of their own accord and how many were compelled to do so because of threat, intimidation or violence.

After World War I the import figures declined. Following a change in colonial policy, public brothels were no longer tolerated to the extent they had been during the heyday of Chinese immigration in the 1890s. Out of 3,911 Chinese women arriving in Singapore to be registered as prostitutes in the years 1919–24, only 252 were repatriated. Many of those sent back to China were too young, as the minimum age to enter a brothel was 18. As the numbers gradually diminished, the type of girl involved in the traffic changed. Traffickers now tried to carry on importing along new lines. The tendency during the 1920s was to bring in fewer but younger girls who were more subservient and of greater value. An older woman by this time was more apt to be aware of changing colonial policy and practice toward brothel prostitution and give the game away, and was therefore considered a higher risk and not as valuable (*CETWCE* 1933 pp. 62, 287).

A major stumbling block for colonial authorities in their efforts to control the importation of women for brothel prostitution were the triads or secret societies and their *samseng* or hoodlums. Singapore was a predominantly Chinese city and Protectorate officials were quick to point out that in terms of percentages, the secret societies or dangerous element was increasing in direct proportion to the rate of Chinese immigration. A powerful underworld had developed that held a vice-like grip on the coolie trade and the importation of women for brothel prostitution (C.M. Turnbull 1972 pp. 109–10; Yen 1981 pp. 62–92). Though a great deal was unknown about the activities and organisation of these societies, Protectorate experts felt there was mounting evidence of close working relationships between Hong Kong's trans-oceanic brokers and the triads, and several important secret societies and business associations in Singapore. The same pattern of exploitation and protection was developed in Singapore as in Hong Kong and China, and ranged from traditional rackets – extortion and prostitution – to the smuggling of women and narcotics. The Hong Kong triads with their *samseng* fed off their own communities first, 'swimming in the sea' of their own sub-communal groups from China before amassing enough money and strength to prey on other dialect groups outside their own territories. The Singapore secret societies, particularly those of the Ghee Hin, Ghee Hock and Hai San, which were often based on residential and occupational principles, followed the same pattern.

The societies also played a fundamental role in the life of the brothels, guaranteeing protection with extortion to increase their influence, membership and capital. While the precise relationship between the traffic in women and the secret societies remains unclear in many respects, there is little doubt that some 'flesh traders' were members of triads, while others were linked indirectly to the activities of these societies (Yen 1986 p. 252). According to Vaughan, what is clear is that *all* Chinese brothels had connections with secret societies in 1879. The authorities also knew that *kwai po* from a full range of brothels – including the Malay Street and Smith Street houses, as well as sly establishments – had met with triad leaders and cemented their relationships by 'burning yellow paper', a ritual ceremony that established the brothel-keeper as a triad member for life (1974 p. 112).

Location and Numbers of Brothels and Prostitutes

In Singapore between the 1880s and 1920s the red-light districts served as a 'natural' form of boundary maintenance (Young to Lord, 13 July 1917, CO 273/ 457, No. 60716). Registered brothels were confined to specific localities catering to Chinese and non-Chinese clients, including Europeans (Schumsky 1986 pp. 665–7). The public brothels for Chinese were primarily clustered in the 'big town' south of the river where the largest number of labourers were found. Registered brothels for non-Chinese were chiefly concentrated at the north end of the city. The primary administrative aim of this 'natural' segregation of brothels into districts for Chinese and non-Chinese was to separate, control and regulate the behaviour of prostitutes and to curb the spread of venereal disease.

While the carefully demarcated brothel quarters were subject to regulatory control, the character of the two 'safe zones' was also shaped by the fact that one, the Smith Street area, was in the heart of Chinatown and the other, the Malay Street area, in an entertainment district and urban slum not far from the business centre of the city. This spatial overlap between Chinatown and the recognised quarters where prostitution flourished was a direct consequence of Singapore's expansion. As the economy and port grew, so did the migrant-labour population of the city – and the *kwai po*, merchants, cabinet makers, clothiers, florists, laundrymen and doctors whose economic livelihood depended on the *ah ku* accounted for only a small fraction of that population, compared to the vast army of Chinese coolies who lived in these working-class areas. Strictly speaking, segregated prostitution did not exist in Singapore, according to the colonial authorities, because there were public brothels both inside and outside the special quarters. But by tolerating the existence of these red-light districts in working-class neighbourhoods, in the heart of the city, the government was inadvertently highlighting the importance of prostitution. This colonial policy of toleration and transgression with respect to the locality of brothels sought to set social and economic boundaries, and regulate the sexuality and behaviour of Chinese and non-Chinese:

> Simply by staying out of this section, one could avoid taking cognisance of the business or its practitioners. But by locating the district at its very centre, the city emphasised its existence and heightened its visibility. In some cities [like

Table 3
Number of 'Public' Brothels in Singapore in 1877 and 1905

Northern Area	1877 Number of Brothels	1905 Number of Brothels
North Bridge Road	11	2
Rochore Canal Road	2	2
Victoria Street	23	4
Sheik Madersah Lane	16	14
Hylam Street		32
Malabar Street		50
Malay Street	1	34
Bugis Street		14
Fraser Street		54
Tan Quee Lan Street		36
SUB-TOTAL	53	242
Southern Area		
New Bridge Road	33	
Hong Kong Street	45	
North Canal Road	20	4
Chin Hin Street	12	17
Upper Hokkien Street	36	36
Chin Chew Street	13	
Smith Street		17
Trengannu Street		7
Sago Street		13
Spring Street		5
Banda Street		12
SUB-TOTAL	159	111
+ Northern Area	53	242
TOTAL	212	353

Source: Compiled from the List of Licensed Brothels for February 1877 Appendix M pp. LXI–III, in Report of the Committee appointed to enquire into the working of Ordinance XXIII of 1870, commonly called The Contagious Diseases Ordinance, in Straits Settlement Legislative Council Proceedings 1877 Appendix 7, and 'Return of Brothels and Prostitute Brothels known as the Protectorate', SSAR 1905 p. 652.

Singapore], citizens almost had to avoid the red light district consciously, thus intensifying their awareness of its existence (*ibid.*).

By the turn of the century the northern brothel area was very clearly defined. It comprised Malay Street, Bugis Street, Hylam Street and Malabar Street, as well as Fraser Street and Tan Quee Lan Street. The first four streets were all public thoroughfares (Young to Lord, 13 July 1917, CO 273/457, No. 60716). The Malay Street quarter was one of the most accessible districts in the city. The area was a grid of grimy terraced shophouses on the seaward side of Singapore not far from the Raffles Hotel, and just off North Bridge Road.

The southern area was located principally around North Canal Road, and in Hong Kong, Chin Chew, and Chin Hin Streets from 1850–80. Cantonese women, who received only Chinese clients, resided in these houses, which were generally ill-ventilated, and dirty. *Teochiu ah ku* also resided in brothels in North Canal, New Bridge and North Bridge Roads, while the 'all nationality' women, primarily European and Malay prostitutes, frequented North Canal and Rochore Roads, and Chin Chew Street.[7] However, by the 1890s the centre of this red-light district had shifted six blocks further south into the heart of Chinatown, the Kreta Ayer area, as it expanded in the last years of the 19th century. The southern area by then comprised Smith Street, Sago Street, Trengannu Street, Upper Hokkien Street and Chin Hin Street (Cowen to the Association for Moral and Social Hygiene, 18 December 1916, CO 273/452). These five streets were peppered with Chinese and Japanese brothels. Sago Street had at least three establishments labelled 'Japanese house' in letters over a foot high above the door (*ibid.*). It was a common sight in this street before World War I to see 10 or 12 prostitutes on view in a brothel soliciting from the doorway. Often referred to as Little Temple Street by Cantonese, because of a local landmark, the Toh Peh Kong Temple built in 1895, Sago Street had at least 28 brothels in 1902 (*Chinatown: An Album of a Singapore Community*, Times Books and Oral History Department, Singapore 1983 p. 100).

Just as the Malay Street quarter was adjacent to North Bridge Road, so the Smith Street brothel district ran into South Bridge Road. The two sections of Bridge Road constituted the principal thoroughfare running through the middle of town from end to end. Europeans did not frequent the southern area, as the northern Smith Street district was located in the centre of Chinatown. Patrons of this area included Chinese, Japanese, Malays, Indians and Javanese. Sandwiched between the Smith Street brothels were great restaurants three stories high, gleaming with new paint and incandescent gas lamps, brightly lit from ground floor to roof (Enc. No. 6, Young to Lord, 13 July 1917, CO 273/457, No. 60716). Li Chung Chu from Shanghai described this red-light area in 1887:

> As far as prosperity is concerned, no area in Singapore can compare with 'Greater Town'. All the foreign firms, banks, Post Office and customs office are found along the seaside there. Although there are also bazaars in 'Lesser Town', they are set up by the natives to sell local products and various foodstuffs. Not a single big market is found there ... There is an area known as Kereta Ayer in Greater Town where restaurants, theatres and brothels are concentrated. It is the most populated area where filth and dirt are hidden. No place in Singapore can compare with it. Along the streets gas lamps are on throughout the night ... Along Kereta Ayer, brothels are as many and as close together as the teeth of a comb. It is said that the licensed prostitutes registered at the Chinese Protectorate number three thousand and several hundred. Apart from these there are countless unlicensed prostitutes and actresses. They are all Cantonese who were either sold at young age and sent to *Nanyang*, or were born and brought up in Singapore (1975 p. 25).

The number of brothels in the tolerated districts rose towards the end of the 19th century, as did the number of houses outside the designated areas, as the city's population expanded. In 1868, 349 brothels were in business and the total number of prostitutes was officially listed as 2,061; 1,644 were Chinese and there were no Japanese women yet.[8] However, the introduction of the Contagious Diseases Ordinance two years later – a government scheme to register brothels and medically inspect every prostitute resident in them – precipitated a marked downturn in growth over the next decade. In 1877, 212 brothels were registered, concentrated in 11 streets and roads. Table 3 shows that in the northern area they were primarily clustered along Victoria Street, North Bridge Road and Sheik Madersah Lane with only one registered house listed for Malay Street: No. 12, run by a women named Miriam. On North Bridge Road all *kwai po* were either Cantonese or *Teochiu*, while in Victoria Street there were keepers of all nationalities in the 23 houses officially listed, including European women on their own with names like Lina, Clara, Rosalie Brown, Utily Schwartz and Omelia Green.[9] South of the river the largest number of public brothels were located along three thoroughfares: Hong Kong Street, 45 houses; Hokkien Street, 36 houses; and New Bridge Road, 33 houses.[10]

But an immense increase in the number of brothels, which invaded parts of the city where they had never been before, occurred in the 1890s as a consequence of the repeal of the Contagious Diseases Ordinance in 1887 and the abolition of brothel registration in 1894. The institutional forces in Britain which brought about the repeal of the CDO in Singapore were formidable indeed. The decade-long purity campaign by Josephine Butler and fanatical repealers in the 1880s, strengthened by personal interests and interests shared with prominent politicians and colonial officials, is a fascinating exploration of the hypocritical morals and double standards of Victorian society and political culture – it was a campaign whose successful outcome was to have tragic repercussions for the prostitutes and the Chinese community well into this century. Consequently, the statistics provided to the government by the Inspector-General in 1898 did not contain all brothels in the city. Possibly as many as half of them escaped his lists, though they were presumed to be more accurate with respect to Japanese and European houses. Nevertheless, he recognised 308 unregistered Chinese brothels, whose inmates were numbered by their keepers as 1,751. The Inspector-General also listed 121 additional brothels containing 335 prostitutes of 'other nationalities' (Swettenham to Chamberlain, 5 August 1898, CO 882/6, p. 52).

There was enormous growth in the Malay Street area at the turn of the century and the locality and its character were redefined by 1905. Earlier the red-light district had been concentrated in Kampong Glam, along Jalan Sultan, Arab Street, Sheik Madersah Lane and Malay Street. These four thoroughfares contained primarily Malay brothels in 1877. In addition to these houses there were Chinese and European brothels which were situated along North Bridge Road and Victoria Street. Twenty-eight years later the principal locality of these brothels in the northern area had shifted a few blocks to the west, centring on the predominantly

Table 4
Size of Brothels in Selected Streets in the Southern Area in 1877 and 1905

Locality	1877			1905		
	No. of Brothels	No. of Prostitutes	Median Size of Brothel	No. of Brothels	No. of Prostitutes	Median Size of Brothel
New Bridge Road	33	205	6.2	0	0	0
North Canal Road	20	95	4.8	4	14	3.5
Chin Hin Street	12	65	5.4	17	133	7.8
Upper Hokkien St	36	360	10.0	36	310	8.6
Upper Cross Street	4	5	1.2	10	32	3.2
TOTAL	105	730	7.9	67	489	7.3
Smith Street	–	–	–	17	237	13.9
Trengannu Street	–	–	–	7	119	17.0
Sago Street	–	–	–	13	194	14.9
Spring Street	–	–	–	5	38	7.6
Banda Street	–	–	–	12	72	6.0
TOTAL	–	–	–	54	660	12.2

Source: Compiled from List of Licensed Brothels for the month of February 1877, Appendix M, pp. LXI–III, in Report of the Committee appointed to enquire into the working of Ordinance XXIII of 1870, commonly called the Contagious Diseases Ordinance, in Straits Settlements Legislative Council Proceedings 1877, Appendix 7, and 'Return of Brothels and Prostitutes Brothels known as the Protectorate', SSAR, 1905, p. 652.

European and Japanese establishments in Hylam, Malabar, Malay and Bugis Streets, and the Chinese opium smoking houses of Fraser and Tan Quee Lan Streets. In the late 1870s, there were 53 registered brothels just southeast of downtown. By 1905 the number of no longer registered brothels had risen to 242, an increase of 350 per cent! One of the sharpest drops in the intervening years had occurred along Victoria Street where brothels were converted into rickshaw lodging houses to accommodate an ever-increasing number of Hockchia and Hengwah rickshaw pullers.

The establishments 'south of the river' in Chinatown also showed marked changes but of a different sort. In the 1860s and 1870s the largest number of Chinese brothels was found along New Bridge Road or just off it, on Hokkien and Hong Kong or 'Coffin' Street. But by 1905 the data on distribution confirms that there were now fewer larger brothels, concentrated outside those thoroughfares, in the 'Smith Street area'. Brothels disappeared off New Bridge Road as more and more merchants opened up shops and small businesses on this main street in the 1880s. The better establishments were now principally located in Kreta Ayer, a few blocks to the southwest between the Bridge roads in the streets running from Smith to Sago; in addition Japanese brothels were established in this period in the neighbourhood of Banda and Spring Streets.

Data on the size of brothels in selected streets in Table 4 for the years 1877 and 1905 discloses that there were a large number of prostitutes concentrated in fewer brothels in the Smith Street area. Smaller houses continued to hold their own in Upper Cross Street and Chin Hin Street but most other establishments showed slight losses in the number of prostitutes they contained. A typical brothel in 1877 had seven *ah ku* in residence, plus the *kwai po*. Sometimes, however, the brothels were large: Gheon Ah Roi, keeper of brothel No. 6 in Hokkien Street, had 14 girls, as did Koh Ah Jam further down the street at No. 33/4. At the other extreme, three out of four houses listed in Upper Cross Street had only one inmate each.[11] The size of public brothels in these streets fluctuated hardly at all between 1877 and 1905, despite the loss of 28 houses by the beginning of the 20th century.

The number of women who could reside in a brothel depended upon the size and accommodation of a house. While the overall number of brothels increased in Chinatown between 1877 and 1905, the dramatic growth occurred in the Smith Street area where the houses were three and four storeys high, and the number of *ah ku* cramped in them rose accordingly. By 1905, a typical house in Sago and Trengannu Streets contained 15–17 women, and the bigger brothels housed as many as 17 or 18 prostitutes.

There is evidence that sly brothels existed prior to 1877, but no statistics are available to indicate how many there were or their distribution. The colonial administration was not unduly concerned about the location of these brothels in the late 1870s, with the exception of those near the Tanglin barracks (Swettenham to Chamberlain, 5 August 1898, CO 882/6, p. 52). By the turn of the century, however, they were far more alarmed at the number of brothels and the rapidity of their spread into the narrow, dusty and unlit streets of a city in the deadly grip of a venereal disease epidemic. This metamorphosis occurred in places like Canal Road and Pasir Lane which were lined with two-storey buildings with clay shingled roofs, small paned windows and smaller doors which framed the heavily made-up *ah ku* sitting in the gloom (SCII of Yeo Ah Lip, 4/4/1908; SCII of Yip Mui Chai, No. 218, 6/11/1908; SCII of That Koh Loo, No. 59, 3/4/1909).

The houses occupied by *ah ku* at the turn of the century were similar in appearance. They were two-, three- or four-storey buildings with large numbers on the fan lights over the door, with a red or other coloured lamp behind the number (Cowen to the Association for Moral and Social Hygiene, 18 December 1916, CO 273/452). The brothel numbers were not always identical to regular street numbers, and in some cases they bore no relation to them. These numbers were not found on any other houses in the city except registered brothels, and not on public houses outside the two designated 'safe' areas. The uniformity of size and pattern of these numbers meant a house was a publicly recognised brothel in the eyes of the Police and Protector of Chinese. But it is not clear whether they were put up over the doors by order of the colonial authorities, and, if so, by which authority, and under what law, or whether they were put up by the keepers at the behest of the police, whose suggestion would have been as good as law to a *kwai po*.

Class and sub-communal origins were important factors separating Chinese brothels into higher and lower grades in Singapore. The more exclusive brothels, with a wealthier clientele, were primarily located in the Smith Street area. Chinese men – merchants, schoolteachers and middle-level public servants – could have sexual relations with a Cantonese *ah ku* overnight, if she was not already booked, in a comfortably decorated setting in these establishments. A black signboard over the entrance attracted the attention of would-be clients to these *lo kui chai* (whore houses) which provided overnight service. A Kreta Ayer resident remembered in his youth being able to distinguish these higher-grade brothels from neighbouring shophouses by the signboard:

> I saw the signboards when I was young. The sign which was hanging outside in a prominent place above the entrance usually had a name on it like 'so and so *Lau*' or 'so and so *Heung*'. Names ending in '*Lau*' or including '*Heung*' were always brothels.[12]

Most of these houses also had ornate bas-relief plaster frames situated directly above the windows facing the street. The rectangular frames were decorated and inscribed with Chinese characters, euphemisms in the language of romance and imagery, advertising the personal attributes of the extremely popular *ah ku* living in the street-side rooms on the upper levels. Usually a soft, poetic phrase like 'fresh breeze' or 'clear moon' had been incised in the plaster frame, describing the qualities of a popular woman, who might peer out of her window or over the balcony along Smith Street.[13] Unfortunately, most of these brothel inscriptions have been badly defaced with the passage of time. A few barely discernible examples still survive, especially in Smith Street, as telltale fragments of the panorama of street-front life in Chinatown at the turn of the century, and a tangible sign of the history of brothel prostitution in Singapore.

The entrances and halls of the Chinese brothels were lit by incandescent gas lamps. Only one brothel in Singapore, a large Chinese house in Smith Street, had electric light by 1917 (Young to Lord, 13 July 1917, CO 273/457, No. 60716). Singapore was not a well-lit city and the higher-grade brothels were certainly no exception to the rule. The less exclusive second-class *Teochiu* houses were more readily found at the northern end of Chinatown closer to the river while lower-grade brothels were located in the Malay Street area: 'The other side of the river was low class.'[14] In these establishments everything was kept to a bare minimum except the number of *ah ku* residing in them, averaging between seven and eight per house in Tan Quee Lan and Fraser Streets in 1905. There was little atmosphere and the sex was convenient, quick and cheap. These inexpensive brothels were locally referred to as *pau chai*; the numerous customers – coolies, sailors, and soldiers – who patronised them were known as *ta pau*, while the *ah ku* in these *pau chai* were called *pau po*. *Pau* means firecracker, suggesting that the sexual service available was as quick as burning a string of firecrackers.[15]

With the exception of some of the more exclusive *lo kui chai*, most of the brothels occupied by *ah ku* were cramped, ill-ventilated and not very clean (Swettenham to Chamberlain, 8 September 1898, CO 882/6, No. 25; Anson to Carnarvon, 21 April 1877, CO 273/91, No. 132). The upper storeys of the houses had narrow passages running the whole length of the building; doors at intervals along the passageway opened into small, dingy, oblong wooden rooms, which were pitch dark even in the middle of the day and had to be illuminated with an oil lamp. The air in these rooms was often stale. The wells and toilets which usually adjoined one another at the back of the houses were in too close proximity for sanitary purposes, especially for washing clothes and bathing (*ibid.*). Besides the main entrance there were in many cases other outlets leading down to the hall below, or to an adjoining brothel, either by back doors, extra side staircases, or steps over the roof which, on the occasion of a surprise visit by officials or a sudden homicide, enabled prostitutes to make their escape (*ibid.*).

The Status and Exploitation of Prostitutes

I will now focus on the status of prostitutes in these houses and the exploitative sexual economy of brothel prostitution as a business. In the 'public' brothels *kwai po* divided *ah ku* into three categories according to their financial relations with the house. Chinese prostitutes were either 'sold', 'pawned' or 'voluntary'. The sold prostitutes, bought by the *kwai po* from traffickers, belonged to the house and were considered, in common parlance, to be 'adopted daughters' of the brothel-keeper. These *kongchu* or *amaksan* were furnished with all the necessaries – food, clothing, pocket money – but everything they earned went to the *kwai po*, and they were absolutely her property to use and dispose of as she saw fit.[16] Those women who were pawned or hired to a house were called *pongnin*, which literally meant 'assist for a term of years'. *Pongnin* were in most cases young girls working off a debt they had contracted on behalf of poverty-ridden parents or a guardian. The *pongnin* were usually bound to prostitute themselves for a minimum period of six years, during which time they had to hand over to the *kwai po* half their earnings, receiving in return only room and board.[17] They were able to retain the remaining half, which they might or might not have the opportunity to use toward repayment of their debt, which in the course of time was progressively increased by the *kwai po* supplying various articles of clothing and jewellery at exorbitant rates. In theory, *pongnin* who were working off a debt were free at the end of the fixed term if they had paid everything they owed, but it frequently happened that towards the end of their term they were transferred or sold to begin another term of bondage for a different house or a new *kwai po*.

The *tap tang* (literally, 'sharing the lamp') or voluntary prostitute had a similar status in the *kwai po*'s eyes to the *pongnin*, receiving food and renting a room in the brothel against half her earnings. The difference was that she had no debt to pay off to the proprietor of the house. *Tap tang* thus had far more autonomy than either *kongchu* or *pongnin*. The remaining half of their earnings usually went to themselves if they were free agents, or to a 'pocket mother' if the *tap tang* happened to be the property of some old woman, often an ex-prostitute. This was not unusual in Singapore as late as the 1920s.

The majority of Chinese prostitutes in Singapore were not free. The conditions under which *kongchu* and *amaksan* lived, and the ties – financial, social and moral – by which they were bound to their *kwai po* made them virtual 'outsiders' with no rights in themselves. The 'sold' prostitutes were in a particularly hopeless position in Singapore, whereas:

> ... one must remember that the prostitute in China is in her own country, speaking her own language, amongst her own people, often backed and supported by family ties, and influenced for good by local surroundings, with the knowledge that she can always appeal to the humanity of her parents, relatives, friends or fellow prostitutes in trouble and sickness; with the direct assurance and comfort in a very large number of cases, that her degradation as a woman is supporting a helpless father or mother or brother and sister unable to support themselves, and that she is doing her duty ... in obedience to the principles of Chinese filial piety (Hare memo, 12 June 1889, in Swettenham to Chamberlain, 8 September 1898, CO 882/6, pp. 83–4).

Prostitutes of the house rarely received a cent of their earnings, unless they could successfully hide any gifts they obtained from admiring customers. *Kongchu* were nearly always forced to work at all times and in all circumstances, in health and in sickness. If they broke down under the relentless routine or contracted a sexually transmitted disease they were invariably sold or set adrift on the streets. A *kwai po* who bought a girl was also not always prepared to release her to a willing customer merely for the return of the purchase price plus interest and expenses. Here the aspect of bondage and the exploitative nature of the relationship between *kwai po* and *kongchu* is crystal clear, because the keeper, like a slave-owner, often believed she was entitled to a commercial price – to compensate her for the loss of future earnings of her *amaksan* for a stipulated period of years. Regardless of her own wishes or of the morality which had previously guided her actions, a Chinese woman, as a *kongchu*, lost all rights over disposal of her own body. Her helplessness in the face of the *kwai po*'s power lends to the *kongchu*'s behaviour an aura of total submission. Speaking on this point, Tan Jiak Kim, a well-informed Chinese resident and Municipal Commissioner, stated in 1889:

> The majority of our unhappy women are not in the strict sense of the term free agents, especially those young girls who form the bulk of our prostitutes; they have been in most cases, sold, trained, and brought up for the sole purpose of earning money for their mistresses ... Taking into account this and the social restrictions imposed upon these poor, wretched women by the old customs of their nation, I am not far wrong when I say that they occupy a position, in a free country like this, nearly equal to that occupied by a bondage slave.[18]

The system of procurement and indenture that brought destitute Chinese village girls to Singapore's brothels under contract was also little better than bondage.

The *pongnin* received food, lodging and some medical care upon entry into the brothel, but the 'debt' system well known in the world of Chinese prostitution, of keepers running *pongnin* into further indebtedness, by offering to provide clothes, jewellery, furniture and rent, flourished in Singapore. During her six years the *kwai po* was obliged to give a contract prostitute only one suit of clothes per year. If the *pongnin* wanted a larger wardrobe she had to purchase it at her own expense or borrow the money. She also had to pay for the small everyday necessities of life like tea, oil, tobacco and matches (Statement of McBreen, 11 May 1898, in Swettenham to Chamberlain, August 5, 1898, CO 882/6, No. 227, p. 78; Niccol-Jones 1941 p. 38). The original debt arising from money transferred on her entry into a brothel as a *pongnin* – the money for which she was 'sold' or was 'selling herself' – was not recognised by the colonial government and was considered the basis of an illegal transaction in China. However, the debt which a *pongnin* incurred with a *kwai po* for the purchase of clothes and finery was considered legal:

> The girls when they get to the place of prostitution have no nice clothes, as naturally they are from poor homes. First they have to borrow money from the keeper of the house, sometimes four hundred or five hundred dollars, in order to buy better clothes and be able to do business, and this is a debt by the girl … a legal debt which must be paid back. In that stage, whenever the girl owes money to the keeper of the house, she must give the keeper … half of her earnings, keeping the remaining half for herself. After the debt is paid, she is free, and all the money she earns is for herself (*CETWCE* 1933 p. 140).

The filial obligation of a young woman to supply her family's needs was too strong in most instances not to comply with repayment of the debt. The brothel-keepers favoured this contract-debt system because they made considerable profit while having to furnish little real benefit or expense to the *pongnin*. The *pongnin* disliked the system intensely. Even though they were moderately cared for, being fed and clothed in the brothels, they were often unable to pay off their debt, having to turn over half their wages until the contract was eventually completed.

If she was able to leave the business, and this was often done on the *pongnin*'s own initiative, to get married, she was rarely allowed to take any of her wardrobe, except what she was wearing to go away in. To be free to do this, though, she had to settle all her debts first. But it was almost as difficult for a *pongnin* to get loose as for a *kongchu*, because of the arbitrary value placed on her body by the keeper. The more she desired to leave, the higher the *kwai po* fixed the price of her manumission, so that she was unable to amass sufficient means to re-purchase her own body, and was obliged to remain a *pongnin* indefinitely, a virtual prisoner of the *kwai po*. The only possibility for a *pongnin* to obtain her freedom under such circumstances, short of absconding, was to find a wealthy man who wanted to marry her and who was willing to pay the *kwai po*'s exorbitant price. If the keeper learned she was attempting to run away with a suitor, the *pongnin* was often drugged, taken to the Federated Malay States or Sumatra and sold into another brothel, where she would have to serve another six years, even if she had already worked off five years of the previous contract with her first brothel-keeper (Statement of McBreen, 11 May 1898, in Swettenham to Chamberlain, August 5, 1898, CO 882/6, No. 227, p. 78). This form of indenture and chronic indebtedness in brothel prostitution flourished at the end of the 19th century because poverty, patriarchy and the prosperity of Singapore compelled Chinese women to enter brothels as *pongnin*.

The circumstances of the lives of *ah ku* who were sold or pawned were complicated by the mere fact of being in Singapore, distantly cut off from parents, kin and friends. They were under the thumb of the *kwai po* and had no one they could appeal to for help against having been brought to the city under false pretences and against their will in many cases, or against the cruelty of their keeper. Fictive kinship terms were used to mask the exploitative nature of relations between *ah ku* and the *kwai po* whose property they were. The *kongchu* and *pongnin* were referred to as 'daughters' of the keeper, and called the *kwai po* 'mother'.[19] These women were obliged to carry on prostitution under the guise of this fictive relationship, which was one of the most enduring intimidating features of Chinese traffic in women and young girls and brothel prostitution, because no sense of free will or choice was possible . The women were usually fearful of the unknown, afraid to disobey their 'mothers', and ignorant of their rights and everything connected with the colonial government under which they lived. While public prostitution was forbidden under the Chinese Penal Code after 1911, it was still recognised by Chinese custom. Under common law, a *kongchu* or *pongnin* was the property of her *kwai po* unconditionally, and almost beyond redemption, and as such she was virtually a legal non-person with no rights over herself (Gronewold 1982 pp. 33–4).

Free women, *tap tang*, who chose the third path of recruitment into prostitution were fully aware of what they were doing when they entered a Singapore brothel. As one said in 1918: 'I am a prostitute in 70 Malabar Street. I have been in Singapore for about 10 months. I went straight to 70 Malabar Street' (SCII of Teng Ah Hee, No. 263, 9/10/1918).

Voluntary prostitutes were motivated by poverty or domestic contradictions to take up the life of an *ah ku*. Many became prostitutes in order to live or find a livelihood for others. There were those who came to Singapore to seek work as domestic servants and wage labourers because of economic hardship, or to escape the sexual harassment of a wanton husband, or the abuse of a tyrannical mother-in-law (*CETWCE* 1933 pp. 140–1; Gronewold 1982 p. 73). They were often induced to become *ah ku* because they could not earn enough income for their kin and themselves except as prostitutes. Some *tap tang*, though, had been victims of the traffic in women and children when they were younger. They had been bought in China as infants or orphans and had remained for quite a number of years under the authority of an adoptive 'pocket mother' or *kwai po*. Ultimately, they had managed to attain their freedom and had chosen to continue their life as *ah ku* on their own account. These women were not always registered, but their names and the brothels they lived in were usually known to the Chinese Protectorate (League of Nations, C. 223 M. 89, to FO, 17 May 1926, FO 371/11871, p. 65). Like the class of free prostitutes in China to which she belonged, a *tap tang* enjoyed far more liberty than was accorded to *kongchu* and *pongnin*, and consequently was better able to assert her rights when necessary.

The treatment of *ah ku* by brothel-keepers varied and did not appear to be generally harsh, although there were instances where great cruelty was shown: for example, sick girls were beaten to make them work. *Kwai po* were capable of punishing an *ah ku* in a brothel by keeping her a virtual prisoner if she was disobedient or did not earn enough money, or by stopping her food. In extreme cases of maltreatment the voices of the *kongchu* and *pongnin* rarely reached beyond the walls of the brothels where they were held in bondage by *kwai po* who regarded them merely 'as part of the furniture'.

The varying status of the *ah ku* and their economic dependence on the brothel-keeper made it easy to transfer a prostitute from one *kwai po* to another for a particular amount, which was in fact often the purchase price. The women were also transferred between keepers on note of hand, in return for or as security against loans, just like a trader bartering his goods (Memo by Hare, 12 June 1889, in Swettenham to Chamberlain, 8 September 1898, CO 882/6, No. 25, p. 83; Weld to Derby, 30 May 1883, CO 273/20, No. 214). The precautions taken by the colonial government to put up notices in brothels stating that the girls were legally at liberty to leave and of giving them 'protection' tickets were of little or no use, as few *ah ku* could read, and the *kwai po* could easily prevent them absconding. Their only hope of release was for a customer to intercede and purchase them.

The Business of Prostitution

Brothel prostitution was a lucrative form of business when Singapore was undergoing rapid economic expansion and development. Before the turn of the century, running brothels in the city was considered one of the easiest ways for Chinese entrepreneurs to accumulate capital (Testimony of Ah Jeok in Anson to Carnarvon, 21 April 1877, CO 273/9). A sign that brothels were an extremely profitable way of making money at this time was the large sums paid for the goodwill of a registered house (*Singapore Free Press* 9 January 1897). To show that brothel prostitution was a source of wealth depending on the number of *ah ku* in a house, let us examine the average expenditure and income of a Smith Street brothel owner around 1905. Allowance has been made in this annual account for rent, which was usually twice that charged to neighbouring lodging houses, the possible illness of an *ah ku* and slack periods in business, leading to a minimum working month of 24 days. Account has also been taken of secret society payments and other 'squeezes' to *samseng*, and of monthly medical contributions towards the welfare and maintenance of *ah ku*. The prostitute usually had to contribute an equal share towards this fund. The figures in Table 5 represent an average net profit of $5,545 to the proprietor of a three-storey Smith Street brothel with 14 *ah ku*.

Table 5
Expenditure and Income of a Smith Street Brothel Owner *Circa* **1905**

Annual income $3/day x 24 days/month x 12 months x 14 *ah ku*	$12,096
Maintenance Food, clothing and jewellery $45/*ah ku* x 14 *ah ku* Rent @ $60/month Secret-society payments @ 50c/day x 360 days/year Brothel medical fees @ 50c/day x 360 days/year	630 720 2,520 2,520
Annual expenditure Annual profit	6,390 5,706

Source: Compiled from various cases in the Singapore Coroner's Inquest and Inquiries between 1883 and 1905.

It could have been far more. Attention must be drawn to the secret society payments which *kwai po* often had to satisfy. When brothel owning did not pay these were the channels, along with dramatic rises in rent, which absorbed profits. Still, once the expenditure for rent and the overall welfare of the *ah ku* was deducted from the owner's gross income, the annual profit was a sizeable one. An average *ah ku* would continue to earn upward of $800 annually for four years barring unforeseen circumstances. The brothel owner would then usually sell her for about $2,000, receiving a net profit of around $1,750 from the resale, on top of the gross income made from her previous four years of labour as an *ah ku* under contract (Hirata 1979 pp. 14–5, 17).

To obtain an estimated overall picture of earnings, we can also calculate how much money would have changed hands on an average night in one section of the Smith Street area at the best places in 1905. If every *ah ku* listed for the 37 houses in Smith Street (17), Trengannu Street (7), and Sago Street (13), numbering 550, were engaged for the evening at the standard rate of three dollars, $1,650 would have been made on the night. This was only the basic earnings for three streets. Assuming the *ah ku* in these 37 brothels worked a minimum of 288 days, the total could easily have been over $475,200 a year.

Conclusion

The coolie traffic, a market for prostitution and Singapore's economic development were interrelated factors crucial in shaping the meaning and experience of the *ah ku*, and the history of the city. The presence of these women was indispensable in maintaining the coolie labour force so necessary for Singapore's growth and expansion. Equally important, large profits were made from brothel prostitution which enabled Chinese entrepreneurs to accumulate capital and diversify their economic interests in Singapore. Agrarian poverty in China, patriarchy and rising urban prosperity in Singapore all had a direct impact in creating a situation of drastic gender imbalance in Singapore at the end of the 19th century. This in turn gave rural Chinese women the choice of becoming prostitutes, and opened a traffic in victims for that market. It also impacted on the lives of the masses of men who visited the Chinese brothels.

The importation of women for prostitution and the control and regulation of brothels was a serious problem for late-19th-century Singapore because of fear of the spread of sexually transmitted diseases. At the same time, brothel prostitution was a necessity for social control and a prop for morality, enabling Chinese society to protect the purity of its marriageable women in both China and Singapore, by sacrificing the majority of *ah ku* to a rising tide of Chinese migrant labour.

It was extremely profitable for brothel-keepers and procuresses to import young Chinese girls as *tap tang*, *kongchu* and *pongnin* for brothel prostitution in Singapore. *Kwai po* who needed fresh girls went to China themselves, sent representatives, or employed traffickers as intermediaries to buy girls and arrange for their passage to Singapore. At the turn of the century the selling price of a common woman in southern China was from $20 to $50. In Singapore the value of these ordinary women increased dramatically. Prices ranged from $150 to more than $500 depending on the woman's age, appearance and origin as Chinese immigration increased, and the traffic in women for brothel prostitution kept pace.

It has already been noted that in Chinese law debts from money contracted on entry of an *ah ku* to a brothel were not recognised. Theoretically, neither *kongchu* nor *pongnin* were under any legal obligation arising out of the act of 'selling' or 'pawning'. However, the classification of prostitutes in China as 'mean people' and as slaves was a legal and economic fact of consequence (Gronewold 1982 p. 33). *Ah ku*, as prostitutes and 'mean people', could not expect the assistance of respectable members of the Chinese community, many of whom were their clients, but were often too busy with their own affairs to concern themselves with the legal status and economic plight of these women. In practice, all concerned – the *kwai po*, who held absolute rights over an *ah ku*, the person who sold her or arranged for her to be pawned to the *kwai po*, the public at large, and even the *ah ku* herself – considered that she was under a legal-moral obligation to serve in a brothel until the original amount of the purchase or pledge, with or without interest, had been repaid.

At the turn of the century, flesh traders in the southern parts of China were engaged in a covert but highly lucrative trade: the selling of women and girls. The profits from trafficking in women were enormous and rising in Singapore in 1900. Thousands of females were either kidnapped or bought in China and transported to the port-city under threat of violence and constraints for debts. After passing the Chinese Protector's examination upon entry, they were sold to a brothel to ply their new trade. The upsurge in human traffic from China and the increased presence of brothels in the Malay Street and Smith Street areas of Singapore symbolised a broader sense of the ascendancy of colonialism and capitalism. The lucrative brothel industry reflected the economic dynamism of Singapore, as well as the disintegration of the agrarian world of Qing China in the face of massive social and economic upheaval.

In a very real sense the failure of the Chinese Protectorate to combat the traffic for brothel prostitution had to do with striking in the wrong place. Critics of the government's policy on brothel prostitution wanted to abolish the public houses which ensured a market for traffickers and secret societies. However, the Colony did not contemplate the abolition of brothels, but tacitly sanctioned them for pragmatic social and economic reasons, and the brothels could not exist without a constant supply of young girls from China. Under these ironic circumstances the officials of the Chinese Protectorate could only gradually make themselves felt in their efforts to eradicate the traffic in women and children and brothel prostitution in the period prior to World War II.

Notes

1   Prostitution is mentioned briefly in Lee Poh Ping 1978 and C.M. Turnbull 1977, while Yen Ching Hwang 1986 deals with it only as a social problem in part of a chapter.

2   On the question of the fundamental inequality of Chinese women and the trade in women as prostitutes in the late Qing and early Republican periods see Sue Gronewold 1982; on Japanese women see Yamazaki Tomoko 1975 pp. 52–60.

3   There have been a number of histories of Singapore but most administrators and historians who have written them, especially those that concern the history of the Chinese, have ignored the position of ordinary women. They have also failed to consider the dynamic between class, ethnic and gender relations in an examination of female immigration, women's work and prostitution. Of the early books by colonial officials, J.D. Vaughan's *The Manners and Customs of the Chinese of the Straits Settlements* contains information on a diverse range of topics pertaining to Singapore Chinese society and culture, ranging from opium smoking, gambling and Chinese chess to the structure and organisation of secret societies. Unfortunately, in this brief account of the Chinese in the Straits Settlements, prostitution is not covered in any detail. Li Chung Chu, a citizen of Shanghai, stayed in Singapore for more than a month in 1887, and wrote a little book entitled *A Description of Singapore in 1887*, published in 1895. Li's record of Singapore is authentic and one of the few written in Chinese at that time. The value of his book from the standpoint of social history lies in his candid observations about the city's street life. He provides background detail to evaluate changes in the popular culture of the *ah ku*.

Song Ong Siang's *One Hundred Year's History of the Chinese in Singapore* commemorates the technical and entrepreneurial skills and the wealth and influence that had come after the first wave of immigration in 1821. Song, in recording the lives and material success of many Victorian-era *towkays* (businessmen), who clawed their way into the unsympathetic environment of the *Nanyang*, reminds us that the tendency of Straits immigrants was towards loyalty to the King and a new Empire – the British. He encyclopaedically records more information about ordinary Chinese in Singapore than most earlier works, but one has to comb the huge index systematically for fragments of the life stories of 'faceless' migrant women - prostitutes, peasants and coolies, who did the difficult, back-breaking work of binding and building a nation. Recent trends in historical writing and the study of overseas Chinese communities make Song's history a mine of information on Chinese society in Singapore.

Lee Poh Ping, Carl Trocki and Mary Turnbull have focused on the formation of a mercantile class and an immigrant society in 19th-century Singapore. In their pioneering analyses of the clash between the Malacca Chinese 'free trade society' and the *Teochiu* 'gambier and pepper society', prostitution is mentioned briefly, as a primary economic activity of the secret societies along with gambling and the control of coolie labour.

Yen Ching Hwang, whose earlier work examined the role of the overseas Chinese in the Straits Settlements in support of the 1911 Revolution and the equally dramatic part they played in late Qing modernisation, has recently written a history of the Chinese in Malaya and Singapore from within. He concentrates on the class structure of the various Chinese groups and the relationship of dialect and class organisations to the social structure of the Chinese society. Yen deals with prostitution as a social problem, focusing primarily on the vested interests of the colonial government in controlling it. His discussion of regulation does not consider the nature of the social relations of the women, or the historiographical significance of the texture and meaning of their experience. Vaughan 1974; Li Chung Chu 1975 pp. 20–9; Song Ong Siang 1923; Lee Poh Ping 1978 pp. 53, 57, 80, 86; Trocki 1979 pp. 32, 211; Turnbull 1972 pp. 86–90; Yen Ching Hwang 1986 pp. 248–83.

4 "Report of Venereal Diseases Committee', Council Paper No. 86, Straits Settlements Legislative Council Proceedings (1923), December 17, 1923, CO 275/109, p. C288.

5 No. C.247, League of Nations to Foreign Office, May 9, 1933, FO 371/17387; League of Nations, *CETWCE* 1933 p. 94; S.E. Niccol-Jones 1941 'Report on the Problem of Prostitution in Singapore' p. 38; R.S. Morton *Venereal Diseases* (Penguin Books, London, 1972) p. 124.

6 Statistics of the Registration Office, Contagious Diseases Ordinance, 1887–1894, CO 275/33; Smith to Knutsford, May 7, 1888, CO 273/152, No. 187.

7. Report of the Committee appointed to enquire into the working of Ordinance XXIII of 1870, commonly called the Contagious Diseases Ordinance, in *Straits Settlement Legislative Council Proceedings*, 1877, Appendix 7, p. XLIII (henceforth Report on CDO, *SSLC* 1877).

8. Appendix N, Abstract of Return of Brothels and Prostitutes of Singapore, in Governor of Straits and Settlement to Colonial Office, 24 February 1869, CO 273/91.

9. List of Licensed Brothels for the month of February, 1877, Appendix M, pp. LXI–III, in Report on CDO, *SSLC* 1877, Appendix 7.

10. *Ibid.*

11. *Ibid.*

12. Fong Chiok Kai, interview with the assistance of Ms Tan Beng Luan in the

Committee Room of the Kreta Ayer Community Centre, Singapore, 1 October 1987; Gronewold 1982 p. 6.

13. *Ibid.*

14. Yip Cheong Fung, interview held with the assistance of Ms Tan Beng Luan, Singapore, 3 October 1987.

15. Wong Swee Peng, interview held with the assistance of Ms Tan Beng Luan in the Ming Yueng (M.B.A.) Home for the Aged, Singapore, 3 October 1987.

16. Minute by the Protector of Chinese on brothels in Singapore in Swettenham to Chamberlain, 5 August 1898, CO 882/6, No. 227, p. 77; *CETWCE* 1933 pp. 44–5, 137.

17. *Ibid.*; Gronewold 1982 p. 70.

18. Report of proceedings of the Municipal Commissioners, Singapore, 12 September 1889, in the Straits Settlement Association to the Colonial Office, 8 November 1897, CO 882/6, p. 464.

19. Report of Proceedings of the Municipal Commissioners, Singapore, 12 September 1889, in the Straits Settlement Association to the Colonial Office, 8 November 1897, CO 882/6, p. 47.

5. Mui Tsai Through the Eyes of the Victim: Janet Lim's Story of Bondage and Escape[1]

By Suzanne Miers (with the co-operation of Janet Lim)

It is very difficult for people to understand what it means to be a slave, to be bargained for and sold like merchandise, to suffer shame and the whips of one's master and mistress (Lim 1958 p. 42).

Introduction

This chapter provides a rare personal account by the victim of the institution known in Cantonese as *mui tsai* or 'little younger sister'. This was a recognised system of transferring unwanted girls, often as small children, from poor homes into rich families, who paid a nominal sum, sealing the bargain with a particular type of contract drawn up on red paper. Most became unpaid servants. Theoretically, their bondage ended when they reached marriageable age, at which time their owners were expected to find them suitable husbands. Their treatment varied directly with the affluence and disposition of their owners (Jaschok and Miers). Some were kindly treated, even genuinely regarded as members of the family. In fact this was the usual happy fate of boys transferred under an identical system. Some of the girls were duly married off and became free women, but others never escaped from bondage.

Janet Lim's story throws light on the workings of the institution at its worst, on the circumstances in which she became a *mui tsai*, and on the policies of the colonial government, which on the one hand did not prevent her importation as a virtual slave into a British colony, and on the other, played a crucial part in her escape and successful rehabilitation, enabling her to find the way to independence through Western education. She graphically describes the trauma to which *mui tsai* were subjected, and also gives us a rare glimpse of the impact on the owners of her escape and the subsequent revelations of how badly they had treated her. Most poignant, she makes it clear that long after her escape and embarkation on a successful career, there remained the social stigma of having been sold, made worse because it had happened not once but twice. Slave origins are kept secret even today by the surviving *mui tsai*, and Janet Lim is careful never to reveal the real names of those to whom she refers.

Her account is particularly important in the context of this volume because it shows how an individual victim of potentially one of the most oppressive institutions to which Chinese girls were subjected could, with courage, initiative and luck, escape, and with ability and determination become mistress of her own destiny. It must be pointed out, however, that few former *mui tsai* achieved such social mobility and that at least in the early days it was only possible for Janet Lim because she moved in Westernised circles.

From Poverty to Servitude

Janet Lim believes she was born in Hong Kong to Chaozhou parents in July 1923[2] and named Qiu Mei – Autumn Beauty. Her father was a traditional doctor from southern China named Kwek Nai Poh. The family moved back to his village when she was only a few months old. Sadly she does not know where it is but believes it is somewhere in Guangdong Province. Her father had his own fields of rice, sugar cane and groundnuts, and the family was prosperous. Janet retains a clear picture of the village and of the neighbouring one where her maternal grandparents lived, whom she often visited. Her early life was happy. The only unusual thing about the family seems to have been that her father was a Roman Catholic and believed in giving girls a Western education, for he promised to send her to school. He had probably been to Singapore, since he taught her a Malay word and told her that girls there went to school.

In contrast, her mother, Chua Gwek Lui, was a Buddhist, who had been married at the age of only 13 to Janet's father, who was 10 years her senior. In the usual way, the marriage had been arranged by her parents through a matchmaker and she did not see her husband before the wedding. She had no formal education and was brought up to do housework and agricultural labour. She worked hard, and not only delivered her own babies alone, but was up and doing all her normal work the very next day. She shared the Chinese views of her day on the worthlessness of daughters, who were marginal members of the family and were usually married out of it by the time they were 15 to husbands chosen by their fathers (Hayes; Watson). Following Chinese convention, she never displayed any affection for her daughter, unlike her husband, of whom Janet has only happy memories. The only indication she ever had that her mother loved her came when she overheard someone complain that she treated Janet as though she was not her own child. To Janet's joy her mother replied that she loved her 'like a pearl deep in the sea' (Lim 1958 p. 30).

The family soon suffered a series of tragedies. Their second daughter was given away soon after birth, before being named, because her horoscope predicted that if she remained at home, Janet would die (Koh). Although at the time many girls were abandoned or killed, the new baby was placed in a convent. However, she died in infancy. To the great joy of the parents the next child was a boy. There followed another girl who died soon after birth. With relatively prosperous parents and a bright little brother, family life was happy until the much loved boy died at the age of four. Soon afterwards, when Janet was only six years old, her father also died.

After this the family fortunes went steadily downhill. Her father's only brother arrived from Singapore and claimed the estate. Janet's mother was soon involved in quarrels with her brother-in-law. One day, in desperation, she sent Janet to fetch her mother, intending, she later explained, to give her her jewellery and other possessions and ask her to look after Janet, and then to kill herself. Had Janet done as she was told she might have lived her life with kindly grandparents. But instead of fetching her grandmother, she went to her father's grave and implored him to return to life. When she finally came home, her mother told her that she had not committed suicide because two butterflies, believed to be messengers from the dead, had appeared and she had decided she wanted to see Janet again. All indications are, therefore, that she truly did love her.

However, now desperate for a livelihood, her mother, escorted by a friend of her late husband, set out with Janet in search of a new husband. They made a long and arduous journey on foot, walking through mountains, taking care to avoid bandits, until eventually they came to a town, the name of which Janet does not remember. There they stayed in a house full of women and children. Here one day her mother and other women paraded in their best clothes twice around the garden in front of prospective husbands. Janet soon found to her deep resentment that she had a stepfather, with whose family they went to live – a stepfather she would never really accept.

Life was not happy for them. Her mother, as a new bride, had to serve everyone at meals and Janet soon discovered that she herself was destined to marry one of her stepfather's nephews – a boy of about her own age. Times were particularly hard as there was a drought. Soon the rice paddy and vegetables dried up in the fields. The family had to dig for water and often went hungry. Janet managed better than the others because her stepfather's father, who lived alone, took a fancy to her and shared his food with her. Her mother was particularly unhappy, and after some months, she and her husband crept away secretly in the night, taking Janet with them. They went to her mother's parents' home where they had a happy reunion. Alas, this was shortlived. Janet remembers celebrating her eighth birthday (her seventh by European reckoning) in her grandparents' house. But her stepfather had no home, no job and only one dollar in his pocket. Her grandfather suggested that he might try selling fish as a hawker. After only a few days, they set off to try their fortunes in Shantou (Swatow) and the whole village turned out to see them off. This was the last time Janet was to see her grandparents. In Shantou life was reasonably happy for Janet. She helped another family, who ran a candy stall.

Life as a Marketable Commodity

Janet's stepfather failed to find work and her parents told her they were returning to his family. Then they broke the devastating news that they would not be taking her with them. Their excuse was that the journey was too exhausting. Over her protests they took her to Ampo, a neighbouring town, to a big house belonging to a wealthy family. There, one terrible day, the memory of which, nearly 60 years later, still reduced her to tears, her mother told her that they were selling her. She explained to the weeping child that she was their only asset – all that stood between them and starvation (interview 1 September 1989).

Janet was stunned and heartbroken, but she believed it was her filial duty to accept her fate. Her mother tried to comfort her by saying that they would come back to fetch her if they were able to get any money. When Janet replied that if they did not come she would run away, her parents, perhaps significantly, did not tell her not to.

Broken-hearted, she watched the transaction. One hundred and twenty Chinese dollars were counted out in front of her and the red paper contract was drawn up in exchange.[3] Her mother gave her 25 cents and said: 'You be a good girl and we will see you again.' Janet followed her parents forlornly across the courtyard, crying bitterly as they went out of the big gate. She watched them disappear into the distance. The fat woman who owned the house and had bought her had the gate slammed, told her brusquely to go inside, and then compounded her misery by breaking the news to her that her mother was pregnant and, therefore, no longer wanted her. This was the last time that she was ever to see or hear of the mother from whom she had never before been separated. She believes that the $120 might possibly have enabled her parents to survive for a year. She thinks that she must have been sold under the name of Lim (meaning forest), which was her stepfather's surname. It is indicative of the shame of being sold into slavery that was to pursue her over the years that Janet did not divulge in *Sold For Silver* that it was her parents who actually sold her or that the deal was concluded in front of her. She did not even tell her own husband and children this until 1989.[4]

In her purchaser's house there were eight or nine children of both sexes, some of them only four or five years old. The pretty girls talked of being 'looked at by men' – the meaning of which Janet did not understand, nor, as a newcomer, did she manage to make friends with them. Feeling utterly deserted, depressed and miserable, she performed the duties of a servant. She was given the distasteful job of massaging the fat owner and his wife when they were in bed and of serving them tea until they fell asleep. Only then could she tiptoe slowly away, closing the door quietly, to go to bed herself. She was also taken by her mistress on her visits to customers. The woman seems to have been dealing in children, because the conversations were about their price. It did not dawn on Janet that they were slaves, she simply thought that the woman was running an orphanage. She never saw an actual transaction but the children were constantly changing.

Her one hope lay in escape and one fateful day, finding the gate open, she made a desperate bid for freedom. She ran out and began to follow the railway line to Shantou, hoping to disappear in the streets of the town. But she was recaptured by a passenger in a passing train who recognised her. He was a dealer working with her owner and he jumped off the train and took her back to the house. She then faced the first physical cruelty of her life as her owner attacked her, pulling her hair and digging her fingernails into her until she fainted. The woman suspected that the parents had told her to run away. She threatened to have them arrested and tried to force Janet to tell her where they had gone. Her captor intervened to prevent the woman from inflicting further injury, and Janet finally persuaded her that her parents were not a party to her escape. In fact she had no idea where they were.

After this abortive escape, Janet's life became a living hell. She was chained up and treated like a dog. As she says, 'like a dog I behaved'. She had to plead for food and water, to wash or go to the latrine. After a month, she persuaded her owner that she was a medium with supernatural powers and was released (Lim 1958 pp. 36–8). About two weeks later she was overjoyed to be told that she was going home. But her happiness was shortlived for she was embarked with the other children on a boat for Singapore.

Her owner, with the man who had recaptured Janet posing as her husband, together with another woman, took the children to Singapore. On the way they were carefully coached to say that the dealer was their 'auntie' and they were coming to Singapore to school. There were about eight or nine children, aged from four to 13. The older girls, destined for brothels, told her happily that they were going to a lovely place where they would have rooms to themselves. How much they understood of what was in store for them is unclear. Janet certainly did not comprehend it.

On arrival in Singapore, officials made a show of searching all the luggage, poking sticks into the big packages, but the most precious cargo – the children – passed without trouble. They were huddled together in one cabin and all they were asked was: 'Where are you going?' Told that their aunt was taking them to school, the officials made no further enquiries, and to Janet's knowledge there were no other formalities. Since the year was around 1930, this is of considerable interest. At that time it was still legal to have and even to acquire a *mui tsai*, but trafficking in children was illegal, and it is clear that little effort was being made by the authorities to check it.[5]

The children were taken to a large house surrounded by coconut trees, where another woman dealer took charge of selling them. Janet heard the bargaining over the sale of the other children. Predictably, the younger boy went first, then the older boy and then the pretty girls, whose fate as prostitutes was clear from the discussions. When prospective buyers sized up Janet they said she was too young and not pretty enough for a brothel. All her life she has thought of herself as plain. Her mother had complained about her looks and she was told that her nose was too flat and her mouth too big. In fact, the photograph at the beginning of her book shows that she was a charming looking girl. However, in Singapore, although her belief in her plainness must surely have affected her self-confidence, her looks saved her from the usually grim life of a Chinese prostitute (Warren; Koh; Hoe n.d.). In retrospect this may be seen as a blessing, but at the time her fate was pitiful.

Eventually a woman came who looked her up and down crudely, then rapped out brusque orders to stand up, walk, and turn around. Janet, carefully trained by her parents, was very polite, and the woman told the dealer that she thought she had a purchaser. She took Janet home, left her to sleep on the bare floor under her own bed, and the next day took her to the prospective buyers. They examined her carefully and the bargaining began. The seller demanded $300 (Singapore) but eventually settled for $250. Singapore currency was worth much more than the Chinese dollars her parents had received for her. This time Janet did not see a red paper drawn up. The profit was considerable as the cost of feeding and housing the children was small, since they ate leftovers and slept on the floor. The only expense lay in their original cost and their fares to Singapore. Janet does not know how the various dealers in Ampo and Singapore split the proceeds.

Life as a Mui Tsai

Janet now found herself as one of two *mui tsai* in a household which consisted of an old man, his second wife – a former servant who had become pregnant by the master and married him – their son, who was about her age, and a girl who was a distant relation. This time she was sold under the name of Lim Ah Mui – superstition demanded a change of name to bring good luck. The two little *mui tsai* ranked lowest on the social scale. Significantly, her companion asked Janet on the day she arrived how often she had been sold. When she replied 'twice', the other child said she had been sold three times, which was socially even worse.

The girls had no beds, ate only leftovers, usually just rice, and were at everyone's beck and call. They dared not even approach the free children who came to the house. Janet did the housework and looked after the poultry. In fact her only friends were the geese, to whom she poured out her sorrows. The other *mui tsai* was their mistress's favourite, so Janet found herself utterly deserted, bereft of love and intellectual stimulation and, until she learnt her owners' dialect, unable even to understand what was being said to her. The master was a rich man with a large circle of friends and many visitors. Janet, imprisoned inside the gates, vividly remembers her insatiable longing to see the world beyond them. No one who has not been a prisoner, she believes, can fully appreciate this longing. Nevertheless, life was not at first unbearable. She learnt to cook and sew, as well as to swear!

It was not until the master began to pursue her at nights to fondle her that her real torment began. Fortunately, he was impotent, but his attentions were painful and the child was terrified of him. She tried to escape him by sleeping in a different place in the 20-room house or the garden every night – under beds, in cupboards, up trees, out with the geese, in the bathrooms – anywhere to avoid him. One night he complained to his wife that he could not find her and the two of them finally discovered her cowering under a platform holding flower pots. Unable to reach her they jabbed her with sticks and poured cold water over her. In spite of the pain she refused to come out until long after they had given up.

Her life had become a living hell from which the only escape seemed to be suicide. She seriously considered this in the belief that it would end her troubles. Only fear of what lay beyond death prevented her from carrying it out. The ill-treatment and particularly the noisy night-time searches attracted the attention of the neighbours. But when one of them asked her what the disturbances were about, the child was too frightened to tell her. The woman clearly understood the situation for she looked at her pityingly and said that she would rather starve than part with her child. Janet was so afraid that her owners would find out that the woman had even spoken to her that she forgot to feed the pigeons and that day, to add to her distress, one of them died from lack of water.

Temporary relief came when a doctor who visited the family prescribed some bromide to help the old man sleep. Since Janet served him a whiskey in the evenings she was able to add bromide to his drink and he would sleep until about four a.m., giving her a few hours of rest. When the bromide ran out she pleaded successfully with the doctor to give her another bottle. Although the doctor obviously appreciated the child's misery he did not go to the authorities because he was a friend of the family. Thus, although both neighbours and outsiders knew the situation, no one took action to protect this helpless little girl from what was clearly iniquitous treatment.

Janet's relations with the son of the household are of some interest. She remembers him without rancour. He was in a sense a fellow victim of the Chinese patriarchal system since he was as frightened of his father as she was. Of course, his situation was in no way comparable to hers. He attended the English school in Singapore and would talk to her and show her his schoolbooks. He let her use his pencil and told her that some of the things she scribbled looked like letters. The very idea of being able to read and write was to Janet a wonder beyond her imagination, a skill that seemed to her forever unattainable.

However, Janet was surreptitiously introduced, along with her fellow *mui tsai*, to Christianity by a nurse who, on her visits to the house, went out of her way to talk to these ostracised children. She taught them and the master's son to pray and told them of Christ's sufferings. But alas, in spite of Janet's fervent prayers, her master continued to pursue her. Only when the family visited their estates on the Malay peninsula was she better treated, as he would have lost 'face' had his conduct become known. After one of these trips, during which Janet cut her hand badly after he shouted at her, her mistress seems to have been sorry enough for her to send Janet for a brief respite to stay with her aunt, named Ah Yee.

Janet was entrusted to this kindly old woman in the hope that she would persuade her to change her mind and sleep with the old man willingly, so that he would be satisfied and the household would be more peaceful. The change for Janet was memorable. She found herself in a kind family who treated her well. Ah Yee not only shared her bed with her but allowed her to sit down to meals with the family. They worked side by side doing household chores, cooking and looking after the poultry. The surroundings were pleasant and Janet once again felt like a human being. Ah Yee even suggested that she might marry one of her own two sons – a prospect which pleased the child.

She also explained to Janet why her master had been forcing his attentions on her. It appeared that he had come to Singapore from the south of China and had made plenty of money. He believed that by sleeping with a very young girl, he would remain young and healthy and have a longer life. This presumably refers to the belief that by sleeping with a virgin a man could cure impotence (Koh). To please him, his present wife had suggested that he 'import' girls. The implication was that Janet would not be freed as *mui tsai* were meant to be at the age of 18, but would become his concubine as well as his servant. She now knew for the first time the appalling prospect in store for her. Soon afterwards her mistress fetched her, exhorting her to be good, and making it clear that she felt that in buying Janet she had made the mistake of her life.

Registration and Escape

Events now moved rapidly to enable Janet to escape her projected fate. In 1932, in response to pressure from the Colonial Office, the government of Singapore forbade the import of new *mui tsai* from 1 January 1933 and ordered that all existing *mui tsai* be registered with the authorities. Moreover, rules were laid down about their conditions of work and it was stipulated that the children were to be paid wages. Heavy penalties were imposed for failure to comply. Janet, of course, was quite unaware of the new laws, but her owners decided to register the two girls. They dressed them up in new clothes and jewellery and painted their faces to make it look as though they were treated like daughters of the family. When they arrived at the registration office a young blue-eyed European woman, whom Janet thought beautiful enough to have come straight from heaven and silently named 'angel-face', held her hands, and told her in private in Chaozhou dialect that she would visit the house once a month and that if the child had any complaints, if she was unhappy or ill-treated, she should not be afraid to tell her. Needless to say, when they got home the children's finery was taken away and they were once again mere drudges.

However, their registration proved to be a watershed in the lives of the two little girls. Seeing their future as an endless sea of drudgery and beatings with nothing to look forward to, they realised for the first time that there was an outside world in which authorities might care about them. Young as they were, they began to plan their escape. The problem was how to make contact with the angelic blue-eyed woman. They decided that one of them would try to slip through the gate and go to a police station. Since Janet had to serve dinner her companion was the one to escape.

The plan worked to perfection. Janet distracted the watchman at the gate while her fellow *mui tsai* slipped out into the dusk. Then Janet served the dinner, full of guilt and anxiety. When the girl was missed a search was mounted throughout the house and garden, but the young fugitive successfully found a police station. A policeman took her home to his wife for the night and then to the registration office in the morning. There she met Mrs Winter of the Chinese Protectorate, who was in charge of *mui tsai* registration. The next morning the blue-eyed European woman arrived at the house and assured Janet that her companion was now in her charge and would not be returned. She then took the frightened child into the house to confront the owners. In front of them she asked her to tell her how she had been ill-treated. Finally, after much talking, she took Janet to the office where she was reunited with her friend.

Life in the Po Leung Kuk

Mrs Winter took the girls in her car to the Po Leung Kuk – an orphanage for girls (Koh; Sinn). After a medical examination, Janet was introduced to life in the institution, which she came to regard as even worse than that as a *mui tsai*. It was noisy and crowded, housing several hundred inmates, mostly Chinese, with a few Indians.[6] Many were prostitutes, who talked incessantly of the money they had earned on the streets. Others were *mui tsai*, *pipa tsai* (Koh) or just orphans. A number were there because they had run away from home, often to marry or to escape an arranged marriage. A few had committed crimes. The inmates ranged in age from infancy to their 20s. Some had babies, who were placed in the nursery. In Janet's section the girls were locked up at night without water and were reduced to drinking out of the toilet bowl, scrubbed for the purpose. They were counted each morning and it really seemed to Janet that she had merely exchanged one prison for another. She spent her time sewing, washing and ironing, gardening and doing other chores.

The Chinese Protectorate in Singapore arranged marriages for older girls in the institution. A prospective bridegroom would come to the home and the girls on the 'marriage list' would be paraded before him for him to take his choice. The girl would have to decide on the spot whether to accept him. Janet witnessed two such marriages. The girls apparently accepted in order to get out of the home. The husband then paid for his bride's trousseau, which the other inmates helped her to make, and when the day came for him to fetch her, they lined the steps to the gates and cheered them on their way (Lim 1958 p. 83).

When asked what she wanted to do, Janet said she wanted to go home to her mother in China. The authorities made an attempt to find out where she had come from but she only knew that she had been born in Hong Kong and no one could recognise the name of her village in China. It was decided that she should stay in the Po Leung Kuk in Singapore, but she was moved to a different building where the girls were younger. They were not locked in but were forbidden to go beyond the guarded gate. Once more Janet stared in longing at a gate hoping somehow to get to the other side of it. The fates were to favour her.

Her owner, who blamed the Christian visitor for the girls' defection and had even laid a curse on her (Lim 1958 p. 56), at first tried to woo the children back by sending them food, but eventually realised it was a lost cause. He then paid $700 in compensation to Janet and $500 to her fellow *mui tsai*. Janet speculates that the disparity may have been because she had suffered more beatings! He may have paid the money to avoid prosecution. She does not think that it was a large sum for him since he was a rich man who owned estates and factories. For her it was to make all the difference. It opened the way to an education and social mobility. Since she now had money, she was sent to classes in Chinese to test her intelligence. When she did well, the authorities decided that she should go to an English mission school.

Western Education: The Road to Freedom

The Church of England Zenana Missionary School

Janet Lim thus entered the Church of England Zenana Missionary School in 1934. The school was both a boarding and day school and had mostly Chinese girls; it took some orphans as boarders. Janet was one of two orphans chosen that year. She was baptised and given a strict Christian upbringing, so Lim Ah Mui became Janet Lim. She was also taught English in a special class until she was able to follow the ordinary curriculum.

With her entry to this school, Janet Lim's life as a *mui tsai* came to an end. She finally realised the education that her father had promised her as a little girl in faraway China and which had seemed completely unattainable in her years of suffering. She describes her bewilderment at finally being able to mix freely with people and her sense of disbelief that she was no longer a *mui tsai*. Her years at the school were happy ones, surrounded by teachers who cared about her and the many friends she made among the pupils. It became in a very real sense her home. The only sad times were the holidays when most children went back to their parents and Janet and the other orphans had nowhere to go.

The Choice of a Career Rather Than Marriage

Like the Po Leung Kuk, the school arranged marriages for the older orphans and vetted young men who went there to choose their brides. Prospective husbands had to be Christian and had to promise that they would only take one wife. Since most Chinese marriages were arranged by the families of the bridal couple, and many of Janet's contemporaries left at the age of 12 or 13 to get married, the school merely acted *in loco parentis*. The husbands provided money for the trousseaux and the brides were expected to become docile, self-effacing members of their new families, ruled by their mothers-in-law.

At the school they were taught domestic work but, true to Chinese tradition, were given no sex education and had little or no contact with boys, to the point that Janet thought that men were either superior beings or evil (Lim 1958 pp. 78–9).[7] Most of the girls who married appear to have accepted their fate quite willingly as part of the natural order of things. Janet, however, at the age of 14, was so upset when told she was being considered as a bride that she was promised that no arrangement would be made without her consent. The other candidate for the same bridegroom, also a former *mui tsai* but aged 16, was willing to marry and was allowed to go for walks with her prospective husband. She subsequently married and returned to show her friends her baby.

At the age of about 16 Janet was told to begin thinking about a career. The school emphasised domestic training and the children did most of the chores, even the cooking, during Janet's first years. Only in 1935, with the arrival of a new teacher, did the school begin to train girls for careers other than marriage and motherhood (Lim 1958 p. 74–5). Unfortunately Janet was not able to realise her academic potential because the school received a government grant-in-aid and this meant that all 'over-age' girls had to leave. Janet had been five years at the school and had reached standard seven. She was too young to work but deemed too old to remain at school to study for the senior Cambridge examination.

This was to limit the range of careers open to her. In fact she had little choice. The school arranged for her to become a trainee nurse at St Andrew's Mission Hospital. After she left the school she was given $200 – what remained of the compensation she had received from her former master. She shared some of it with the girls at the school and she bought herself a watch, a Parker pen and a pair of shoes. She put the remaining $60 in a stocking. She still had it with her when she was shipwrecked during World War II.

Adult Life

Janet has graphically described in *Sold For Silver* her life at the hospital, beginning in 1939, and her subsequent terrible experiences during the war. She narrowly escaped death when the ship on which she was being evacuated from Singapore was sunk. She reached Sumatra after an ordeal at sea, only to face horrendous treatment by the Japanese in their efforts to turn her into a 'comfort girl' for the troops. Once again she spent her nights hiding from her tormentors, just as she had as a little girl. She fled but was recaptured. Her stubborn refusal to prostitute herself led to her being accused of being an American spy and taken to a place of execution – only to be 'spared' at the last minute, to suffer 'slow death'. The brutal imprisonment which followed drove her to attempt suicide. After great suffering she was finally released and allowed to resume nursing.

With the end of the war in 1945 she returned to Singapore and finished training at Kandang Kerbau Maternity Hospital, taking her general education certificate. She embarked on a highly successful career and became the first Asian matron of the St Andrew's Mission Hospital in 1954. She subsequently married an Australian doctor. They have three children. They lived for many years in Hong Kong she has spent the last 21 years in Australia.

Janet tried to return to China to try to trace her family, but on the point of leaving for Guangzhou in 1948, she was warned that the city was falling to the Communists. Thus, tragically, she could not make the journey while her mother might still have been living. Now she believes there would be no chance of even tracing the village where she lived as a child.

In a material sense she has clearly prospered far beyond what her expectations might have been had she remained in China. However, the scars of her early life remain with her. She makes it clear that even today she feels very insecure (letter 11 July 1990). Looking back, she still loves her mother in her heart, in spite of her vivid memories of the trauma of her sale. She recognises that her mother suffered the terrible blows of losing her husband and son and then of being forced into poverty, to the point of selling her only child, all while still in her 20s. Janet believes, however, that her own fate has been worse, rejected as she was by the parent she loved, forced to suffer physical and mental abuse at a very young age and to bear the shame and social stigma of slave origins for the rest of her life.

The Enduring Social Stigma of Mui Tsai

Janet had been warned by the Chinese woman in charge of the Po Leung Kuk that she should not mention that she had been a *mui tsai* once she got to the Zenana Mission School because the other girls might laugh at her. This struck her as cruel, but she was soon to discover that slave origins carried a stigma, and, in fact, the six girls in the school with her who had been *mui tsai* never even discussed it amongst themselves. One girl, however, did tell her that she had been sold when, on a school outing, she saw the father who had sold her and her sister. This girl was fortunate, ending up in the home of a Chinese midwife who sent her to school and treated her as her own child. To the day of her death in 1986, however, she never contacted any member of her family or revealed her origins, except to Janet. Former *mui tsai* rarely tell even their own children about their past. Throughout her young life, when friends asked Janet where her parents were she would lie: 'They sent me to school in Singapore and then were killed during the war in China' (letter 11 July 1990).

The social stigma was to endure well beyond her school days. People would make sly remarks about her origins and many years later an English friend at a dinner party in Singapore heard a Chinese woman say: 'If you only knew her past you would have nothing to do with her' (interviews, letters 11 July and 29 September 1990). It was said with such scorn that he wondered what terrible crime she had committed. She explains today that it is considered more shameful by the Chinese to have been sold (compounded in her case since she was sold twice) than to have been abandoned, the reason being that her parents had made money out of her. They thus betrayed her to a greater degree than those who abandon children they cannot support. Janet, in the face of these rumours about her 'shameful' past and the speculation that she might be a criminal, tackled the problem head-on with characteristic courage by writing *Sold For Silver*, giving us a rare firsthand account of the workings of the *mui tsai* institution from the point of view of the victim. The reactions of the Chinese community to its publication are of interest. Some parents wrote suggesting she might be their lost daughter, but none were her parents. Many were sympathetic to her sufferings.

The Impact of Janet Lim's Escape on Her Owners

Particularly significant was the effect of her escape on her owner and his family. She never saw either him or his wife again. But the old man was so ashamed that he did not leave the house for three months and the family changed their name to avoid loss of face. He managed to keep out of court and the case was not published in the press presumably because he made a cash settlement. The son of the house visited her with their Christian friend when she was at school. After the war, in London, she met him again and heard that his parents had died during the war. He apologised for the way they had treated her. Out of consideration for him, she has to this day kept their name secret. Before *Sold For Silver* was published she telephoned him to assure him that she had not revealed the family's identity. He thanked her and said he would be the first to buy the book.

Reflections on Mui Tsai

Janet Lim does not believe she would ever have escaped from her bondage had she not been registered. As a *mui tsai* she had no opportunity to learn anything of the outside world, and any suggestion of leaving or marriage, even when she was older, would probably have been severely punished. Only for those in kindly homes was there a chance that their owners might arrange a suitable marriage, and hence their escape from a life of servitude. Janet thinks that she might have been resold, perhaps as a concubine. Marriage to the master's son would have been unheard of. She believes, therefore, that without British intervention she would never have escaped and might not even have survived, given the hard work and the constant undernourishment she suffered. She ate only rice and vegetables and the scant fish and other protein left over. Although a cow was regularly brought to the house to provide milk for the master's son, the girls were never given any.

Janet has kept in touch with some of the other *mui tsai* who grew up with her. As far as she knows, all keep their origins secret. Most did not get more than a standard five education and hence became domestic servants or children's nurses, usually working for European employers. The school is still their home when they have holidays. Most are married with children of their own, who probably do not know that their mothers were *mui tsai*.

After the war, when the government took greater care to enforce the laws (Koh), poor families continued to abandon their infant daughters in hospitals and clinics, and Janet has a number of unmarried nursing friends who adopted these infants and gave them a good education (letter 11 July 1990).

Today the practice of *mui tsai* is almost forgotten by most Chinese in Singapore. Janet Lim finds that her origins are no longer considered shameful and when she reveals them she is greeted with intense surprise and great interest.

Notes

1. Janet Lim (Mrs Errol Strang) published an account of her experiences in *Sold For Silver*, Collins 1958, reprinted Oxford University Press, Singapore 1985. The references here are to the reprint. This chapter is based on the book as well as interviews with Janet Lim conducted in Brisbane on 1 and 2 September 1989, and on letters from her. I am profoundly grateful for her help and co-operation, without which it could not have been written.

2. Janet Lim does not know the exact year she was born. When she wrote *Sold For Silver* she calculated that it must have been 1923. However, she remembers that her eighth birthday (by Chinese reckoning) was before she was sold and she spent about a year with the dealer and then some three and a half to four years as a *mui tsai* in Singapore (letter 30 July 1992). This would make her nearer to 12 in 1933.

3. This paper was the customary contract drawn up to confirm the selling or 'adoption' of a child as a *mui tsai*. For examples see Maria Jaschok, 1988, pp. 146–9.

4. Janet Lim revealed it to me in our interviews in Brisbane and then told her family, letter 11 July 1990.
5. For information on the laws in force in Singapore at the time see W.W. Woods 1937.
6. In 1933, 423 girls were admitted and 375 discharged.
7. Only in Janet Lim's last year was she allowed to join a mixed club (Lim 1958 pp. 83–4).

Part III: Social Remedies and Avenues of Escape
A. The Official Response

6. Implementing Government Policy for the Protection of Women and Girls in Singapore 1948–66: Recollections of a Social Worker

By Koh Choo Chin

The Social Welfare Department and the Protection of Women and Girls

After World War II ended in August 1945, 'Syonan-To' became Singapore again. The war had impoverished and demoralised the population and displaced many people. Hundreds from Malaya, Thailand and Indonesia had been stranded on the island when they failed to board ships evacuating people to Australia and elsewhere. Survivors of ships bombed in Indonesian waters returned to Singapore homeless and unemployed. People had lost homes and family through air raids, illness, the conscription of labour, and massacres by the Japanese army.

The Social Welfare Department came into being in June 1946. After nearly four years of Japanese occupation with its scarcity of food and medicine and the disruption of education and commerce, it had to take on work for which no other government department was specifically responsible, such as housing, repatriation, tracing of relatives, providing cheap restaurants for city workers and communal feeding centres for undernourished children, and teaching them the three R's while schools were being reopened. It also took over the functions the Chinese Protectorate had carried out before the war. The Protectorate had handled all matters Chinese, including family disputes, family maintenance payments, the custody and adoption of children and the suppression of trafficking in women and girls for prostitution or as *mui tsai*.

The disruption of education had caused children to go out to 'make' money by any means they could, and juvenile delinquents roamed the streets. The conscription of teenaged girls to serve the Japanese troops in 'Comfort Houses' had created juvenile prostitutes, who now solved their economic problems by continuing to prostitute themselves. Trafficking in female children for immoral

122

purposes increased. Before the National Registration of Citizens came into force in 1948, there were any number of people besides Chinese immigrants moving in and out and even settling down in Singapore. Girls were brought in from Thailand, Malaya and Indonesia by traffickers and sold as prostitutes or as *mui tsai*. Such cases were discovered only when ill-treatment was reported by neighbours, or when the victims ran away and sought assistance from members of the public or the police, or through police anti-vice raids. With the prevalence of crime, the police had little time to attend to anti-vice work, so the Women and Girls Protection Section of the Social Welfare Department began to build up a framework to tackle it.

By 1947 the department had shifted from emergency to permanent work and the Women and Girls Protection Section took over the protection of women, girls and children. The rescue and rehabilitation of juvenile prostitutes, cases of ill-treatment, the screening of female immigrants under 18, the investigation of guardianship cases and the management of homes all came under the Section. At this time there were several homes for girls (see below), as well as a home for destitutes and persons awaiting repatriation to India, Hong Kong and other countries with the aid of the United Nations Relief and Rehabilitation Administration. A Boys' Home and Boys' Hostel catered for problem boys and others requiring assistance.

To meet these additional demands the Social Welfare Department began to recruit and train new investigators with the highest appropriate local academic qualifications. In 1948 six were recruited. I was one of the three women attached to the Women and Girls Protection Section. The three men went to the Relief Section but were called upon to help whenever required by the Women and Girls Protection Section.

The Women and Girls Protection Section was under the Assistant Secretary, who had been the Lady Inspector at the Chinese Protectorate before the war and had wide experience of work with *mui tsai* and with immigrants. She spoke several Chinese dialects as well as Malay. Initially she was assisted by a supervisor who had also been with the Chinese Protectorate, and by a Lady Inspector, who conducted interviews with and paid home visits to *mui tsai*, and dealt with miscellaneous cases resulting from the separation of parents or adoption. In those days, English was not widely used and not many local Chinese were bilingual.

The majority of cases dealt with illiterate or semi-literate Chinese and it was necessary to have a Chinese-educated woman to write notices in Chinese calling clients for interviews, to read letters or documents and to write names in Chinese characters. An interpreter was seconded from the police courts to translate for the Lady Assistant Secretary and interpret statements and Statutory Declarations for clients. Since the three of us knew seven Chinese dialects between us, we helped in interpreting, which was something new to us. By accompanying the Lady Inspector on home visits we learned how to interview, and to master the bus routes and streets in sections of Singapore unknown to us. We also saw the seamy side of life in the crowded areas in town as well as the conditions under which the rural folk lived. We felt that, compared to these, the *mui tsai* were fortunate, until we realised how appalling their lives could be even in comfortable homes.

After working with the three senior officers in rotation for some time we were able to work independently, except for the screening of immigrants, which had to be carried out with the Assistant Secretary, who was the gazetted 'Protector' of Women and Girls empowered to detain girls for investigation or commit them to one of the homes. When the Children and Young Persons Ordinance was enforced in 1950, lists of babies given away were sent in by maternity clinics and other institutions as required by the new law. Until the Children and Young Persons Section was set up, each of us covered around 50 cases monthly, visiting both the natural and adoptive parents' homes. This did not include investigations we conducted on the days spent in the office writing reports. We also witnessed marriages during weekends. Female immigrants betrothed in childhood (*san po tsai*, see Hayes) used to be sent to Singapore for eventual marriage. Such girls were put under the supervision of the Women and Girls Section until they were married according to Chinese customary rites, so it was necessary for us to see that the marriage was genuine before closing the case.

These duties sent us to all corners of Singapore, as well as the islands. We went over creeks and swamps to squatter settlements, some of which could only be reached by motor launch or rowing boat. Once my shoes were nearly carried away by the tide when I left them on the bank to wade across to a house on stilts. Public transport was inadequate then in rural areas, the few buses being infrequent. Moreover, the clusters of unnumbered huts were a long way from the bus-stops. On one occasion, in order to get to my case, I had to leave my car as collateral for the loan of an old bicycle without brakes.

After the Children and Young Persons Section was adequately staffed, the Women and Girls Section took on anti-vice raids on hotels and brothels. By this time the section had more investigators to cope with the increased work and I became the Lady Inspector when the former one resigned. I conducted more office interviews and accompanied the Assistant Director, as the head of the section was then called, on anti-vice raids. These were usually carried out at night up to the early hours of the morning. To facilitate investigations, I was gazetted the 'Protector' with authority to send suspected pimps and others living on the immoral earnings of juveniles for fingerprinting and photographing in the Police Records Office, as well as to remove young prostitutes from brothels in the absence of the Assistant Director.

In 1960, the Women and Girls Section was divided into Women and Girls (Protection), for the suppression of brothels and the prevention of trafficking, and Women and Girls (Welfare), to deal with rehabilitation and requests for assistance from parents or girls. Since follow-up was now thought necessary, I was appointed the Lady After-Care Officer to begin the rehabilitation program from the time of a girl's admission into a home.

By then the Women and Girls Section was in charge of three institutions. The Girls' Home for juvenile prostitutes catered for about 40 inmates, training them in general domestic work and teaching basic courses in English and Chinese. The Girls' Homecraft Centre accommodated over a hundred, ranging from abandoned babies and miscellaneous other nursery cases, to juveniles, including schoolgirls, who were in moral danger, and others who had requested protection. This home was formerly the Po Leung Kuk (see Sinn), which in the 1930s took *mui tsai* who had been rescued from ill-treatment (see Miers) as well as runaways and others who sought protection voluntarily. After the war it began to accept orphans and immigrants detained on arrival after investigations had proved them to be victims of traffickers. It had become known for producing good, well-trained wives, and when contact with China was no longer possible, its girls were in great demand. The third institution was the Muslim Women's Home, which catered primarily for the reception and rehabilitation of Muslim women and girls in moral danger. It accommodated about 40 persons.

The Women's Charter came into force in September 1961, replacing the Women and Girls Protection Ordinance.[1] The age for the detention of girls was raised from 18 to 21. Those below 18 could only marry with the approval of the Minister of Culture, whose ministry was now responsible for the Social Welfare Department, and after investigation by the Women and Girls Section, mainly carried out by the After-Care Officer. The Girls' Hostel was opened in 1961 as a halfway house for girls discharged to daily jobs or taking training, and for those whose home environment was unsuitable. Some were schoolgirls. The Discharge Committee under the Women's Charter met monthly to discuss the After-Care Officer's reports and recommend discharges from all these homes.

The Screening of Immigrants

Chinese female immigrants arrived in Singapore by the shipload after World War II while China was going through political turmoil. Earlier, other than small groups of women from Guangdong seeking employment, there had been only a trickle, mostly betrothed females or wives with children joining husbands who had found employment or established businesses in *Nanyang*.[2] Men would return to China periodically to visit their families, and to marry, and some left their brides until they could send for them later. As political conditions in China worsened, parents who could not leave, usually for financial reasons, entrusted daughters from the age of eight upwards to relatives or fellow-villagers to take them to relatives or friends in *Nanyang*, to seek a better future through marriage or employment, usually in domestic service. Other girls were sold via lodging house agents to provide for the rest of the family. These agents did a roaring business arranging passages to destinations in Borneo, Malaya and Indonesia via Singapore, and trafficking in girls at the same time. These immigrants were screened by the Women and Girls' Protection Section.

Screening was tedious when large numbers arrived on one ship. The Immigration depot was a warehouse or godown on the wharf, built to contain cargo. The poorly ventilated metal structure was an oven when temperatures went above 30 degrees Celsius. With a steaming mass of humanity bubbling with excitement and anxiety after a voyage on a crowded deck with limited facilities, individual interviewing was not pleasant or easy. Immigrants came from different parts of China and communication was a problem though the two Social Welfare Officers each spoke four dialects.

Doubtful cases were asked to report at the Social Welfare Department for further questioning as unsatisfactory replies could be caused by nervousness. There was rarely any documentary proof of age or relationship so the lodging houses were made responsible for producing the girls' relatives and proof of relationship, such as letters, photographs or the red paper documents customary in cases of transfer or marriage. When there was strong evidence that a girl had been bought as a *mui tsai* or for prostitution, a bond, supplied by a reputable person or firm, would be executed and the girl would be placed under supervision to ensure that she would be well treated. She might then be used for domestic work, or be trained for a respectable occupation. Should the terms of the bond be violated – that is, if she was physically ill-treated, or was often away at an undisclosed address when visited, or was found in undesirable company – the bond would be estreated. The girl would then be committed to a 'place of safety' – namely the Girls' Homecraft Centre. Persons who failed to get guarantors would also have their wards committed to the centre and, if they were young enough, they were sent to school.

Such girls were medically examined before admission, not only to ascertain that they were healthy, but also to have a record of virginity. This was important because defloration of a virgin could bring in thousands of dollars to whoever bought the girl for immoral purposes. Supervision ended when the girl reached 18, or married, or when she had been trained in a respectable occupation like sewing, cooking or hairdressing.

Protecting Mui Tsai

Among the girls in greatest need of protection were the *mui tsai*. A *mui tsai* was easily distinguished from the members of the family owning her. She was usually dressed in cast-off clothes or in a garment of the coarsest material, with a round neck and button-up front, worn over loose trousers, and she was often barefooted. Her hair would either be plaited behind or be cut short like a skull cap. She would be left to sleep on a mat in any available space in a storeroom or corridor, unless there was an adult servant to share a room.

Her duties were varied and endless. Forced to be at everybody's beck and call without a murmur, she bore the brunt of any discord in the family. One duty she was certain to be given was to empty and clean the porcelain or enamel spittoons and the pots used to contain urine in the bedrooms at night. Some families allowed toddlers to defecate while playing and the *mui tsai* would have to go on all fours cleaning up after the infant. After a long day of activity, often slapped or pinched for being slow or daring to make excuses, the *mui tsai* would frequently have to relieve her mistress's aches and pains. Sometimes there would be grandparents who needed massaging too. The greater part of the evening would be spent kneading and rubbing lethargic bodies. Should she drop off in a sleepy moment or show resentment, she might get a kick, if convenient, or be subjected to pinching, twisting of eyelids, or even the smearing of a cut chilli on her eyelids or genitals.

To the older generation of Chinese women accustomed to the use of *mui tsai* (some were given them by their parents with their trousseaux), or familiar with the practice, the interest of the authorities was an encroachment on their privacy, so the Social Welfare Officer was an unwelcome visitor. The innocent *mui tsai*, often told that the officer would 'arrest' and 'punish' her in an institution, was usually unco-operative and even hostile. This hostility could sometimes be an intelligent girl's way of pleasing her mistress. The child's hostility could sometimes be diffused by subsequent visits, or sometimes by making her report at the Social Welfare Department, where she would be interviewed alone and physically examined.

This establishing of rapport with the girl had to be subtle so as not to encourage her to be wayward or arouse the suspicion and resentment of the mistress, who would certainly take it out on her. Hence on home visits, while ostensibly checking to see if her nails were kept clean, the girl's hands were felt to establish whether or not she was given rough work to do, and her scalp was examined, on the excuse of checking for lice, to see if there were bumps caused by knuckle knocks – a convenient and invisible form of punishment. Sometimes by turning the girl's shoulder on some excuse, a wince would indicate that a trip to the office was necessary for a thorough examination. Very often the girl was slapped or punched from behind so hard that serious injury could be caused. Another part of the body where weals and bruises could be found was the inside of the thighs.

As the *mui tsai* grew into her teens, treatment could change for the better or worse depending on her disposition. In a businessman's home a mournful face would be unpropitious, so she could expect harsh treatment and blame for unfavourable events or failure in business. The better-endowed girl would have a different role to play. Her mistress could use her to induce her husband to stay home instead of spending his time and money on women outside the household beyond her control. Such a *mui tsai* would be kept for life to serve the sexual needs of the entire family with, perhaps, better treatment but no authority over any children she produced, until the demise of her mistress. Even then her powers were limited.

Marriage would be out of the question as it would be a disgrace to the family to marry her after she had lost her virginity, unless a poor man could be found who would take a bride without paying the customary betrothal money and on condition that her defloration would only be known to him. This sexual abuse of female servants had been practised in Chinese households for a very long time, so, unless forced by circumstances, few mothers chose domestic service for young daughters and it was not easy to find local girls to live in. The wealthy could avoid the difficulties of employing young domestics by simply acquiring *mui tsai* who had no relatives to watch over them.

One example will suffice. Two girls, aged 16 and 17, were bought by a Chinese businessman through relatives in China. They were under supervision and in between home visits, they reported at the Social Welfare Department. They looked cheerful and well-fed, and though they came from different villages, they were friends, having travelled together from China. One day, after nearly a year of supervision, they both turned up at the Social Welfare Department looking nervous. They had run away because an attempt had been made to get the elder girl to sleep with their master. She had been given wine after dinner and ordered to spend the night in his room. They asked the Department for shelter. Both were put into the Girls' Homecraft Centre until they took up domestic employment found by the Department. They continued to keep in touch until the older girl was married to a driving instructor and the younger one continued in domestic service with proper wages, part of which she was encouraged to put into a savings account in a bank.

Sometimes a *mui tsai* was turned out on the streets. There was a sad case of one *mui tsai* who knew nothing about herself except that she had been with the same family 'for a very long time'. She was stunted, bow-legged and had a perpetual frown. Communication with her was not easy as her vocabulary was limited to instructions to carry out duties, as she had hardly ever spoken to anyone. Her owners had found that she was mysteriously pregnant and had chased her out of the house. All she had was an old handkerchief when she was directed to the Social Welfare Department. The scanty information she gave about her predicament was inconclusive but she was taken into the Girls' Homecraft Centre. She was not interested in her baby and agreed to have it adopted.

By that time she was estimated by medical examination to be about 20, so she was consulted when a carpenter applied for a wife. Girls outside, he thought, were getting too modern and demanding, and now that he was over 30 he had saved enough money to marry, and was delighted to have a bride from a place known to have 'good' girls. He did not mind her looks so long she was normal. He was a happy man for only a short while. Marital discord surfaced when he discovered that his wife was not the virgin he had expected. He felt cheated after all his years of hard work and his initial happiness. The disappointment caused his health to suffer and he became violent, off and on. They returned a few times and became a case for the Family Dispute Section. The wife worked hard to bring up their three children and the blow was somewhat softened by two of the children being male.

Marriage for some *mui tsai* was a release if they found husbands who were independent and liberal-minded. Otherwise, it might mean servitude under domineering mothers-in-law, with the cruelty of the rest of the clan to contend with. The fortunate few whose mistresses took an interest in their welfare were matched with care and married off as adopted daughters with trousseaux and some jewellery. Thus they were given 'face' and their in-laws were less likely to ill-treat them.

Girls Betrothed (San Po Tsai), Given Away or Abandoned

The rural girls were usually sold by debt-ridden, gambling, opium-smoking fathers or by those who needed money to fulfil filial duties like paying medical or funeral expenses for elderly parents. These girls were usually adopted as 'little daughters-in-law'. Some were betrothed in infancy to young sons. Some were taken in by families without a son, who hoped to have one later. Hence such girls among the Fukien were named *Lai Di*, which means 'come younger brother'. Whether she lived up to her name or not, she would be trained to work like a *mui tsai* until she was about 16 and old enough for marriage. Before the customary marriage ceremony, the girl was treated no differently from a *mui tsai*. She would be trained to be submissive and to accept whatever was doled out to her by the entire family, and the son – her future husband – could reject her when he came of marriageable age. She could then be sold to another family or married later, or kept for service for the rest of her life. One dialect group could even sell a daughter-in-law who had had children if she was considered disobedient or had not produced a male child. She might thus lose contact with her children.

Being a daughter-in-law was not a better deal than being a *mui tsai* unless a woman bore sons and faithfully served the entire family in return for one or two new outfits during the Lunar New Year and, perhaps, an outing with her husband and children occasionally. Whatever she collected from her own labour, such as eggs from a few fowls or vegetables she planted in her free time, belonged to the family. If her husband was a philanderer, she would be blamed and humiliated in the presence of neighbours.

Some girls were given away, particularly those born in the Year of the Tiger, a much dreaded animal in the Chinese zodiac. If a daughter arrived in the night, when tigers prowl for prey, it was feared that she would devour her parents or siblings (depending on their horoscopes) and marrying her off would be a problem. If there was a sickly parent or sibling in the family, a new-born girl's horoscope would be checked, and if it clashed with that of either one, she would be given away. If she was the only female, however, she would be given in name only, and would become the godchild of someone with a flourishing family. Many such girls were readily adopted by Malays and Indians, but the fate of those who went to Chinese couples was precarious unless they were childless or unsuperstitious Christians.

Country folk work hard on their farms tending poultry, livestock, vegetables and fruits or tapping rubber, so a girl, however acquired, was an extra hand whatever her status. I particularly remember one such girl I first saw carrying banana trunks on the carrier of her bicycle. She was under five feet and could not reach the seat but pedalled standing. Her trousers were rolled up above her knees and her blouse was stained with grey-brown patches, probably from banana and sweet potato sap. Her shoulder-length hair was tangled with damp wisps hanging over her face.

In those days, timber houses were not numbered and several houses used the same number, as extensions were built close to the main house. I usually found cases by mentioning the occupation of the person I was looking for, or the purpose of my visit, for instance, to check up on an adopted baby. Names were not helpful because neighbours knew each other by nickname or in the case of a married woman by part of her husband's name, but they knew the goings and comings of the neighbourhood.

I stopped this girl to make such an enquiry, and also asked her about herself. Her palms were raw with sores and so were her bare feet, and there were insect bites all over her arms. She was 19 by Chinese reckoning and had been given away because she was born in the Year of the Tiger and her horoscope had clashed with her father's. She accepted her lot as dictated by fate. At her age, and with her attitude, there was little that could be done to help her, so I suggested she should visit the government outpatients' clinic in the district to treat her sores, as the friction from the rough coir rope of the bucket used to draw water at the well, and the sap from the banana trunks and sweet potato vine, could cause an infection. She thanked me but said she would never find the time to make such a trip. This girl occupied my mind for a while as her fatalistic attitude disturbed me. Being over 18 she could only be helped if she asked for shelter in the Social Welfare home. All I could do was to enquire about her sore hands and feet and offer some ointment on subsequent contacts.

Abandoned girls might be treated like *mui tsai*. Thus bar waitresses who had given up their jobs to be kept by men would abandon their children to return to their former occupation or take up prostitution if their relationship turned sour. Boys, being in demand, could be sold, but a girl was a millstone around her mother's neck. At best she would only fetch a low price, and at worst she might simply be given to whoever was interested, or taken home by her putative father. In these cases, woe betide the little girl if she became the object of her stepmother's resentment.

A letter from a neighbour written in Chinese to the Social Welfare Department reported one such case. The stepmother used to make the child of eight or nine boil water on a firewood stove. While waiting for it to boil, the child had to crouch in the kitchen to watch the fire, pick up the burnt-out firewood with iron tongs and put it back into the stove. She had been badly beaten for spilling the boiled water. Her brother was attending school but this girl, though of school age, had to stay home to help with the housework and look after a toddler. I went to investigate and found a terrified girl, crouching in a corner of the kitchen screaming as I got closer that she would not do it again and begging me to leave her alone, while at the same time inching away with her back against the wall. It was obvious that her stepmother had threatened her with 'arrest' and 'punishment' by the Social Welfare Department. In fact this woman, who had gone to hang up her laundry, told me on her return that I could take the child away. The little girl began to howl on hearing this.

I told her softly that I could not take her away as the department only sheltered destitute people and she had parents and a home. I was there after hearing about her accident with the kettle of boiling water, to find out if she had been badly scalded. She calmed down and the woman then explained that her husband had dumped this unwelcome child on her when she could hardly cope with her son while expecting her second baby, and the girl's constant whining for her own mother irritated her. It seemed that the mother had been kept by her husband for a while but had abandoned both the child and father to resume her former job as a bar waitress. It was not clear whether the child was actually his. The stepmother seemed relieved to have unburdened herself of her unhappiness and even thanked me when I told her I would visit periodically to help build their relationship, as I felt that the girl might be a help later. I advised the girl to be obedient and more careful in her duties, to half-fill the kettle, for instance. I asked her to smile a little so that she would not have an old lady's face. She giggled.

The case was registered for visits. Although the child had not been bought as a *mui tsai*, she was definitely being used as one. After two years of monthly visits, supervision was reduced to her reporting with her father every two months until she was able to do so on her own. One day when she was about 15, she hesitantly asked during the usual chat at my desk, whether she could be considered a destitute girl. Neighbours had speculated that she might soon be married off to a trishaw pedaller. She was accepted by the Girls' Homecraft Centre, where her father visited her only once. She completed her training very well and at 17 was discharged to domestic work. She married a fruit stallholder who had worked his way up from doing odd jobs in the market. She was cheerful and held her head erect as she walked in to inform me of her marriage. She had come a long way from the cowed little girl I had first met.

Improvement in the Position of Girls from 1950

By 1950, immigrants had stopped coming from China, though some did come from Hong Kong. With the Children and Young Persons Ordinance in force, *mui tsai* ceased to be so called. Those under 14 not living with their natural parents were now known as Transferred Children. Transfers were registered by the maternity clinics if decisions were made early, or as soon as red paper documents were signed and the children taken over. They were under the supervision of the Social Welfare Department until they were 14 or were legally adopted. Though no longer *mui tsai* in name, some continued to be used for unpaid labour. However, severe physical ill-treatment was less evident.

With family planning being encouraged and the government helping with ligation and even abortion, there were fewer babies for adoption. People were more enlightened, sending girls to school and allowing them to take up jobs in factories. Girls were no longer a liability but an asset, benefiting the family economically. This newly found freedom however, brought new problems which neither parents nor daughters could handle, resulting in a wave of 'uncontrollable' adopted and natural daughters in our case load.

Pipa Tsai, Prostitution and 'Paternal Aunts'

Like *mui tsai*, which means little younger sister in Cantonese, *pipa tsai* is a diminutive term meaning little *pipa* player. These were young girls trained to play and sing to the accompaniment of the *pipa*, a Chinese guitar, at parties in clubs and brothels where businessmen entertained. These girls were also taught poetry and jokes and witticisms fitting for such functions. As they grew older the entertainment included prostitution and soon the *pipa* was not used but the girls continued to be paid hourly for their company at the table and elsewhere, at a play for instance. *Pipa tsai* then became synonymous with call-girl or prostitute.

Since elderly Chinese men believed that sex with a virgin would rejuvenate them more effectively than traditional medicine like ginseng or the organs of animals like the tiger or deer, they were prepared to pay highly for one. This led to a lucrative business for pimps – the so-called 'third or sixth paternal aunts' who worked in or even owned establishments themselves. These 'aunts' would find girls by going to places such as temples where desperate women went to pray for such things as jobs for their husbands or sons or for the recovery of sick relatives, and where men would ask the gods for winning lottery numbers or other types of assistance. The prosperous-looking 'aunts', usually dressed in neat outfits with gold, jade and pearl ornaments stuck in oily buns at the back of their heads, would show interest and express sympathy. Thus a contact would be made and the family circumstances investigated, special interest being taken in the daughters. In the evenings, while serving businessmen, they would sound out the demand, or they might do this over a game of mahjong, having arranged to sit in for one of the players.

These 'paternal aunts' originated among the spinster domestic servants from Guangdong, some of whom went to work in clubs or brothels. The more enterprising ran brothels, taking commissions from prostitutes and charging for services rendered. When it was time to consider retiring, some would use their nest eggs to invest in an adopted daughter, or even more than one, so that they could 'collect eggs' in old age. Juvenile prostitutes were called 'chicks'. Thus, another category of virtual slaves emerged. Soon women of other dialects, usually Fukien opium addicts and gamblers, were also living on the immoral earnings of girls.

Unlike *mui tsai*, the adopted daughters of these 'aunts' were sometimes pampered before the slaughter in their teens. Such a girl would be sent to a private Chinese school for a few years to become literate as training for the profession. She would be encouraged to enjoy a life of comfort with a servant to attend to her every need, trailing along whenever she was given permission for an outing and handling the money for shopping. This indulgence was, of course, to prevent her from being influenced unfavourably, and most important, to ensure that her virginity was kept intact. Girls adopted when they were older were examined by midwives before payment to ensure the collection of the defloration fee.

Depending on a girl's age and appearance, it would cost a man anything from S$2,000 to S$3,000 – a hefty sum 35 years ago (1950 to 1960) – to deflower a virgin. He would then be charged around S$1,000 monthly plus extras for services, to keep the girl for as long as he wished. At the same time, while he was at work, the 'aunt' could get clients for the girl using other rooms, which might also be owned by her, and collecting from S$30 to $50 per client. After the initial stage, there would be a sliding scale of charges for subsequent clients, both for keeping the girl and for her short-term services.

One such girl was found in a brothel in a residential district with a client during a raid resulting from a tip-off. On investigation, she was found to be in the charge of a certain 'third paternal aunt' who evaded an interview by the Social Welfare Department but sent the girl's aunt to claim her. This old, crippled ex-rubber packer said she had been left with her niece when her seaman brother died. After an accident, she could not work and her teenage niece took over her job, but as a minor she brought in less than S$2.00 a day, which was hardly sufficient for food. They owed rent and had borrowed money from friends for medical expenses. Through sympathetic friends her niece had been found a job with a kind prosperous *San Gu* – 'third paternal aunt' – to attend to her and accompany her on outings. The benevolent *San Gu* advanced S$2,000 to pay the debts and rent, and the aunt was to be paid S$60 monthly for the girl's services, and all her personal needs were to be supplied, plus any additional assistance the aunt might need. The aunt went to the temple to give thanks with a bundle of expensive joss sticks. She was relieved to see that her niece looked well-fed and happy whenever she returned. But these visits became less frequent and her monthly allowance began to come through the *San Gu*'s servant. Finally her niece stopped coming.

With deep emotion the old aunt related how she had been tempted in her desperation to take advantage of the kind offer which turned her niece into a prostitute. The girl was detained. She was thus saved from further exploitation, and her aunt from harassment for not leaving her for the agreed period. The *San Gu* could have been taken to court for living on the immoral earnings of this girl, but such girls were usually poor witnesses as their sense of obligation and fear of the underworld connections of the pimps were a deterrent. After a year in the Girls' Home, the girl was apprenticed in a hairdressing salon, which employed her when she qualified. Supervision had to end since she was then over 19; besides, it was known that the Social Welfare Department had a home for juvenile prostitutes at the time, and the stigma of any connection with it could jeopardise her future.

Among women such as *San Gu* some had sworn sisterhood. These left their hair in single plaits done loosely from the nape of the neck and dressed themselves in white, neatly ironed tops worn over black cotton trousers, or silk ones on special occasions. They used 'elder sister' after their names, like Yu Jie – Elder Sister Jade – and hence they were known as *amah jie*. Another group who had confirmed their spinsterhood did their hair up in shell-shaped buns decorated with pearl- and jade-studded ornaments. The ceremony was described as *shu qi* (Cantonese *saw hei*), meaning combed up (hair). Other status symbols were gold wrist watches or expensive jade earrings, and the sponsorship of the philanthropic programmes of the temples where they worshipped at all religious festivals. Such temples were their resting place in their twilight years, when the rich ones could devote all their time to prayers in comfort as the services were provided according to their donations. Poor ones had to do all the chores and earn money from performing religious rites outside.

One of these *shu qi* paternal aunts had arrived, so to speak, but was not ready for full retirement as she still had two or three girls at the height of their profession. Being in semi-retirement, she had left her wards in the care of an old servant in one of her establishments in town, visiting periodically just to check on the business. One of the girls left the premises one day after spending the night with an elderly client whom she had asked to help her leave the profession. He agreed to give every assistance as he knew someone in the Social Welfare Department. This friend referred them to the Women and Girls' Section. Since the girl had made the request for shelter, and her 'paternal aunt' did not come forward, there was no investigation other than getting her statement, with as much history as she could supply. She was put in the Girls' Home for juvenile prostitutes for training to fit into society.

However, she was unable to fit in at the Home because, from her statement, she had been adopted at the age of seven, sent to a Chinese school for a few years and had been ordering a servant around for all of 10 years. She had been earning good money, being young, attractive and intelligent, and she had been pampered and spoilt, so life in the Girls' Home did not appeal to her, especially as she was with other former prostitutes and wished to sever ties with such people and start a new life. She asked to be put in a home where she could learn to live a respectable life. It seemed a reasonable request, so when the elderly man who had brought her in came to enquire after her, he was told of her request and he readily offered to employ her to help his family run a school tuckshop which his wife was handling alone.

The family accepted her and she was happy when I visited her the first few times, but one day she seemed different. When we were alone, she said, with a touch of coyness: 'It's no good here!' She explained that the old man had harassed her to leave his wife's room to share his bed. Why would she abandon a better deal with her paternal aunt if she wished to continue living in the same way, she asked? It was not easy, with her background, to fit her into a job. Fortunately, there was a small family of four which required a young girl to help them. She fitted in well as she was pleasant and affectionate, and was allowed to go out on her own and even went to church with neighbours. The family were not told of her past and she appreciated this.

One day she informed me that she had been visiting her 'paternal aunt' who seemed resigned to her choice and had even said that she could return to live with her and she would not insist on her resuming the profession. Her aunt appreciated the fact that she had not reported her vice business. The girl asked if I had any objection to her returning. By then she was past 18 and, judging from her conduct so far, I thought she would be able to manage, so she returned to her aunt. She visited me at the office sometimes, informing me of her activities. The company she kept was at a higher social level through her contact with the church youth groups, and she seemed pleased with herself for having achieved what she had set out to do.

After a period of silence, she appeared one day to get my help in finding a servant to look after her first child, a boy! She had married a businessman and was living in the family house in an elite residential area. She expressed relief that she had been able to conceive as she had been worried that her past life might have left her barren. Her happiness was complete, and so was mine, since her confidence in me and her co-operation had brought my case to a successful end. We met about 10 years later in a furniture shop and she looked every bit a lady; she had three children and informed me that since her mother-in-law had died the family had separated into different units and she and her family had moved into a small house of their own. Though she gave me her new address and telephone number, I chose to fade out with her past.

Those girls who did not have enough courage to escape the clutches of their 'aunts' sometimes remained until they were motivated by harsh treatment, when they had outlived their popularity, before finding a way out. Some found their freedom by marrying regular clients or were kept by clients until they found other employment. This could never be in their former profession, or both parties would be harassed by underworld protectors.

There was a case of the prospective daughter-in-law of a farmer. She was attracted by the comfortable life young women led in the apartments from which she collected slop for her family's pigs. There were a few brothels on her circuit and she would look longingly at the well-fed and beautifully dressed girls of about her age, wondering why fate was unkind to her. She took matters into her own hands, and since she knew the servants in the apartments well, she found her way into a job in a different district so that her future husband would not be able to locate her. However, the humble-looking servant who had helped her was an 'aunt' running a brothel, and the naive country girl was deflowered and did not dare go home. She had to continue prostituting herself just for food and lodging, and was given jewellery and clothing on loan. She found a sympathetic client one night and told him her story. He was touched as he was a family man and he bought her freedom for about S$2,000. Ostensibly, he was to keep her as a mistress, but actually he arranged with the girl that she would take a domestic job and repay him in instalments.

Without any experience in domestic work other than her farmhouse routine, she was miserable when she worked out how long it would take to settle her debt with her low wages. So she drifted back into prostitution. Before she could begin paying him, her saviour was stabbed to death one night. News reached her former pimp that she was back 'on the line' and it was assumed that her benefactor had begun to live off her. The girl was so upset that she took her life by drinking caustic soda.

Some girls just hoped to escape their 'aunts' by being taken in by the authorities in raids, getting their freedom via detention in the Girls' Home for a period of training. The outcome depended on their strength of character and the environment to which they were discharged. At least this escape route freed them from the danger of retaliation. The Sunday school in the Home touched a few of those who attended and they joined evangelistic groups and became full-time workers. Others were trained as beauticians and either took up jobs or, if they married men who could finance them, opened their own salons. Many returned to dancing but married as soon as they found suitable men and became housewives.

Some married well. One young woman from a country town in Malaya, who had come to look for domestic work in Singapore, was introduced to prostitution and fleeced by her chief tenant, a former dance hostess. She was saved by a raid on the premises and detained for a period. After a few months in a domestic job, she took up dancing just to meet a suitable man. One day she drove up to my office in a sports model Volvo looking sophisticated and dressed in the latest fashion. She requested that I stop visiting her as she had found a man who would take her as his secondary wife. He had bought her a house and the car. As he was a Thai subject he was not bound by the Singapore law of monogamy.

Changing Times: Dance Halls, 'Aunts' and 'Mummies'

When dancing became popular in the 1950s, cabarets sprang up in the amusement parks and some hotels. They catered to British soldiers, European and American seamen and English-educated local men. Dancing was an occupation taken up by young women with little or no qualification for other jobs. It was, like other forms of employment, a means of livelihood. Dance hostesses confined themselves to the regular hours.

Soon older *pipa tsai* joined in. Some graduated to become 'mummies' who took up supervisory positions booking dances, but who also went out themselves with clients who preferred to skip the dancing. A coupon system was used and the hostesses changed them for cash. Clients usually took the hostesses out an hour before closing time so that whatever they gave them afterwards was their own, excluding charges for nights spent on the premises. Some 'mummies', besides carrying on prostitution themselves, also ran apartments to accommodate dance hostesses who preferred to stay away from home.

Soon the 'paternal aunts' also sent their wards to attend English schools and dancing classes. Ballroom dancing became a popular form of entertainment and classes sprang up in various parts of the island, but many were exclusively for training entertainers.

The former 'paternal aunts' and the 'mummies' learned business methods from each other. From the 'mummies', the 'aunts' learned to use the cabarets as points of contact, as businessmen began adjourning to dance halls after dinner and thence to the girls' apartments. Brothels began infiltrating residential apartments in town and later bungalows, all under the name of 'hostels'. The 'mummies' in turn used the 'aunts'' methods of squeezing both their lodgers and clients for services offered, as well as for favours in the cabaret like getting better clients. With the protection of underworld brothers, 'aunts' and 'mummies' could keep dance hostesses, especially the more popular ones, as lodgers as long as they wanted.

Sometimes 'mummies', in order to provide for themselves in their old age, adopted little girls, usually training them as hostesses. Some were sent to English schools and ambitious girls even went as far as secondary school, or trained as office workers, in order to get access to a higher stratum of society. Not all these girls turned out as their guardians expected, as some examples will show.

A simple domestic servant working in a brothel adopted a female toddler with no particular idea of what she would do with it besides serving her as a companion to while away her free time during the day as she was only attending to one prostitute. The little girl was brought up in the brothel and became a pet on the premises, and complimentary remarks from visitors gave the adoptive mother some ideas. When the girl was found during a raid by the Social Welfare Department she was put on cash bond after investigations, and was closely supervised. She was later sent to a mission school. Her adoptive mother tried to take her out of school once or twice but she was finally left to continue until secondary school.

Through her frequent reports at the office we formed a friendly relationship and often discussed her future plans. She decided to take up typewriting as she felt that she would not be able to cope with more study, and besides her adoptive mother, whom she addressed as paternal aunt, could not afford more money for her education. The bond was cancelled and she was helped into a job as a typist in the civil service. She married a colleague. It was heart-warming to witness the couple walking up the aisle of the church with the adoptive mother of the bride beaming proudly amongst her friends, most of whom worked in brothels. To them, a 'veiled' bride was something to talk about for it was a symbol of chastity, much admired even among their class. The couple have both retired now, living happily in their own apartment with grown-up children, the eldest of whom is a trained teacher in a girls' school.

Another girl of similar upbringing was more ambitious. She was sent to a Chinese school up to secondary level but was fortunate in that by this time extra-curricular activities had been introduced in schools and she mixed freely with the boys. Her English was good and so she was bilingual, and being sociable she had many friends. She lived in one of the apartments occupied by dance hostesses/call-girls managed by her adoptive mother, and when she was found during a raid she was taken away. By then there was a Girls' Hostel run by the Social Welfare Department, so she was placed in it and continued attending school. She returned to her adoptive mother later and managed to go to Nanyang University. The last I heard of her was that she had gone abroad.

There are others who have done well and are now in various countries around the world. Some severed relationships with their adoptive mothers, but one, I have been told, had settled her adoptive mother comfortably in a house she had bought before she went away to get an extra degree. She married a European and remained abroad, remitting a regular allowance to her adoptive mother.

'Boyfriends' (Male Pimps)

As time passed, the female pimps found rivals in their trade. Young educated men began gradually enticing girls from school and home to work in bars, giving them a taste of independence and luxury and then leading them into prostitution. Some were found office jobs as cover. These men were more ruthless than the 'paternal aunts', who at least treated the girls better as long as they brought in the money. If the girls did not get enough clients calling for them, the 'aunts' would punish them by scolding them or making them miss a good meal, or having them kneel on the spiky skin of a durian. The so-called boyfriends would threaten and even assault the girls if they refused to entertain the clients brought to them. The anti-vice raids were a boon to some of these girls, but others found the training for other work too irksome and soon returned to what they considered the lesser of the two evils.

The boyfriends used to stalk around the Girls' Home outside the fence, trying to get the girls to escape, passing messages or throwing notes into the compound. A few girls escaped more than once but were recovered each time, until they were too old to take in. When the girls were discharged to work or for training, the boyfriends would harass them and threaten their parents to try to get them back.

Vice is so lucrative that even religious institutions were exploited. In one case two girls from a Malayan rubber estate left in the care of a temple worker were brought to Singapore by the nun who owned the temple, where they discovered to their horror that she had arranged for them to be deflowered. They escaped and were handed over to the Social Welfare Department. The nun was prosecuted but, with money to engage a good lawyer, she was acquitted of the charge. In another case a girl was deflowered by a monk while collecting illegal lottery bets.

Opium Dens and Prostitution

In the crowded districts of Singapore near the wharfs, labourers and sailors shared accommodation with families in the shophouses. They took up rooms or the entire floor and all slept on platforms built along both walls, leaving a central passage leading to the bathroom and lavatory behind. Those who had rooms usually had opium smoking paraphernalia on the floor or on makeshift beds made of planks placed on wooden benches. Families occupied cubicles partitioned with plywood, cardboard or even jute sacks sewn together. To save electricity, some people used oil lamps or just wicks in cups of oil. Sometimes people just crawled into these hovels to sleep. Children wandered all over and together with adults ate their meals on the pavement by the road or on the stairs. If the women sold vegetables, they took their younger children along, so they practically lived on the streets. Sometimes, out of curiosity, children would stand around to watch the opium smokers and listen to their yarns. Many girls of around 10 years old were introduced to vice in this way.

The smokers would invite them in, petting them a little, and in time, with a dollar or so, they could do anything with these innocent children. Some were even offered the pipe for a puff just to satisfy their curiosity. After the initial unpleasant effects and drowsiness, the girls would begin to enjoy the puffs, and would also like earning money which their parents could not give them. Some were 'employed' to prepare the opium, sticking the little melted lumps into the bowls of the pipes and, after drawing out the first puff, passing the pipe to the smoker. Many girls were deflowered in their drowsy state and also became addicted. If they married or just lived with an addict, they would, in time, run such dens for a livelihood. Such women would prostitute themselves until they were too old to do so and became pimps. The girls in such districts were exposed to moral danger all the time while their parents tried to eke out a living. There was no one to protect them. Some of their mothers worked the night shift cleaning ships in the harbour. Others carried earth on construction sites, working right up to the moment that their labour pains began, while the children's fathers were also working, or smoking opium, or gambling.

The Women's Charter

By 1961, the Women and Girls' Protection Ordinance was incorporated into the Women's Charter. The charter greatly improved the status of women by introducing monogamous marriage. However, by dealing a blow to traditional customs, it also caused some unexpected complications and hardship during the initial stages. For instance, some secondary wives or concubines, living under the same roof with principal wives, had taken the traditional acceptance of the family's duty to support them, implicit in the tea ceremony, for granted. They were caught unawares when their husbands died intestate and they found that the principal wife or 'grass roots' wife could legally drive them and their children out of the house, unless they had produced sons for the family. These secondary wives (concubines) were usually from poor families whose only means of giving their daughters a better life was to marry them off as secondary wives. Some of them went through rough times when they were thus left destitute.

On the other hand, shrewd concubines who went in search of such opportunities were better prepared. They scooped up all they could get, bargaining to live in houses rented or even bought for them. As time passed and the law on monogamous marriages began to sink in, marriages by customary rites performed at home or in clan associations were registered at the Registry of Marriages. There were a few cases in which the 'grass roots' wives were outwitted by mistresses who had their union registered, leaving the principal wife destitute when the husband died. In such a case, she would have to depend on her children to take up the legal battle for her property.

Time has brought many changes since then and the normal procedure now is reversed. Many marriages are first registered at the Registry and then a more convenient or auspicious date is picked for celebration with the traditional ceremony before the couple live together.

Reflections on my Work with the Social Welfare Department

This has been a nostalgic journey, going back more than four decades to the beginning of an interesting and enlightening career with women and girls in Singapore. Not only did it bring me into contact with a cross-section of Singapore society, it also gave me an insight into the problems of others and tapped my resourcefulness. The stories I had heard from my parents, relatives and neighbours of different dialect groups all came alive during these years.

Working against the traditions of a different culture and against ignorance was challenging and demanding. Success is difficult to assess as each individual case required a different approach, leading to objectives just as varied. Results sometimes took years to emerge, either via the grapevine or when cases reappeared with fresh problems. It is understandable that few girls returned to report success or to express gratitude; these were the kind of episodes in life everyone would prefer to forget. I found my work during those years rewarding enough, as, after all, I was merely a faint light appearing during a dim period of life, and a stepping stone, perhaps helping the unfortunate towards goals which, hopefully, they have finally realised.

Notes

1. The Women's Charter 1961 introduced monogamous marriage and gave women rights to property and divorce. However, it did not apply to Muslim women, who were given more limited rights.
2. *Nanyang*, the Chinese term for the South Seas, included Singapore, Malaysia and Indonesia.

B. The Chinese Patriarchal Response

7. Chinese Patriarchy and the Protection of Women in 19th-century Hong Kong[1]

By Elizabeth Sinn

The Po Leung Kuk, the Society for the Protection of Women and Children, founded in 1878, is one of the oldest and most highly regarded welfare organisations in Hong Kong. Today, it operates an extensive range of services including schools, nurseries, training and hostel services for the mentally retarded, day care centres for the aged, holiday camps and paediatric clinics. Many people have forgotten its earlier role and functions, and in particular the original motives for its foundation. It is fascinating to reconstruct the early history of the Po Leung Kuk, which, beyond telling us how women were protected, also reveals how the Chinese social elite attempted to uphold patriarchy in a British colony. The essential nature of Hong Kong society in the 19th century thus becomes apparent.[2]

When the British occupied Hong Kong Island in 1841, Captain Elliot proclaimed that the Chinese on the island, though now under British sovereignty, would be governed according to the laws and customs of China. The British made this declaration to minimise resistance to colonial occupation. It entitled Chinese who later arrived to work in the new colony to enjoy, to a large extent, freedom from an incomprehensible and alien legal and judicial system, and to perpetuate Chinese patriarchal society. When the Registrar-General's office began specialising in the management of Chinese in the 1850s, it further cushioned the Chinese community from the intrusion of English law (Sinn 1989). Moreover, the Tung Wah Hospital Committee, formed by the most influential Chinese merchants in Hong Kong, also sought to speak on behalf of the Chinese community. The hospital, dedicated to the use of Chinese medicine to the exclusion of Western medicine, was founded to cater to the medical needs and cultural bias of the Chinese in Hong Kong, fully demonstrating how much they felt distinct as a community, and how determined they were to stay apart (*ibid.*).

Under these circumstances, Chinese social customs, which often clashed with English social and legal ideals, managed to survive. One area where the differences were most conspicuous and irreconcilable was in the concept of and

---

The author wishes to thank Ms Susanna Hoe, Dr Veronica Pearson and Dr James Hayes for reading this paper and for their helpful comments.

141

attitude toward individual freedom and slavery. The Po Leung Kuk's early history illustrates these conflicts and attempts to contain them.

Chinese Patriarchy

Patriarchy as a family form characterised by the supremacy of the father and the subordination of women prevailed in many parts of the world in the 19th century, but manifested itself differently in different societies.[3] In China, the central tenet of patriarchy was that the male parent, as the head of a definite household, was the representative of the 'family', the principal organised expression of the Chinese State. His supremacy was enhanced by the necessity of continued sacrifices to the spirits of deceased ancestors. The patriarch was thus invested with a power over every member of his family, consisting of one or more wives, children, grand-children, younger brothers, their wives and children and so forth, as well as of hired and purchased servants, every one of whom had a fixed relation to the 'family', guaranteed by the whole social state, and all were subject to the same *patria potestas*. In a state thus based on patriarchy, the idea of personal liberty, of absolute rights possessed by every individual as conceived in the modern West, was entirely alien. Every member of the family or household merged his or her individual existence into the 'family', which was legally the only 'person' existing in China. In a family thus constituted, none could be free in the Western sense. The idea that every woman in China must be owned by someone was especially prevalent (Eitel Report 1879 pp. 49–56).

Another feature of Chinese society which had historically evolved from patriarchy was that almost every social arrangement – betrothal, marriage, concubinage, adoption, servitude – was professedly based on a money bargain. Given his absolute power over members of his household, and the right of holding property in persons, the patriarch's right to sell his children was unquestioned. Even the temporary pledging of a wife, concubine or daughter to another family for domestic servitude was not interfered with by the law in China, regardless of the written penal code. This gave rise to the general belief that people could be traded, a belief held not only by those who purchased and sold, but by the object of sale as well. The use of the term *ming mai*, *ming mai*, meaning open, legitimate purchase and sale (of persons), with written documents confirming the trans-actions, clearly indicates the wide acceptance of the system.[4] It is said that until the foundation of the People's Republic in 1949, China had one of the most comprehensive markets for the exchange of human beings in the world (J.L. Watson 1980 p. 223).

The holding of property in persons of course contravened English law, which had abolished slavery and upheld freedom of the individual . But though the first ordinance enacted in Hong Kong was against slavery in any form, it was a dead letter. The selling of girls as *mui tsai* (*mei zi*, girls purchased for domestic servitude) and as concubines, and of boys for adoption, was transacted in Hong Kong without fuss. Moreover, as early as 1856, the Secretary of State for the Colonies, H. Labouchere, had noted that the large numbers of prostitutes in Hong

Kong were nothing short of slaves ('Correspondence re Chinese Slavery', p. 81), but instead of concentrating on liberating them, official attention was diverted to designing better medical control to ensure the colony's public health.[5]

The practice of human trafficking did not attract attention again until emigration abuses were uncovered. In 1871, Chief Justice John Smale condemned the coolie trade as a slave trade, and created a great stir by declaring Kwok Asing, an emigrant from China charged with murder and piracy, innocent on the grounds that as a kidnap victim, he had a right to liberate himself even by killing the officers on board the kidnapping ship. In this, Smale was supported by the Tung Wah Hospital Committee (Sinn 1989 pp. 103, 114). In the fight against emigration abuses, other forms of human trafficking were exposed.

Emigration, Migration and Resulting Problems

From the 1840s, Chinese emigration, stimulated by the growing demand for Chinese labour abroad and the discovery of gold in America and Australia, was also intensified by the worsening economic conditions in many parts of South China. While many emigrants went voluntarily, the insatiable demand for cheap coolie labour, especially in destinations with horrible conditions such as Peru and Cuba, drove labour recruiters to resort to kidnapping by force or by decoy.[6]

At first, with few exceptions, Chinese emigrants were male, but from the 1860s, demand for Chinese females grew, and so did abuses related to female emigration.[7] By the early 1870s, kidnapping had become a major problem, the kidnapping of girls being so rampant that girls going to school in Hong Kong disguised themselves as boys, and every day offers of rewards for missing girls were posted in the streets (Eitel memorandum, *HKSP* 34/93 p. XXVIII). Hong Kong, an important embarkation port for Chinese emigrants, was naturally the place where numerous kidnap victims were taken. Moreover, as internal migration in China accelerated, Hong Kong, being a major shipping centre, was also the transit point for kidnapped persons taken from one Chinese port to another. From the 1880s, women kidnapped from Southeast Asia for the China market added another dimension to the problem.[8]

As early as 1872, leaders of Hong Kong's Chinese community, represented by the Tung Wah Hospital Committee, seeking to fight emigration-related abuses, alerted Governor Kennedy to the prevalence of kidnapping, particularly of women to be sold as prostitutes in Hong Kong or overseas.[9] In this, they may have been prompted by Chinese officials on the Mainland. Interestingly, the Hospital Committee focused its attention on the problem chiefly where it was related to emigration, and did much less for the many local prostitutes, the majority of whom had clearly been sold into prostitution. It will become obvious that Chinese community leaders were more concerned about some forms of human trafficking than others.

The Hospital Committee's efforts clearly show that British attempts to regulate Chinese emigration in Hong Kong were neither comprehensive enough nor implemented effectively enough to deal with abuses. The committee even asked

Kennedy for permission to employ detectives to watch out for kidnappers, and this was granted. In addition, the US Consul in Hong Kong, instructed by Washington in 1875 to forbid Chinese women from sailing to America for immoral purposes, also asked the committee to screen all women emigrants for would-be prostitutes (Sinn 1989 pp. 107–8); this naturally involved the committee more closely with detecting kidnap cases. The government, in response to strong representation from Chinese community leaders, enacted new ordinances in 1873 and 1875 against kidnapping and the purchase and sale of persons.

The 1875 ordinance, the Chinese community leaders soon discovered to their horror, went far beyond what they had originally asked for. It was directed not only at kidnapping and the sale of 'pigs' (people kidnapped for emigration) and of women for prostitution, but at *any* form of buying and selling of human beings. After the ordinance was passed, the police began bringing suspected cases of illegally detained children before the magistrates for investigation, although, when the child appeared to have been properly treated and the defendant had acted with the parents' consent, the case was dismissed. This was enough to 'put all native residents of Hong Kong in a state of extreme terror'. It was claimed that for the well-to-do who invariably had purchased *mui tsai*, and sometimes adopted sons, and for the poor, who saw the sale of their children, especially daughters, as a means of survival when destitute, the strict enforcement of the law meant constant fear of prosecution, squeeze and interference ('Petition of the Committee-members and Merchants', 25 October 1879, in 'Correspondence re Chinese Slavery', pp. 44–9).

The arrival of a new Governor, John Pope Hennessy, in 1877 aggravated the situation. Filled with humanitarian ideals and ready to help underdogs wherever he went, Hennessy was at first shocked to find that women were frequently sold as prostitutes, but the Registrar-General told him that it was useless to try and free them. A year later, in May 1878, Hennessy learnt about a case in which a child was sold, and, seeing this as an illegal transaction, he pressed the Attorney-General to prosecute the purchaser. Like the Registrar-General, the Attorney-General refused to act, claiming that the magistrate had no jurisdiction – which was not true, as he could have prosecuted under Ordinance 2 of 1875 (Hennessy to Hicks-Beach, 23 January 1880, *ibid*. pp. 1–4). No legal action followed. Even so, the Governor's hostility to these transactions, so far unprosecuted, caused further concern among the Chinese community, and its leaders soon forced the issue.

Proposal for an 'Association for the Suppression of Kidnapping and Traffic in Human Beings'

A few months later, in November, several prominent Hong Kong merchants from Donguan county, Guangdong, petitioned Hennessy for permission to form 'an association for suppressing kidnapping and traffic in human beings' ('Memorial of Chinese Merchants', 9 November 1878, *ibid*. pp. 26–8). They stated that kidnapping, accompanied by the selling of kidnapped women as prostitutes in

Hong Kong, overseas or to different parts of China, and by the selling of young boys as adopted sons, was becoming unbearably rampant. As most of the kidnapping occurred in Donguan, (the county closest to Hong Kong after Bao'an), the petitioners, knowing their home county well, felt obliged to help stamp out the crime by employing special detectives. These would be paid rewards out of a fund raised among Donguan natives, and three persons would be elected to manage the fund. They asked authority from the Governor to institute enquiries in suspected kidnap cases, and for their detectives to be able to make arrests before handing over the suspects to the police. Kidnapped persons thus rescued would be sent home by the association.

We can see from this petition that despite the Tung Wah Hospital's initial success in suppressing kidnapping, especially of males, the kidnapping and sale of women for prostitution continued. This resulted partly from the changing pattern of Chinese emigration in the 1870s. As the Straits Settlements overtook the United States as the prime destination, new markets were created for Chinese women as prostitutes, *mui tsai* and concubines, with a consequent rise in kidnapping and human trafficking. Economic troubles, caused partly by floods in South China, exacerbated the situation (*ibid.* p. 27). By 1878, it was clear that kidnapping syndicates were in operation, with regular depots for their victims in different parts of Hong Kong (*ibid.* p. 31). The intensified crime wave may have overwhelmed the Hospital Committee, whose hands were already full with other duties, and this probably explains why the Donguan merchants saw the need to start a new association specifically to tackle the problem.[10] And yet, the presentation of the petition at this particular juncture seems to be more than a response to the crime wave. Like many Chinese petitions in Hong Kong, this one needs to be read between the lines.

No doubt the petitioners believed that kidnapping was an evil which had to be combated, and were clearly dissatisfied with the way the police and courts were handling it. But it should be noted that it was not a question of efficiency: it was a question of *definition*. The dissatisfaction appears to have arisen out of a basic difference between the Chinese and the police and courts about *what constituted kidnapping*. The Chinese proposal was therefore not simply to suppress 'kidnapping' but to suppress it as *they defined the crime* according to patriarchal principles.

Defining Kidnapping

Where physical abduction was involved, kidnapping was easy to identify and there was little room for disagreement. However, apart from these 'straightforward' cases, there were many 'grey areas' which needed qualification.

For example, many of the kidnap cases the Chinese referred to were really *guaiyou* cases, 'kidnap' by enticement rather than abduction. These crimes were difficult to detect, especially because, in English legal terms, so long as the 'victim' declared that she was travelling voluntarily and not under compulsion by the 'kidnapper', she was considered free to go, and no one was prosecuted.

Sixteen cases of kidnappings of women and children that came before Hong Kong magistrates in the first six months of 1883 produced only one conviction – and the kidnapper was subsequently turned over to the Singapore Government (*HKSP* 1/1887 p. 18). From the Chinese point of view, women, whether they were wives, concubines, daughters or *mui tsai*, were always someone's property, never free agents, and therefore were never entitled to move about 'voluntarily'. Therefore, the enticer inducing women to leave their rightful owners must be prosecuted, and the women censured (Eitel memorandum, *HKSP* 34/93 p. 101).

In fact, since neither adultery nor desertion was criminally punishable in Hong Kong as they were in China, and since the Hong Kong Government had refused to change the law despite repeated representation by leaders of the Chinese community,[11] the only resort left to a Chinese husband whose wife had deserted him was to sue for kidnapping. In this way, he would get the police to trace the 'kidnapped' woman, who, when returned to him, might be prosecuted on the Mainland. The lover, if there was one, or other go-betweens, would hopefully be charged and convicted of kidnapping. It is safe to assume that this was one of the areas the Po Leung Kuk was set up to deal with because the police could not be relied on to tackle them effectively.

At the same time, there were cases the police considered kidnap cases which the Chinese did not. The Chinese took very seriously the sale of children by persons other than their parents or legitimate guardians, and in China, this was punishable by death (Meijer 1979 p. 331). However, as long as the child was sold by a legitimate party such as a parent, the purchaser was entitled to its possession. By the same token, even if a child had actually been kidnapped, as long as the purchaser was not aware of this fact, he was not guilty of any offence. Moreover, the sale must be honoured, so that if the child had to be taken away, the purchasers would be entitled to a refund (*HKSP* 1/87 p. 6). The Hong Kong police, however, did not accept any form of human trafficking, so disagreement over kidnapping followed. For example, the police could prosecute any purchaser of a child for kidnapping and illegal possession since the transaction was considered illegal.

In the final analysis, different views on kidnapping rested on different ideas about individual freedom and bondage. The Chinese, threatened by Hennessy's attitude, may have felt compelled at this point to stem the intrusion of English law into their patriarchal system.

To them these were specifically Chinese crimes which must be tackled by those familiar with Chinese social conditions, especially of family life, and according to social customs.[12] 'Social customs' are the operative words, and where women were concerned, the Chinese blamed English law and the English judicial system for encouraging their women to believe they were free, and making them susceptible to promises of escape from bondage. They were exasperated by women seeking 'refuge under the British flag' and taking advantage of the freedom available in Hong Kong (Bowen to Derby, 6 August 1883 #175 CO 129/211). They believed that 'Hong Kong had already acquired for itself a bad name for immorality from a Chinese point of view' (Norton-

Kyshe 1971 Vol. 2 p. 201), and took it upon themselves to defend Chinese moral standards as best they could under these difficult circumstances.

Defining Good and Evil Human Trafficking

The Chinese also had very specific views about human trafficking. In a subsequent petition presented to the Governor in October 1879 they pointed to a clear distinction between *good* and *wicked*, guilty and non-guilty, human trafficking. In the first category were the sale of boys as adopted sons and the sale of girls as domestic servants. The petition reiterated the patriarchal premises by referring to Confucianism and the imperative to continue the family line, so that families without heirs needed to acquire a son through purchase. To the petitioners, this institution was completely justifiable. So too was the *mui tsai* system. They thought the *mui tsai* did not have such a bad deal. The girls, being young, had to be taught and tended, and when they reached maturity, they had to be given in marriage. They did little hard work and were generally treated well. These practices, the petition argued, had existed in China since time immemorial, and where no kidnapping or decoying or compulsion occurred, the law did not interfere. They prevailed among common people as well as the families of scholars and high officials. If this was forbidden, poor people would have no relief, and many girls from impoverished families would be drowned as infants.

Though concubines were not mentioned in the petition, one can judge from the Po Leung Kuk's subsequent work that the purchasing of women as concubines, too, fell into this category of non-guilty trafficking. On the other hand, the petition admitted, the selling of free persons for purposes of prostitution, as well as decoying, kidnapping, or use of compulsion, were obviously wicked acts and should be severely punished ('Petition of the Committee-members and Merchants', 25 October 1879, in 'Correspondence re Chinese Slavery' p. 210).

This hard-hitting petition, stating so unequivocally the Chinese community leaders' views, was a reaction to Chief Justice Smale's recent actions.

The 1879 Crisis

In October 1879 Smale had convicted a number of persons of kidnapping, detention of children with intent to sell them, and of selling and purchasing a child for the purpose of prostitution.[13] It was the first time that any prosecution had actually been brought against slavery in the colony. In delivering sentence, Smale hit at the very core of Chinese patriarchal authority by proclaiming that according to English law:

> … no one can acquire any right over the person of another, that no man can sell his own person into slavery, that a parent has no saleable property in his child; moreover that every such sale *nudum pactum* absolutely void, that money paid on any such sale cannot be recovered back, but that the man bought must be restored to liberty, and the sold child to his parent, as if no money had been paid; that no purchase money can be recovered back and that the crime in buyer and seller must be punished.[14]

He challenged the Chinese custom of buying and selling young girls as *mui tsai* and women as prostitutes, declaring that slavery, both domestic slavery and brothel slavery, was in fact the cause of kidnapping. He pointed out that if the Chinese community leaders intended to fight kidnapping, it would only be logical for them to begin by fighting slavery; and unless they did so, kidnapping would persist.[15] He might have added that the *mui tsai* system was a main supplier of prostitutes (Kani 1979 p. 314), and that polygyny, practised openly and extensively in Hong Kong, was another vital link in the trade in women, and a source of endless abuses.

Indeed, cases before and after 1879 indicate the close interrelations between kidnapping, domestic servitude, concubinage and prostitution. So often, girls were sold from hand to hand, from port to port, first as *mui tsai*, but only to end up being sold as prostitutes and concubines.[16] Cases of three or four resales were common and there were even cases of reselling up to six or seven times (Kani 1979 p. 311; PLK Vol. 1, 22 May 1884). The transactions could also occur over great geographical distances. The situation was fluid, for women were a veritable commodity of trade which could be sold in many forms. It would be illogical to combat some forms of human trafficking and not others. Thus Smale was correct in pointing out the central contradiction in the Chinese community leaders' thinking.

Smale was aware that the Chinese had long used Elliot's Proclamation of 1841 to defend many of their practices which otherwise contravened English law. But he felt that even the proclamation could not be used to justify the perpetuation of slavery. If, he observed, according to the penal code of China, slavery was outlawed, there was no reason for the Hong Kong Government to tolerate it.[17]

Not surprisingly, the leading Chinese, feeling threatened by Smale's views, were forced to state their own, and presented the petition mentioned above. To strengthen their stand, they ended the petition by threatening that, unless their advice was taken, Chinese merchants who had been attracted to Hong Kong by 'the equity of the administration of law' and 'the absence of vexatiousness on the part of the executive', and who had helped the colony to prosper, might leave.

Hennessy, faced with two sets of arguments, turned to E.J. Eitel, his Chinese secretary and adviser on all things Chinese. Eitel, in a long report on domestic servitude in relation to slavery, argued that the term 'slavery', bound up with the peculiar development of the social life and legal theories of the progressive societies of the West, was not applicable to the Chinese situation. Human relationships operated so differently in China that 'to deal justly with the slavery of China, we ought to invent a new name for it'.[18] Thus he concluded that legally, since Chinese domestic servitude differed so widely from negro slavery, police prosecution of the former under any law with reference to the latter would constitute an act of very doubtful legality. Politically, it should be tolerated as a low form of social development; because it was a necessary part of Chinese patriarchy, absolute condemnation of it would be an act of moral injustice. Besides, practically, it would be difficult to implement without causing disturbance among the Chinese and embarrassment to the government (Eitel Report pp. 49–57).

Governor Hennessy was persuaded to change his mind about human trafficking – in any case, by now he was convinced that the Chinese merchant community was the key to Hong Kong's prosperity. Even the Secretary of State for the Colonies, Lord Kimberley, after initial misgivings, came round to the view that the sale of a child, which might possibly be 'advantageous to the child, both immediately and in afterlife' should not be made a misdemeanour (Kimberley to Hennessy, 18 March 1882, No. 22, in 'Correspondence re Chinese Slavery', pp. 100–4). Thus, despite protests from Smale and other Britons in Hong Kong, no charges for slavery *per se* were made. The issue of slavery was not to reappear until the late 1910s.[19]

In the meantime, the Chinese dichotomy between 'good' and 'wicked', or 'honest' and 'immoral', human trafficking prevailed (see minute by acting Police Magistrate Ng Choy in 'Correspondence re Chinese Slavery' pp. 83–4). This was now not only the operating principle of the Po Leung Kuk, the police and court acted accordingly.

The government's theoretical position was ambivalent. On the one hand, where a child was sold *voluntarily* by a parent or relative, the mere fact of a money payment was not sufficient ground for prosecution. On the other, the government paid lip service to anti-slavery principles by declaring that the payment of money for a child did not confer any title that British officials would recognise, and that 'no opportunity was lost' to proclaim the right of every Chinese subject, man, woman and child, to freedom (*HKSP* 1/87 p. 4). The fact remained that human trafficking was not, *prima facie*, an offence. As for kidnapping, the Po Leung Kuk detectives were employed to uncover cases of kidnapping according to the Chinese definition of the crime, though not all cases brought before the court led to conviction. Thus after a year-long struggle, the Po Leung Kuk, with the Governor's blessing, settled down to operate within this ideological framework, and maintained the Chinese patriarchal system in colonial Hong Kong.

The Formation of the Po Leung Kuk

The Society which came into being in January 1880 differed from the one originally proposed in several ways.

After reading the Donguan merchants' petition, Hennessy asked them to discuss their proposal with two police magistrates[20] and some of the original ideas were modified as a result. First, the society's focus was shifted from kidnapped persons to women and children. Its English name became the 'Society for the protection of women and children', but its Chinese name remained the '*bao liang ju*', 'Society for the protection of the innocent', which is more comprehensive. The reason for the change in name is unknown, but its later work would show that, though the Society offered refuge to men as well as women, it *did* spend much more time over women's cases, which tended to be more complicated and demanded more of the directors' attention and time.

Second, in terms of structure and funds, J.J. Francis, the police magistrate, recommended that the Society should acquire corporate status by registering as a company under the Companies Ordinance. Instead of three managers, he suggested a management committee of seven members to be elected annually by subscribing members, each to pay $10 or more. In this way, the Society would have a more permanent, formal and responsible management structure. In fact, the Society was not incorporated until 1893; up to that time, it had an annual committee of 10 directors elected annually. (See below, p. 164 for organisation after 1893.)

Francis also suggested ways for the Society to care for kidnap victims. If possible it should restore them to their lawful guardians in the interior of China, but it should provide for women or children who had actually been sold by their guardians, who would only sell them again if they were returned. It must also consider how to deal with persons who were absolutely friendless, by marrying them off or setting them up in life ('Correspondence re Chinese Slavery', p. 31). Thus, he redirected the Society's focus from the primary objective of suppressing kidnapping to the care of victims. As it turned out, this part of the Society's work was a far greater and more lasting achievement than the suppression or prevention of the crime.

The government, having found it difficult to care for kidnap victims, was naturally glad for an institution to come forward to take over that responsibility. The Society's work was to show that the job could not be done without a deep knowledge of Chinese society and its peculiar customs, without money and organisational ability, social status and authority, and widespread connections with institutions and individuals in China and overseas. In other words, it was best done not by the Hong Kong Government but by Chinese community leaders, with government support. But there was a trade-off – the Society would accept these responsibilities only if the government would let it operate within a Chinese ideological framework, at the expense of English justice, and the tension inherent in these circumstances may be imagined.

It was immediately obvious to the petitioners that Francis' suggestions, which made the Society's work more comprehensive than at first envisaged, would also require far more money. Though Francis told them they would not need to pay rewards to detectives because the government would do so, the expanded functions would still be expensive ('Correspondence re Chinese Slavery', p. 29). In view of this, they found it necessary to approach other members of the Hong Kong Chinese community through the Tung Wah Hospital.[21] As a result, Donguan natives would no longer be the only donors of funds; nor would they alone be the managers. Thus, from very early on, the Society ceased to be merely a Donguan county concern, but became, like the Tung Wah Hospital, a community-wide one.

The initial subscription drive only raised $1,330, and no further attempt was made to enlist more members or to start an annual subscription (*HKSP* 34/93 p. xii). Instead, the Society sought assistance from the Tung Wah Hospital. Until 1892, it depended on 'loans' from the hospital and the Man Mo Temple[22] as its main source of income. It was suggested that the Po Leung Kuk did not feel it necessary to seek financial support from the Chinese community independently because people saw that in subscribing to the hospital they were also subscribing indirectly to the Po Leung Kuk (Wai Yuk's opinion, *HKSP* 34/93 p. 15). The Society itself employed two detectives, but accounting and clerical work was done by hospital staff. Despite this, the administration of the two institutions was carefully kept apart.

Hennessy had promised to grant land for building premises, but this fell through, and until 1896, when the Po Leung Kuk's own premises were finally completed, all persons the Society rescued were housed in one of the wards at the hospital, which also provided them with food and clothing.

The first Committee of Directors was elected in 1881. Although it was proposed that members who subscribed $10 or more should have the right to elect directors, they were elected annually at a public meeting held at the Tung Wah Hospital, at which the Chinese community was invited to vote for nominated candidates. In fact, the selection took place among the leading merchants of Hong Kong, and the public meeting was largely ritualistic. Nonetheless, by conferring legitimacy on those elected as representatives of the Chinese community, the meeting was significant. Since both the Tung Wah Hospital and the Po Leung Kuk committees targeted the most wealthy and powerful merchants in Hong Kong, it is not surprising that there was a frequent overlap in membership.[23] Of the 128 Po Leung Kuk directors from 1878 to 1900, 78 had served or would serve on one of the Tung Wah Hospital committees. More important, they also shared the Chinese local elite's sense of mission: to ensure the material wellbeing of the locality and spiritually to raise the morals of the community by upholding existing orthodox social values. Needless to say, in the 19th century, all directors were men. The first woman director did not sit until 1937, and the first woman chairman was elected in 1971 (PLK 1978, Chinese section, p. 139).

The first chairman of the Po Leung Kuk (1881) was Leung On, who was also the hospital's first chairman. Leung's reputation for compassion, earned from his rescuing people from being sold as 'pigs' overseas, had won him the nickname of 'Bodhisattva', one who postponed his own entry into Buddhahood in order to help others. In fact, the first meetings of the Society were held at the offices of Gibb Livingston's, where Leung was comprador (*HKSP* 34/93 p. 10), before they later adjourned to the hospital.

The Protection of Women

Given its small size, the scale of the Po Leung Kuk's work is staggering. In 1893, the Registrar-General summed up its work thus:

> [It] co-operates with this department in detecting cases of kidnapping and kindred practices, and in bringing to justice the offenders in such cases; it provides a

Table 1
Girls & women detained under Ordinance for the Protection of Women and Girls, and the Ways they were dealt with 1891–1920.

	1891–9	1900–7	1909–20
1. Released after enquiry	282	1,188	1,343
2. Conditionally released	—	12	69
3. Fetched by relatives	480	264	157
4. Fetched by husbands	194	111	61
5. Awarded to guardian	98	76	—
6. Repatriated	537	576	343
7. Taken by school, orphanage or convent	79	77	39
8. Delivered to French consul	17	1	3
9. Delivered to Japanese consul	22	12	—
10. Adopted	57	47	7
11. Married off	273	212	70
12. Adopted and awaiting marriage	—	—	27
13. Escaped	1	—	8
14. Died	21	7	5
15. Repatriated overseas	2	8	—
16. Kept at Po Leung Ruk	45	—	—
17. Case pending decision	18	111	190
18. Others	5	4	—
Total	2,181	2,701	2,322

Source: Kani Hiroaki, Kindai Chugoku no Kuri to Choka, *p. 266, Table 52.*

temporary home for men, women and girls who have been inveigled into the Colony under false pretences for the purposes of emigration; for women and girls brought into the Colony for improper purposes, but who are found to be unwilling to enter on or who wish to abandon a life of shame; for children who are being brought up in vicious surroundings by persons who have no legal claim to them; for destitute women and girls found by the Police or sent back from places outside Hongkong, such as the Straits and San Francisco (*ibid.* p. XLIII).

The amount of work can also be seen from Tables 1, 2 and 3. But figures alone cannot fully reflect the variety which characterised its operations nor the different types of cases with which it dealt, nor the geographical from which the victims came and to which they were delivered, nor the vicissitudes of individual experiences (see Table 2). Its work reveals the incredible prevalence of kidnapping and human trafficking, with each case reconfirming the cheapness, degradation and misery of human life in China, and not just among the poorest classes. Together they reveal not only the misfortune and helplessness of women, but of men as well. In this article, however, we shall concentrate on the protection of women.

Here is a typical situation. The Po Leung Kuk detectives watched for cases of kidnapping at the piers or by boarding ships; when suspects were discovered,

Table 2
Persons accommodated by the Po Leung Kuk and how they were dealt with 1894–9.

Year	Adopted	Women sent home	Died	Married off	Men sent home	Being accom- modated	Total
1894	13	6	275	181	31	3	509
1895	22	5	160	155	41	2	385
1896	36	5	110	219	59	2	431
1897	21	12	83	220	48	1	385
1898	30	7	106	205	64	—	412
1899	43	7	114	207	35	5	411
Total	165	42	848	1187	278	13	2,533

Source: Kani Hiroaki, Kindai Chugoku no Kuri to Choka, *p. 49, Table 12.*

Table 3
Numbers of Persons Dealt with by the Po Leung Kuk, 12/7/91–3/7/92

Number of men, women and children remaining in Po Leung Kuk at the commencement of the year.	52
Girls sent to the Society by the Registrar-General and married under the auspices of the Society, security being taken by the Registrar-General.	47
Destitute women and girls sent to the Society by the Registrar-General. Particulars, stating how disposed of (16 girls adopted under security).	339
Women and girls sent to the Oi Yuk T'ong Canton to be sent home.	17
Men and boys sent to the Oi Yuk T~ong to be sent to their homes.	18
Males sent to the Society by the Registrar-General. Usual particulars, stating how disposed of. (Ten boys adopted under security.)	104
Males received into the Society, who were dealt with by the Police Magistrace.	18
Do., females.	18
Females received into the Society, who were dealt with by the Police.	1
Women and girls received into the Po Leung Kuk in Hong Kong or sent from other ports, who were sent home or restored to their relatives by the Society.	51
Do., men and boys.	399
Total number of persons.	1,005

Source: Summarised from the Annual Report of the Po Leung Kuk from 12 July 1891 to 3 July 1892; printed in appendix 42 of Hong Kong Sessional Paper 34/1893.

they and their victims would be taken to the Registrar-General's office,[24] which would hand the suspect to the police and transfer the victim to the Po Leung Kuk. The woman would be questioned about herself and her family, and if she expressed a wish to return to her family, the Society would make contact with her parents or relatives through a network of institutions and individuals in different parts of China or overseas. Finally, a family member would come to fetch her. Where it was impossible for a family member to come to Hong Kong, the woman would be sent off accompanied by a Po Leung Kuk employee, most often to Guangzhou, and especially to the Aiyutang, the city's most respected merchant-operated charitable organisation, where she would be met by family members. If the relatives were very poor, the Society defrayed the costs (*HKSP* 34/93 p. XX).

Always, a bond, or security, had to be produced by the person taking charge of the woman to ensure that he was the legitimate party. In some cases, the recipient undertook to present the girl to the Society at intervals for 'inspection', even at 24 hours' notice (Kani 1979 p. 340; *HKSP* 34/93 p. XII). Thus, many cases involved long-term vigilance.

Records show that each case was carefully and intensively investigated, and meticulously recorded, making the Po Leung Kuk archives a priceless asset to historians.[25] Every woman was interviewed by at least two directors, usually the chairman and vice-chairman. Often it was a long time before the woman, either too frightened to tell the truth or coached to tell lies, told the whole story. The interview, which usually started at 7pm, sometimes went on until 1am, during which time the investigators would have heard many sets of truths. At the committee meeting on the following Sunday, the evidence would be laid before the other directors for a decision (*HKSP* 34/93 p. 123).

The Society also sent for information to verify the stories, sometimes by writing to the woman's native region, which could be very remote, asking for information from local organisations, minor officials or individual members of the local gentry (PLK Vol. 8, 29 November and 8 December 1887).

The Registrar-General entrusted the investigation to the directors knowing that it was more likely that women would confide in them than in British officials. Moreover, he did not have the wherewithal to obtain information on the Mainland. The Society instigated dozens of kidnapping cases, and one can only speculate that, without the Society, many of these cases would have gone undetected. Obviously the Registrar-General regarded the Society as useful in helping to maintain law and order in Hong Kong.

The Society was able to operate only by maintaining close working relationships with many institutions and individuals. To begin with, there were the Tung Wah Hospital and the Registrar-General's office in Hong Kong, as we have seen. In addition, there were many categories of institutions, including government offices on the Chinese Mainland and Chinese consulates overseas, the Protector of Chinese office in Singapore, charitable organisations, local militia organisations, shops and firms, overseas Chinese chambers of commerce, and regional associations. Among institutions which worked most closely with it were the

Aiyutang and Guangrantang of Guangzhou and the Jinghu Hospital of Macao (for other institutions, see PLK 1978, Chinese section, p. 152).

Interestingly enough, after the Po Leung Kuk was founded in Hong Kong, a number of similar institutions appeared overseas. In 1881 a Po Leung Kuk was established under the aegis of the Protector of Chinese in Singapore (Memo by Hare, in *HKSP* 34/93 pp. LXVI–VIII) and later also at Kuala Lumpur, Ipoh, Malacca and other Malay cities. Societies to fight kidnapping and protect the victims were also formed in Bangkok, North Borneo and Annam. More significantly, in their planning stages, they wrote to Hong Kong's Po Leung Kuk for copies of its charter. The Hong Kong Society's influence is manifest, and the emergence of similar institutions enhanced its work (Kani 1979 pp. 79–80).

The extensive network of institutions the Po Leung Kuk dealt with covered a wide physical area, reflecting the geographical expanse of human trafficking. In China, it covered Guangdong, including the remotest parts, Guangxi, Fujian, Shanghai, Hainan, Hunan; overseas, it spread from Hong Kong to San Francisco, Annam, Singapore, Sandakan, Siam, Japan.[26] Some localities where the women were taken were so remote that no one had heard of them or knew where they were (PLK Vol. 5, 28 February 1889). As an intermediary situated at the shipping centre of the region, the Po Leung Kuk played a pivotal role.

The network of institutions was important for disseminating and gathering information – through it, the Po Leung Kuk heard about kidnap cases and other missing persons, searched for family members of victims and sought reliable information about them. It was also indispensable for actually transporting the women home, for if their home was outside Guangzhou, they were taken by relay through a series of institutions, each of which would assume responsibility for passing them on to a legitimate party (Kani 1979 pp. 203). Women who had to be sent over long distances would be entrusted to the ship's staff, who often took on the responsibility as a social obligation. Always, the basic operating principle was trust, and a common faith in the need to uphold orthodox moral values. Thus, this network did not just implement social and charitable services, *but was an ideological network for upholding Chinese patriarchy regardless of the physical locality.*

The Variety of Cases Handled

Besides the 'classic' cases, there was an endless variety of situations, far beyond the scope outlined in the original petition. The Po Leung Kuk not only handled cases discovered by its detectives or referred to it by the Registrar-General. Requests to find missing persons came from all quarters, sometimes from family members or owners of *mui tsai*, or from charitable organisations on their behalf. Witnesses of suspicious incidents also reported to the Po Leung Kuk, and it is significant that many reported to it rather than to the police.[27]

Not all cases involved 'straightforward' kidnapping, and the large number of 'grey area' cases the Society had to deal with shows why its founders were so keen to emphasise the peculiarity of Chinese crime. The cases are not easy to classify, but I shall attempt to do so.

Married Women

There were many cases involving wives, concubines and widows. Some were enticed to leave their homes by promises of high wages, or of finding their husbands who were working in another town or abroad. They went willingly with the 'enticer', only to find themselves sold as prostitutes or concubines on arrival in Hong Kong or elsewhere (Kani 1979 pp. 167–89, 234).

There were also cases where women were actually sold by their husbands. The Qing Penal Code allowed husbands to sell adulterous wives or concubines (Meijer 1979 p. 331). Though there was no formal mechanism to stop a husband or father-in-law selling a primary wife, this was rare. The concubine was likely to go first in cases of poverty, and wives would only be sold in destitution (J.L. Watson 1980 p. 231). However, there were instances when they were sold for being stupid or 'loose' (Kani 1979 pp. 202–4, 234).

In one of the most pathetic cases, a woman claimed that her husband had first sold her to Singapore, and when she escaped and returned to him, he sold her to Guangzhou, and again she escaped and returned to him. It was only when the husband sold the daughter that the woman, disgusted, finally ran away from him. This highlights one of the most basic problems: the women themselves were so imbued with the value of obedience and submission, and so convinced of the husband's right to sell them, that they tolerated the situation without resistance except in extreme cases (*ibid.* pp. 201–2). Moreover, given the social and economic conditions of the time, there were few alternatives open to them.

In one case, a husband, instead of suing the kidnappers of his concubine, proceeded to blackmail them for the crime (*ibid.* p. 237). This gives some idea of the complexity of the situation.

In some cases, women ill-treated by husbands or mothers-in-law, or because of the jealousy so common in polygynous households, left the husband's home voluntarily and chose to stay away (*ibid.* pp. 186, 190–5, 197–8). Fleeing in this way was an act of desperation, perhaps only short of suicide as a means of self-liberation, for these women, even the most innocent, would almost automatically be condemned as wayward and self-indulgent.

There were also cases of elopement, which the Po Leung Kuk took most seriously, but their wish to deal harshly with the woman and her lover was often frustrated by the leeway given them by English law (PLK Vol. 4, 31 December 1888). According to Hong Kong law the wife could not be prosecuted for desertion or adultery, and the only way to punish the elopers was to charge the man with kidnapping and send the woman back to her husband. In one case the woman drove the directors to exasperation by simply refusing to admit that she had been kidnapped (PLK Vol. 5, 15 March 1889). As a result the lovers went unpunished.

Another difficult case was that of a woman the directors described as 'ferocious', who refused to return home. Her husband was working abroad, and though the father-in-law came for her, she refused to go with him. As she was married, the Po Leung Kuk could not dispose of her either through marriage or adoption. There was nothing the Society could do short of insisting that the father-in-law came again (PLK Vol. 5, 15 March and 5 April 1889). This case dragged on, unresolved, and illustrates the multiplicity of situations the Po Leung Kuk had to deal with.

Girls Procured Ostensibly to be Married

Marriage was often used as a cover-up for procuring girls as prostitutes. In some cases, the girls themselves were aware of the deception, but collaborated with the procuress by telling the emigration officer in Hong Kong, who questioned them at embarkation, that they were going overseas to be married. But the Society also rescued many girls who had been unwittingly given or sold, often by their parents, as wives or concubines to men living in another town, only to find that they were to be sold as prostitutes. The case of Tsau Kung-wan and Cheung Luk shows how entrenched this practice was.

Cheung Luk's mother, to defray her husband's medical expenses, sold her in Guangzhou to Cheung Tsing for $290 to be taken to Hankou to become the fifth concubine of Cheung's husband, Tsau Kung-wan. However, when the steamer reached Hong Kong, Cheung Luk and Cheung Tsing were taken by a police inspector, who suspected kidnapping, to the Registrar-General and then to the Po Leung Kuk. Cheung Luk's mother, summoned to Hong Kong to give evidence, admitted to the sale, but now that she found that Tsau was much older than she'd thought (75 instead of 63!) and had heard other stories about him, she changed her mind and decided to take her daughter home. She repaid part of the money, had the ceremonial marriage cards cancelled and took the girl back to Guangzhou.

It was revealed in the course of investigation that this was not the first occasion that Tsau had procured young girls as his concubines in order to sell them as prostitutes afterwards. Eight years earlier, in 1883, a girl from Shunde district, after only a few days of marriage to Tsau, was taken to Shanghai by his fourth wife and sold to a brothel. On another occasion, four Cantonese girls, taken to Shanghai ostensibly to be married, were all seduced by Tsau. Afterwards two of them married Cantonese policemen and the other two were put in brothels (*HKSP* 34/93 pp. LXX–IX).

Mui Tsai

Many cases involved *mui tsai*. Some were reported missing by their owners, or by their parents or guardians (Kani 1979 306–8); others were sent to the Po Leung Kuk by the police while their owners were being investigated for assaulting them; still others were discovered when being sold as prostitutes (*ibid*. pp. 308–9, 312–3). Much has been said about the tragic *mui tsai* system (Jaschok 1985; Koh; Jaschok & Miers; Miers); suffice it to say here that once a child was sold as a *mui tsai*, her future was fraught with uncertainty. She could be sold and resold, or mortgaged, still as a *mui tsai*, or as a prostitute or concubine, and it was common for a girl to change hands three or four times, and cases of six or seven resales are recorded. She was subject to ill-treatment by her owners (Kani 1979 pp. 308–9) and sometimes forced to become the owner's concubine. It is therefore not surprising that many escaped, either on their own volition or they were persuaded to flee by others.

Prostitutes

Under Hong Kong law, women could choose to be prostitutes, but only if they were of age, unmarried and had not been sold or coerced into the profession (*ibid.* p. 121). Nominally, every prostitute in Hong Kong had to be registered at the Registrar-General's office, and there she would be asked if she was entering the profession of her own free will. In addition, in every room in every Chinese registered brothel, a printed notice was exhibited explaining that the girls were free, and that if they had been deceived, pledged or sold, they could get their liberty at once. It is difficult to know how many women took advantage of this. It is known that in many cases women who had been bought and brought up as prostitutes were so imbued with a sense of obligation to their 'pocket mothers' that they felt compelled to work to repay them. There were also many ways brothel-keepers intimidated or terrorised them into submission. Conversely, there were few other avenues open to them. In some cases, where prostitutes decided to leave with customers they fancied, they were soon abandoned, or taken overseas and sold to brothels (*HKSP* 1/87 p. 5).

Laws enacted to protect prostitutes had not been enforced vigorously before the founding of the Po Leung Kuk, and earlier Registrars-General had little faith that they could use the laws to deal with the question of their freedom (Report on CDO 1880 p. 56). After the Society was established, more cases of brothel slavery came to light. Suspected cases were taken to the Po Leung Kuk and through careful interrogation, the directors were often able to establish whether or not the women had been sold. James Russell, a former Registrar-General, reported in 1882 that the number of women leaving brothels without paying their mistresses what they owed had risen (*HKSP* 1/87 p. 5), possibly because they felt they could go to the Po Leung Kuk for refuge. On the other hand, many women were allowed to return to the brothels because they insisted they were doing so out of their own free will. It should be noted, however, that no attempt was made either by the Society or the Hong Kong Government to outlaw prostitution (Miners 1987 pp. 191–206).

Disposal of the Women

The Po Leung Kuk naturally had no intention of keeping its wards longer than was absolutely necessary; space, food and clothing were important considerations, and ultimately the responsibility was overwhelming, and could not be relieved until they were disposed of in the most appropriate way. Tables 1, 2 and 3 show that most of the women rescued by the Po Leung Kuk were fetched by family, relatives or owners when they could be identified or were considered suitable. Otherwise, young girls were put up for adoption or sent to other institutions and the women were married off.

Those returned to their parents included prostitutes who were suspected of having been sold (Kani 1979 pp. 121–2).

Adoption

Girls were adopted by institutions such as schools and orphanages run by missionaries or convents, or by individuals. In 1892, a regulation for adoption was laid down by which the adopting parents had to swear an oath before the martial god, *guan di*, that they would not use the child as a *mui tsai* (*ibid.* p. 344). The Society also investigated them, and their particulars had to be presented to the Registrar-General.

Return to Husband

Given the patriarchal bias of the Po Leung Kuk, it is not surprising that returning married women to their husband's home was regarded as by far the most satisfactory solution. Between 1891 and 1898, 194 women were so dispatched. Cruelty, except in extreme cases, was not thought sufficient reason for women to leave their husbands and every effort was made to coax women who had run away to return. The Po Leung Kuk simply asked the husband to swear an oath never to mistreat his wife again (*ibid.* p. 193). However, if a case of ill-treatment came to the notice of the police, the man might be flogged for assault (*ibid.*).

Some women had left the husband's home because he had died, or had gone to work abroad, and they were unhappy living with their in-laws. Even then, the Society would try to arrange their return, and sometimes it found itself in a dilemma if the women resisted. The Society might wish to detain them until they complied, but it had no legal power to do so indefinitely. Indeed, its right to detain at all was often queried. As one of its critics said, the women were 'imprisoned without trial' (Whitehead's evidence, *HKSP* 34/93 p. 25). It was always conscious that under British law it had no right to detain anyone against his will. Thus it could do little but urge members of the husband's family to come for a woman while reminding them that she was free to go at any time. In one case, a woman whose husband worked in San Francisco had been in the Po Leung Kuk for a whole year, and the directors had to plead with her father-in-law to come for her (PLK Vol. 4, 26 September and 20 December 1888).

Zhang Ba's case shows how keen the Society was to return women to their husbands (PLK Vol. 1, 21 February 1884). Zhang was sent to the Po Leung Kuk by the Registrar-General, and after investigations the directors ascertained that she had indeed left her husband to become a prostitute, for economic reasons. They recommended that she be returned to him in order 'to teach those who fled to distant places to be afraid, and not to repeat the mistake' (PLK Vol. 1, 23 February 1884). Zhang at first agreed to return, but she later changed her mind. According to the committee, this was because a man she was seeing behind the hills of the hospital kept dissuading her. The committee, much dismayed, was eager to return her to her family before she changed her mind again.

The Registrar-General, however, as a matter of routine, asked for a surety from the husband or mother who might come to fetch a woman. But the Po Leung Kuk made a special plea to waive the surety in this case, arguing that since Zhang's husband and mother were strangers in Hong Kong they would find it difficult to obtain a surety there whereas it would be much easier for them to do so in Guangzhou. Moreover, Zhang had shown herself to be wayward, and should be sent back as soon as possible. She was finally sent to the Aiyutang in Guangzhou to await a surety. It is apparent that Zhang was sent back double quick to avoid complications, and possibly without her full consent.

Married Women Freed or Returned to their Parents

But despite the Society's predominant intention to return women to their husbands' homes, it was not always possible or expedient to do so.

Sometimes the women themselves refused to return. There were cases where a man would ask the Po Leung Kuk to trace his wife, whom he alleged had been 'kidnapped' when in fact she had eloped, hoping that the Society would find her and send her back to the Mainland where she could be charged. If the woman, when found, absolutely refused to comply, there was little the Society could do except to lament that under British law adulterous women could get away scot-free (PLK Vol. 4, 31 December 1888). Both the Po Leung Kuk and Tung Wah Hospital were troubled by 'kidnappers' who were 'so audacious' as to employ lawyers to demand the production and acquittal of the women (*HKSP* 34/93 pp. XXXIX–XL, LXI–IV). As mentioned, since adultery was not a criminal offence in Hong Kong, the only way the husband could get at the lover was to charge him with kidnapping (PLK Vol. 6, 6 October 1889). This was one of the 'grey areas' of kidnapping which the Hong Kong Chinese community believed the Hong Kong police least able to cope with.

But there were also cases where the husband refused to come for a wife who had been 'kidnapped' because he considered her immoral (PLK Vol. 4, 22 November 1888). In fact, it is always difficult to determine in these situations whether the woman was an innocent victim or a willing accomplice.

Exceptions to the general practice were also made on compassionate grounds. In cases where the husband was obviously a scoundrel, and it was believed that the woman would be miserable if returned to him, she might be given to the charge of her parents instead (PLK Vol. 6, 9 December 1889). There was a case of a concubine who ran away after fighting with the primary wife. She was then sold as a prostitute. When the Society found her and heard her story, it sent for her father to take her home. In another case, both the Po Leung Kuk and the Guangrantang in Guangzhou believed that a concubine who had been sold by her husband, who ran a brothel-cum-opium den, would probably be sold again if returned to him, and decided to marry her off in Hong Kong. This particular case became complicated when the husband protested and the magistrate of Nanhai county, the British Consul at Guangzhou and the Hong Kong Government all became involved, but eventually the Society's decision was upheld (Kani 1979 p. 346).

Chu A-ying's case is also instructive. Chu was the concubine of a blind man, Chan, who took her away from a brothel at Guangzhou for 25 taels, about $32. They came to Hong Kong, and while he smoked opium Chu became a prostitute with his knowledge and gave him all her earnings. As he became more demanding, they quarrelled a lot, and after begging him many times to release her for a small sum, she finally ran away. Her husband then went to complain to the Registrar-General of her desertion. Sensing some domestic squabble, the Registrar-General asked the Po Leung Kuk Committee to arrange an amicable settlement, but the pair could not be reconciled. The Registrar-General, in the presence of her husband, told Chu she was free to do as she liked. But it seems that the Society persuaded her to pay him $20 as a final settlement, and Chan gave her a written receipt and release for it (*HKSP* 34/93 p. XXXII–III).

It is significant to note that though the Registrar-General and the Po Leung Kuk agreed that Chu should go free, they treated the matter very differently. For the Registrar-General, who did not recognise the money payment by the husband in the first instance, it was 'no strings attached'. But for the Po Leung Kuk, the woman still had an obligation to her husband, which could only be cancelled by a money settlement. As a piece of property, she could only be freed through a monetary redemption. Despite the apparent co-operation between the Registrar-General's office and the Po Leung Kuk, there were irreconcilable differences in principle.

Marriage

One of the most unconventional ways the Society dealt with women was to marry them off. In an age when only the parents and guardians had the right to do this, it was truly a radical departure from Chinese tradition. It was also an innovation in that the women did have a say – they could choose from the applicants for their hand, or could decide not to marry at all (e.g. PLK Vol. 8, 3 September 1887). To this extent, some measure of freedom was provided.

Young women of marriageable age whose parents could not be traced or identified, or whose parents and guardians were likely to resell them, were recommended for marriage. As with adoption, the Po Leung Kuk took pains to prevent abuse. Men wishing to marry its wards had to register at the Society in person, and a date would be set for the man and woman to meet. If both parties were agreeable, the man would find a guarantor. The Society would investigate his character and the guarantor's as well, and if these were found acceptable, the man would be summoned, and he would eventually apply to the Registrar-General's office for permission to marry. Everything was under the Registrar-General's scrutiny; applicants were turned down for a variety of reasons, for example, if the guarantor was suspect or from out of town (Kani 1979 p. 344–7).

The bridegroom-to-be was required to swear on oath that the couple were marrying of their free will without coercion from a third party; that after marrying, he would not sell his wife, nor let her become a *mui tsai* or concubine; if this happened, he would be willing to be punished, and the guarantor would be fined $500 (*ibid.* p. 349). The Registrar-General was empowered to call at any time for the production of women so married (*HKSP* 34/93 p. 108).

Another important stipulation was that the Society's wards could only be married as primary wives. This was to cause a dilemma, as we shall see below, but it ensured the status and self-respect of the women, and made certain that the Po Leung Kuk was not turned into a supplier of concubines.

Some prostitutes were also married off, and this the Registrar-General regarded as important since it was a way for them to start a new life, though the cynic may see it as transferring them from one form of bondage to another! When women repatriated from the Po Leung Kuk were married off by the charitable organisations receiving them, the Society still required a copy of the 'receipt' for the bride for its files (Kani 1979 p. 350).

By giving them away in marriage, the Po Leung Kuk did provide an opportunity for girls to start a new life. As a rule, of course, the Society did not think it proper to marry off women who were already married, but in extreme cases, exceptions were made, such as the case of Xi Yuehao. Xi was brought to Hong Kong by her husband and his brothers, who were detained by the police on suspicion of being kidnappers. The husband obviously intended to sell her as a prostitute. The Po Leung Kuk returned her to the Aiyutang in Guangzhou. Then the Aiyutang realised that if the husband took her back, he would sell her again, and that if the case was taken before officials, she would still be handed back to him. With the parents too frightened to come for her, the Aiyutang sent her back to the Po Leung Kuk, reasoning that, since under British law women had the right of self-determination, there was nothing the husband could do to her in Hong Kong (PLK Vol. 4, 2 September 1888).

In the case of Xie Ruilan, it was the Registrar-General who noted that, being a married woman, she should not be married off by the Po Leung Kuk. However the directors replied that they had discovered that her first husband had died, and though she had nominally remarried, she had never seen her new husband, and his family had decoyed her to Hong Kong and sold her to Singapore. Only then was the Registrar-General's permission given (PLK Vol. 1, 14 May 1884).

The Registrar-General, obviously, was deeply involved in all the workings of the Society, and particularly so regarding marriage, and this is best illustrated by the bridal sedan controversy.

In Chinese marriage custom the bridal sedan was an indispensable accompaniment. No legal marriage was complete without it. On one occasion, both Frederick Stewart, the Registrar-General, and James Stewart Lockhart,[28] the acting Registrar-General, were very upset to find that one of the wards had been given away in an ordinary street sedan rather than a red bridal sedan. The directors' defence was that since some girls had led improper lives, they could not be treated in the same way as respectable girls. The Registrars-General, on the other hand, were adamant that girls married from the Po Leung Kuk must be given full recognition of their primary-wife status and not be treated as inferior to other brides-to-be.

Related to this was the issue of marrying women off as second wives or concubines. Lockhart claimed that the office had never sanctioned the taking of a girl as a concubine as there was not enough security for the girl concerned, because among the Chinese the union with a concubine was not considered as binding as the union with a legal wife.

The dilemma was that many of these women had been prostitutes, or previously married, and were, according to Chinese thinking, inferior to virgins, and so did not deserve red bridal sedans. It was difficult finding men who would concede them full primary-wife status, with the result that many of these women would be stuck at the Po Leung Kuk with little prospect of finding a husband at all. This wrangling between the Po Leung Kuk and the Registrar-General went on for a long time, creating much hard feeling.

Stewart and Lockhart, however, believed that since the women had come under the protection of the Society, they should be shown proper respect. As a result of their insistence, henceforth whenever a wedding was celebrated, the document for hiring the bridal chair had to be produced and then filed in the Registrar-General's office with the other documents (*HKSP* 34/93 p. 32; PLK Vol. 1, 24, 26, 28 May 1884).

Return to Brothels

In a number of cases women expressed their wish to return to the brothels. As each 'rescued' prostitute was questioned intensively to determine that she had not been sold or coerced, these women must have made these decisions deliberately. The committee's comments on these cases were invariably that since these women had shamelessly chosen to continue indulging in this, there was little they could do but to release them (Kani 1979 pp. 125–6).

Chinese Patriarchy in a British Colony

We may say that one of the Po Leung Kuk's major achievements was to uphold a peculiarly Chinese form of patriarchy at a critical point of its development in Hong Kong. In the 1870s, Smale's condemnation of slavery in any form, the mid-decade ordinances and Hennessy's initial antagonism to human trafficking could have seriously undermined Chinese patriarchy. But after some fanfare for anti-slavery principles and in face of strong opposition from the Chinese community, official inertia set in again. In practice, to have actually enforced the law against human trafficking would have put an end to the *mui tsai* and brothel systems, and affected concubinage as well. In principle, it would have eroded the very basis of Chinese patriarchy, which was the patriarch's supremacy over members of the household, manifested in his right to hold property in them.

The triumph had long-term consequences. The *mui tsai* system was left unquestioned until 1917, and even then, despite Colonial Office pressure on the

Hong Kong Government to abolish the system, and despite various commissions and ordinances, the Hong Kong Government succeeded in procrastinating. It was only after World War II that the system finally disappeared in the urban area;[29] in the New Territories, the practice went on for another decade or so. Only in 1923 was prostitution regulated, with a view to ensuring that the women were entering the profession of their own free will. Before this the main aim of the regulation had been to check venereal diseases (Miners 1987 pp. 196–7). And concubinage persisted until 1970 when marriage laws were overhauled and monogamy enforced (Jaschok & Miers above).

One reason for the Society's success was the policy and attitude of the colonial regime. Britain was interested in Hong Kong primarily as a trading post. The colonial government, mainly responsible for maintaining law and order and maximising conditions for trade, did not even pretend to be concerned with the moral quality of people's lives.[30]

The segregationist policy Elliot had proclaimed in 1841 provided the grounds for the Chinese to be ruled by their own customs. The Registrar-General's office further cushioned them against the intrusion of English law, which, unless public order was affected, left the Chinese alone and was not always vigorously enforced. Colonial rule in Hong Kong was a form of indirect rule through an established native elite. In order to collaborate effectively with it, the government needed to accommodate its social if not political values. The fact that it could assist in maintaining stability without financial cost to the government, and lighten the administrative load, made it all the more welcome. It was also clear that the directors of the Po Leung Kuk with their extensive contacts were able to achieve much that the government could not. The constant warning that if the Society was abolished its work would be left on the government's lap was enough to make the government appreciate the value of its existence.

Even though the Po Leung Kuk had no legal status before 1893, its close association with the Registrar-General's office created the impression that the Society had official or quasi-official powers, and allowed it to wield influence in wide circles. Despite their occasional disagreements, the Po Leung Kuk directors fully realised the value of this association, and pushed the government for a grant to place it on a firm and lasting basis (*HKSP* 34/93 pp. 38–9). The Po Leung Kuk Incorporation Ordinance of 1893 established a Permanent Board of Directors, including the Registrar-General as *ex officio* President, and the Chinese Legislative Councillor as *ex officio* Vice-President. In addition, a committee was to be elected for the term of one year only and to consist of not less than six and not more than 12 members of the Society. This enhanced the status and influence of the Po Leung Kuk; the Ordinance for the Protection of Women and Girls of 1897, which increased the Registrar-General's powers in this area, also indirectly increased the Society's.

Moreover, it must be remembered that, apart from the few radical expatriates raging against slavery and human trafficking, many government officials tolerated the Po Leung Kuk's work because they had much in common. Fundamentally, authoritarianism was a tendency common in both colonialism and patriarchy. In fact, it is argued that the mid-19th century saw the height of patriarchy in Britain among the middle classes, with an intensification in the domestic ideology. Victorian men's condemnation of women's non-marital or extra-marital sexuality contrasts sharply with the view that their own sexual lapses were excusable on the grounds that they were a natural result of their virility. Violence against wives by husbands was condoned as legitimate 'so long as the rod was no thicker than a man's thumb'.[31] Thus, we may safely assume that many of the Britons in Hong Kong, both in public and private sectors, shared these views. They might not agree with the extreme features of Chinese patriarchy, such as the *mui tsai* system, concubinage and brothel slavery, but they would not have been uncomfortable with the general male-dominated attitudes of the Po Leung Kuk directors.

The few expatriate critics complained more about the Po Leung Kuk's *modus operandi* than its operating principles. Some criticised its extra-judicial powers when investigating cases before they came to the magistrate, and complained that the fact that evidence was not taken in public made the situation even more unjust (*HKSP* 34/93 pp. 47, 136). It interfered with police work, some thought, by making policemen neglect their duties regarding kidnapping. Its great influence among the Chinese population stirred up fears of an *imperium in imperio* and it was feared that individual directors might abuse their influence (*ibid.* p. 134; Sinn 1989 pp. 171, 181). Above all, its close relations with Mainland Chinese officials caused alarm and dismay among the European community. Much less, however, was said about the injustice of patriarchal practices *per se*.

However, even though it may be assumed that the colonial government shored up patriarchy, we should note in all fairness that the latter was not left completely uncurtailed. Despite segregation, English law was not completely without effect on Chinese lives in Hong Kong. The many occasions women were allowed to go free testify to this. This is why, though the Society successfully helped to prosecute many cases of kidnapping, it was often frustrated in the 'grey area' cases of *guaiyou*, which had been one of its primary concerns. Moreover, the system of marrying women off, introduced at the Po Leung Kuk and under the close supervision of the Registrar-General, also gave women a degree of self-determination uncommon in China. In addition, since the Registrar-General tolerated but did not officially recognise concubinage,[32] and since the union between a man and his concubine was regarded as less binding than that with a primary wife, many concubines were also allowed to leave their husbands if they wished. Freedom for women, however limited, was more attainable in Hong Kong than on the Mainland, and the many cases of women fleeing to Hong Kong show that Chinese women did take advantage of this. In time, employment and educational opportunities also provided potential for freedom from controls and for change.[33]

Despite the leeway given Chinese social customs, the colonial state restricted its scope of action and, however non-interventionist, could act as a direct mechanism or mediating structure affecting social relations through legislation and the specific way administrators enforced the law. The interaction between the state, individual officials and the local elite played a vital role in moulding Hong Kong society in the 19th century.

It is only too easy for us living a century later to censure the Po Leung Kuk for upholding what appear to us unjust and inhumane principles, and perhaps this is not the place to make judgments. However, we may criticise the Society solely from a pragmatic point of view. It had been set up to suppress kidnapping, and was not more successful in this because it did not try to eradicate the real roots of the problem. Though it tried to differentiate between legal and illegal human trafficking, it could not bring itself to face the fact that they were interwoven. Prostitution, concubinage and the *mui tsai* system were, so to speak, points on a spectrum, and the different forms of women as property shaded into each other. As long as these institutions were allowed to exist, human trafficking would continue and so would kidnapping.

Postscript

Anyone examining the Po Leung Kuk's records cannot help but marvel at the directors' dedication, conscientiousness and deep sense of responsibility. They did protect the women in the way they believed best. Typical of the social elite operating in countless localities throughout China who undertook the mission to ensure the material and spiritual wellbeing of the common people, they were conditioned to uphold, not to criticise or challenge, orthodox moral values. More important, a sense of compassion and high seriousness pervades the records. It is said that 'Patriarchal behaviour is incompatible with autonomy, but not with love'.[34] This perhaps epitomises the work of the Po Leung Kuk in the 19th century.

Abbreviations

PLK Vol. 1 – 'Laiwang xinbu' (Incoming and outgoing letters) 1884, to 6th lunar month.

PLK Vol. 2 – 'Laiwang xinlu' (Records of incoming and outgoing letters) 1884, from 6th lunar month.

PLK Vol. 3 – 'Dinghai nian gebu laiwang xin chaoteng bu' (Copies of incoming and outgoing letters from all ports for the *dinghai* year) 1887, from 8th lunar month.

PLK Vol. 4 – 'Wuzi nian gebu laiwang xinbu, yihao' (Incoming and outgoing letters from all ports for the *wuzi* year, part 1) 1888.

PLK Vol. 5 – 'Wuzi [sic] nian gebu laiwang xinbu, erhao' (Incoming and outgoing letters from all ports for the *wuzi* year, part 2) 1889, from 1st lunar month.

PLK Vol. 6 – 'Jichou nian gebu laiwang xindi bu, yihao' (Copies of incoming and outgoing letters from all ports for the *jichou* year) 1889, from 6th lunar month.

PLK Vol. 7 – a volume with no title, but with '*yi'an*' added on the first page subsequently; contains copies of minutes of meetings and records of cases of special interest, 1880–5. It includes some early material before 1879 copied from the Tung Wah Hospital files.

PLK Vol. 8 – 'Zhi shi lu', 1887; this contains records of daily events and copies of correspondence with the Registrar-General and copies of incoming letters.

PLK 1978 – Po Leung Kuk, Board of Directors, 1977–78, Centenary History of the Po Leung Kuk Hong Kong 1878–1978 (bilingual), Hong Kong 1978.

HKSP 1/87 – Hong Kong. 'Correspondence respecting Child Adoption and Domestic Service among Chinese', Sessional Paper, 1 of 1887.

HKSP 34/93 – Hong Kong. 'Reports of the Special Committee ... to Investigate and Report on ... the Bill for the Incorporation of the Po Leung Kuk ... ', Sessional Paper 34 of 1893.

'Correspondence re Chinese Slavery' – 'Correspondence respecting the Alleged Existence of Chinese Slavery in Hong Kong' (March 1882) [C.-3185], Great Britain, Parliament. British Parliamentary Papers: China (Irish University Press, Shannon, 1971) Vol. 26.

Notes

1. While pursuing my research on the Tung Wah Hospital during the early 1980s, I was delighted to discover the Po Leung Kuk Archives. This is perhaps one of the richest holdings of source material on the social life of Hong Kong as well as of modern China. I am therefore most grateful to the two editors, who by proposing such a compelling subject for this book, have provided me with the opportunity to return to them. The records date from 1878 when the institution was first planned and organised. They contain the inmates' testimonies and voluminous correspondence related to them. Together they reflect the function and role of the Po Leung Kuk Committee as a patriarchal elite in a British colony. Moreover, they enable us to reconstruct the lives of ordinary Chinese men and women in the Pearl River delta from the late 19th century. These people, whose voices are so seldom heard in historical records, speak loudly and clearly through these documents. The Archives can be used to tell many stories besides this one and I hope that other scholars will now study them.

2. For an official history of the Society, see Po Leung Kuk, Board of Directors, 1977–78, *Centenary History of the Po Leung Kuk Hong Kong 1878–1978* (bilingual), Hong Kong, 1978 (PLK 1978). For a more critical account, see J.H. Lethbridge, 1978a pp. 72–103. A lesser known, but extremely important, work on the Po Leung Kuk is H. Kani 1979, which is extensively based on the Po Leung Kuk's archives. A Chinese translation has recently appeared – Sun Guoqun and Chao Congpo (trans.) *Juhua – bei fanmai haiwai di funu* ('Juhua' – women sold abroad).

3. See P. Laslett (ed.) *Patriarchia by Sir R. Filmer* (Blackwell, Oxford, 1949) and Katherine O'Donovan *Sexual Divisions in Law* (Weidenfeld & Nicolson, London, 1985).

4. Kani 1979 pp. 217, 307; Niida Noboru, 'Mei sei jidai no hitouri oyobi hitojichi monjo no kenkyu' (The study of documents relating to the sale of persons and hostages in the Ming and Qing dynasties), *Shigaku zasshi* (Tokyo) Vol. 46 (1935) No. 4, pp. 69–98, No. 5, pp. 49–100, No. 6, pp. 58–86. The examples of transaction documents, some actual and others taken from guides to letter and

document writing, in Hayes 1990 pp. 33–47 testify to the prevalence and openness of the transactions.

5. An account of the workings of the prostitution system in Hong Kong is given in Report on CDO 1880.

6. The best accounts of Chinese emigration and its abuses is given by Kani 1979; see also Irick 1982, Campbell 1923.

7. Generally, the trend of female emigrants followed male emigrants; thus before the 1870s, the majority of women headed for North America. From the 1870s onwards, as *Nanyang* (Southeast Asia) became the major destination of Chinese male emigrants, it also became the major destination for female emigrants (Kani 1979 *passim*; Chiang).

8. See Kani 1979 pp. 223–8. In fact, the first group of kidnapped women from Annam (Vietnam) were sold probably as early as 1867 (*ibid.* p. 224).

9. For the Tung Wah Hospital's role regarding emigration, see Sinn 1989 pp. 101–17.

10. Another reason, it seems, for a specialised association was that the Tung Wah Hospital was under fire for taking on too many extra-hospital duties (Sinn 1989 p. 113).

11. Bowen to Derby, 6 August 1883, #175: Great Britain, Colonial Office, Series 129/211. A Tung Wah Hospital Committee deputation met Bowen, and one of their strongest grievances was that there was no law in Hong Kong as in China to punish adultery criminally. They urged moreover that it was the plain duty of the executive government of the colony to arrest Chinese wives from the neighbouring provinces of China who sometimes took refuge under the British flag, and to hand them over to the authorities at Guangzhou to be dealt with according to Chinese law. Also see Norton-Kyshe 1971 Vol. 2 p. 201.

12. See evidence given by Ho Fook, *HKSP* 34/93 p. 21; Eitel quoted in *HKSP* 1/87 p. XXIX. The Chinese also believed that kidnap cases were dealt with more efficiently by Mainland magistrates (PLK, Vol. 4, 6th lunar month/19th day [27 July] 1888). In this as in other cases, they were bewildered by the loopholes in the British judicial system.

13. In fact, the sentences were provided for by ordinances of 1865 and 1872. 'Declaration by the Chief Justice', 'Correspondence re Chinese Slavery', pp. 5–10.

14. *Ibid.* p. 9.

15. This view was shared by J.J. Francis in a Memorandum, 'Correspondence re Chinese Slavery', pp. 100–4.

16. Kani 1979 pp. 142–3. Kani also gives the story of a girl who, after being kidnapped, was taken to Singapore, then to Penang and then Deli in Sumatra, and not finding a purchaser there, was finally taken to Sabah (*ibid.* p. 218). For the sale and resale of *mui tsai*, see *ibid.* pp. 134–5, 298–9, 311. Also see PLK Vol. 1, 1st lunar month/18th day (14 February) 1884.

17. Actually there was much discrepancy between the written penal code and practice in China. See Meijer 1979; Jamieson 1921.

18. Interestingly, James Watson, writing in 1980, agrees that the *mui tsai* system was not slavery. J.J. Francis, however, thought that 'if these girls [prostitutes] are not

slaves, in every sense of the word, there is no such thing as slavery in existence'. See his memorandum in 'Correspondence re Chinese Slavery', p. 100–4.

19. See Jaschok 1988 for the *mui tsai* system. For an account of the abolition of the *mui tsai* system, see Miners 1988 pp. 153–90, and 1990 pp. 117–31; Smith 1981 pp. 91–113.

20. 'Correspondence re Chinese Slavery', p. 28. In fact, the Captain Superintendent did not attend the meeting.

21. Relations between the Po Leung Kuk and the Tung Wah Hospital had been close from the beginning. One of the original petitioners, Fung Ming-shan, was a founding director of the Tung Wah Hospital and its director in 1872 and chairman in 1879. Another, Lu Li-p'ing, had been director in 1874. See PLK Vol. 7, 9th lunar month/7th day (2 November) 1887. In PLK Vol. 8, the early Po Leung Kuk records up to 1880 were copied from the Tung Wah Hospital files.

22. The Man Mo Temple Committee had been the leading Chinese elite group in Hong Kong until the Tung Wah Hospital was founded. Again there was an extensive overlap of membership. See Sinn 1989 pp. 15–7.

23. Table 59 in Kani 1979, p. 355, lists the occupations of the directors.

24. In some cases, the suspects were first taken back to the Po Leung Kuk where they would be questioned to determine if there was a real case against them, before sending them to the Registrar-General's office. This caused resentment among some people who felt the Po Leung Kuk should not perform such police functions, and even judicial functions in deciding whether the suspects should be sent to the police or not. The detention of suspects was also seen as unconstitutional.

25. Kani's preliminary checklist of the Po Leung Kuk Archives is invaluable (Kani 1979 pp. 99–104). Sinn 1984 pp. 195–223 also describes the archives briefly.

26. In 1898 the Japanese government presented the Po Leung Kuk with a silver bowl to thank it for returning a total of 40 Japanese women over the years. PLK 1978, Chinese section, p. 326.

27. A sample notice offering rewards for a missing girl can be found in PLK Vol. 2, 7th lunar month/24th day (2 September) 1885.

28. James Stewart Lockhart was acting Registrar-General in 1884 and 1885, Registrar-General in 1887, a post he held until 1901, and Colonial Secretary in 1895, a post he held concurrently with the Registrar-Generalship. An accomplished Sinologist, he was often more Chinese than the Chinese. See Lethbridge 1978b pp. 130–62; Atwell 1985; Airlie 1990.

29. Miners 1987 pp. 153–90; compare the difficulty Shen Jiapen felt in any immediate manumission of domestic slaves when he was commissioned to revise the law in the 1900s and abolish slavery in China (Meijer 1979 pp. 345–6).

30. Compare the policy of the Singapore Government toward the Chinese community in the 19th century in R.N. Jackson 1965.

31. Lewis 1986 p. 112; Walby 1990 p. 179.

32. *HKSP* 34/93 p. 32. The anomalous situation in Hong Kong was that the government did not recognise concubinage and polygyny but did not prosecute offenders.

33. In the last decade, there have been many studies of women in colonies to see if their conditions were improved or worsened by colonisation. The essays in

Etienne and Leacock (eds), *Women and Colonization. Anthropological Perspectives* (Praegar Publishers, New York, 1980) clearly show that it is difficult to generalise because conditions differed so widely from colony to colony. Lai 1986 also points out the variation *within* a society, in this case, British Malaya, because of the varied roles women played.

34. Lewis 1986 p. 112.

C. The Christian and Feminist Patriarchal Responses

8. Chinese 'Slave' Girls in Yunnan-Fu: Saving (Chinese) Womanhood and (Western) Souls, 1930–1991

By Maria Jaschok

Wer verlaesst, der bekommt [1]
  (Who giveth, shall receive)

In the Province of Yunnan, slavery is universal, and there is no philanthropic institution where girls who have been maltreated can find a refuge. Many Chinese are reluctant to interfere with a custom which has the sanction of antiquity, even though it has become a crime against humanity, but happily an increasing number of Chinese are prepared to join in any effort which has as its objective the amelioration of the conditions of the slave girls.

(Petition signed by China missionaries and others resident in Yunnan-fu for the funding of a Home for Freed Slaves in China, sent to the Treasurer of the Anti-Slavery and Aborigines Protection Society in London, 1 June 1930; papers of the Anti-Slavery and Aborigines Protection Society, Rhodes House, Oxford.)

This chapter explores the aims and attitudes of individual parties to the trade in *yatou* (slave girls, see also *mui tsai*), and their response to the various solutions offered to the girls' plight. This is a key to understanding the conflict over progressive and enlightened, as opposed to backward and unenlightened, womanhood (and thus nationhood) in which missionaries in China engaged. The missionaries worked from positions of social or ethnic privilege, yet they opened up avenues of change for some of the most oppressed and deprived groups of women. These changes clashed with remedies offered by the Nationalist Party and later, more fatefully, by the Communist Party. Under the Communist Party the sexual revolution brought the enforced submission of women whose lifestyles were at variance with what rapidly became a new patriarchal orthodoxy, in which the question of women was ultimately not for women to resolve.

The historical context in which the missionaries worked was extremely complex. Tensions accompanying political and economic modernisation, together with rivalry for control of the country under the Nationalist (Guomindang)

Government (1927–49), led to the politicisation of the cultural and familial spheres. With urgent demands for reform, the threatened erosion of patriarchal control of females – and thus of reproduction and domestic labour and of women as objects of social exchange – encountered deep resistance (Siu 1982).

It has been authoritatively argued that, where they had any impact, Guomindang policies to redress sexual inequality in the public sphere mainly touched urban and professional women, leaving rural and working-class women with progressively deteriorating lifestyles and falling expectations.[2]

Nevertheless, cultural changes – and changes in sexual mores – slowly spread beyond the centres of social change. Change came through the manifestos of political parties, and through the early revolutionary ideals of sexual emancipation to which the Nationalist Government was an heir, however diluted they may have become (Siu 1982). Progressive education and literature and the impact of educated professional women affected even conservatives, who could no longer always exert the customary male prerogatives over women unchallenged. The evangelical, educational and social (and thus political) work of Western missionaries contributed to this tension between patriarchal traditionalism and the embryonic, but stubborn, reform movements.

Chinese women intellectuals were often ambivalent over the missionaries, but for many professional women, missionaries rendered 'great service to the women of China', providing them with education and approaching women with a 'consistently liberating attitude' (Tseng 1931 p. 286).[3] Not all women activists shared this view. Some argued that Christian humility amounted to an irritating colonial arrogance which, by cultivating 'a slave-mentality' of admiration and dependency in relation to everything Western, stood in the way of women's revolutionary activism (Guangdong Funu Jiefang Xiehui 1926 p. 6).[4] In the end, it was not for Chinese women to decide. When the Communist Party deported the last missionaries in 1951, it also insisted, on behalf of women, that the path to sexual equality was non-negotiable. After the missionaries left, the fate of Chinese Christian women shows the unforgiving rigidity with which the Communist Party enforced its road to the salvation of women.

Following its victory over the Guomindang in 1949, the Communist Party consolidated its claim to the loyalty of women, building on its early advocation of women's rights. Addressing sexual equality as national policy, the Party reached back to its political work among women in the Jiangxi (1928–34) and Yanan (1935–48) soviets (Spence 1981 ch. 11). Through legislation (the New Marriage Law of 1950) and social intervention, notably in a series of *hunyinfa yundong* (Marriage Law campaigns) culminating in 1953, family control over the fate of its female members was drastically curtailed. Women won the legal right to conclude, and dissolve, monogamous marriage, and the transfer and sale of minors were prohibited (Davin 1975 pp. 84–94). But these advances in the status and rights of women came at a price. A growing Party monopoly of political life led to a monopoly of the path to the liberation of women, symbolised by, and institutionalised in, the appointed official flagship, the All-China Women's

Federation (Croll 1974; Davin 1975; Parish & Whyte 1978; for self-represen-tation, see APDC-ACWF Proceedings 1987).

The Party claim to sole legitimacy led to the denunciation of achievements officially identified as imperialist, feudal and bourgeois, and thus to the silencing of women who might have contributed to a gender inequality discourse more deeply rooted in women's experiences and visions. Among these were women such as appear in this chapter, women whose lives had been touched by missionary, rather than Communist, intervention, who had been saved from death or neglect, had benefited from training and schooling, and had come to identify with a creed which, though Western, was an indispensable source of consolation – their point of view did not count. When the Communist troops arrived to take control of Yunnan, these women were the enemy. Anger over the subsequent deportation of missionaries and fear for their own fate compounded the Christian women's sense of alienation.

Establishing a Home for Slave Girls and Setting a Christian Example in a Heathen Country

Apart from its first year and from 1932 to 1934 (see below), the Slave Girls' Home in Yunnan-fu was run by sisters of the small German Protestant Marburg Yunnan Mission, then affiliated to the British China Inland Mission, which founded the Home in 1930. It continued to be financed from London despite the presence of German sisters (a situation which later gave rise to tension). The main financial support came from the Anti-Slavery and Aborigines Protection Society (henceforth the Anti-Slavery Society) in London, then headed by John Harris, while the sisters were funded by their own Mission.[5] The Marburg Yunnan Mission involvement with the Home for Slave Girls began in 1930 and, despite difficulties and changes (it became a Girls' Industrial Home in 1934) it severed links only when, in 1951, the last missionaries were deported.

The missionaries were not the first to introduce homes for slaves. The Qing government had outlawed public and private slavery in 1910, but only after the establishment of the Republic in 1911 did action begin to match legislation. Homes such as the Home for Runaway Slaves in Yunnan-fu were established by various provincial governments. The Republican Government introduced further laws against the sale of women and children in the Penal Code of 1928.

It is arguable that missionaries in China were 'predestined' to find fault with native welfare provisions. Unquestioned belief in Western superiority and the imperative to 'save' and 'enlighten' in line with a Christian, and thus Western, way of life were compounded by a need to justify the missionary presence (Lum 1985 p. viii).

The China Inland Mission missionaries' emphasis on the need for social change, and the role of a home such as they envisaged in initiating change, particularly in the realm of women's lives, contrasts with the German Marburg missionaries, specifically Sister Frieda Wehle, whose concern was to promote a spiritual revolution. Missionaries in Yunnan disagreed from the start with the motives they attributed to those who set up the government-sponsored homes. They believed the authorities simply wanted to raise the market value of the girls by providing them with a few years of training before arranging marriages for them, and they preferred not to be compromised by working with the authorities to improve the primitive conditions in which slave girls were kept.

Mrs Maud Dymond, a New Zealand missionary working for the Bible Christian Mission in Yunnan, later famed for her dedication to the abolition of slavery in China, provides an insight into the missionaries' attitudes to Chinese efforts at social change (Dymond 1928). About 1922, accompanied by a Chinese bible teacher, she went to a government-run Industrial Home for Runaway Slave Girls which had been in existence since about 1911. As she tells it in her letter to John Harris of the Anti-Slavery Society in London, her purpose on this occasion was to 'teach these girls about the Gospel' (Dymond to Harris, 13 December 1929).[6] What she found she described as 'hell on earth'. She gives an account of it and of her abortive attempt to persuade the people running the home, and the city authorities, to introduce Christian principles and to stem the sale of the girls:

There were between 60 and 70 girls there, of ages between six years and 17 years. They were in a filthy condition and treated like animals. Most of them had been brutally treated, and many died because of their condition and no medical aid. Some were covered with festering sores, caused by being burnt all over with hot irons, some had an eye blinded, or gouged out, some an ear wrenched off, and other horrid brutalities. They slept on bare boards, had no tables, nor basins, nor chopsticks, some were almost naked, and nearly all were in filthy rags. There were a few who had not been so brutally treated, they were waiting to be sold. The money given by the public never reached these poor slave girls, it was all used up by the officials, and the only capital was the sale of the girls. For some years now, joined by other Missionaries, we have gone on trying to save these girls. Six years ago, we petitioned the Governor Tang, to stop the selling of these girls, to make the home habitable, and to provide teachers, to teach weaving, tailoring, etc. He readily complied, and granted most that we requested, and pasted outside the doors of this Institution large placards saying the sale of slave girls was prohibited. There was a public opening at which the Mayor presided, and said that we were going to teach the 'new religion', and dispense medicine. However, it was all a fiasco, nothing came of it, girls were sold, and brought better prices, because teaching made them more valuable. One day the Mayor bought about 20 girls in my presence, and when I protested, he said, 'I am only buying them for wives, they are all going into good homes.' This work is so disheartening, we cannot go on with it, the girls are always changing. We teach them and get interested in them, and then find they are sold into immoral houses. The only good we do is that our continually visiting them is a restraint, they dare not act so cruelly.

... We feel that we must establish a Christian Home and work with Christian Chinese, we are hoping to find a house very soon, but that is slow work, because so many houses, including one we had decided upon, were destroyed by the explosion. The home will be an Industrial Home, which we hope in time to make self supporting and we also feel that this home will demonstrate to the Chinese what slave girls may become, and so help them when they really begin to work in earnest for the abolition of slavery.

Thus the battle lines were drawn. Having been offered the opportunity of collaborating with the Chinese authorities to ameliorate social problems, the missionaries opted instead to challenge both the social system itself and those invested with the traditional authority to protect kinless unattached girls of the lower classes in customary ways. That Chinese officials regarded this as an acute threat to the social order is not surprising.

Whereas the British regarded all trading in women as slave dealing, the Chinese distinguished between the 'legitimate' rights of the *pater familias* to transfer women and their illegitimate appropriation by persons other than the head of the family or the appointed guardian (Sinn, above). And whereas Article 313 of the Penal Code of 1928 prohibited the sale of children and females, it did not touch the customary prerogatives of the *pater familias* (or of his representative) to transfer female members of the family if it was deemed that circumstances dictated such a measure (Cheng 1980 pp. 78–81).

The Chinese officials saw it as their duty to marry off these girls as wives to the poor, or as concubines into comfortably-off families. To progressive patriots and traditionalists alike, the Christian home must have seemed a gross interference by Western missionaries whom they had not wanted in their country in the first place. On the other hand this deepened the missionaries' conviction that these 'trials' were meant by God to test their dedication, and that 'truly benevolent institutions are only found in Christian countries' (Lum 1985 p. 110; see Lum for a discussion of 19th-century missionary perceptions of Chinese charitable traditions).

The consequence of this independent action taken by the missionaries was a relationship with officialdom fraught with tension and at times mutual distrust. Difficulties in enlisting the support of the local community in Yunnan-fu emerged right from the start. A petition sent to the mayor asking for protection for the girls and for police assistance in the liberation of cruelly treated slave girls elicited no reply. Similarly, the appointment of Chinese ladies, Christian and non-Christian, to the Christian Slave Girl Home's board of directors proved frustrating as all the ladies, without exception, kept slaves and were unwilling to go beyond helping to eradicate abuses. Despite these difficulties, within weeks, progress was reported on the setting up of a Christian-run Home for Slave Girls. A complex of low buildings, with 24 rooms, surrounded by a sizeable garden, had been rented, and before the necessary repairs and furnishings were complete, the first girls were admitted (Tindall to Harris, 13 May 1930). A day teacher was employed to teach the gospel and handicrafts. Skills such as making shoes and clothes were taught, initially to add to the Home's self-sufficiency, and weaving machines were bought for the small-scale production of clothes for sale, to bring in badly needed funds.

Even with the Home developing apace, the founders did not lose sight of the imperative to impress and educate the Chinese community. In June 1930, Maud Dymond noted a general interest in the venture to make the slave girls independent by teaching them useful skills. 'This Home will give a lead to the Chinese, because they do not know what they could do with slaves if they freed them' (Dymond to Harris, 6 June 1930). To which Harris might have replied that 'the Chinese' knew all too well what to do with freed slave girls. But references to resistance among local people to the abolition of slavery suggest complex and diverse reactions to the Christian alternative model set up in their midst. The governor of Yunnan did not free his slaves, and his response to the missionaries' exhortations to follow the example of his aunt, a converted Christian, and abolish slavery on his estate, was characterised by Maud Dymond as 'quite apathetic'.

According to another former missionary in Yunnan, the greater resistance came from private individuals who had no wish to lose their source of cheap and abundant labour.[7] Members of the government had often stressed their desire to adhere to the law, outlawing the transfer and enslavement, but so intense was local hostility that the missionaries did not always dare to venture outside, fearing that slave-owners might attack them. This deeply-felt local antagonism against Western residents weighed still more heavily on the Marburg sisters when the Slave Home itself became the target of several break-in attempts. At times the situation was so tense that the missionaries were removed from the Home.

Yet scarcely a month after Maud Dymond had denounced the governor for his moral apathy, the mayor of Yunnan-fu received much praise from her for announcing to the population at large official approval of the Home and his intention to support and assist the missionaries wherever possible. She wrote to Harris in London: 'So now we will not have any difficulty, in owners turning up and claiming abandoned girls after they see we have made them profitable' (Dymond to Harris, 11 July 1930). However, as a letter written by Harris in October of the same year shows, in the end the authorities refused to grant 'protector's rights' to the Home management (Harris to Bascom, 14 October 1930).

By November, there were 15 girls in the Home and more soon came, many of them in poor health and in need of nursing. (For case histories of some of the inmates in 1930, see Appendix A). Those girls who were healthy or sufficiently recovered from their ordeals were subjected to a highly regulated regime of both spiritual and more mundane training.

There are now 15 of them able to go through their days' programme, we have weaving machines, stocking machines, towel machines, and lace looms. They are making their own clothes and shoes from the cloth they weave, and we hope within six months to have stockings, towels and cloth on the market ... We have been very fortunate in some of the girls we have, they are intelligent and industrious, and with girls like these in a year or so they will support themselves and help the Home also. In the mornings until 11.30 they attend to domestic duties and have two hours learning to read and write. In the evenings they learn to embroider, an industry in which Chinese girls excel, they also learn Scriptures and to sing. The girls are very happy, and it was pathetic to see the gratitude they showed over a bed and a wadded quilt, and clean garments, and regular meals.

One girl cried, are those things really mine and she had never slept on a bed, nor had a covering, nor a meal where she sat down at a table, tears of joy streamed down many of their cheeks (Dymond to Harris, 13 January 1931).

At the end of 1930, reports were sent to England on the girls' first Christmas. Optimism was voiced that these girls were just the spearhead of social change: '… this work will grow, and these girls are worth saving, they will raise the status of Chinese womanhood, and China cannot rise higher than her womanhood' (*ibid.*). All around Yunnan-fu placards put up by the authorities denounced the sale of girls as a punishable offence but, as Maud Dymond noted wistfully, people did not take any notice, proclamations pasted on notice boards were torn off in a few days, for yet another proclamation to be pasted on. Despite this keenly felt indifference and at times outright hostility there was a sense of satisfaction at the progress made and a firm conviction that obstacles existed only to be surmounted.

The Missionary Frieda Wehle: 'When God Calls … '

In January of 1931 Maud Dymond joyfully informed Harris that 'an Associate of the China Inland Mission, a young German lady, is going to take charge of the Home'. She was to be funded by the Marburg Yunnan Mission, which made it clear that it was more than ready to face the new challenge: 'We are glad to have been entrusted with this wonderful work.' The British had not wanted control of the Home to slip from their grasp, but financial considerations had triumphed and Sister Frieda Wehle was appointed in place of an 'unsatisfactory' Chinese matron.

To use the missionaries' favourite metaphor, the 'darker' the forces of 'heathen' life, the greater the opportunity for missionaries to 'shine' in it – and to suffer gloriously. This dialectic of suffering and resultant spiritual happiness forms a continuous theme in Frieda Wehle's reminiscences of her China years. Published in 1974, they provide a fascinating testimonial to her formative years and to a personality which compelled her to eschew joys and comforts she craved (Wehle 1974). Dominated all her life by a strong attachment to homeland and family, she was driven to missionary work in a country of which she had little knowledge, that required arduous studies in English and Chinese for which she had little aptitude. She recalls the journey out to China as a voyage away from civilised shores into a world uncharted by the real, that is, God-given, codes of moral and social conduct. Her visit to the first Chinese temple she saw on arrival in Hong Kong elicited the response: 'The world of paganism. Into this God had led me, in order to carry into it the bright light of the gospel. Was I ready? No, not me. Moreover I could not speak a single Chinese sentence!' (Wehle 1974 p. 19).

After a period of introduction to work in China, and of Chinese language training to get her to the stage of giving a sermon in Chinese, she was sent to Yunnan, the China outpost for the Marburg mission. Her account of the journey conveys impressions of a thrillingly exotic country of great distances, its strangeness (read 'darkness') relieved only by all-too-sparse mission outposts – Christian oases inhabited by familiar shapes and intelligible sounds.

Her first posting was to Oshan (Eshan), a small town three days' walk from Yunnan-fu. Wehle was carried there in a sedan-chair. There she gathered her first experience of missionary work in a small Chinese community, working in a polio clinic and as a bible teacher, but her indifferent health gave rise to some concern in Marburg. She was transferred to Yunnan-fu to do work that would be physically less taxing and in a climate more conducive to a quick recovery.

Sister Frieda ran the Home for a comparatively short, but from all accounts stormy, period of Germanic *Sturm und Drang*. As played out in Sister Frieda's mind, the drama featured most prominently God and the Devil, all too often locked in cosmic battle, with the Home and Sister Frieda as a war-zone. This made for a more emotionally charged atmosphere than had been the case with her more prosaic predecessors. Under Sister Frieda social change took second place to the saving of souls. This arrayed her against the mighty forces of evil, in the shape of stubborn Chinese officials, unrepentant heathens of all classes and persuasions, and even some of the girls themselves.

It is not easy to piece together the end of her association with the Home and the town, after about a year. Indeed her own account of the years in China, published nearly 25 years after she left the country, and more than 40 years after she left Yunnan-fu to work in Yuki (Yuxi) in Yunnan, reveals little of the conflicts of that time, suggesting a conscious or sub-conscious attempt to avoid acknowledging what must have seemed to her a devastating failure.

The reports written from the Home to the Mission at the time are much more candid because they are spontaneous and emotional and reveal something of local people besides the 'dear Christian bible teachers' and 'grateful converts', references to whom fill the pages of her later book. The early reports from Yunnan-fu are written from the heart, from an angry heart at that. More information comes from Maria Wehrheim, who assisted her for a time in 1931 and whose letters to her family include personal impressions of life in the Home under Sister Wehle and of the girls in their care.

Female Fates: Challenge and Resistance

Frieda Wehle's reports to Marburg include stories told by the girls on admission to the Home. For example, there was 12-year-old Pao-chen whose parents died when she was six years old. Her grandfather, an opium addict, sold her soon afterwards for 20 dollars.[8] By the time she was 12, she had been sold five times; the last seller had received 100 dollars. Because of a frail constitution, she was unable to do the work her owner instructed her to do. Every day her mistress or the master's children would tie her to a pole and beat her with sticks. Her owner's house was close to the China Inland Mission, and one day the girl fled to the Mission and was brought to the Home. After much care, her health improved. But a stutter remained as well as a nervous condition which made her burst into tears quite suddenly and for prolonged periods (Report, Wehle to Marburg Yunnan Mission, 7 April 1931).[9]

A 13-year-old slave girl was brought to the Home so undernourished that she could no longer be saved and she died a few days later. She had been sold by her mother for 50 dollars. When she no longer had the strength to do the work her master demanded of her she was thrown out into the street, and 'a compassionate heathen man' brought her to the Home (Report, Wehle to Marburg Yunnan Mission, 4 June 1931). Other girls were found in the streets, abandoned, and Frieda Wehle would take them home. This had happened to Ai-lien, who had been sold by her relatives at the age of eight when her parents died. She had to look after her owner's child and was then accused of causing her charge to fall ill by bringing bad luck into the house; she was beaten and her hair torn out. She became one of Wehle's favourites; Wehle saw in her an instrument 'through which God glorifies Himself' (*ibid.*). At times other missionaries would send an abandoned slave girl to the Home, often in a state of total destitution and bearing the marks of maltreatment (Report, 3 December 1931; see also Appendix B for a detailed account of the story of Lien-Min).

The Home also lost girls, usually due to lack of support from the authorities when parents demanded a child back. Ching-hsiu had been brought to the Home when her mother, the sixth concubine of the would-be seller, was in prison. On her release from prison, the mother succeeded in getting back her five-year-old daughter, who was certain to be sold, according to Wehle (Report, 5 August 1931).

Not only the Chinese authorities, but also the British Consul in Yunnan-fu proved less than helpful to the sisters in their attempts to gain legal protection for their wards. They saw the consul as 'lacking guts', and as slow and ineffectual (Wehrheim to family, 19 December 1931). Sometimes girls were caught by former owners when out on an errand, never to be seen again. The sisters' and inmates' anxiety increased late in 1931, when yet another girl failed to return to the Home.

> Now the people of Yunnan-fu seem to know of our Home and are very cautious. Two of our children have already given us much anxiety, we no longer dare to leave the house. How dreadful it would be if an owner came to claim his runaway slave as happened to Sister Frieda last May! The children are so afraid (Report, Wehrheim to Marburg Yunnan Mission, 7 November 1931).

Chinese staff were approached and offered money to tell owners the whereabouts of runaway slave girls. Sometimes the situation was so bad that the only source of consolation, or so sighed Maria Wehrheim, was prayer (Wehrheim to family, 19 December 1931).

On the whole, missionary accounts of the inmates tell of callous abandonment of little girls by guardians and relatives and of their sale for reasons that include the need for money to buy coffins, to finance weddings and to buy expensive opium. They tell of buyers whose disregard for the humanity of a slave girl led to brutal treatment and callous neglect, in 'a heathen society' in which respect for the rights of ownership made public intervention very rare – even where a death occurred.

God and the Devil: Discipline, Prayers, and Domestic Sciences

The Home provided a refuge for girls maltreated by their masters and mistresses, and a place where slave girls could expect to increase their chances of a better life. They were taught reading and writing, with a strong emphasis on the literature supplied by the missionary societies, and some training in basic skills such as sewing, embroidery, weaving and general domestic tasks. Naturally, the greatest attention was paid to religious training and appropriate conduct, the hope being that at least some of the girls, on leaving the Home, would repay the effort by becoming the local religious (as well as domestic) mainstay of the Western missionaries.

Life in the Home not only provided the girls with an escape from their old servitude, it also brought challenges quite unlike those within their native culture. When the girls entered the Home, they entered a way of life that must have seemed as incomprehensible as it was alien. The routine of prayer, study, work and housework went by a clock of a different origin, and some of the girls, however grateful they may have been for their escape from persecution or hardship, resisted. Thus wrote the secretary of the Home Committee, Nurse Tindall, after having drawn Harris' attention to photographs of Sister Frieda and her charges:

> I am sure when you see the picture of the girls you will realise that work among them is very difficult, their natures are so spoilt and hardened by the cruelty they have received that they are little better than animals, and we feel Sister Frieda has a very difficult task. They are difficult to manage and quarrelsome amongst themselves, and several are mentally deficient or in such a condition physically that they will never be able to work (Tindall to Harris, 9 June 1931).

Scarcely three months after the start of her work, Sister Frieda found herself in 'a vale of tears'. It appears that, more than the others working in the Home (whether the Chinese bible teacher Hannah Liu or the young helper Maria Wehrheim), she attracted tantrums, hysterical outbursts and alliances of girls and staff opposed to her regime. The usual response was prayer, with the sinner left alone to ponder her wrongdoing. An often tearful resolution followed with more prayers and earnest sermonising about the devil's handiwork. Such was at times the effect created by the missionaries' exhortations to follow the right path, and the evocation of the consequences visited upon those who did not submit to God's laws, that girls were wont to throw themselves on the floor and cry copiously in repentance of their sins. Their spiritual guardians were no less capable of passion – each perceived deviation from the conduct they so tirelessly endorsed seemed a closing in of the all-pervasive powers of darkness. 'Yes, these are battles with the flesh and with Satan,' wrote Maria Wehrheim in an account of such an incident, '… the manifestations of the Holy Spirit' (Wehrheim to family, 18 November 1931).

When an incident was seen as serious, one woman would talk to the recalcitrant sinner while the other went to her room to pray. When some time had passed, Maria Wehrheim would go to the girl, now left alone, and after telling how much she had hurt *Jiaoshi Wei* (Missionary Wei, as Sister Frieda was called), the girl would then be told to ask for forgiveness. By that time the girl was totally malleable and ready to demonstrate 'such a readiness' to repent that Maria Wehrheim felt moved to declare this a unique capacity of the Chinese people – once properly enlightened.

But even given this heavy combination of prayer and psychological regiment-ation to enforce submission, not all girls could be moved, particularly since not all girls were 'as they should be' (Wehrheim to family, 14 October 1931). Among these were girls whose sexuality obviously troubled the missionaries. Nowhere are there explicit statements, but emphatic references to the desirability of moving the Home to another site less close to the grounds used by the military to drill the troops suggest a great deal of concern: 'This is not lacking in danger. You know about Chinese soldiers. We have to be careful with some of our girls.'

Tense relations with staff compounded the problems Sister Frieda was having with the girls. Teachers were found to have appropriated funds that should have gone to the Home, and some were apparently supporting girls in resisting discipline. They were, as Sister Frieda put it, 'doing things differently from us'. Thus, disagreement with two Chinese teachers in the Home led to conflict with certain girls. One of them, a 16-year-old, departed in the wake of the teachers' dismissal, but not before threatening to murder Sister Wehle if she did not leave Yunnan-fu. A dramatic episode followed which led to police involvement, with Wehle pleading with other missionaries and the Home Committee for support. It eventually ended in a jail sentence for the girl (Wehrheim to family, 19 December 1931; Report, Wehrheim to Marburg Yunnan Mission, 30 June 1931).

Much frustration also arose over the seeming inability of most of the girls to display the virtues cherished in German culture: disciplined and conscientious application to the task in hand. After five months of patient instruction in weaving and knitting, Sister Frieda admitted defeat and put a temporary stop to teaching. But she reported that a few of the girls were learning to embroider. She sighed: 'Much patience is needed to teach them. As it requires quite some skill to get them to take to work. Among them there are only a very few who work with motivation' (Report, Wehle to Marburg Yunnan Mission, 30 June 1931). Sister Frieda was so frustrated in her attempt to instil the work ethic that she had to remind herself that it was her mission to cultivate seedlings on hard (because heathen) soil, and to accept these 'embittered children, whose cold hearts only the love of Jesus could overcome' (Report, Wehle to Marburg Yunnan Mission, 6 October 1931). What she did not admit to was personal defeat: she had not succeeded in reaching the children's hearts, her most fundamental duty.

Sister Frieda's battle with the forces of evil was fought ceaselessly and untiringly. The very problems posed by her relations with the staff and the girls were another sign from God that she must try harder to wrest control from the 'enemy' – an enemy she thought was growing more desperate as the Saviour made his presence felt. The unruliness and lack of discipline, the listlessness with which the girls seemed to approach their daily responsibilities, were to her a worldly manifestation of a cosmic battle between good and evil in which only prayers could help.

The turning point came with the temporary stay at the home of the Chinese bible teacher Sister Hannah Liu, who led the prayer sessions and gospel readings held twice daily, morning and night. As Sister Frieda joyfully put it: 'It is an intervention in the Empire of Darkness, but we are certain God will triumph' (Report, Wehle to Marburg Yunnan Mission, 5 August 1931). In subsequent weeks Sister Frieda was ecstatic to see what she felt to be the spiritual conversion of sinful creatures into children of God. Not all of the girls underwent the miracle, she admitted, but with many she now felt able to talk about the life they could expect in heaven, 'the hopelessness of heathenism', and the joys of being among the Chosen.

> What before I had not dared to hope for, I could now experience when individual girls with tears streaming down their cheeks were lying on the ground and prayed for forgiveness.

She was now able to relate many incidents of piety displayed by the girls: how they prayed for each other in hours of need and visited the sick and the freshly admitted girls to encourage them to turn away from idols to the living god (see Lien-min's story, Appendix B); how proudly they now overcame the temptations to sin and to fall back into their old ways.

It would be interesting to speculate how much the familiar features and accents of Sister Hannah Liu and a more generous personality might have had to do with this change which Sister Frieda credited to God's divine intention, and whether Sister Frieda's failure to establish a rapport with the children did not stem from the strict and dogmatic way she treated them – the result of her conviction that God manifested himself through her.

The Fruits of Salvation

Considering the visions that missionaries such as Mrs Dymond, Miss Tindall, Sister Frieda, Maria Wehrheim, and others brought to their work with the slave girls, and the wider context in which they viewed this responsibility, how were those girls who proved particularly open to Christian teaching to carry the fruits of missionary education back into their society?

There were a number of girls who, because of their physical or mental sufferings, could only ever be a burden rather than potential helpers. The Marburg sisters' preference for healthy and industrious girls gave rise to some criticism and fears in later years that the girls in greatest need of care – the mentally or physically impaired – would be rejected by the sisters as useless (Dymond to Harris, 2 July 1933). These misgivings arose in 1932 when Sister Frieda left the Home, taking with her six or eight of the best working girls (Dymond to Harris, 24 August 1933). When Maria Wehrheim talked about her work with slave girls, she expressed the hope that after one year she would be in a position to take one of them home with her, 'for our household [duties]', but it had to be 'one of those who are loyal and grateful for having been set free' (Wehrheim to family, 14 October 1931).

Truly successful 'liberation' is here based on a mixture of criteria derived from the evangelical mission – conversion to Christianity, gratitude and loyalty to missionaries, and an understanding of proper feminine conduct based on the ideal Christian woman, manifesting itself in a love of cleanliness, order and good housekeeping. Girls who met these requirements were taken into the missionary orbit and prepared for duties which ranged from domestic work in the households of missionaries to helping disseminate the gospel.

Approved Christian families were sought for them to marry into, so as to lay the foundation for a larger Christian community. And the most 'chosen' among the girls were recruited to carry the gospel to people living in remote areas, ethnic minorities and those speaking languages not known by the missionaries.

For the girls, the missionaries offered a rare escape route from lives of suffering and neglect.[10] They also opened up opportunities for an improved livelihood and material security. If left with their owners the best they could hope for would be to become the wife of a poor man or the concubine of a rich one. Girls from the Home, however, could marry into a Christian family where they would be the sole wife, and where Christian precepts demanded that they be treated with a respect their social station did not command. They might also become preachers or bible teachers, with a standing in the Christian community ordinarily unattainable in Chinese circles.

One such success story, both in terms of the missionaries' criteria of success and of the slave girl's expectations of the future normally in store for her, is the case of Phoebe (*Fei-bi*).

In a letter home, Maria Wehrheim identifies her as a 'loyal, intelligent girl, from a good family'. Phoebe excelled in all the qualities Maria Wehrheim found desirable in a good helper. At the time of writing, she was 15 years old. Her mother had died when she was 10. Such had been the father's grief over her death that he took to opium. In due course, he sold all his property to satisfy his cravings and was left with only his daughter, who he intended to give to the highest bidder. A friend of the family took pity on the daughter and managed to persuade him to send her to the Home for Slave Girls, to free himself of the financial burden of supporting her (Wehrheim to family, 28 October 1931).

At the Home, Phoebe became one of the model students and a favourite with the missionaries. And not surprisingly she was the one Maria Wehrheim sought to take with her into the household she hoped soon to set up with her fiancé.

The Ladies' Committee of the time consisted of Christian and non-Christian Chinese ladies, all members of the slave-owning class. Sister Frieda Wehle and Maria Wehrheim had already complained that they were not the sort to make sacrifices, and no 'spiritual rapport' existed between them and the missionaries (Wehrheim to family, 28 November 1931). Moreover the Committee was too supportive of unco-operative Chinese staff, to the detriment of discipline and good housekeeping. Due to persistent conflict with the committee and its unwavering support for the well-connected but unco-operative Miss Shang, a Chinese teacher, the two German missionaries left the Home on 30 January 1932, and Miss Shang took charge.[11]

They went to the nearby School for the Blind, run by a Marburg sister. A few days later, Phoebe and three other girls requested permission to leave the Home and join them. Initially, the German missionaries worried about the effect this might have on their presence in Yunnan-fu. Miss Shang, with tears in her eyes, had begged the girls not to leave but Phoebe responded: 'I must leave for the sake of my soul.' And in this way, writes Wehrheim, 'I got my Phoebe back with me' (Wehrheim to family, 1 February 1932). Phoebe's emotional identification with the missionaries, particularly with Maria Wehrheim, made it 'unbearable' for her to stay with Miss Shang. She had all along taken the side of her *Jiaoshi* (missionary) and firmly opposed Miss Shang. Even now, in her 75th year, she refers to her departure from the Home with a spirited pride (1991).[12]

Miss Shang was a native of Zhejiang Province, a baptised Christian who must have been recommended to the Ladies' Committee as the missionaries seem to have played no part in her appointment. She appears to have come from a privileged family. Her father was a pastor and she herself 'had many years [of teaching] experience in orphanages and boarding schools' (Tindall to Harris, 30 August 1930). Maria Wehrheim characterised her as 'nominally a Christian', and 'unfriendly to foreigners' (Wehrheim to family, 16 December 1931). Miss Shang was accused of trying to influence the girls against the *Jiaoshi*, although, notes Wehrheim, she knew very well that the Home was supported through the generosity of foreigners.

Miss Shang's resentment may have had its roots in personal animosity. On the other hand, it may have been based on nationalistic sentiments – sentiments shared by patriotic educated women throughout China (Guangdong Funu Jiefang Xiehui, 1926). Thus a close reading of the conflict between Sister Frieda and the Chinese teacher Miss Shang suggests that she feared that the missionaries' ultimate objective went beyond the care and rehabilitation of slave girls and entailed, under the cloak of Christian care, a process of 'Westernisation' unpalatable to educated Chinese women.

Phoebe joined Wehrheim's household after Wehrheim married Johannes Dietrich, to help with general household duties, and stayed until her own engagement to a preacher. They were in touch until the Dietrichs' departure in 1950 and re-established contact by letter after the Cultural Revolution ended, in 1978. Maria Dietrich died early in 1990, and the now 75-year-old Phoebe wrote to the widower:

> Although Mrs Dietrich [is] in Heaven, I think [of] her and miss her forever. I lived with her when I was a little girl and you showed your concern for me all the time. There is nothing I can bring to you, but [I] still keep your kindness in my mind forever. I have no chance to see you and do something [for] you. Please, take care

of yourself (Phoebe to Dietrich, 17 October 1990; in the possession of the Dietrich family; original in English; uncorrected).

Discourses on Saving and Being Saved

In its original conception my interpretive framework suggested a one-way process of 'appropriation' of the cultural identity of a class of Chinese women by missionaries who strove to save their own souls as they engaged in the rescue and rehabilitation of the souls of non-Christians – a difficult, and thus, by their Christian logic, a particularly meritorious, vocation. Almost by definition, the missionaries' work with these most vulnerable women brought them into contact with the most 'accessible' and most marginalised women, the *yatou*. As Nurse Tindall noted in 1934:

> ... We find from the experience of the few years we have had the Home open, that it is only the girls who are incapacitated through mental deficiency or physical deformity or illness, very often caused by the neglect or cruelty these girls are made to suffer, who are unwanted and who we are therefore able to rescue (Tindall *et al.* to Harris, 8 February 1934).

There was a contradiction between the moral duty of the missionaries to support the abused and abandoned *yatou*, and the aim to Christianise the Chinese. Missionaries did whatever they could to grant refuge to all who sought them out, but the women with the greatest potential to assist in conversion were cultivated with the greatest care.

However, it was the rescue of sufferers that appealed to the congregations in the missionaries' homelands, who saw the rehabilitation of 'pitiable slave girls' as the rescue of helpless creatures from dens of 'heathen' darkness. The more appalling the circumstances, the more sympathetic the believers.

In my interpretive framework, the Chinese women at the receiving end of missionary activity may be seen as the helpless victims of religious zealots, ignorant (unlike many of their educated compatriots) and brainwashed by 'God's imperialists' (McCutcheon 1991). What is missing in my interpretation, however, became apparent only when I met the former protégés of the Marburg mission. Then I realised that their relations with missionaries had evolved over years of close, often intimate, interaction in the course of which both parties had changed and been changed.

In the summer of 1991, I visited Phoebe and her family, and Sister Hannah Liu and her companions, in Yunnan. Their lives since the departure of the missionaries from China are now proving crucial to my documentation of change. I became aware of the need to record both the early formative years of their assimilation under the cultural, religious and emotional influence of the missionaries, and the post-missionary time when they devised independent, creative, adaptive and flexible strategies to cope with China's political fluctuations and the regimentation of religious expression.

This shift in interpretive emphasis does not deny the consequences of unequal historical constellations which made the 19th century the 'great century of missions' and engendered the overriding goal of 'Christianisation of the world in one generation' (McCutcheon 1991 p. 1), and which cast the missionaries as the spiritual and cultural ambassadors of religious teachings so deeply embedded in Western ways of life that one presumed the existence of the other: Christianisation inexorably entailed Westernisation (John H. Connor 1991). Nor can one overlook the subjective, psychological imperatives which compelled so many missionaries to rescue heathen souls in faraway countries from the fires of eternal hell.

More narrowly defined, the missionaries' work of saving and rehabilitation, with its premise in the vocation to spread the gospel among heathens, imperceptibly gave them a personal stake in conversion. Success required the refashioning of the Other in a culturally familiar image. The claiming of Chinese souls for heaven became invested with an emotion which made each conquest a personal triumph. Sister Bertha Preisinger from Marburg tells of the conversion of a little girl shortly after her arrival: 'Thus I received the gift of my first little Chinese' (Pagel 1979 p. 12). Once converted, these souls 'belonged' to the sisters as God's creatures. Their fates, worldly or eternal, were to be decided by the sisters. With this claim, the missionaries reached deeply into patriarchal prerogatives.

The more gentle Maria Wehrheim expresses convictions as unshakeable as Sister Frieda Wehle that although she would have liked to work in a different field, she had been put to work in the Slave Home for a reason. In her words, to work with God's most oppressed and miserable creatures is a 'delicious service' to God. Her natal family, from whom she was separated by such a long and painfully-felt distance, was fortunate to give their daughter to such a cause, and she herself was blessed to be so given. She gave expression to her sentiment in the homily 'who giveth, shall receive' (Wehrheim to family, 19 December 1931). For Sister Frieda and Maria Wehrheim, the saving of Chinese souls was inseparable from the salvation of their own souls.

But the sisters were not the only makers of history. What about the part Chinese women played in these transactions with God? How do they perceive the merits of the 'delicious service' rendered to them? How do they look back at their saviours? And where have they steered their lives since the last missionaries left in 1951? Not all of the women are alive, not all can be traced. The picture is thus a partial one, composed largely of those personable and talented enough to have engaged the sisters' emotions and professional interests.

Phoebe, the woman who was to be sold as a *yatou* but was saved from the hopeless grind of daily servitude, fear of ill-treatment and an uncertain future (which she thinks she would not have survived), became instead a bible teacher and the daughter-in-law of a respected Chinese family. Thus not only was her soul saved but she emerged into a life which gave her security, safety and love. Even in 1991, the small group of missionaries who took her into the Home, foremost among them Maria Wehrheim, were her 'mothers', her teachers, her source of identity and her emotional centre. When she went to the Home as a little girl, the Western women in their strange black garb (the sisters were wearing the headdress and long coat of their order which are still worn today) were at first frightening to behold. But it was different from the fear she had felt when her father was preparing to sell her. This was more strange than upsetting to her – and the strangeness wore off quickly. Even now, in 1991, my Western features seemed more familiar (homelike, as she put it) than the features of the people around her. I reminded her so strongly of her beloved Maria Wehrheim that in the end, during our last conversation together, we sat by the table as the two had often sat: side by side, and hand in hand.

Phoebe's position in the sizeable Protestant community is that of a respected Elder. She goes to church regularly, and attends meetings held to discuss the appointment of much-needed bible teachers or the renovation of the church. Her opinions are listened to as one of 'the Early Ones' whose direct contact with Western missionaries grants her a special legitimacy in the church. She enjoys this so much that she refuses a comfortable retirement at her daughter's home outside Kunming. Her more crucial ties are with other Christians, many of whom she knows from the Marburg mission days. She also regards it as her sacred task to report regularly to Pastor Dietrich on the state of the church in Yunnan. She is conscious of the thread she is weaving between the old missionary society in Germany and the Chinese congregation, and she does not want it broken.

She does not resent the roles Westerners have played in China. She is grateful to her saviours, whom she misses deeply. She cannot forget, or forgive, the deportation of those she loved as her family. It engendered in her a deep hatred for everything Communist. The Communists may also have abolished the enslavement of women, but for Phoebe the personal and formative experience of liberation at the hands of the missionaries pre-empted any other claim on her loyalty. Her family is around her, but incomplete. And it was the Communist Party which broke up the most loving family she has ever known. Yet, interestingly, she also remarks proudly how 'Chinese' the church has become. Whereas 'in the old days' foreigners and rich Chinese occupied the front rows in her local church, now 'any ordinary Chinese' can sit there. She is patriotic and proudly self-reliant, and she is also emotionally loyal to the guardians of her childhood. For her, there is no contradiction. On the contrary, she is proud to have witnessed the development towards independence, which she believes could not have happened without the missionaries' intervention in her life and the lives of others.

Sister Hannah Liu says: 'I am God's instrument.'[13] She went through fire for her faith and her attachment to foreign missionaries. As an orphaned child, around 1913, she was given to Sister Bertha Preisinger, later Sister Frieda's fellow missionary, to save her from 'the danger unprotected young girls were faced with'. She grew up to become a highly skilled helper to the Marburg missionaries, and, when a young woman, she herself chose to become Sister Hannah, a mainstay of the German sisters. When the last missionaries were deported in 1951, she carried on with the work of preaching and baptising. Because of her high public profile, she was most cruelly interrogated by Party officials in the wake of the Three-Self Reform Movement of 1951 which was initiated to expel any remaining traces of Western influence from the churches in China.[14] When in 1954 she was sentenced to 21 years of hard labour, it did not break her, nor did she ever renounce her long association with the German sisters. Her faith in God, her chosen path of celibacy, the ties of sincere affection, even love, which bind her to the missionary sisters she knew both as child and adult, the loyalty which cost her so dearly when one statement condemning foreigners might have shortened her sentence – they all contribute to what makes her an extraordinary, even a charismatic person.

It is in a language of love that she speaks of Sister Bertha Preisinger, who took her in when she was a helpless six-year-old orphan and who became her 'mother': 'She did everything but give birth to me.' She addressed Sister Bertha Preisinger as *lao renjia*, literally Old Dear One, a form of address expressing both respect and a loving familiarity. The unmarried status of both the missionary sisters and Chinese women allowed for a direct and very personal bonding where mission-ising became inseparable from socialising. The women created extraordinarily close relationships. Missionary sisters adopted 'daughters', and their Chinese wards acquired 'mothers' and 'aunts'. More than 40 years after Sister Bertha's enforced departure, and many years after her death, Sister Liu, now in her 92nd year, is still 'homesick' for her *lao renjia*. 'We all lived so well together.'

The missionary sisters gave Sister Liu a cause to live for, supported her through school and college and thus gave her much-appreciated access to learning. She can never forget the gift of schooling. 'One must have a clear head, otherwise it is easy to go wrong.' The sisters also provided her with a source of strength which she is still tapping today: her communication with God through prayer. This capacity to derive consolation and direction from prayer made her self-sufficient and self-reliant when the whole political system weighed against her, and her own society castigated and disowned her 'as a foreigners' tool'. Ultimately, it was this closeness to Westerners, and her unrepentant refusal to denounce and revile them when pressured to do so in endless criticism sessions, which brought her agonisingly long years of hard labour. In prison she was ridiculed for her loyalty. But, as Hannah Liu puts it, she 'had to speak from the heart', and she refused to put down the women she loved. She was thus classified as a particularly hardened and stubborn reactionary and her sentence was accordingly harsh.

On several occasions despair made her want to end her life: despair over the mission station and its dependants, in her care since 1951; over the fate of the orphaned children she had adopted; over the patients she had nursed as a midwife, now without expert care (there was no other midwife in the district). Each time, 'God intervened' and something occurred to prevent her committing suicide. She relates these incidents wistfully. She does not say (she may not know, nor care) that her sufferings have made her a legend, a powerful symbol of endurance, in the Christian community in Yunnan (and beyond), where people speak of her with touching admiration although they have never met her in person.

Nothing seems to have diminished her passion, her energy, her gratitude to her saviours, and the stubborn determination to carry on with God's work in the face of recalcitrant Party leaders in her town. Her conviction that despite her advanced age she would outwit the atheist town cadres and expand the Christian congregation to include intellectuals as well as workers (to provide for future religious leaders) inspires the small flock to whom life without her is unthinkable. She is physically frail, but she has the heart of a lioness. Daily worship, prayers, bible classes, counselling of believers and would-be believers, correspondence with authorities for recovery of missionary property, devising strategy for the future of Christianity in the area, these are still her daily tasks. When she wanted to tell me what sustains her, she cited her last letter to Sister Bertha, written shortly before her arrest in 1954, in which she assured her *lao renjia*, 'I can never get lost, do not worry about me. Even if I must fall, I will fall into God's hands.'

The German sisters who departed so long ago from Yunnan still function as a vital source of reference, as role models who continue to provide guidance to the small community of women around Hannah Liu: whether in secular life, where drinking afternoon coffee and eating cake (albeit a pale shadow of German pastry) are an integral part of the domestic routine of old women in a remote county town in Yunnan, or in the religious sphere, inhabited in communal solidarity, where the unchanging pattern of individual prayer and group prayer continues to be a testimony to the past.[15]

The half-dozen women around Hannah Liu have been with her since the inception of the Home for Slave Girls. One of her helpers was saved from enslavement when she found refuge in the Home in the days when Hannah Liu took on the role of a mediator between Sister Frieda Wehle and the inmates (see above). They all remained unmarried and attached themselves to the community of the mission station which has become Hannah Liu's household, and a surrogate family for each one of them.

Are they 'wrong', misguided, misled by zealous white women who, following in the footsteps of generations of proselytising predecessors, merchants and soldiers, driven by their private urge for a release their own societies could not provide, came to project their religion onto those women who by virtue of race and class were the ideal 'virgin territory' to work on?

A. Albrecht-Heide suggests that colonial values and valorisations shaped social constructions of femininity and feminine duties that gave women's collaboration in the masculinist colonisation process a 'metaphysical' dimension. 'Male hordes colonise, female camp-followers 'culturise'' (Albrecht-Heide 1988 p. 12). Should we see women's contributions to alleviating suffering and social injustice in the colonies as testimony to their noble nature, or as the traditional feminine contribution to the task of nation-building?

In a wider historical perspective the personal motivations of parties to the process may appear of secondary consideration. And yet these women, in their reports, letters, official submissions and private musings, show a capacity for initiative and action, loyalty, valour, and endurance which must inform any recording of history if it is to do justice to their lives.

Furthermore, and equally crucial, many of the women whose lives were affected by missionary workers were saved from drudgery, neglect and highly uncertain fates. Nor did their gratitude diminish in subsequent years when it would have been opportune to suppress the memory of their saviours, revealing a lack of pragmatism which earned them societal outrage and selective punishment. Some of the women utilised opportunities granted by literacy, professional training and status in the religious community by virtue of association with the German sisters (who were increasingly regarded more like revered 'ancestresses') to bring about momentous qualitative changes in their own lives, and in the lives of those close to them. They did not feel in need of another source of liberation.

Chronology decided the engagement of loyalties. A person of the intelligence, organisational skills and commitment of a Hannah Liu might have done excellent work in the Communist-directed mass movements of the 1950s. On the other hand, she argues, and crucially so, that she might not have been alive to greet the arrival of Communism had it not been for missionary intervention.

The small number of missionaries in China and their relatively limited social engagement render comparisons between their impact and that of the Communists on women's lives not very meaningful. Nonetheless, the testimonies of women such as Hannah Liu and her companions, of Phoebe and the other women still alive who were saved by the Home make an eloquent case: Communist monopolistic claims on the liberation of women was not merely a negation of Christian beliefs and sentiments, it became a devastating negation of the identity of the persons so denounced.

Now less saliently anti-foreign, less rigid on the whole in its treatment of officially recognised Christian churches, the Chinese government permits Christian women and men to worship openly and profess their beliefs without fear of political reprisal, even if membership of a church is not conducive to career prospects.

Current estimates of the size of Christian churches in China suggest a total of about six million believers. Protestants account for about half of the total (Han Wen-zhao, quoted in C. Tremewan 1985 p. 15). Phoebe's granddaughter, now in her early 20s, is a baptised Christian and churchgoer because, as she told me, 'Our lives are so empty. We are so bored. What can we hope for? At least believing gives some meaning to our future.'

It seems to me that the active implementation of such Christian precepts as human compassion and charity for the needy and socially vulnerable by the heirs of the missionaries has, through the mediation of time and space, turned a historical situation, tainted by colonialist co-option, into a social process *within* Chinese society.[16] What is taking place now is the resolution of the conflict between different codes of conduct in which the women actively engaged claim 'kinship' (and proudly so) with non-Chinese, but equally fiercely claim the right to legitimate space in Chinese society. Looking into the future, one might speculate whether their social and religious identities will not become entirely (and non-controversially) Chinese, with the Western 'ancestry' progressively of value or relevance only to a dying generation of the missionaries' spiritual descendants and, conversely, hardline Party ideologues.

As for the younger generations of Christians, and particularly the women, as the most active among them, claims to social relevance will be judged by their conduct and enacted beliefs, and their contribution to a society in which the search for meaning is no longer mechanically derived from a centrally-steered, Party-loyal propaganda apparatus.

While Albrecht-Heide's critique of women's collaborationist roles in the colonial enterprise, of which the task of religious conversion constituted a major facet, is all too persuasive, a microscopic treatment of the relationships of these women reveals the importance of treating relationships dialectically and dynamically, acknowledging the capacity of all the parties to mediate the processes by which history and life-histories are constituted. Thus the 'metaphysical' contributions made by certain missionary women, riding on the crest of a last wave of colonialist enterprise in China, are grasped as an opportunity through which women like Hannah Liu and Phoebe could come to discover and develop their potential for strength, compassion and charity.

Archives

Marburg Mission Archive, Marburg an der Lahn.

Papers of the Anti-Slavery and Aborigines Protection Society, Rhodes House, Oxford.

(Private collection) Wehrheim letters in the possession of the Dietrich family, Marburg. By permission of Pastor J. Dietrich.

Interviews

Pastor Dietrich, December 1989, December 1990.

Pastor Zhang, Shanghai, June 1991.

Phoebe and family, Kunming, 1991.

Sister Hannah Liu and community, Eshan, 1991.

Notes

1. Letters from Maria Wehrheim, in the possession of the Dietrich family.
2. For the best account of the period, see Bobby Siu 1982. Also, Margery Wolf 1985.
3. Although the number of Protestant Christians never rose above 0.2 per cent, in the 1930s 35 per cent of the Chinese elite had received a Christian education, 90 per cent of all nurses were Christians, and 70 per cent of all hospitals were mission institutions (Barrett 1982 p. 233).
4. As James McCutcheon points out (1991), unlike missionary success in the Pacific in the 19th century, where missionaries preceded colonial governments, 'in Asia the linkage of missions with Western colonialists has been a major factor for the slow growth of Christianity in that region' (p. 2). Around 1900, Chinese folk-religionists constituted 79.7 per cent of the population, Christians made up 0.4 per cent (Protestants about 0.1 per cent) (Barrett 1982 p. 231).
5. The origins of the Marburg-based Protestant mission can be found in the late 19th-century Prussian revivalist movement (*Erweckungsbewegung*) which in

1899 inspired four young women to form the first community of deaconesses. Guided by the charismatic Pastor Theophil Krawielitzki, the community later moved from Vandsburg in West Prussia to Marburg, where an astonishing spiritual growth resulted in the foundation of several more convents (*Diakon-issen-Muetterhauser*), in Germany and abroad. In 1909, the first sister departed for Hunan in southern China. She was later joined by three more sisters sent by the Vandsburg Mission. In 1928, after a long break caused by World War I, a group of sisters, among them Frieda Wehle, departed for China, this time to Yunnan, designated by the London-based China Inland Mission as their new field of missionary activity. In 1929 the Vandsburger Mission changed its name to the (Marburg) Yunnan Mission. The Yunnan Mission annually sent out missionaries, deaconesses and pastors, until in 1939 their presence in Yunnan totalled 57 adults and 20 children. Connections with Germany were severed during World War II, creating great difficulties for the missionaries, cut off from funding and spiritual support at a time when conditions in China were deteriorating. In 1951 the remaining missionaries were deported, one of them Sister Frieda Wehle, who spent the rest of her active years, and her retirement, in Germany, where she died in 1984 (Arno Pagel 1979 p. 6; interview with Pastor Dietrich, December 1990).

The British China Inland Mission began its activity in 1865 under the leadership of Hudson Taylor and grew to be the largest mission in China, with over 1,000 missionaries in 1914. They adopted Chinese dress and customs, concentrated on small inland cities and towns, and eventually built up a self-supporting church of over 85,000 members (Barrett 1982 p. 233).

6. Unless otherwise stated, letters and reports to London from Yunnan-fu are in Brit. Emp. Mss. S.22, G691, Anti-Slavery and Aborigines Protection Society, Rhodes Library, Oxford.

7. Interview with Pastor Johannes Dietrich in Marburg, December 1990. His late wife, Maria Dietrich nee Wehrheim, assisted Sister Frieda in her work with slave girls.

8. It is difficult to estimate the value of $20 as it is unclear whether the currency referred to is in Yunnan dollars, Yunnan pounds, Hong Kong dollars, or Mexican dollars – all of these are mentioned in the Anti-Slavery Society files. All one informant was able to tell me was that 20 Yunnan dollars would have bought several weeks' supply of opium.

9. All reports to Marburg subsequently cited will be from the Yunnan Mission newsletter, *Bandsburger Zweig der Liebenzeller Mission im Verband der China Inland Mission*. In the possession of the Marburg Yunnan Mission, now called Marburg Mission. Marburg-Lahn, Germany.

10. For a discussion of women's marginality in traditional Chinese households, see Rubie Watson, 1991.

11. In 1934, Sister Nanny Bethge was appointed the matron of the Home and thus re-established its connection with Marburg.

12. Interviews with Phoebe, at the time about 75, and her family, in Kunming, Yunnan, in June 1991.

13. Based on interviews conducted in Eshan, Yunnan, in June 1991. Sister Hannah

Liu lives with her co-workers and helpers close to the former mission house, now inhabited by the families of Party cadres. The fact that the local government has been so reluctant to restore former church property to the Christian community is a constant thorn in the flesh of the small congregation of about 300 Christians. It is not a very hospitable environment in which to carry out proselytising. But the indomitable spirit of Sister Liu, despite her advanced age, carries the community. A large signboard over the front entrance of the house (rented by the adopted grandson of Sister Liu) announces the presence of a Christian household. In this private house, prayer-meetings, baptisms and bible classes are held. Public worship is prohibited in Eshan.

14. In 1950, the Christian Manifesto signed by over 1,500 church leaders and eventually by 400,000 Christians acknowledged the contribution of missionaries but also attacked them as a part of Western imperialism. While Article 88 of the Constitution guaranteed religious freedom, it did so with the proviso that the churches eradicate all legacies of Western imperialism.

    In 1951, following the departure of all Western missionaries from China, the Three-Self Reform Movement was set up. Led by the YMCA (Young Men's Christian Association) executive Y.T. Wu, the Movement's objective was to assist churches in expelling whatever remained of imperialism, feudalism and bourgeois influence. Denunciation meetings were carried out where former missionaries and Chinese Church leaders were attacked; study sessions to bring about ideological thought reform were obligatory. Churches which succeeded in meeting Communist Party requirements were given permission to continue with their worship (Barrett 1982 p. 233).

15. The closeness and intimacy of which the Marburg sisters were capable contrasts strongly with Grimshaw's portrait of women missionaries in the Pacific whose anxiety over cultural 'contamination' and the possible consequences for the 'moral purity' of their families created a situation where the world of the missionaries was strongly segregated from the 'native' world (P. Grimshaw, 1983). The missionising, and thus fraternising with the natives, was left to male missionaries who, after their day's work was done, returned to the bosom of the family.

16. While it is not disputed that China has its own indigenous tradition of welfare and charitable concern, as documented in Raymond Lum's study (1985), its current diffusion into a state-run welfare system has depersonalised what in the case of my Christian informants are daily enacted personal rituals of compassion, a celebration of their 'difference' as believers in a non-Christian society.

Appendix A

Case Histories of Girls in the Slave Home 1930
(Tindall to Harris, Yunnan-fu, 14 November 1930).
Perhaps you would be interested to hear a very short account of the girls we have already admitted.

On May 3rd the first two girls were admitted.

Chang Shui Chen, age 16 was brought to the Home by an old Christian woman who had bought her when she was 4 years old, she has not been ill-treated and is therefore a quick intelligent girl.

Chang Shoe Ing, age 11 was brought from the country by her Uncle at her father's death and sold to a woman who has since become a Christian and has freed her.

Wong Ru Uie, age 11 was found on the streets for sale, her mother had just died and her father did not want to have to keep her.

Iang Ping An, age 21 was found on the streets by a C.I.M. missionary who brought her to the Home. When 6 years old she was sold by her mother for $40 (6/6) and later re-sold to a woman who treated her most cruelly, this woman beat her continually and finally threw her out of the house as unwanted. Her legs were a mass of ulcers due to the beatings.

Chang Mei Ing, age 14 was being sold by her mother but found and brought to the Home by a Church Member.

To Chia, age 12 was brought to the Home by a man who said she had been lying out in the street outside his house for several days, she is dumb and we think deaf, but she was in a terrible condition and on her head each side there are large deep scars like the scars from the burns of hot irons.

Ling Lu Teh, age 13 was brought from the country by her mother and sold when she was 8 years old, her owner would not let her have enough to eat so she ran away and hid in the Methodist Chapel.

Chiai Lu Chia, age 13 was owned by a woman who was a great opium smoker, for some offence she beat the child and turned her onto the streets.

Luh Neng En, age 18 was sold as a child by her brother when her parents died, her owner died and she was left to beg on the streets for a few months till she came to the Home.

Kao Chao Ti, age 16 was sold at 6 years old, she has always been very badly treated, she is nearly blind and lame and very undersized, we are going to keep her for a time and if her sight does not improve we are thinking of sending her to the Blind School.

Loh Ching Ih, age 20 and her sister age 12 were left without any parents, their elder brother who is a rickshaw coolie put them up for sale but they ran away, they wandered about the country for three weeks then found their way to a boy's orphanage kept by missionaries who sent them into the Home.

Wong Lan, age 15, was sold by her relatives at her parent's death, she was bought by some very cruel people and finally ran away and came to a Christian gentleman's home for protection. Since she has been in the Home her owner has been trying to get her back and we feel sure that if they could once get hold of her they would kill her, they are so angry.

Wong Ching Chen, age 13, was brought by her father from the country when she was 10 years old and sold for $25, she was found homeless in the streets by a missionary who kept her for a time then sent her to the Home, later some people came to claim her, but when they were told they must pay for her board during the time we had had her they refused, she was not worth that much.

Appendix B

Lien-Min: The Story of a Pitiable Little Chinese Girl.
(Told by the Missionary Frieda Wehle.)[a]

'In a very dark part of the old China lies – two hours by road from the town of Yuki (pronounced Uschi)[b] – a village, whose inhabitants are all called 'Liang'. About 50 families live there, descendants of one and the same ancestor.

'About 15 years ago [ca. 1935] something horrible took place in this village: one night all members of one of the 50 families were murdered in cold blood. Twenty-one persons found their death through the hands of murderers. Only one adult daughter escaped their fate because she resided in Yuki, where she lived as the married Mrs Ren. What were the reasons for such a horrible deed? Ah, at times things happen in heathen lands which we cannot comprehend and find it difficult to explain.'

Frieda Wehle then explains that it was the wealth of this family that had so aroused the hatred and jealousy of the other families that only murder could avenge their feelings. The murderers on the whole managed to escape justice. Among them was a man whose wife died soon after the bloody events took place. On her deathbed she told her one surviving child, a seven-year-old girl, that her father was a murderer. The man, needing money for his opium addiction, sold his daughter for good money to the one survivor of the family he had helped to annihilate. Mrs Ren lived close to the mission of which Frieda Wehle was in charge.

'Although she was one of our closest neighbours, she had never been willing to attend the nearby prayer service. Yet day and night she was haunted by the miserable fate of her murdered kinsfolk, whose death allowed her no peace. Her heart and soul were dedicated to revenge for the murder, so that her dead relatives might find peace. As a dedicated idol worshipper she sought secret guidance from pagan priests and sorceresses. They gave her advice to gain control over a family member of the murderers – even if she were a child – in order to perform the act of revenge. Only this way would the ghosts of the dead be pacified. This she agreed to do, and from that time on she only waited for a chance to execute her plan.

'It happened that Mrs Ren heard of the planned sale of the child. This was the opportunity she had waited for! A satanic glee now shone in the dark pagan heart. The woman hurried to offer the father of the child, through a go-between, six times the usual sum for such a girl. The heartless father agreed with joy, and the transaction was concluded. Without suffering a pang of conscience, the greedy man delivered his child into the hands of this woman; because nothing mattered as much as money for opium. What did he care about the child and its fate?'

Frieda Wehle then laments the destiny of so many slave girls who, like this girl, are sold by an addicted father and, without protection, are subject to the whims of their master. If they are lucky, their fate may be bearable, but more common, says Wehle, were stories of girls dying of maltreatment and malnutrition and neglect. Sometimes they were found by the missionaries and taken into the slave homes to be cared for. And even in these cases their lives could not always be saved as hunger and neglect had already taken their toll.

'From the time of her arrival at Mrs Ren's house, days of fearful suffering commenced for the pitiable little creature. Every night she had to lie down on a hard wooden plank to be beaten mercilessly by the vindictive woman all over her body with a hard wooden stick. Whenever Mrs Ren ran out of energy, her grown son continued the cruel treatment. At the end the victim would be deposited under the stairs where she had her austere resting place.

'During day time, the poor thing was made to work! Although the heathen neighbours heard the child's cries and moans so that they would shudder at it, no one dared to interfere with the evil Ren family. Was not the child their property with which they could do what they liked? And did not everything happen in accordance with the pagan priests' counsel? It was clear that only death could release the child from its suffering.

'The front part of the land was occupied by a Christian, Mrs Dwan. She had rented a shop from the Ren family. One day she confided to us the poor child's tale of suffering. But what was one to do? We sought advice from a Christian town official. This official informed the mayor and his wife of this matter, and he found a hearing. The mayor took the matter in hand. One evening, to the shock of the Ren family, their house was surrounded by soldiers. The child was forcibly removed and brought to us at the mission. What a pitiful creature lay there before us! What indescribable misery. It was questionable whether the child could be kept alive. The whole body was covered with weals and bruises, the hair in great measure torn out, an arm broken. But after a few days of dedicated nursing some improvement could already be detected. The friendly chief consultant from the hospital of the French consulate in Kunming, Dr Peret, came personally the long way to Yuki in order to look after the maltreated child. He too was deeply moved by the fate of the poor thing. No trouble was too much to bring about improvement. Progress was slow, but eventually energy returned. With what joy did we observe the first grateful smile on a face marked by pain!

'Now the Little One had to be given a name! What was more obvious than to give her the Chinese name of "Lien-min", of which the meaning in German is "Mercy". Bitter suffering she had endured, but she was granted mercy.

'I once asked her in a quiet moment: "Lien-min, what is your family name?" She answered: "Actually, I am from the Liang family; but I must not use the name Liang. This my mother ordered before she died. Thus I have no name. Ah, Lady Missionary, may I not take your name and call myself 'Wei' (pronounced Waj) like you?" I was content. From that moment onwards the Little One was called "Wei Lien-min", and she was pleased.

'Soon Lien-min learnt to understand how important it is for us human beings that, as the bible says, our names are known in heaven. In order that this may be so, a member of the yellow race must do the same as one of the white race: he must believe in the Lord Jesus and follow him. This Lien-min wanted to do with all her heart. The love she had experienced touched her innermost being. The other children at the mission had visited her conscientiously in her little room, told her of the love of Lord Jesus, and not only prayed for her, but also taught her to pray.

'During the time when the patient was still unable to move, the children knelt down beside her bed and thanked the Heavenly Father that Lien-min had been saved so miraculously. One day [the other girl] Ai-li said to her: "Now you must lie there praying; but when you are up again, you must pray on your knees. And when you are all well, then you can bow down before the Lord to thank Him. Before, we also lay down before idols, and they are only made of wood and clay. How much more must we pray to Lord Jesus who is our true God and Saviour."

'So she learnt to thank her Lord from the depth of her heart for the salvation of body and soul.

'When Lien-min was sufficiently recovered in strength, I brought her to Kunming to Sister Adele at the orphanage. We had been advised by friends and teachers that she should under no circumstances be sent to school in Yuki. The vindictive crone would scarcely stand the sight of the child whose death she desired. It would be safer in the provincial capital of Kunming.

'A few days before my departure for home I visited Lien-min a last time in the orphanage. How much she had to show and tell me about! "Lien-min," I then said to her, "now we want to pray together. And tomorrow morning, when you see the plane fly over the town, then you know, it carries me home. Pray that I can soon come back." And then we knelt down together, and she said among other things: "Dear Saviour, protect the plane that it doesn't hit against a stone on the way." A child's prayer.

'After long air travel, we landed safely in Europe. The plane before us, which had travelled the same route, had crashed, and the 32 people on board all died. How the grace of God had protected us!'

This pious sentiment is followed by a final paragraph in which Sister Frieda tells us that Lien-min was adopted by a Swiss family, members of the Friends of the Yunnan Mission.

a. Translated from German by Maria Jaschok. Originally published in 1950. *Lien-min. Die Geschichte einer erbarmungswuerdigen kleinen Chinesin*. Erlebnis-berichte der Yunnan-Mission. Marburg/Lahn.
b. Present-day Yuxi.

9. Social Christianity, American Feminism and Chinese Prostitutes: The History of the Presbyterian Mission Home, San Francisco, 1874–1935

By Sarah Refo Mason

Introduction

In 1885, a San Francisco-based trafficker in Chinese women bought a young girl of 14 years, Liang May Seen, in Guangdong Province on the southeast coast of China, the birthplace of many of the girls and women bought and sold in the profitable trade in prostitutes in the Chinese American community. The circumstances of Liang May Seen's procurement were typical of the transactions that brought young women to the United States from China during the second half of the 19th and the first decades of the 20th century. The death of Liang May Seen's father, reported to have been a German sea captain, had left her Chinese mother and family destitute. Liang May Seen's mother was approached by the San Francisco procurer with an offer to buy her daughter, ostensibly to marry her to a Chinese merchant in San Francisco. The trafficker showed her a photograph of the avowed merchant, and Liang's mother consented ('Register of Inmates' 1889 p. 121;[1] Culbertson 1890 pp. 41–2). There is no record of the amount the procurer paid Liang May Seen's mother. Typically during the 1880s, however, young girls were bought for $50 in Guangzhou, the provincial capital, and after the enactment of the Chinese Exclusion Act in the U.S. in 1882, sold for as much as $2,000 (Hirata 1979 p. 12).

Arriving in San Francisco, Liang May Seen discovered the procurer's promise that she would marry a Chinese merchant was a hoax. Instead, she was sold to the owner of a Chinatown brothel for $2,500, an unusually high price reflecting her market value as an attractive young girl, as well as the rising cost of importing Chinese women and girls into the U.S. After serving as a prostitute for four years, Liang found an opportunity to flee from her owner to a refuge for Chinese women and girls in San Francisco, the Presbyterian Mission Home, an event that changed her life, eventually bringing her to the midwestern United States as a pioneer in

Research for this study has been supported in part by a grant from the Women's History Grants Programme of the Minnesota Historical Society with funds provided by the State of Minnesota.

the small Chinese American community in Minneapolis, Minnesota (Culbertson 1890 pp. 41–2).

The story of Liang May Seen is typical of the early lives of many of the three thousand Chinese women and girls estimated to have lived at the Presbyterian Mission Home for varying lengths of time between 1874 and 1935. The destitution of the families who sold them, their use as prostitutes, their deception and exploitation at the hands of procurers and brothel owners, and their flight to the Home tended to be common elements in their lives.

I first encountered the career of Liang May Seen in 1979 while researching the early years of Chinese American settlement in Minnesota, as part of the Minnesota Historical Society's Ethnic History Project. The older members of the Chinese community were especially eager to tell their stories, and those of Liang May Seen and other pioneers, whose lives and experience had been neglected by Minnesota's historians. Having lived in Guangzhou, China, during my childhood and adolescence, I was also eager to hear their stories, and we developed good rapport during the course of the interviews. Through interviews with Liang May Seen's descendants I learned that she was the first Chinese woman known to have settled in Minnesota, and that prior to her marriage to Woo Yee Sing, an early Chinese resident in Minneapolis, she had lived in a San Francisco mission (Mason 1981; interview with Howard Woo, 9 October 1981, St Paul, Minnesota; interviews with Margaret Woo Chinn, 29 August 1979 and 27 May 1982, St Paul, Minnesota).

Ten years later, I was able to follow up this fragment of Liang May Seen's earlier life in San Francisco. As I searched the records of the Presbyterian Mission Home (renamed Cameron House in 1942), I became increasingly interested in the Mission Home itself, and its rich history in San Francisco's Chinatown. The handwritten records kept by the missionary women in charge of the Home and the published annual reports of the directors of the Home, the Women's Occidental Board of Foreign Missions, provided the evidence I needed to piece together Liang's early life as she described it to the missionaries following her escape from the Chinatown brothel. The records also provided documentation of the religious values of the missionaries, as expressed in their views of prostitution, and in the religious and educational programmes they conducted in their efforts to influence the lives of the Home's residents.

Interviews in 1991 with Lorna Logan, director of the Mission Home from 1934 to 1942, were particularly useful in casting light on the role of the American missionary women in the Home's cultural environment, and interpreting the religious zeal and commitment to social reform of the missionaries who provided the Home's leadership during its first 60 years. Interviews, also in 1991, with the present director of Cameron House, Harry Chuck, whose grandmother had been a resident at the Home, and with other descendants of Mission Home women in California and Minnesota were useful in understanding the response of the Chinese women themselves to their Mission Home experience, and its effects on their lives following their departure from the Home (interviews with L.E. Logan,

23 April, 4 and 9 October 1991, San Francisco; interview with Harry Chuck, 30 April 1991, San Francisco).

The main focus of this chapter is on the training of residents of the Mission Home for Christian marriage or for work in a Christian setting. A secondary focus is on the cross-cultural interaction of residents, Chinese assistants, and American personnel in the Home, and its influence on the lives of the residents after leaving the refuge.

The first part gives an overview of the larger social environment of the young Chinese prostitutes and *mui tsai* (young girls sold by their parents into domestic servitude at an early age) who found refuge in the Presbyterian Home. It draws on both scholarly and popular sources as well as on accounts of missionaries. Helpful sources have included the recent research of Lucie Cheng Hirata, the earlier scholarship of Mary Roberts Coolidge, and the observations of Otis Gibson, a missionary in San Francisco's Chinatown in the 1860s and 1870s (Hirata 1979; Coolidge 1909; Gibson 1877).

The second part focuses on the training and cultural environment of the Presbyterian Mission Home. It is based on primary sources, including the 'Register of Inmates' and other records at the Home (now Cameron House); personal interviews with descendants of the women who lived at the Home; interviews with Lorna Logan, former director of the Home; correspondence and reports of the missionaries and their Chinese associates; and annual reports compiled by staff and board members each year from 1874 to 1920.

The Chinese Community in San Francisco

When news of the discovery of gold in California reached South China in 1849, thousands of labourers in Guangdong and Fujian provinces left their villages to seek work in the *gum shan* ('Gold Mountain'). For generations, young men of the coastal areas of South China had sought work abroad, supporting their families with remittances sent home from Singapore, Penang and elsewhere in *Nanyang* (Southeast Asia). During the late 1840s, the number of men compelled to seek overseas work increased dramatically because of overpopulation, exploitation by landlords, foreign imperialism, and calamities brought about by the ineffectiveness and corruption of the Qing government (T. Chen 1940). Emigration from South China to California during the Gold Rush peaked in 1852, when 20,000 Chinese arrived in San Francisco. By the turn of the century, more than 200,000 Chinese, mostly male, had settled in the state of California (Chan 1986 p. 37).

While most of the early Chinese immigrants were bound for the gold mining region of the Sierra Nevada, San Francisco served as the main gathering place for California's Chinese community. During the 1860s, when the racism and violence of European American miners drove many Chinese workers from the mines, large numbers of Chinese settled more permanently in San Francisco, where light manufacturing work and jobs serving the white population as cooks, servants, and laundrymen became available (Hirata 1979 p. 5; Chan 1986 pp. 42, 45).

Between 1860 and 1870 the Chinese population in San Francisco increased from 2,719 to 12,022. By 1880 the number of Chinese reported by the census in San Francisco had grown to 21,745, overwhelmingly male in composition. With this growth, social organisations emerged in the Chinatown district, including merchant guilds, surname and regional associations, benevolent societies and *tongs*, or secret societies. While many of the associations provided social services and mutual assistance, *tongs* were often involved in illegal activities, including gambling, importation of opium and the trade in Chinese women and girls as prostitutes and *mui tsai*. Although other *tongs* also engaged in the trade, the Hip Yee Tong in particular capitalised on the market for prostitution in San Francisco's predominantly male Chinese community. From the early 1850s it developed a lucrative trade in women and controlled much of the traffic in prostitutes for at least two decades (Ma 1990 pp. 14–29; Chinn 1989 pp. 3–8; Chan 1986 p. 48; Hirata 1979 p. 10; Gibson 1877 p. 144).

During the third quarter of the 19th century the traffic in Chinese women and girls was run by a highly organised network of procurers, importers and brothel owners, controlled by the Hip Yee Tong, extending from California to Hong Kong and South China. Procurers, and sometimes brothel owners themselves, obtained young women and girls from their families by kidnapping, enticing or purchasing them in Hong Kong and in Guangdong and Fujian provinces. Importers transported them to San Francisco, where brothel owners bought them. Some women were also recruited by means of a contract made by a San Francisco-based agent and a contractor in China, who would recruit women from the contractor's native district for a specified period of service (Hirata 1979 p. 8–9; Holder 1897 p. 288–91).

In the view of young male Chinese immigrants, whose wives traditionally remained in the village, prostitution was a minor vice. Elders in the emigrant community often warned young men before their departure to avoid prostitutes, but largely for economic reasons. For the elders, maintaining the institution of the arranged marriage was most important for the perpetuation of lineage, and tacit approval for frequenting brothels or even taking a second wife abroad was seen as a means of pacifying young men and maintaining stability in the emigrant community. In the patriarchal society of 19th-century China, wives of overseas workers were carefully watched by relatives in the community to assure their purity, but the export of young women to provide prostitutes for male Chinese immigrants in San Francisco was generally acceptable (T. Chen 1940 pp. 142–4; Yang 1965 pp. 54–8; Hirata 1979 p. 7).

In the social hierarchy of prostitution in San Francisco's Chinatown, young girls bought to serve in the more exclusive brothels, like their counterparts in Shanghai and Guangzhou, were selected on the basis of their youth, beauty and entertainment value, especially their singing abilities. The high prices paid for young women with these attributes indicated their higher value in terms of the profits to be generated in a higher-class brothel serving a wealthier clientele of Chinese men (Hirata 1979 p. 14; Hershatter 1991 pp. 257, 264).

Higher-class prostitutes were often sold under contract for a period of four years' service. These contracts, between the brothel owner and the prostitute, were designed to appeal to young girls by limiting the period of service, thus lessening the likelihood of escape. They were also designed to disguise the exploitation and illegality of the practice of selling women in the U.S. Typically, after the girl was sold at the auction and an agreement on price was reached, a four-year contract was drawn up on red paper. The contract stated the name of the purchaser and that of the young woman, and the period of time she would be required to serve her owner. Under the terms of the agreement, the young woman would usually acknowledge her indebtedness for the price of the steamship ticket and the cost of the food consumed during her trip to San Francisco. The brothel owner would agree to lend the money to pay the woman's debt, while she in turn agreed to provide sexual and other services to the owner's clients for four years without wages. The transaction would be accompanied by a ritual of placing the amount of the purchase in gold into the young prostitute's hands by her purchaser, the brothel owner. The woman would then immediately place the gold coins in the hands of her seller, followed by the signing of the contract by the seller and purchaser, with the young prostitute usually signing with her thumb mark (Gibson 1877 pp. 137–40; McLeod 1947 pp. 180–1).

Most Chinatown prostitutes had lost their ability to attract customers after four years of service because of the ravages of disease and abuse, and owners had little interest in retaining their services beyond that period of time. In some cases, however, prostitutes entering a brothel at a very young age could still be attracting clients and generating high profits when their contract term was completed. In these cases the owner often refused to release the woman, as a higher-class prostitute in late 19th-century Chinatown could earn $250 per month or more for her owner (Hirata 1979 pp. 14–5).

Higher-class prostitutes provided sexual services in the luxurious rooms of brothels catering to a clientele of wealthier Chinese men. They would dress in bright-coloured silks and be adorned with jewellery given to them by admirers. Some women were also allowed to leave the brothel occasionally to sing or perform scenes from Cantonese operas at *tong* banquets or parties organised by Chinese merchants. Despite their silks and jewels and the apparent luxury of the higher-class brothels, women serving these establishments were not allowed to forget their status of servitude. They worked without wages, could not leave the brothel without permission and were sexually abused or beaten at the whim of their owner or clients. At any time they could be taken to the auction block, stripped of their clothing, examined in a humiliating manner and sold to the highest bidder (McLeod 1947 pp. 180, 183; Hirata 1979 p. 14; Dillon 1962 p. 230).

Lower-class prostitutes had often previously served in brothels catering to a wealthier Chinese clientele, but were perceived to have lost value because of age, disease or abuse. They were often confined in small rooms facing alleys, with only a few shelves, a chair or two, a washbowl, and bedboards for sleeping. The only door to the room usually had a barred window from which prostitutes called to passersby, offering their services for as little as 25 cents. Controlled by the Hip Yee Tong, these brothels served a mixed clientele that included the poorest Chinese labourers, sailors, transients and drunkards (McLeod 1947 pp. 182–3).

Chinese prostitution in San Francisco peaked toward the end of the century's third quarter, with the census of 1870 reporting 1,426 Chinese prostitutes in the city, or more than two-thirds of all Chinese women. Subsequent years saw a substantial decline in the number of Chinese prostitutes for reasons that included the evolution of a more established Chinese community, enforcement of legal constraints and the arousal of public sentiment in the moral reform movement led largely by Protestant women missionaries (Hirata 1979 pp. 24–7).

As anti-Chinese agitation grew in California, Chinese prostitution was often singled out for attack and legislation. In 1875 Congress enacted the Page Law, which made the importing of women for prostitution a felony. The Chinese Exclusion Act was passed in 1882, severely restricting immigration to the U.S. from China to those who had been born in the United States and to women and girls who were the wives or daughters of merchants, teachers, students or tourists. While these laws resulted in a decrease in the number of women brought into the U.S. from China, they also enhanced the opportunities for corruption and bribe-taking among American immigration officials (Hirata 1979 pp. 24-26; Coolidge 1909 p. 419; Dillon 1962 pp. 318–20).

One example of a corrupt American official contributing to the organised trade in women and girls was the American consul in Hong Kong, who was given the responsibility of certifying the character of all Chinese women emigrating to the U.S. following the enactment of the Page Act. Initially, David H. Bailey entrusted the investigation of women to a local group in Hong Kong, the Tung Wah Hospital Committee, who were committed to ending emigration abuses. Soon, however, he took on the responsibility of examining the women himself, charging a fee for merely asking them whether or not they were going to the U.S. voluntarily and issuing a certificate to that effect. When Bailey's successor, John S. Mosby, arrived in Hong Kong in 1879, he found that the consul had been personally pocketing the fees, enriching himself by thousands of dollars at government expense (Coolidge 1909 p. 419; Mosby 29 June 1879[2]).

Origins of the Presbyterian Mission Home in the Chinese Community

Emerging within this larger context of anti-Chinese sentiment, restrictive legislation and the changing social and economic environment of Chinatown in the early 1870s was the organised response of reform-minded Presbyterian women in San Francisco to the condition of Chinese women and girls living in bondage as prostitutes in their city. Like their contemporaries among the religious women of other denominations, the Presbyterian women definitely viewed prostitution as sinful, yet they did not consider the Chinese prostitutes to be 'fallen women' because they had been forced into a morally degrading life. On the other hand they were appalled at the conditions in which Chinese prostitutes were compelled to live and work, describing the situation as an 'affront to God's love for all people' (interviews with L.E. Logan, 22, 23 March 1990, San Francisco).

Protestant missionary women in the U.S. had crusaded against prostitution as early as the 1830s, describing their campaign as 'moral reform' and prostitutes as women fallen into a life of sin. After 1865, however, missionary reformers began to look upon prostitutes more as victims of a faulted environment than as victims of their own wrong decisions. This emphasis on the environmental sources of prostitution, which the San Francisco missionary women reflected, had originated among Protestant middle-class women reformers in eastern and midwestern cities in the post-Civil War period, predating the Social Gospel movement by several decades (Noble 1981 pp. 81–2; Keller 1981 pp. 242–3).

The idea of establishing a women's missionary organisation to rescue and provide an alternative environment for Chinese prostitutes in San Francisco took root at a time Protestant women in cities across the country were organising their own missionary societies. This was due not only to the rising missionary fervour among Protestant women, but also to the fact that prior to the 1870s denominational missionary organisations did not appoint single women as foreign missionaries, and only sent out married women as 'assistant missionaries' (Condit 1893 p. 8; Beaver 1980 pp. 87–8).

The Women's Occidental Board of Foreign Missions, as the San Francisco women later named their organisation, grew out of a women's prayer meeting held in the city on 10 March 1873, during which three women – including two who had served with their husbands as missionaries in Guangzhou – decided to organise the religious women of the city to rescue and provide refuge for the Chinese prostitutes and *mui tsai* of San Francisco. While they clearly hoped that the Chinese women and girls would eventually become Christians, and thereby be 'freed spiritually', their primary commitment was to minister to the Chinese as an 'expression of Christian compassion'. At an initial meeting on 14 April 1873, a larger group of interested women adopted a constitution and established themselves as an auxiliary branch of the Woman's Foreign Missionary Society of Philadelphia, which had been established in 1870. The official name of the new organisation was 'The California Branch of the Woman's Foreign Missionary Society of the Presbyterian Church of San Francisco'. Sixteen years later, in 1889, the connection with the Philadelphia Society was severed and the Occidental Board became an auxiliary of the Board of Foreign Missions in New York. Thereafter the official name was 'The Woman's Occidental Board of Foreign Missions of the Presbyterian Church' (interviews with L.E. Logan, 22, 23 March 1990, San Francisco; Condit 1893 pp. 8, 15).

The first year of the work of the Occidental Board was one of perplexity. Initially a conflict arose among the women as to whether to support a missionary at the Door of Hope in Shanghai, China, a refuge for prostitutes and *mui tsai* in that city, or to establish a rescue home themselves for Chinese prostitutes and *mui tsai* in San Francisco. The women increasingly favoured the latter course, especially following the Philadelphia Society's appointment of a missionary, Sarah Cummings, to work in San Francisco instead of Shanghai as had been originally planned (Condit 1874 pp. 7–8).

In August 1874 the Occidental Board rented the upper floor of an unfinished house on San Francisco's Prospect Avenue to serve temporarily as the rescue home, or Mission Home, as it came to be known. Sarah Cummings, already working as a home visitor in Chinatown under the auspices of the Philadelphia Society, was appointed the first missionary in charge of the Home. Several board members who had served with their husbands as missionaries in China, or in Chinatown, played a vital role in the operation of the Mission Home during its first years. Mrs I.M. Condit,[3] who had served in Guangzhou and spoke Cantonese, and Mrs A.W. Loomis, who had served in Ningbo, were especially active in teaching classes and resolving problems that arose (Logan 1976 pp. 8, 10; Cummings 1877 pp. 8, 9).

From the earliest years of the Mission Home, Chinese women were engaged as staff assistants. Mrs Ching Yuen, one of the assistants, had been brought to San Francisco in 1859 as an hereditary slave (see J.L. Watson 1980 pp. 223–50) and had been sold and resold to various owners until a Chinese merchant who had attended the Presbyterian mission school in Chinatown bought her to be his wife. Another early assistant, Mrs Tam Ching, was raised in Guangzhou in the family of Andrew Happer, founder of Lingnan University in that city. She was the wife of a Chinese pastor in San Francisco, Tam Ching, who had also studied at the Presbyterian mission school in Chinatown before returning to Guangzhou for theological training (Robbins 1874 p. 14).

Chinese prostitutes sought refuge at the Home soon after its doors were opened in 1874. In late 1875 Cummings reported that 10 women were already occupying the four small rooms. In these rooms the residents slept, ate, attended classes and did needlework. By 1876 the original residence on Prospect Avenue could no longer accommodate the Mission, and a more spacious building was acquired on Sacramento Street with the assistance of the Philadelphia Society. From 1874 to 1876 a total of 36 women and girls resided at the original quarters of the Mission Home for varying lengths of stay (Cummings 1876 p. 20; 'Register of Inmates' 1876 p. 19).

In 1878 Margaret Culbertson, a native of upstate New York and an acquaintance of Mrs P.D. Browne, president of the board, became superintendent of the Mission Home. During the next 19 years, Culbertson became known for her daring rescues of Chinese prostitutes and *mui tsai,* and for the rescue techniques she developed. Rescues of prostitutes were usually undertaken in response to requests for help from the women themselves. Typically, messages from women seeking help were brought to the Mission Home by sympathetic friends, or even by clients, specifying a time and place for the rescue. With the help of co-operative police officers and trusted Chinese assistants, Culbertson was instrumental in rescuing and aiding several hundred young prostitutes and *mui tsai* between 1878 and 1893. Altogether, between the founding of the Mission Home in 1874 and

1893 when Culbertson became ill and left for a time, 392 Chinese women and girls found refuge there (Houseworth 1894 p. 37; 'Register of Inmates' 1893 p. 185).

During the 1880s increased numbers of *mui tsai* were brought to the Mission Home for protection, often by the Society for Prevention of Cruelty to Children, following the enactment by the state legislature of a law protecting minors in service work, including girls serving 'in houses of doubtful character' (Condit 1893 pp. 13–4; *San Francisco Bulletin* 13 August 1880 p. 12). In seeking to establish guardianship of the children, who would presumably be forced by their owners into prostitution on reaching maturity, Culbertson and the staff and board members of the Home assumed a difficult and time-consuming responsibility. With the commercial value of each child reported to be from $300 to $3,000, owners did not give up the girls without considerable effort by the Home, including recourse to the courts and the use of writs of habeas corpus to establish guardianship. Staff and board members were required to appear in court with the children in each case, and several appearances were usually necessary before cases were settled (Condit 1893 p. 14). These efforts, involving court battles and risk to the missionaries, Chinese interpreters and rescued *mui tsai*, were dramatic expressions of what the missionaries called 'Christian compassion' (Cameron 1920 p. 22; interviews with L.E. Logan, 22, 23 March 1990, San Francisco).

Training Residents for Christian Marriage and Christian Work

The everyday tasks, personal relationships, school work and religious activities that made up the daily schedule of Home residents reflected the religious beliefs and values of the missionaries. From the 1870s residents of the Mission Home assembled each day after breakfast for morning worship. This included a bible reading in English, a hymn sung in English, followed by a recitation of the Lord's Prayer in both Cantonese and English. Morning worship was followed by the daily Home School, conducted in Cantonese and English each weekday morning. In the afternoons residents worked on their sewing projects, followed by hymn singing in Cantonese. During the evenings they attended worship services held in the schoolroom, usually led by a missionary. The bible was read together, and the residents were led in hymns and prayer. On Sundays all attended the Chinese Presbyterian Church in Chinatown, and on Sunday evenings the residents and staff gathered for bible study and hymn singing in Cantonese, led by Mrs Tam Ching (Robbins 1878 p. 75; Phillips 1876 p. 21).

While Culbertson and other missionaries were committed to providing a Christian atmosphere for the Chinese women and girls at the Home, they were also concerned with their preparation for a productive Christian life after their departure. The residents were trained in cooking and housework, sewing and knitting. They made their own clothes, for which they received small sums of money, and made fancy items for sale at the Home's annual bazaar. In the earlier years of the Home's history there were few employment opportunities for Chinese women in San Francisco, with the exception of domestic service. Some of the younger women sought domestic employment to earn money, and others made domestic work a career, but for most of the women, marriage was often the only avenue to a normal life after leaving the Home (Robbins 1878 p. 8; Phillips 1876 p. 21; interviews with L.E. Logan, 22, 23 March 1990, San Francisco).

Culbertson and others involved in negotiating marriages for the women were especially anxious to protect them from further exploitation. Because so few Chinese women were available for marriage either in San Francisco or elsewhere in the U.S., it was not unusual for bitter contests to develop between suitors for the women at the Home. Women who had escaped from brothels were also in danger of being kidnapped and returned to their former owners, while unscrupulous men might marry a woman and later sell her to pay off a debt (Robbins 1878 pp. 10–11).

The Christian values of the missionary women influenced the guidelines they established for the marriage of the Home's residents. Strongly supporting the Christian doctrine of marriage as a sacred covenant between a man and a woman, they opposed marriages to men who had wives in China or elsewhere. They insisted that none of the women would become second wives of San Francisco merchants. While non-Christian residents were not expected to marry Christians, the missionaries were concerned that women who had become Christians at the Home would also seek marriage with Christians. The missionary women feared that with so few months of religious instruction, Christian women might not be able to withstand anti-Christian influences without the nurturing of a larger Christian community (Robbins 1878 pp. 10–12).

While the missionaries were committed to protecting the women at the Home from exploitative marriages, they often found the task difficult. In an early example, a former owner of a young woman, A Ngo, who had escaped from a brothel in 1877 and had taken refuge in the Home, described himself as the woman's husband, and continuously sent letters to Sarah Cummings, the superintendent, over a period of seven months, asking her to return his wife, and promising to treat her well. When A Ngo refused, the former owner threatened her life. When threats failed, he sent friends to persuade her, and a succession of suitors followed, asking to marry her. One such suitor was a traditional Chinese doctor, who impressed A Ngo, and an interview was arranged. A missionary fluent in Cantonese overheard the doctor tell A Ngo that he had a wife and children in China, which persuaded the missionary not to negotiate a marriage between the two. Another suitor, a merchant, pleased both A Ngo and the missionaries, and negotiations for marriage were completed. Following the marriage, the merchant thoughtfully provided a gift of $40 for the Home 'to pay for her rice' (Robbins 1878 p. 10).

Pauline Robbins, an active board member, described the problems involved in the marriage of young women from the Home in the organisation's Annual Report for 1878. 'The work of the missionary would be greatly lessened,' she wrote in her account of the experience of A Ngo, 'if the inmates could include only young girls and children. Several years (of) instruction would thus be insured, and these matrimonial negotiations avoided. With A Ngo the vicissitudes of her life have been such that she could not hope to be the chosen wife of a Christian man; we were thankful that she could be lifted from the position of a slave to a home of her own choosing, where she carries new ideas of woman's capabilities, and especially of woman's freedom' (Robbins 1878 p. 11).

By the 1880s, as word of the Mission Home spread among Chinese American communities across the country, Chinese men who had been converted to Christianity came to the Home in search of wives. Some were residents of San Francisco and other West Coast cities, while others came from more distant places: Philadelphia, Chicago, New Orleans, Minneapolis and other cities. The prospective husbands brought letters of introduction written by their pastors, confirming their Christian faith and ability to support a family. In addition, the missionary women conducted their own investigations, always seeking to match their 'daughters' with well-recommended Christian men, while also trying to select women who had been at the home long enough to have had sufficient training and religious instruction to succeed as Christian wives and mothers (interview with Howard Woo, 9 October 1981, St Paul, Minnesota; interview with L.E. Logan, 9 October 1991, San Francisco).

Woo Yee Sing, a young Chinese Christian from Minneapolis, was typical of the men who sought wives at the Mission Home. Arriving in Minneapolis in 1880 at the age of 18, Woo attended English classes at the Westminster Presbyterian Church, where he was converted to Christianity by an elder of the church in 1882. An enterprising young man, Woo had established a popular hand laundry serving an upper middle-class clientele in the vicinity of the church. When he heard about the Mission Home, he secured a letter of introduction from his pastor confirming his reliability and departed for San Francisco. He apparently made a favourable impression on the Home's superintendent, Margaret Culbertson, who introduced him to Liang May Seen, the attractive young woman Culbertson had rescued three years earlier. Liang May Seen, who had become a Christian while living at the Home, was apparently also pleased with Woo Yee Sing, and a wedding was arranged for 23 July 1892. The ceremony was conducted at the Mission Home by Reverend I.M. Condit, a pastor of the Chinese Presbyterian Church, with Culbertson serving as Liang May Seen's witness ('Register of Inmates' 1889 p. 121; Culbertson 1890 pp. 41–2).

While some residents of the Mission Home were married in traditional or civil ceremonies held elsewhere, Christian weddings were conducted at the Home, where they were occasions of joyful celebration for all of the residents. In preparing for weddings held at the Home, formal invitations were sent to friends in the community from the 'Ladies of the Occidental Board'. The Home was decorated with flowers and simple refreshments were provided. During the earlier decades of the Home's history, the marriage services were usually conducted by one of the local pastors who had served in China, most often Reverend I.M.

Condit or Reverend A.W. Loomis, both pastors of the Chinese Presbyterian Church (Logan 1976 p. 17; 'Register of Inmates' 1874–1902).

Following the marriage of young women at the Home, Culbertson and her successors maintained close contact with them, visiting those who lived in the Chinatown community and being available to assist the women and their families if needed. Former residents who had married and had left the Home, also returned to visit their friends or to seek advice or counsel. By 1889 there were 46 families on the West Coast that had been established by the marriages of women at the Mission Home. In several cities former residents organised monthly meetings and raised money to send to China for flood and famine relief (Culbertson 1890 pp. 246).

Married former residents living in more distant cities also made an effort to maintain contact among themselves and with the missionary women at the Mission Home. In Los Angeles, Portland, Chicago, Boston, New Orleans, Philadelphia and Minneapolis, families established through the marriage of women from the Home formed supportive communities with continuing ties to the Mission Home (Pascoe 1990 p. 159; interview with L.E. Logan, 4 October 1991, San Francisco).

Chinese Assistants as Cultural Intermediaries

The Home's first long-term superintendent, Margaret Culbertson, initiated the policies and practices that fostered the development of the Home's open cultural environment and its innovative programme of basic education, practical training and religious instruction for women and girls of all ages and varying capabilities. The key to Culbertson's method appears to have been her use and training of Chinese assistants drawn from among the most promising women in the Home, especially those who had grown up in the Home and were fluent in both Cantonese and English (telephone interview with L.E. Logan, 20 January 1992).

Chinese assistants were initially employed to serve primarily as interpreters for the Home School classes held on weekday mornings. Culbertson enlarged their role, giving them the responsibility for overseeing housework, nurturing young children and new arrivals, counselling younger residents, and for the discipline of the residential life of the Home. One assistant was trained as Culbertson's personal assistant and interpreter, working with her on rescues and assisting in court hearings and community contacts. All assistants were expected to have a good education and to speak both Cantonese and English, and were paid a small wage for their work. The Chinese assistants were important role models for the younger residents, who called them 'Auntie' or 'Ah Yee' (interviews with L.E. Logan, San Francisco, 23 April, 4 October 1991; 20 January 1992).

The first assistant selected and trained by Margaret Culbertson was Ah Tsun,[4] who took refuge in the Mission Home shortly before Culbertson became superintendent. On her arrival at the Home Ah Tsun had described herself to the missionaries as a slave, owned by a woman who had brought her to San Francisco illegally by shaving her head, dressing her as a boy and claiming she was her son.

Several years after her arrival in the city, when Ah Tsun was 16, she became aware that her owner had made plans to sell her into prostitution and she fled to the Home ('Register of Inmates' 1877 p. 28).

Employing a ruse often used to regain custody of runaway girls, Ah Tsun's owner went to the police and charged the young girl with theft. Ah Tsun was arrested and taken to prison, where her owner subsequently posted bond and obtained an order for her release, expecting to take Ah Tsun back to her residence. However, through the intervention of the Mission Home board and staff, Ah Tsun was released to the Home, to whom custody was given, following several court hearings ('Register of Inmates' 1877 pp. 28–30).

At the Mission Home Ah Tsun proved to be an eager student at the Home School, becoming sufficiently proficient in both English and Cantonese to serve as a competent translator. Working under Culbertson's guidance, the young woman assumed a number of the superintendent's responsibilities. She became an expert in all aspects of housekeeping and cooking, including the preparation of both Chinese and American food, and supervised the residents in performing their assigned household tasks. Becoming a Christian in 1878, Ah Tsun also learned to play the organ for worship services, and often led the services as well. Most important, she was popular among the residents and served as a role model for the young girls (Phillips 1878 p. 9).

In 1884, following her marriage to Gon Wing, Ah Tsun left the Home to live in the Chinatown community, where she was also known as Muriel Wing. After her departure she was employed by the Occidental Board as a home visitor, initially as an interpreter accompanying an American missionary on home visits, but later working on her own. This position involved visiting women in their homes, teaching English, conducting evangelistic work and talking with them about footbinding and other issues ('Register of Inmates' 1884 p. 30; Cameron 1920 pp. 22–3; Wing 1903 p. 44).

Later in the 1880s the Occidental Board provided Ah Tsun with an opportunity for further education in China in order to enhance her skills for missionary work in San Francisco. Ah Tsun and her husband travelled together to Guangzhou, where Ah Tsun entered the True Light Seminary, a school for girls and women established in 1872 by the Board of Foreign Missions of the Presbyterian Church in the U.S. to provide basic education and training for Christian work. From the point of view of the American missionaries in San Francisco, further education at True Light would enhance Ah Tsun's reading ability in Chinese, enabling her to read the bible in Chinese with greater proficiency. Bible study classes at True Light, it was felt, would also enhance her ability to discuss Christian teachings with the women she visited in the Chinatown community (Cameron 1920 p. 23).

Gon Wing, Ah Tsun's husband, died during their stay in Guangzhou, and Ah Tsun returned to San Francisco with her two young sons after completing her course of study. In 1900 Ah Tsun was again employed by the Occidental Board for home visiting in Chinatown, and in 1906, following completion of a course in kindergarten training, she became a teacher in the Occidental Board's Day School, a school initially established to provide education for Chinese children excluded from the public schools. She continued to teach in the school until her retirement in 1935, and is believed to have been the first trained Chinese kindergarten teacher in the U.S. (Cameron 1920 p. 23; Muriel Wing, Biographical Files 1925, 1958, Presbyterian Historical Society).

Chun Fah was another early assistant trained by Margaret Culbertson. As a six-year-old *mui tsai,* Chun Fah had been rescued from a notorious dealer in young girls in San Francisco's Jackson Street by officers of the Society for the Prevention of Cruelty to Children, and had been brought to the Mission Home for protection in 1878. Information regarding the abuse of the child had been provided by a Chinese resident in the community, leading to her rescue. Soon after Chun Fah arrived, a writ of habeas corpus was served on the Mission Home. After several court hearings, during which it was revealed that she had been sold to the dealer two months earlier by her parents, guardianship of the child was granted to Culbertson ('Register of Inmates' 1878 p. 42).

Despite the ill-treatment she had received from the dealer, evidenced by scars and bruises on her arms and back, Chun Fah was an attractive child who soon became the favourite of the residents. They gave her the name Chun Fah, meaning Spring Flower, in place of her former name, Tong Cook. On the day of her arrival she also became the 'spiritual child' of Charlotte Van Cleve of Minneapolis, who was captivated by the new resident during a visit to the Home. Van Cleve was a member of the Westminster Presbyterian Church in Minneapolis, actively engaged in women's missionary activities, and assumed the support of the child as a personal project. Returning to Minneapolis, she remained in close touch with Chun Fah, writing encouraging letters and advising her that she was praying for her daily ('Register of Inmates' 1878 p. 42; Robbins 1913 p. 8; Culbertson 1881 p. 20; WOBFM, *Annual Report* 1891, SFTS, p. 51).

Two years after Chun Fah's arrival, Culbertson described the child, then eight years old, as 'the light of our home'. She reported that while Chun Fah had not been able to speak a word of English when she had entered the Mission Home, in two years she had become more proficient in reading, writing and speaking English than most of the older girls. She also noted that Chun Fah was very fond of stories and could repeat stories from the bible quite accurately (Culbertson 1881 p. 21).

By the age of 15, Chun Fah had become a Christian and was taking an active role in the religious life of the Home. Among her activities, she served as secretary of the Light House Mission Band, a missionary society for young girls, writing reports on the group's monthly meetings, to be included in the annual reports of the Occidental Board. Like the women's missionary societies, the bands focused on promoting interest in missionary activities abroad and in raising funds for missionary projects. In addition to experience in organising and fundraising, the organisations provided an important source of group identification for their youthful members (Chun Fah 1888 p. 40; Beaver 1980 pp. 44, 98–9; Keller 1981 p. 245).

In her report of the Light House Band for the year 1887, Chun Fah noted that the group met each month at the Mission Home, opening the meeting with prayer and singing and continuing with a discussion of overseas mission activities. She reported that the Band, then in its seventh year, had raised $73, of which $56.35 was to be sent to China in support of a bible teacher, $10 was to go to a mission serving American Indians, and the remainder was to be presented as a token of appreciation to an older Presbyterian congregation which had left its church building to the Chinese community when it had moved out of San Francisco's downtown area (Chun Fah 1888 p. 40).

At about the age of 16, Chun Fah was employed as an assistant at the Mission Home, working closely with Culbertson in rescues and in court, where her language abilities in Cantonese and English were particularly useful, and helping with the Home School and religious instruction. She was popular with the women of the Home, and was seen as a source of encouragement for residents and a nurturing spirit for those arriving at the Home in distress (Culbertson 1890 p. 24; Wilson 1974 p. 44).

In 1892 Chun Fah married Reverend Ng Poon Chew, a respected minister and Chinese-language newspaper publisher in Chinatown, who was also the first Chinese graduate of the San Francisco Theological Seminary. An important event in Chinatown's Christian community, the marriage was moved from the Home to the larger Chinese Presbyterian Church, where Reverend I.M. Condit performed the ceremony and Qui Mooi, the Mission Home's latest arrival, sang a Chinese song, accompanying herself with a traditional Chinese instrument (*The Occident* 18 May 1892, SFTS).

Chun Fah and Ah Tsun were seen as unusually capable women, establishing Christian families and becoming Christian wives and mothers, exemplifying an important goal of the founding missionaries of the Mission Home. Like other married women who had been residents of the Home, both of these women were active in the Chinese Church and the Christian community, and remained in close contact with the missionaries and with their 'American mothers', women who had undertaken their support at the Mission Home. In 1882, M.L. Berry, a member of the Occidental Board, visited the families of four married women from the Home, including those of Chun Fah and Ah Tsun. She commented on the 'cheerful Americanised home' of Chun Fah, as well as the neatness of Ah Tsun's home. She also praised the cleanliness of the home of Ah Mui, another of the households she visited, and the good behaviour of Ah Mui's children. She was especially pleased to find books on the table in the home of Ah Yoke, a fourth former resident, and also noted an organ in the parlour, a treasured gift from Ah Yoke's 'American mother' in Pennsylvania (Berry 1893 pp. 47–8; Culbertson 1888 p. 54).

Social Christianity and Feminism

In 1893 the Mission Home was moved to a new three-storey building in Sacramento Street, built with the assistance of women's missionary societies in

Presbyterian churches throughout the U.S. Four years later, Donaldina Cameron, a teacher at the Home and a young friend of Evelyn Browne, the daughter of the Occidental Board president, became the Home's superintendent. Cameron continued the rescues of individual women initiated by Culbertson, as well as most of Culbertson's training programmes, but introduced a new approach that reflected the theology of late 19th-century Social Christianity. The new superintendent was convinced of the need to move beyond individual charity to efforts to correct or change unjust institutions in American society. Reflecting her feminist ideals, she envisioned the day when women whose lives had been influenced by the Home would play a larger role in American society, both as women and as reformers, through collective action within church organisations and structures, or by furthering their education to become teachers, lawyers, doctors, nurses and members of the other professions (Pinney 1894 p. 11; Cameron 1908–9 pp. 77–8).

Outraged by the exclusion of Chinese children from the San Francisco schools, Cameron made education a special concern during her first years as superintendent. As early as the 1870s the Occidental Board had established the Home School for girls and young women at the Mission Home, as well as the Occidental School for Chinese children in the community, to provide basic education. While a few young women who received their education at the Home School were able to obtain jobs as interpreters because of their language skills in English and Cantonese, neither the Home School nor the Occidental School provided education beyond an elementary level. For most of the young women growing up at the Home or in the Chinatown community, lack of access to secondary education restricted their employment options to domestic service or sewing on consignment from local enterprises (interviews with L.E. Logan, 23 April, 4 and 9 October 1991, San Francisco).

The San Francisco earthquake of 1906 demolished most of Chinatown and left the Mission Home in ruins, and plans to confront the issue of Chinese secondary education were temporarily laid aside. The following year a new building was built on the site of the destroyed Home, financed by gifts from the Philadelphia Society and the Pacific Northwest Board, and in April 1908 the Mission Home family of staff and residents moved in. Almost immediately, the question of secondary education for girls was again raised. Several residents of the Home approached Cameron stating that they were interested in teachers' training because they wanted to return to China to teach in mission or government schools. Acknowledging that there were openings for teachers in China, Cameron encouraged the girls' aspirations, and recommended to the Occidental Board that mission education in Chinatown be extended to include instruction at the secondary level. Already burdened with the responsibility of raising funds for existing programmes, the board decided that providing high school education for their constituents was beyond the scope of their commitment (Cameron 1908–9 pp. 77–8; Logan 1976 pp. 28–32, 35–6; interview with L.E. Logan, 20 January 1992).

Another approach to the secondary education issue was made in 1909, when Cameron encouraged several girls who sought advanced instruction not provided by the Home School to enrol in the local public school. A few days later, the principal of the school sent a note to Cameron stating that under Californian law Chinese children could not attend public schools. Members of the Board's school committee responded by noting a provision of the law requiring the establishment of a separate school for Chinese children if such a school was requested. The request was then made by the Occidental Board, who also offered space at the Mission Home for classes to be taught by a teacher provided by the San Francisco Board of Education, serving Chinese girls from the Home and from the Chinatown community. While the class provided by the Board of Education did not provide instruction on the secondary level, it brought the girls' education to the level of that provided for American-born children preparing to enter high school. The class led to the establishment of the Oriental School several years later, a public elementary school which served several generations of children in Chinatown and which also served as a symbol of the city's segregated school policies (Logan 1976 p. 36; Cameron 1908–9 p. 77; Chinn 1989 pp. 44–5).

In 1911 three Mission Home girls graduated from the eighth grade in the new public school class. In the same year two other young women from the Home entered higher education, with the help of sponsors the Home had been instrumental in providing. Margaret Woo entered the University of Arizona in Tucson, and Lon Lee entered the nurses' training programme of the Presbyterian Hospital in Philadelphia (Crown 1911–2 p. 19).

Models of Service

Cameron was a strong advocate for the women at the Home, and in several instances she was successful in finding wealthy sponsors who made it financially possible for some of the Home's residents to continue their education beyond the elementary level of the Home School. Cameron and her assistants also provided models of single women committed to lives of service to others as an alternative to marriage. Two Chinese assistants, in particular, exemplified those for whom Cameron served as a model: Tien Fuh Wu and Leung Yuen Qui. Both played an important role in the cross-cultural interaction and relationships that were part of the daily life of the Home under Cameron's leadership (interviews with L.E. Logan, 22, 23 March 1990, San Francisco).

Tien Fuh Wu, a former *mui tsai,* was born in Ningbo, Zhejiang Province, in about 1884. Her father had sold her at the age of six for gambling money. She was taken to Hong Kong, and from there she was brought to San Francisco and sold to a well-known Jackson Street dealer in *mui tsai.* In San Francisco, Tien Wu was treated harshly, her mistress often twisting the flesh of her face and burning her arms with a lighted wick dipped in oil. The abuse of this child became a scandal in Chinatown, and Chinese neighbours reported the situation to the Mission Home. Subsequently she was rescued in 1894 by A.M. Houseworth, Florence Worley and a Chinese assistant, Ah Cheng, accompanied by two officers of the

Society for Prevention of Cruelty to Children ('Register of Inmates' 1894 p. 432; Houseworth 1894 p. 39; interviews with L.E. Logan, 22, 23 March 1990, San Francisco).

Growing up at the Mission Home, Tien Wu was full of enthusiasm, making up games for all to play, and always taking the lead in the younger residents' activities. She was also seen as a difficult child who resented authority, but she grew attached to Leung Yuen Qui, a close associate of Donaldina Cameron and one of the Home's 'Chinese aunties'. Leung Yuen Qui had fled from a Chinatown brothel in 1890 and had since become a special assistant and interpreter (interviews with L.E. Logan, 22, 23 March 1990, San Francisco; Wu 1943;[5] 'Register of Inmates' 1890 p. 142).

As a teenager in 1906, Tien Wu was sponsored by a wealthy businessman in Philadelphia, whose family took her into their household for four years, enabling her to attend Stevens Academy. After graduation she studied at the Toronto Bible College in Canada for an additional year. Returning to San Francisco in 1911, Tien Wu found offers for both employment and marriage, but elected to return to the Mission Home to work as an interpreter and assistant to Cameron. She was influenced in this decision by her admiration for Cameron's former assistant, Leung Yuen Qui, who had befriended her during her rebellious childhood, and whose early death from tuberculosis had especially saddened Tien Wu during her youth at the Home. In her child's grief, Tien Wu had resolved someday to take Leung Yuen Qui's place as Cameron's interpreter and assistant, and to become a 'Chinese auntie' with whom other young girls could identify. Like Leung Yuen Qui and Cameron, Tien Wu remained single, committing herself to a life of service. Years later, when asked by Cameron to take her place as superintendent, when the latter was planning to retire, Tien Wu refused, stating that she preferred to continue as an assistant and 'Chinese auntie' (Wu 1943, see [5]; interview with L.E. Logan, 23 April 1991).

In the decade after Tien Wu's return to the Mission Home, from 1911 to 1921, educational opportunities for Chinese girls and young women continued to grow at the Home School as well as in public and private high schools in San Francisco. During this period the Home's educational programme was enhanced when Leung Mo Yuen, a graduate of the True Light Middle School in Guangzhou, joined the Mission Home staff in 1910 through the assistance of a Carnegie gift to the Home. Her Chinese language classes and bible study classes in Cantonese in particular were important additions to the Home's cross-cultural education services. In 1919, a typical year of the decade, three girls from the Mission Home began high school and two enrolled in the Lux School in San Francisco, a school requiring high scholastic ability for entrance. Of the 40 women and girls who entered the Home during the year, the majority were children. Five women left the Home for domestic service, three found business positions and five married and left to establish their own homes (Cameron 1920 pp. 24, 42; K.Y. Chen 1972 p. 104).

While both Tien Wu and Cameron were pleased with progress made in educational programmes during the period, they were increasingly concerned by the number of requests for rescues in the 1911–21 decade and in subsequent years, clear evidence that the trade in Chinese women had not ended, despite the legislation of the 1870s and 1880s. In 1923 Tien Wu wrote to Edna Voss at the Board of National Missions in New York that she and Lo Mo ('Old Mother'), as the residents affectionately called Cameron, had been pressed with rescue work ever since her return to the Home in 1911. Cameron also reported in 1920 that she hoped to relieve Tien Wu of household responsibilities as much as possible because of her 'important duties of interpreter and assistant in rescue work' (Tien Fuh Wu, letter to Edna Voss, Board of National Missions, 31 August 1923, p.3, biographical file, Presbyterian Historical Society; Cameron 1920 p. 50).

Another source of concern for Cameron and Tien Wu in the early 1920s was the change in board governance that left the Home without the direct support of the San Francisco-based Occidental Board. In 1920 delegates from Presbyterian women's missionary boards across the country met in Philadelphia to form a new Women's Board of Foreign Missions as part of an initiative to unify the denomination's missionary boards. Several years later the Presbyterian Board of Foreign Missions, administered by men, decided that all work in the U.S. should come under the responsibility of the denomination's Board of National Missions, which after 1923 was based in New York City. This was a significant change for the women of the Mission Home, who had always seen themselves as foreign missionaries, serving a Chinese constituency. Most important, the reorganisation meant that the Occidental Board, which had met monthly at the Mission Home since 1873 and provided strong personal and financial support for the Home's programmes, ceased to function as an independent jurisdiction (Logan 1976 pp. 41–2).

In the early 1930s requests for rescues became less frequent, and immigration officials and missionaries believed the traffic in women was waning. Donaldina Cameron was approaching mandatory retirement in 1934, and Lorna Logan, a young journalist from Seattle, had been recruited by Evelyn Browne Bancroft, Western Area Secretary of the Board of National Missions, to become her successor, serving as Cameron's assistant during a transition period beginning in 1932. When Logan arrived at the Home there were about 40 women and girls in residence. Tien Wu had become the Associate Director, and May Wong, a young woman who had been rescued in Portland by Cameron and Tien Wu in 1922, was a Chinese assistant who would later work closely with Logan (interviews with L.E. Logan, 22, 23 March 1990, 23 April, 4 and 9 October 1991, San Francisco).

Efforts to End the Traffic in Women

While Tien Wu and Cameron continued their rescues of individual women in the 1920s and early 1930s, their larger commitment became that of ending the traffic in Chinese women altogether. They were in close contact with federal Immigration Service officials, who often advised the women on how to proceed in bringing traffickers to justice, including securing information from prostitutes who had escaped to the Home about owners and procurers that could be crucial in the arrest and prosecution of importers. Lorna Logan's own history of the Home's transition from a refuge for women and girls to a church-related community centre provides an account of such a trial. This occurred soon after her employment by the Mission Home, and marked the waning of the traffic in women (M.C. Martin 1977 p. 256; Logan 1976 p. 47–9).

On 13 December 1933, Logan related, a young girl named Leung Gwai Ying appeared at the door of the Mission Home with a staff member of the Methodist Home for Girls. The latter explained that the girl was looking for Donaldina Cameron, but had mistakenly gone to the Methodist Home. The girl told Tien Wu and Cameron that she had been brought from Hong Kong and sold in San Francisco for $5,000, and was seeking to escape from her owner. When she told her story, Cameron asked if she would be willing to tell what she knew to federal immigration officials and thereby help to bring importers and owners to trial. Although she feared retribution from her owners, she agreed to reveal the names and other pertinent information regarding individuals involved in importing her. Immigration officials were particularly interested in the information Leung Gwai Ying provided because she named several individuals already under investigation (Logan 1976 p. 48).

After many months of further investigation and preparation, an initial trial opened in federal court in San Francisco on 5 March 1935. The defendants included a man and three women: a well-known hardware merchant, Wong See Duck; his wife, Kung Shee; a moneylender, Fong Shee; and a procurer, Yee Mar. During the first days Leung Gwai Ying presented her testimony, including names, dates, and addresses of individuals involved in importing her into the U.S. However, when one of the American lawyers hired by the defendants began to attack her personally, Leung Gwai Ying floundered and was not able to continue. The first trial ended with the jury unable to agree on a verdict (*San Francisco Chronicle* 6 March 1935; Logan 1976 p. 48).

A second trial opened on 31 April. In the interim, Leung Gwai Ying's 'sister', Wong So, one of two other girls brought into the U.S. with her, was found in the Salinas Valley of California and brought to the Mission Home. Wong was a more assertive witness, and the defence lawyers were unable to intimidate her. Moreover, Immigration Service officials had conducted further investigations of the ring in China and were able to present evidence to substantiate the testimony of the two girls. On 2 May 1935, all four defendants were found guilty. Wong See Duck was sentenced to two years in prison followed by deportation and a fine of $5,000, while Kung Shee, Fong Shee and Yee Mar were each sentenced to one year in prison. During the following month Cameron found Leung Gwai Ying's second 'sister' in New York and brought her to the Mission Home, where she gave birth to a daughter (Logan 1976 pp. 48–9; U.S.A. vs. Wong See Duck *et al.* 3 May 1935 [6]).

By 1938 it was becoming clear that efforts such as Logan described in her history of the Home had contributed to a demise of the traffic in Chinese women.

For a few years rumours of sales of Chinese women continued, but the requests for rescues virtually stopped. While the number of residents at the Home in 1932 averaged about 55, in 1938, the average number was 15 and these were mostly American-born girls with family problems (Logan 1976 pp. 49, 61).

Sustaining Values and Relationships for New Generations

With the passing of the need for a rescue home in Chinatown, the old brick building that had been the Mission Home became a community centre within the larger Presbyterian ministry in Chinatown, which also encompassed the Chinese Presbyterian Church and its Christian education programme. In tribute to her leadership of the Home from 1897 to 1934, the building was renamed Cameron House in 1942. Donaldina Cameron exemplified the missionary women who shaped the history of the Home from its founding in 1874 to the late 1930s. They were committed to both evangelical Christianity and social reform. They engaged in daring rescues and provided a Christian refuge for Chinese prostitutes and *mui tsai* as an expression of Christian compassion. Finally, they and their closest Chinese associates and assistants provided a feminist model in a Christian context for their Mission Home constituents, who often remained in contact with the Home and the values of its leaders throughout their lives and in places far from San Francisco.

One such constituent was Liang May Seen, who, as has been seen, had been imported from Guangdong Province to California in 1885 at the age of 14 and had been a resident of the Mission Home from her rescue on 21 July 1889 until her marriage to Woo Yee Sing of Minnesota on 21 July 1892. Beginning their life together in Minneapolis in the early 1890s, the couple settled in the downtown area where Woo had earlier established a hand laundry. Woo's laundry and its colourful horse-drawn delivery wagon were well-known in the nearby Lowry Hill district, where many of the upper middle-class residents were his customers. Later Liang May Seen also entered business, opening an import shop next door to the Westminster Presbyterian Church, where Woo Yee Sing had first attended English-language classes and been converted to Christianity in 1882 (interview with Howard Woo, 9 October 1981, St Paul, Minnesota; Bushnell 1938 pp. 76–7).

Liang May Seen and Woo Yee Sing both took an active part in the Westminster Church. Although the church had provided both English lessons and religious programmes for Chinese immigrants since the 1880s, Liang and Woo attended the regular English services and Sunday School classes. Woo had a close friendship with the minister, David Burrell, and enjoyed making contacts with influential citizens among the church members. Liang also developed close friendships with feminists in the church, including Marybeth Hurd Paige, the first woman to serve as a member of the Minnesota state legislature. Paige's sister-in-law, Emma Paige, a teacher at Central High School in Minneapolis and an active member of the women's missionary society, also took an interest in Liang May Seen (interview with Howard Woo, 30 October 1991, Minneapolis, Minnesota).

Liang May Seen played an important role in the extended families of Woo Yee Sing and his brother Woo Du Sing in Minneapolis. She was especially helpful to her brother-in-law's wife, who had come directly from a village in China, spoke no English and rarely left the home, in keeping with village tradition. Liang often took her sister-in-law's children with her own to special events at the church or at school, and when her niece and nephews needed advice about school they usually asked May Seen, who understood American ways (interview with Margaret Woo Chinn, 27 May 1982, St Paul, Minnesota).

Liang May Seen's son, Howard Woo, remembered family visits to San Francisco to visit Donaldina Cameron and other missionary women at the Mission Home during his childhood. He also remembered Cameron's visits to Minneapolis, during which she usually stayed with the Woo family. She often complimented Liang May Seen on her immaculate housekeeping, and for being a serious homemaker rather than playing mahjong all day. Howard Woo recollected that in addition to visiting his mother and her family, Cameron had come to Minneapolis to try to locate and expose dealers in the white slave trade in that city, which was reportedly a centre of transactions in women (interview with Howard Woo, 30 October 1991, Minneapolis, Minnesota; Rosen 1982 pp. 117–8).

In 1920, 27 years after the arrival of Liang May Seen and Woo Yee Sing as a married couple in Minneapolis, another young woman from the Mission Home, Minnie Jun Soo, moved to the city with her husband. Born in San Francisco, she had been brought to the Mission Home in 1908 after falling into the hands of dealers in *mui tsai* after the death of both of her parents. Described by Donaldina Cameron as a bright child with a gentle nature, Minnie Jun Soo lived at the Home until she was about 18, when she married Frank Hin Chan, a San Francisco-born Chinese businessman. The couple lived in Chicago for several years and then moved to Minneapolis, where Chan managed the well-known Nankin Café, and where their son, Warren, was born (Cameron 1908–9 pp. 74–5; Warren W. Chan, letter to the author, 29 August 1991). Despite age differences, a bond developed between Liang May Seen and Minnie Jun Soo, because of their common background at the Mission Home and their shared fondness for Donaldina Cameron. The two women and their families often visited each other's homes and frequently talked by telephone. The Woo family also urged the Chan family to participate in the activities of Westminster Church, where they found acceptance and a network of supportive friends (interview with Lolita Young Woo, 30 October 1991, Minneapolis, Minnesota).

Conclusion

Reviewing the history of the Mission Home and the family histories of its former residents, such as Liang May Seen, Chun Fah and Minnie Jun Soo, one searches for the effects of the Mission Home experience on the later lives of the residents, the choices they made and the values they taught their children. Descendants of the women who lived at the Mission Home, interviewed for the present study, presented an almost romantic view of the Home as a place where their mothers had found refuge from harsh treatment and bondage. At the same time, Howard Woo's recollection of Donaldina Cameron's praise for his mother's serious homemaking and immaculate housekeeping appears to substantiate the appraisals of recent historians, who have emphasised the degree to which American missionary women in the U.S. and China, especially during the earlier period, imposed their 19th-century values of morality and domesticity on their constituents. Nevertheless, Woo also described his mother's stay at the Home as 'a more or less happy time for her', where she learnt English and became a Christian, pointing to the fact that the Mission Home and its independent American lay women missionaries provided an important link to the larger society for the Chinese women and their families (Pascoe 1990; Flemming 1989; interview with Howard Woo, 30 October 1991, Minneapolis, Minnesota).

Notes

1. 'Register of Inmates', 1874–1908. A handwritten record of arrivals at the Mission Home, including information provided by the Chinese women concerning the circumstances of their escape or rescue. Record in possession of Cameron House, San Francisco.
2. John S. Mosby to Stilson Hutchins Esq., 29 June 1879. John S. Mosby, Collection, Tracy W. McGregor Library, University of Virginia.
3. In the records maintained by the Mission Home, as in other missionary records of the late 19th and early 20th centuries, married women, including both Chinese and Americans, were customarily identified by their husbands' names or initials, prefaced by the conventional title 'Mrs'. Single women were identified by their birth names or initials, prefaced by the title, 'Miss'. In identifying the married women who appear in this study, I have used the conventional form for the purpose of clarity. In the identification of single women, I have used their birth names, if they were recorded.
4. At the time of the initial arrival of the young women and girls at the Mission Home, the missionary in charge entered their names in the 'Register of Inmates' as the women and girls identified themselves. The records indicate that many of the women used aliases, reflecting the dangers in revealing their true identities. Many did not reveal a family name. A large number used the prefix 'Ah' with their given name, a traditional usage in rural villages in South China to show familiarity. The Chinese assistants at the Mission Home often later gave 'religious names' to residents. These were Chinese terms reflecting the Christian experience of the residents at the Home, such as 'transformed' or 'converted'.
5. 'Life History Blank', submitted to the Board of National, Missions; Tien Fuh Wu, 11 June 1943. Biographical file, Presbyterian Historical Society.
6. U.S.A. vs. Wong See Duck, 1935. Records of District Courts of the U.S. Northern District of California, Criminal Case Records, 1912–1935, Group No. 21, Case No. 25295-K. National Archives, San Bruno, California.

10. Protected Women in 19th-Century Hong Kong

By Carl T. Smith

Introduction

The opportunity to become a 'protected woman' offered a choice beyond those normally open to Chinese women. Most accepted the usual progression from daughter to bride, daughter-in-law, mother, mother-in-law and perhaps widowed grandmother. The later stages of this progression brought increasing powers of decision-making and authority.

However, there were other positions for females in the Chinese social structure, one of which was that of protected woman – a woman acquired by and living with a foreigner. This opportunity was limited to the coastal port cities where different races and cultures met. In Hong Kong, some protected women were bought from brothels. Most, however, came from the Tanka[1] boat people, a marginalised group living in the Pearl River delta and coastal area.

The boat people's lifestyle on the edge of the social structure offered some of their women opportunities for independent choice and activity. Though the work was probably controlled by the males of the family, women could earn money by operating sampans carrying passengers and freight to and from ships, providing foreign shipping with fresh vegetables and fruit, fowls and pigs, and with services such as washing and mending clothes. Some of the women, called the 'Salt Water Girls' (*haam sui mui*), may have earned an independent income by providing sexual services to sailors.[2]

The boat women's contact with foreign ships facilitated the emergence of protected women on the China coast. These women, living an active life in the open air, would have been healthy, and if the pictures of them by China coast artist George Chinnery are reasonably representative, they had a natural beauty. They had little to lose by associating with foreigners because of their marginal position in Chinese society.

The term 'protected woman' arose from the Hong Kong Government's system of licensing brothels and suppressing unlicensed establishments. Young Chinese women living in a household where there was no male adult might well be

---

Acknowledgement is due to Richard Irving, Department of Geography, Hong Kong University, who prepared the maps for this chapter.

suspected of operating a 'sly brothel'. The Registrar-General, reporting in 1868 on a new ordinance for the prevention of contagious diseases, complained that:

> There are whole streets of what may be considered the most pernicious establishments of all, viz. houses full of kept women, where, nevertheless, common prostitutes are maintained for chance comers, or are sent out if needed. And the employers of the women so kept are exceedingly jealous and resentful of any interference with the house in which they reside, giving them written certificates to serve in case of a visit from the police and of course these papers become marketable articles. What makes these houses most impregnable to the law is their invariable habit of never admitting any person they do not know, or who is not introduced by one of their known customers (Hong Kong Government Blue Book 1868 p. 128).

This gave rise to a practice by which a woman, if suspected of being a prostitute or of operating a brothel, could claim that she was supported – thus 'protected' – by a foreign male and produce a certificate to prove it.

Origins of Protected Women

Although there is scant evidence of the commencement of the practice, it is safe to say that protected women appeared almost as soon as the British occupied Hong Kong in 1841, because there were so few European women in the early days of the colony (Hoe 1991, n.d.). One of the earliest documentary mentions of such a woman is in the will of William Stewart, dated 2 September 1845 (Hong Kong Record Series Will File 79 of 1847 (4/14)). He was a partner in the firm of Jardine, Matheson and Company, and bequeathed to Alloy, 'a Chinese female known to my executors in China', the sum of $7,700. Out of this, $2,700 was for the purchase of a house in a location of her choice and the rest was to provide her with a monthly payment. Unlike provisions made by other protectors for the financial security of their women, the money Stewart left was not under Alloy's control. The terms set down show his deep affection and concern for her: 'My executors will invest the sum as to yield a pension for her future support, she having no one but me to look to for the means of diverting starvation in her old age.' Further evidence of the bond between them was his bequest of a portrait of Alloy to Andrew Jardine along with one of the 'late' (probably Dr William) Jardine. We do not know when the connection between Stewart and Alloy began. He arrived in China in October 1835, became a partner in Jardine's in 1842 and died in Hong Kong on 10 September 1846. At the time there were few women in Hong Kong, either Chinese or European. Openly acknowledging an association with a protected woman would not have brought the same degree of social stigma as would later have been the case. It is doubtful if even a decade later a partner of Jardine's would have displayed a portrait of his Chinese woman in his home.

The first newspaper notice of an alliance between a foreign man and a Chinese woman also contains the first evidence of a change in attitude. It is the account in the *Friend of China* on 13 October 1849 of the 'Cumsingmoon Affair'. This concerned opium trading by Ng Akew, a Chinese woman living under the protection of James Bridges Endicott, master of an opium receiving ship at the Cumsingmoon anchorage in the Pearl River. The editor was embarrassed to expose a practice that was normally kept under cover; hence the account was prefaced with a moralising editorial apology:

> While there is little to commend, there is much to condemn; and though we run the risk of offending many, we probably will please none. Irregularities have grown out of the demoralised conditions of the foreign residents in China, partly from a branch of their traffic (the smuggling of opium), partly from the long term during which society was nearly without the influence of educated and refined European families. The last few years have seen wonderful changes in the social conditions of the foreign residents, and we now speak more of what was than what is; but though what once was the rule may now be the exception, the evils of the exception are still felt, and its shameless immoralities are too open and too observable.

The editor was too sanguine in his opinion that alliances between foreigners and Chinese women were in decline. Missionary correspondence contains frequent references to the bad example set by the immoral conduct of foreigners in China. However, the presence in Hong Kong of more foreign women with conventional moral standards meant that the foreign male who wished to be accepted in 'society' became more circumspect about irregular alliances.

The relationship between Endicott and Ng Akew continued until 1852 when he brought a woman out from England to marry. He and Akew reached a separation settlement. Their offspring were divided between them. Those who went to Endicott were received and cared for by his new bride, who subsequently had children of her own. These two sets of children grew up together. The boys found positions in Shanghai and the Philippines with foreign commercial firms while the girls later went to England and the United States. They thus lost their Chinese heritage. Unfortunately the lives of the children left with Akew cannot be documented but they must have become part of the Chinese/Eurasian community of Hong Kong.

The Rev. J.E. Eitel, in his history of Hong Kong published in 1895, discusses the role of the Tanka or boat people in Hong Kong. He states that they had a near-monopoly of the trade in girls and women, and that:

> The half-caste population in Hong Kong were, from the earliest days of the settlement of the Colony and down to the present day, almost exclusively the offspring of these Tan-ka people. But, like the Tan-ka people themselves, they are happily under the influence of a process of continuous re-absorption in the mass of Chinese residents of the Colony (1895 p. 169).

This reabsorption process, however, is not supported by my own research, which shows that the children of the protected women and their descendants developed into a distinct Eurasian community, although it is true that, at first, it was identified more with the Chinese than the European members of the Hong Kong population.

The Anomalous Position of Protected Women in the European Community

A protected woman occupied an anomalous position between the European and Chinese communities. She had little connection with the European community other than with her protector and his most intimate friends, particularly those who also had relationships with Chinese women. Most Europeans were reluctant to receive the Chinese woman or her Eurasian children into their circle. The children were the tangible evidence of moral irregularity. A letter in the *Hongkong Telegraph* of 26 September 1895, in reply to one from a Eurasian condemning European fathers who deserted their protected woman and their children, expressed this view clearly:

> It is unfair and absurd to blame Europeans for abandoning a certain class of women and their illegitimate children. In the first instance the mothers of Eurasians are not as circumspect as they should be, and therefore all their offspring are, of course, illegitimate. In many cases Europeans are, too, quite unable to detect any traces of European parentage in their children which claim to be their offspring. All women and young girls – whether here, in China, or otherwise – can earn an honest living by needlework, etc., or they can marry respectable Chinese, if so inclined. This is a free Colony. No one can force them to adopt a life of ill-fame. If they choose to be classed with 'unfortunates' then they must bear the consequences of such madness.

This correspondent signed himself 'Fairplay', though in throwing all the blame on the women and none on the men who used them and then abandoned them, his letter seems less than fair.

The connection protected women had with European life in Hong Kong was tenuous. Most did not even have a lifelong relationship with their protectors. After acquiring a competence on the China coast, foreigners usually returned to their countries of origin. The woman in the relationship would always have before her the prospect of her partner leaving her and their children. Her future depended on whatever provisions he chose to make for her. After his death or departure, her only contact with Europeans would probably be merely with his close friends if they chose to watch out for her welfare. If he made no provision for her she might find herself in desperate straits, particularly in old age when she would have no one to support her. If she had children she could look to them, and in lieu of natural children she could adopt them. If childless she would have nowhere to turn as it was unlikely she would receive support from her natal family.

The Anomalous Position of Protected Women in the Chinese Community

Once a woman had chosen to live with a foreigner she was no longer fully accepted in her own community. Evidence of the Chinese attitude appears in press reports of a police court case in 1870 – a case which also illustrates the sensitivity of European officials on the subject:

Seen Aleen, a fine looking Chinese female living under the protection of a foreigner in D'Aguilar Street complained of Yeong Kan Sun, a shopman, for styling her a 'sow', insinuating tender relations of an unpleasant description and finally cracking her scull with a billet of wood. The defendant said the remark was to apply to a fellow shopman (*China Mail* 8 December 1870).

The magistrate sentenced him to 21 days hard labour. The case was reopened when new evidence showed that the shopman had called the woman a 'sow' living with a 'dog', thus disparaging a European – a more serious offence. The magistrate found that such epithets were coming into common use, and this:

… was dangerous to the peace and safety of the Colony. Styling a woman of this description the mistress of a dog, was only another method of gratifying the insane hatred to the foreigner, who by implication was the 'dog' (*ibid.* 14 December 1870).

The magistrate went on to imply that the harsher sentence he now imposed was in order to protect the reputation of women:

In this Colony no woman, no matter to what class she belonged, should be insulted in the public street with impunity. If Chinese saw fit to resort to this Colony for their own purposes … they must learn to respect English law in regard to the protection of females, or they must expect to have the penalties of those laws fall on them (*ibid.*).

However, it is more probable that his main concern was to protect the reputation of European protectors.

In certain sections of the Chinese community there was a strong prejudice against Chinese women who lived with foreigners and against their children, placing them on the margin of the Chinese community. However, by force of circumstance they were a part of that community and were bound to maintain contact with it. If a woman came from a brothel, she might keep in contact with those she had known in former days. Some women married Chinese men after their protectors left them and thus re-established themselves in the Chinese family structure, or they entered into other arrangements with Chinese men (see below). This was clearly easier if they had property.

That many protected women retained contact with their natal families is clear from the fact that they left their relatives money. Thus a woman who died in 1891 made provision for her children, fathered by a European, and then left money to her brother, niece, nephew and sister-in-law (HKPRO Series Will File No. 59 of 1891 (4/841)). A single woman and property owner mentioned her son and daughter and also her mother, sister, nephew and several friends in her will when she died in 1893 (HKPRO Series Will File No. 40 of 1883 (4/481)). Nevertheless, they remained marginal to the Chinese community.

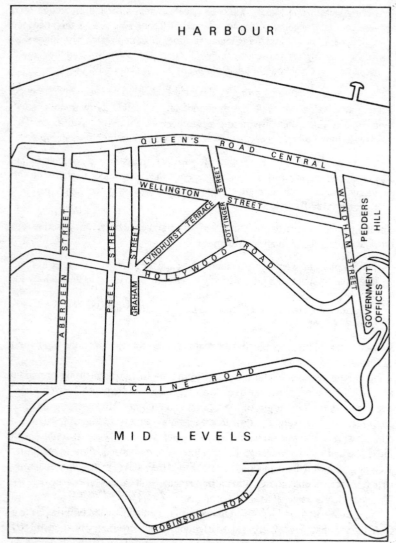

Map 4. Principal Streets in Central District, Hong Kong Island

Marginal Residence

Having marginal status, the protected women lived in a marginal section of Hong Kong, in the sense that it was neither exclusively European nor exclusively Chinese. It was between two European sections of the town, the business district in Queen's Road Central and the large residential mansions in Caine, Robinson and Bonham Roads. The area between was populated by a mixed and polyglot group composed of middle-class or wealthy Chinese, Chinese prostitutes serving non-Chinese,[3] European prostitutes, Indian, Parsee and Muslim merchants and shopkeepers, a few scattered Portuguese and Macanese, and protected women. To the west was Tai Ping Shan, a densely packed, almost entirely Chinese section, and to the east Pedder's Hill, government offices and the military cantonment.

When the area was first developed the buildings were of European style, set in large lots. With the pressure of an increasing population these residences were replaced by buildings of a style between the Chinese and European. Lawns and gardens vanished and rows of connected houses faced the streets. Within the larger blocks back alleys and lanes appeared with similar buildings. The ground floors of the buildings on through-streets were mostly occupied by Chinese shops – carpenters, washermen, provision stores, bookbinders – and by Parsee, Indian and Muslim businesses.

The cosmopolitan nature of the neighbourhood dated from the removal of two lines of ramshackle houses near a stream running down the hillside. These were thrown up when the first Chinese flooded into Hong Kong after the British occupation of the island. After a few years the government decided to move the Chinese to a different location to the west of the European section, as this unsightly settlement separated two European residential sections – Aberdeen and Gough Streets to the west and Lyndhurst Terrace, Pottinger Street and the east end of Hollywood Road to the east. After the area was cleared, lots were marked off and sold at auction. The lots were not as large as those in the adjacent European sections. Several wealthy Chinese bought lots and subsequently built family houses on them. Other lots were bid-in by Parsees, or obtained by Europeans for speculation. The presence of Chinese, even wealthy ones, and of non-Chinese Asians set the tone of the area. Most Europeans were averse to having such neighbours.

When foreign businesses were first established in Hong Kong the European staff often lived above the offices and shops in the Queen's Road area, but as the Caine/Bonham/Robinson Road area developed, more Europeans moved up the hill.[4] The 'area between' became a convenient location to put protected women. Social disapproval prevented the men from having the women in their own quarters. This 'area between' was a discreet stopping-off place between business and residential establishments.

In this marginal cosmopolitan neighbourhood, a Chinese woman was a step removed from the general Chinese community. The 'in between' character of the area suited the protector, who, like his woman, had entered into an unconventional relationship which might be tolerated by his compatriots but which it was still prudent to keep in the shadows. Moreover, the comings and goings of a non-Chinese at the residence of a Chinese woman was not as obvious here as in a totally Chinese neighbourhood. A marginal community could also be of advantage to the woman's children, whose playmates would come from various backgrounds – Eurasian, Asian, European, Chinese – and the sharp end of prejudice would be less felt.

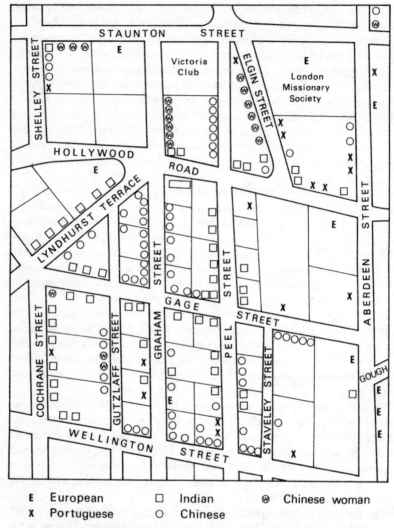

E   European   □   Indian   ⊗   Chinese woman
X   Portuguese   O   Chinese

Map 5. Ethnic distribution of Population in Central District and Premises occupied by Protected Women, 1872 (Rates and Collection Book 1872, HKPRO)

Protected Women's Associations

To counteract exclusion from the European community and marginality in the Chinese community, protected women tended to strengthen their ties with their own kind. Two groups of such women bought property in Graham and Peel Streets for their common use. Thus in 1868, a property developer sold two sections of Inland Lot 450 (43 and 45 Graham Street) for $4,160 in trust to 10 single women. The trust was dissolved in 1913 when the properties were sold (Hong Kong Land Office, Memorial 4561).[5] Another group of women bought a property in the same neighbourhood in Peel Street in 1872 for $2,000, which they sold for $3,550 in 1881 (Hong Kong Land Office, Memorials 5508 and 10365).

The mutual support they found among themselves was expressed in a number of wills in which the testator named other protected women as her executrices or as guardians of her minor children. The relationship becomes evident when a knowledge of the status of the women named by the testator is correlated with other data which establishes their identity as protected women. Their wills also show that many of them became prosperous property owners and business women (e.g. will of Lau Kwai, HKPRO Series Will File No. 14 of 1899 (4/1219)).

Protection as an Avenue to Independence

The position of a protected woman enabled her, under favourable circumstances, to achieve personal and financial independence. Her primary relationship was to a single male, her protector. This freed her from the domination of a mother-in-law, a primary wife, or males in the Chinese patriarchal family; but her independence was in proportion to the degree of control her protector wished to exercise over her. Independence, however, could become absolute with his death or absence.

An example of the freedom given to a protected woman is demonstrated in the 'Cumsingmoon Affair' (*Friend of China* 13 October 1849; see also above). While living with her protector Endicott, the captain of an opium receiving ship, Ng Akew traded in opium in a small way. In 1848 she had bought eight chests of the drug which Endicott and another captain of an opium hulk had recovered from a vessel sunk in a typhoon. But in April 1849 her cargo was seized by pirates. A determined woman and, as a boat woman, acquainted with the haunts and methods of the pirates, Akew visited them and threatened them with the vengeance of her foreign friends. The pirates gave her a quantity of betel nuts, which did not cover her loss. Against Endicott's advice, and in his absence, she went again to the pirates' den to demand compensation.

This example shows that protected women were not only capable of independent action but that they might accumulate capital to use for business transactions. Indeed this is also clear from their wills.[6] The woman who was able to accumulate personal capital by savings from her allowance, from gifts, trust funds, rents from properties or management of loan schemes, and who exercised good business judgment, could increase her capital and further strengthen her financial position. Financial security opened a door to independence. In the inter-cultural setting of the China coast cities, the protected woman, under certain circumstances, could create her own place. If she had been locked into the traditional patriarchal domination of females in the Chinese family, she would have been denied this road to independence. Although, while living with their protectors, not many had the capital or freedom enjoyed by Akew to do business in their own right, these women had more liberty than their sisters in a Chinese family. Protectors were in

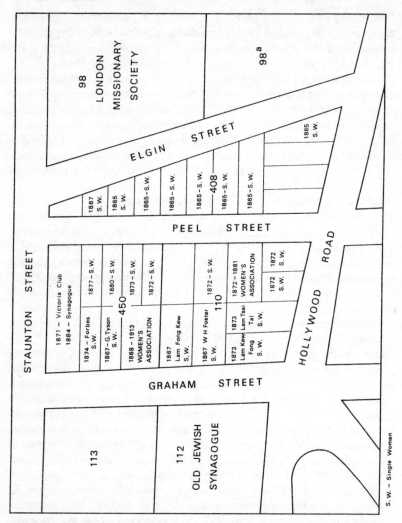

Map 6. *Properties Occupied or Owned by Single Women in the Graham/Peel/Elgin Street Area in Central District, Hong Kong Island*

Hong Kong for varying periods. Ship's officers came and went, and merchants would take business trips or visit their countries of origin. During these absences the women would be free from male domination.

They usually attained full freedom when the protector died, left Hong Kong permanently or, as in the case of Endicott and Ng Akew, severed relations. If he left or died, he would sometimes leave instructions for friends or business associates to oversee or assist her. Sometimes the mistress was taken on by another European protector, although there is little evidence of this. Some found Chinese protectors. Thus one Leen Aho, whose protector did not provide for her, came under the protection of the nephew of the wealthy Chinese comprador of the P. & O. Company, who gave her food and rent (*Daily Press* 10 January 1871).

Sometimes they married Chinese men. An example of this was Leung Akiu, who lived with a European clerk of the Supreme Court from 1846 to 1852/53, when he left Hong Kong. On his return he introduced her to Wong Achau, a small merchant, intending that she should become his concubine or second wife. The couple lived together for two years before there was a formal Chinese marriage ceremony in 1857. Since Wong's first wife had now died, Akiu was able to take her place as his primary wife. That she had accumulated capital is clear from his attempt to break her will after her death in 1881. She was alleged to have kept a brothel in one of her properties and bought girls as prostitutes under the guise of adopting them (*China Mail* 21, 22, 23 December 1881).

Some women, when left by their protectors, entered into non-marital relations with Chinese men, like the ubiquitous Ng Akew. She, as has been seen, already had some capital and the settlement with Endicott in 1852 provided her with considerable income from properties. From 1855 to 1856 she formed a profitable business association with one Fung Aching, a building contractor who also traded coolies to Peru. Like Leung Akiu, she was also engaged in the brothel business (J.W. Norton-Kyshe 1971 Vol. 2 p. 317).

In most cases, upon the departure of a protector, his woman managed her own affairs. She could find herself in relatively easy circumstances or enslaved by poverty, depending on the provisions he had made for her and on her own business acumen during the time they had lived together. Normally while he was with her she would have control of the household and would receive an allowance for personal and household expenses. Depending on his inclination she would control the household funds, with varying degrees of accountability, so long as she ministered to his needs. With good management she might accumulate her own savings. When one adds to this the provisions made for them, some women came out of their relationships extremely well. Thus Leung Akiu was able to maintain a large household of some 15 persons, consisting of servants, natural and adopted children, purchased children, some of whom were bought to work as prostitutes, and at times relatives from her natal family. Another enterprising woman, whose protector had been a prominent European provision store keeper in early Hong Kong, made extra money by 'adopting' daughters whom she trained to become mistresses of men from Scotland (personal communication from a descendant).

The auction of the household affects of Ng Akew after her bankruptcy in 1878 illustrates the lifestyle of a prosperous protected woman. For sale were custom-made marble-top blackwood tables, chairs and stools, carved blackwood sofas, chairs and a table, chimney glasses, engravings, pictures, lamps, carpets, clocks, bookcases, sideboards, crockery, glass and plated ware, vases and ornaments, Guangzhou-made blackwood bedsteads, teak wardrobes, a toilet table and glass, washstands, and one iron safe (*Daily Press* 29 March 1878).

The principal assets of financially successful protected women were landed property, household furniture, cash and jewellery. Those who became property owners were in a fortunate position. Customarily Chinese women did not own property in their own name, though as widows they usually had a life interest in the property left by their husbands. The protected woman, on the other hand, often owned property in her own name. Protectors would convey properties outright or in trust to the women they lived with. The Hong Kong Land Records show these transactions (see Appendix). Where a property was transferred by a foreigner to a Chinese woman for a nominal consideration – say one to five dollars – it usually means that the grantor was her protector. Conveying property absolutely to the woman suggests the vendor had confidence in her ability to manage her own affairs. Otherwise a trust was created with friends of the grantor as trustees. The first documentary evidence of a grant of land by a foreigner to a protected woman was recorded in July 1845 when a merchant, F.J. Porter, conveyed a lot in Queen's Road West to one Akew for the nominal sum of five dollars. She sold it the following year for $700 (Hong Kong Land Records, Memorial 121, 23 July 1845).[7]

The first large-scale venture by a protected woman was the development of Inland Lot 408, bounded by Hollywood Road, Elgin Street and Peel Street, by Ng Akew in partnership with Fung Aching. He obtained the lease in 1855 and conveyed it to Ng Akew. They built 13 dwellings on the property and rented nine on Elgin Street to single Chinese women. They sold off the last parts of the lot in 1858 at a profit. Protected women continued to live in this part of Elgin Street for many years (Hong Kong Land Records, Memorials 1104, 1115, 1203, 1417). Many other lots in the neighbourhood were bought by them or their protectors. Some were held in trust for the benefit of the women and their children. The Land Records show numerous such transactions.

Although many protected women achieved independence through their relationships with foreign men, others were not so fortunate. The departure of a protector could leave his woman independent of male control, but if he had not provided for her, she and her children might be enslaved by poverty. A letter by an abandoned child who signed himself 'Eurasian' published in the *Hongkong Telegraph* on 24 September 1895 put the problem cogently:

Our lot is anything but a happy one … Practically without home or blood relations in true sense of the term … deserted in nine cases out of 10 by heartless fathers who seldom give us even a fair grammar school education; thrown at an early age on the slender resources of our fine mothers who … are not in a position to rear us up in the same manner as our heartless fathers were reared, neither can they see to it we associate only with desirable school fellows and playmates … and the wonder is, truly, that we are as well off and as educated as many of us find ourselves today. It certainly reflects the utmost credit on our unfortunate mothers and stimulates one and all of us to leave no stone unturned to render the existence of our mothers as happy as it is possible under the peculiar circumstances. True, in some cases our mothers have only themselves to blame for what they are wont to speak of as 'cruel desertion', but I cannot shut my eyes to the fact that many of us have cause to curse the memory of our fathers and say in the bitterness and anguish of our souls, it were better we had ne'er been born ... I freely admit some of our fathers act like *men* and have either settled a dowery on our mothers and have left us the means of keeping the family respectable but there are, unhappily, many shocking cases calling aloud for the closest inquiry by the authorities and for justice.

The writer proposed that an association be founded to promote the welfare and improve the social status of Eurasians and that a law be passed by the Legislative Council to protect their mothers. He also suggested that the association should keep a careful record of members and their parents and, when necessary, provide a monthly grant to needy mothers.

The Children of Protected Women

Clearly the welfare of their Eurasian children, upon whom many protected women had to rely for support in their old age, was of prime importance to them. Their offspring's position in relation to the Chinese community is of particular interest since it was the result of the patriarchal system. Had their fathers been Chinese and their mothers foreigners – a rare situation – they would have been accepted into the Chinese kin group provided the father had registered his child in the usual fashion. Since this was impossible for women, the children of protected women were a group apart. Like their mothers, they were called derogatory names. For example, a Eurasian complained in court in 1875 that a constable who had arrested him for firing crackers during a religious celebration had called him 'a foreign devil's child'. Equally they were held in low esteem by the European community.

They were also faced with the difficult problem of adjusting to the very different cultures of their parents. Their solutions were influenced by many factors. The length of the parents' relationship was important. If they were together only a short time, the child was deprived of the presence of the father during his or her formative years, and would have little opportunity to share in the paternal heritage. Moreover, the child's neighbourhood, although ethnically mixed, was predominantly Chinese.

Before the 1911 revolution in China and the abolition of the queue, the hairstyle of the children, particularly the boys, and their dress influenced their sense of identity. If they were educated in Hong Kong, the degree of Western influence at school, the language of instruction, the Western content of their textbooks, the nationality of their teachers, all affected identity formation. At home, the diet and eating customs of the family – Chinese or Western cooking, chopsticks or knives and forks – were a determining mark of which world the child was expected to live in. This would, of course, depend upon the relationship of the parents, including the degree of acculturation of the father.

The cumulative impact of these and other aspects of the child's environment and lifestyle could work in several ways. The children could embrace their Chinese heritage and compensate for the marginal niche they occupied in it by trying to out–Chinese the Chinese, or they could reject it and try to enter the European world of their fathers, or they could take a position between the two cultures and let circumstances and the natural course of life determine which part of their dual inheritance they incorporated into their personal lives and views.

Thus Sir Robert Hotung took the first course and wore the traditional gown of the Chinese gentleman and scholar, and used the family's Chinese name, although he attended Queen's College, Hong Kong. His younger brother, on the other hand, used his father's surname, received a scholarship to study in England and spent most of his adult life as an engineer in a British colony in Africa, cut off from his Chinese heritage. Unlike his brothers, who remained in Hong Kong and married Eurasians, his wife was an Englishwoman.

One pattern which emerged was for the child to use the Chinese surname when young but in adult life to change to the father's name. There were several reasons for this. Since the relationship between the parents was not socially acceptable to the European community, the use of a Chinese name was a way to keep the relationship from being publicly advertised through the child's surname. Once the father had left the colony permanently this impediment was lifted and his progeny could feel freer to use his name, thus expressing a choice about identity. Alternatively the choice might be based on the practical consideration of the value of a European or Chinese name for business or professional advancement. Thus if a son moved into a comprador's office he would use his Chinese name, since traditional Chinese merchants would have confidence in someone they felt was similar to themselves and would understand the Chinese mode of conducting business and social relationships. Similarly, Chinese speakers would prefer to deal with a legal firm or a lawyer with a Chinese name. In other circumstances a European name might be preferable. Even Sir Robert Hotung, when he travelled, found it convenient to dress in European style and register at hotels under his father's surname. Of the 15 Eurasians who attended a meeting held in 1929 to discuss the establishment of an association to assist needy Eurasians, half had Chinese names, one had a Parsee name and the others Western names.

Although on the face of it these children had a choice of identity denied to others, their lot was not particularly happy. They were despised by the Chinese and European communities alike. Like their mothers they felt the need of a support group, as expressed in the letter of 1895 by 'Eurasian' quoted above, who envisaged an association which would not just look after mothers in need but would bind the Eurasians together, improve their social status, help find jobs for the boys and education for the girls. He also expressed confidence that there were successful and wealthy Eurasians who would, at the proper time, build a strictly non-sectarian temple where Eurasians could worship. This suggests that many found themselves in a spiritual vacuum. Some, under the influence of the Diocesan Home and Orphanage, where many of them studied, had become Christian. But others felt cut off from the ancestral worship which provided a centre for expression in the Chinese community. This form of worship was essentially patriarchal as it continued only in the male line of descent. With a foreign father, the Eurasian had to find a substitute. A temple for Eurasians could provide some of the functions of an ancestral hall. One Eurasian family solved this problem by having a private shrine for soul tablets in its mansion and an elaborate Chinese-style grave where traditional ceremonies were held at Qing Ming, the time set for 'sweeping graves' (I. Cheng 1976 p. 97). Some protected women evidently also felt the need to be remembered in the traditional way and left money for their beneficiaries to worship at their graves.[8]

A speech by Charles Graham Anderson in 1929 shows some of the basic insecurities suffered by the Eurasians. Although the difference in their attitudes to their dual heritage tended to split the community into factions, Anderson claimed that, while 'it has been said of us that we have no unity', on the contrary 'there is no gulf between a Chan and a Smith amongst us ... Underlying the superficial differences in names and outlook, the spirit of kinship and brotherhood burns brightly'. Of the most telling of the prejudices they faced, he went on to say:

... with the blood of Old China mixed with that of Europe in us, we show the world that this fusion ... is not detrimental to good citizenship ... We are a force to be reckoned with, a force to be respected and a force to be better appreciated (E.P. Ho 1990 p. 9).

Conclusion

In conclusion it may be stated that becoming a protected woman was an avenue of escape from traditional marriage and male domination open to a few Chinese women on the China coast. In Hong Kong they benefited from the colonial situation in that they were able to become property owners and many achieved financial independence. However, they were under male dominance as long as their protectors were living with them and their ultimate welfare depended largely upon the provisions their male partners made for them and the degree to which they could accumulate savings. The price they paid for taking this avenue was that their future was precarious and both they and their children were poised between two cultures and socially acceptable to neither.

Appendix

Female Landowners in Early Hong Kong

Based on data from registered memorials in the Hong Kong Government Land Office. There have been female landowners in urban Hong Kong almost from the date of its first settlement. These women are designated as 'female', 'single woman', 'spinster', 'married woman', 'householder', 'boat woman', 'mother', 'wife', 'widow' or 'concubine'.

Between 1843 and 1852 there were 18 women landowners designated as 'females', four as 'spinsters', and one as a 'boat woman'. Their place of origin is often given. Fourteen were from Macau and one each from Guangzhou, the district of Heung Shan (Zhongshan) and the district of Sun Ui in Guangdong Province.

From the years 1856 to 1862 neither the place of origin nor the sex of vendors and purchasers is given. After 1863 the designation 'female' does not appear; instead there are the classifications of 'single woman', 'spinster' and 'unmarried woman', all of which may be grouped together in the class of unmarried females. From 1863 to 1884 a total of 205 such women are listed as landowners. Protected women belonged most likely to this group. Within this same time span another 144 'married' or 'widowed' female landowners are listed. Thus over a period of 21 years a total of 349 women were landowners with the greater percentage so-called unmarried women, who were largely protected women reaping the rewards of their labour.

However, a perspective is provided by statistics from the Hong Kong Land Records taken from annual transactions recorded between the years 1844 and 1887. The highest percentage of women buying or selling land is recorded in 1861, amounting to 2.73 per cent of the transacting population. Thus the general impact of women on commercial life might be considered minimal.

It is more meaningful here to establish that the few women who came to be property owners in their own right did so against the most striking social odds. The first female landowner on record was from the Heung Shan district of Guangdong. In May 1843, Ko Sam Mui bought a seaside lot from the principal Chinese landowner in an area known as Shueng Wan (the area of urban Hong Kong where the first Chinese settled after British occupation of the island). Her name, 'Third Sister Ko', suggests a woman of humble origins. The purchase price of the lot was $150. Two years later she sold the lot for $850. The large difference between purchase and sale price may have been due to the improvement of the lot while in her possession. If so, it would mean she must have had the capital at her disposal to make such improvements.

A small group of female landowners held lots on Crown Lease from the government on two streets on the hillside above the Queen's Road area of the Lower Bazaar. These streets are now known as Upper and Lower Lascar Row. The women were from Macau and were probably boat women; one, at least, was so designated. It was government policy to grant Crown Leases in the Chinese section of the new settlement to Chinese who had assisted the British by providing provisions and other services during the recent conflict with China. These women must have rendered such service. The women, however, soon disposed of their lots to Muslims who opened lemonade shops and boarding houses for Lascar seamen. Several of the Chinese women became wives of these Muslim businessmen.

Notes

1. The term Tanka, or *dan jia* in Mandarin, is now rarely used. The usual reference is to boat people. Tanka houseboats, both places of residence and of work, were found on the seashores and shallow river banks in the provinces of Guangdong,

Fujian and Guangxi. The Tanka were a marginal people suffering various social and economic disabilities. Barbara Ward suggests that the term Tanka, literally meaning 'egg families', may be derived from the use of the 'egg' character to represent the sound of a term by which the boat people were known. Ward describes the Tanka as 'people who live on boats and speak Cantonese' (*Through Other Eyes*, The Chinese University Press, Hong Kong, 1985, p. 3). See also Eugene N. Anderson, *Essays on South China's Boat People* (Orient Cultural Service, Taipei, 1972); Hiroaki Kani, *A General Survey of the Boat People in Hong Kong* (Southeast Asian Studies Section, New Asian Research Institute, Chinese University of Hong Kong, 1967); Chen Xujing, *Danminde Yanjiu* (Research on Tanka People), Shanghai, 1946.

2. I am indebted to Dr Maria Jaschok for drawing my attention to Sun Guoqun's work on Chinese prostitution and for a reference to Tanka prostitutes who served Western clients. In this they were unlike typical prostitutes who were so unaccustomed to the appearance of Western men that 'they were all afraid of them'. Sun gives two explanations for the term *haam sui mui*: that the name was derived from the salty waters on which the women lived and worked, and that it might be a transliteration of the English word 'handsome', pronounced much like the Cantonese *haam sui mui*, an allusion to the beauty of the boat women (Sun 1988).

3. The brothels for Chinese were concentrated in Tai Ping Shan with a smaller cluster in Wanchai.

4. The Peak had not yet been developed as the preferred location for wealthy Europeans.

5. Ng Akew was one of the original trustees until she went bankrupt in 1878.

6. Lau Kwai, designated a widow, died in 1899. She names four women to act as her executrices, one her own daughter. Lau Kwai bequeathed to her heirs two properties in Bonham Strand, two in Hollywood Road and one in Upper Station Street (HKPRO Series Will File No. 14 of 1899 (4/1219)).

7. Cases can also be found of non-European protectors. In 1883, a deed of settlement was drawn up by the merchant Mahomed Ebrahim Hajee Asgar to provide for his protected woman Hung Assoo, and for their five children, all under the age of 21. About to leave the Colony, Mahomed Ebrahim Hajee Asgar appointed Hajee Mahomed Sadeck Hajee Esmail, also a merchant, as trustee for Hung Assoo, to be responsible for overseeing the management of a piece of property, Inland Lot 125, which constituted the compensation for 11 years of cohabitation with Hung. Hong Kong Land Records, Memorial 12699, 4 October 1883.

8. See for instance the will of Lau Kwai HKPRO Series Will File No. 14 of 1899 (Note 18). The will of a single woman who died in 1882 provided for the burial expenses of her mother and grandmother and for annual visits to her own grave, suggesting that they were not integrated into the Chinese traditional family structure yet were anxious to be remembered in traditional style. HKPRO Series Will File No. 91 of 1882 (4/477).

11. Female Migrants in Singapore: Towards a Strategy of Pragmatism and Coping

By Claire Chiang

Introduction

This chapter is not about female bondage and women's inescapable fate. It is about women who had the freedom and courage to choose their own means of livelihood, achieving a control over their lives which has significant implications for our understanding of women's choices and constraints in the Singapore of the 1930s.

This chapter looks at women as active agents capable of utilising the resources surrounding them to carve out their unique identities, their *raison d'etre*, their hopes and dreams. It focuses on coping, pragmatism, human resilience and individual control; it also focuses on limitations, fears and disappointments. It aims to tell a human story.

Female Immigration Patterns in Singapore

Large-scale male immigration accompanied the development and expansion of colonial economic interests in Singapore (Lee P.P. 1978; Yen C.H. 1986; Cheng L.K. 1985). Propelled by alluring tales of *Nanyang* (Southeast Asia), impoverished male migrants left their villages in China in hordes, dreaming of a brighter future for themselves and their families. Their dreams were a 'collectivised' phenomenon, transmitted and energised by storytellers, travellers, passage brokers and successful emigrants, embracing a heightened pioneering spirit which made migration a norm of the times, even 'a way of life' (Garth 1973).

Female migration, on the other hand, had no role models to engender a collective movement with similar dreams. There were no tales or songs or success stories which celebrated, applauded and energised female migration. Those who migrated became invisible sojourners in an alien land, toiling away day by day, shaping history in silence. As latecomers, small in number and constrained by their class background and gender, female migrants were peripheral in the economic struggle of newcomers in *Nanyang*.

These patterns were a result of the different status of men and women in the feudal-patriarchal social conditions in the villages of China. Families restrained women from leaving, husbands demanded that wives stay to look after their households, and the Chinese government prohibited female emigration to ensure the return of male migrants (Ee 1955; Davin 1975). Consequently, the sex ratio in the early colonial period was highly unbalanced. Only in the late 1920s and the 1930s did economic conditions become so bleak in China that women were forced to leave their villages to seek their livelihoods elsewhere. It has been argued that the 1933 Aliens Ordinance in Malaya, restricting the entry of male migrants because of unemployment, resulted in an influx of female migrants, forced in place of the men to support the families left in China (Ginsberg & Roberts 1958 p. 251).[1] This inflow of female migrants continued until 1938 when severe unemployment led to immigration restrictions being imposed on women as well.

Female migrants were of various types. One category consisted of women who were free, unindentured and came voluntarily. These were the wives and relatives of men already settled in Malaya as traders, merchants and employers in the early decades of the 20th century (Lai 1986). Another category was single women from Guangdong's silk industries, partisans of an anti-marriage movement who rejected marriage and attained economic independence through work. They engaged in many kinds of work: pan washing for tin ore, rubber tapping, pineapple factory work, domestic help, hawking and construction. The more unfortunate categories of women were those in bondage – young and single women 'selected out', sold as prostitutes and *mui tsai* (child domestic workers in servitude) by a complex underground network of secret societies, procurers, brokers, pimps and brothel keepers (L. Jackson 1983; J. Lim 1958; Lai 1986).

The Inadequacy of Existing Studies of Female Migration

The literature on female migration is sparse and does not explore the themes of this chapter (Lim S.H. 1983; Lim J.H. 1967 pp. 58–110).[2] Songs, rhymes, prose and poetry relating to migration are mainly about male sufferings (Yeo 1986 pp. 175–97). The invisibility of women in migration literature is lamentable, given their tremendous contribution to raising the fares of many of the male migrants.[3]

Conversely a number of studies on overseas Chinese communities in colonial Southeast Asia focus on male migrants, their motivations for leaving China, their histories and successes and how they evolved social structures to cope with the new environment (Livingston 1977; Pitt 1978 pp. 31–59; Lee L.T. 1988; Yong C.F. 1977 pp. 195–209). When Chinese female migrants are included in labour analyses, they are invariably viewed as dependants, wives, daughters or slaves. This overlooks single and married women who voluntarily migrated, as independent migrants rather than dependent or 'associational' migrants, and created work roles and social structures that provided them with economic sustenance and emotional support.[4]

One exception in Singapore literature on female immigration is a preliminary investigation of the work of Chinese women in colonial Malaya written by Lai Ah Eng. It provides a general overview of the origins and conditions of Chinese women's work in the colonial era. Using a socio-historical approach, she examines each work sector in which women were involved and explores the dynamic interplay between class, ethnic and gender relations, concluding that women did not always respond as 'passive victims' to sources of subordination and 'are capable of taking action for self-determination' (1986 p. 107). What is interesting, although not explicitly argued by Lai, is the positive relationship between working and self-determination.

I chose the female economic role as the focus of my analysis for several reasons. I find two of the levels of interpretation of women's work inadequate. First, the conceptual dichotomy between primary and secondary labour markets corresponding respectively to male and female work often makes female work seem unimportant and unproductive. The second inadequacy is the underestimation and lack of appraisal of female competence, at both the personal and collective levels. As a result, women's history is always 'hidden', 'placed apart' or 'marginalised' from mainstream historical analysis.[5]

At the substantive level, there has been greater interest in exposing social problems commonly associated with women, such as prostitution, *mui tsai* or slavery and nightlife entertainment. James Warren looks at prostitution as an economic activity providing many women with their main source of livelihood and giving them an identity (above; see also Lai 1986 pp. 27–55). He suggests that Chinese prostitutes must not be seen as total victims, that some exploited the system as much as the system exploited them. He contextualises prostitution within the colonial economic framework of a growing, expanding economy. With the expansion of economic opportunities, there was an increasing demand for male labourers, generating more brothels and other social diversions. Hence, economic growth, while benefiting the male-dominated economic order, was often achieved at the cost of subjugating women in a flesh trade so lucrative that women and young girls were kidnapped and purchased by unscrupulous and illicit means.

Methodology and Sources

Against the backdrop of a declining agrarian order in Chinese villages and the lure of the flesh trade in Singapore, working-class women not involved in prostitution offer good comparative material for historians, particularly for feminist historians interested in women's options and the constraints under which they operated. For my study, I chose four individuals who in many people's eyes were ordinary workers. However, their courage in stepping out of their home surroundings was a liberating first move towards achieving autonomy away from the patriarchal dominance of rural China.

The four women did not conform to the traditional roles of daughters-in-law, wives and mothers (Topley 1975) and they were not sold as *mui tsai* or as prostitutes. They were arbiters of their own fate who looked at marriage with secondary interest and saw work as the primary avenue for individual independence and family sustenance. As much as anyone else, their work ethos was positive and their economic value was productive and at least self-sufficient.

Their fundamental belief was a strong adherence to self-help: you earned your own livelihood. These were the central orientations guiding my analyses of the lives of four Shan-shui women who came to Singapore in the early 1930s with nothing to offer but their labour: Leong Ah Hou was a domestic servant, and Sin Tai Mui, Lock Fong Kheng and Wong Sau Heng laboured as earth-carriers on construction sites.[6]

In each case, I asked the following questions: what made the woman abandon her familiar village environment? What features in this environment shaped her independent thinking? What made her different when women elsewhere were hardly allowed out of their households? Without the assurance of clan protection, how did these female migrants, with little skill and no education, adjust to local life and male patriarchy? What social institutions did they develop to manage their lives in Singapore?

I used several sets of raw interview data in the form of typed transcripts (in Chinese) and cassette tapes (in Cantonese) at the Oral History Department of the Singapore Government's Ministry of Information and the Arts.[7] I did not carry out the interviews or structure them. I organised and interpreted these life histories applying concepts borrowed from selective theoretical perspectives that allowed me to make links between the individuals and their society in their methods of coping with the external world.

Culling insights from the words of the interviewees, I examined how the self emerged, how it adapted to external forces and resolved basic conflicts. I focused my analysis more on meanings and interpretations than on the problems of validity, reliability and representativeness of biographical data. I believe that the spoken words of these women are as real and as meaningful as any documentary evidence. Without their words, we would not have their histories.[8]

Although words are not a 'neutral mirror of reality', in the absence of other information, oral data may be the only data that can give us a historical and personal knowledge of a particular individual. However, it only includes the information the informant wishes to express and share. Despite all the ambiguity, ambivalence, dissonance and conflict they have to confront, individuals attempt to give coherence to their lives in their thoughts and actions. In reading oral data and presenting them in an organised fashion, I tried to capture the thoughts and actions of the women's experiences.

I have presented the verbatim data of Leong Ah Hou as a domestic servant in chronological order, from her account of her village days in China to her experiences in Singapore. By following a life history approach, I hope readers will gain a total picture of the individual. As in all research interviews, it is difficult to cover all the areas of a person's life. I have had to make do with the information which had already been collected and analyse it with extensive interpretations.

I have then summarised some major findings about Shan-shui women as earth-carriers and presented three other case histories, drawing out comparative themes and highlighting their differences and similarities.

Leong Ah Hou as a Domestic Servant: Lessons in Pragmatism

Village Background: Early Economic Independence

I was born in Samsui [Shan-shui district] in 1917. I lost my mother when I was seven years old. As a child with no mother to take care of me, I had to earn my livelihood by looking after other people's cows. After a few months in this work, I returned to my father. A household without a mother was difficult, so I went to stay with my grandmother (mother's mother). When my grandmother died, I was 16 years old. I went back to my father after that but he was too old to look after me ... he was 70 years old so I came to Singapore.

As a child, I went to collect mulberry leaves to feed silkworms. I used to go to the market to buy silkworm cocoons ... which were placed on small sheets of paper one foot in length and breadth ... whitish in colour ... I then kept them in a pot ... After many days the silkworms were born and they gradually grew. The mulberry leaves I plucked to feed them were huge pieces ... I collected them, piled them up one on top of the other and cut them to fine portions like our hair strands to feed them to the silkworms. After feeding, they shed their wastes. When the white paper was soiled it had to be changed because the environment for raising silkworms had to be absolutely clean, without even a speck of dust. Any dust particle would attract ants which could eat up the silkworms. The air had to be good and the premises clean and tidy ... By 20 or more days, the silkworms would grow ... from green colour to yellow ... that was when they were ripe enough to spit up silk. They would spit out silk threads which bundled up their bodies. The healthy ones turned out smooth and thick cocoons; the weaker ones had cocoons which looked tattered and filthy in colour. The ugly ones could not be sold in the market, only the lovely ones were accepted by traders who then spun them into yarn.

In a year, I could raise silkworms six times. Each maturation process took a month. In January we started to raise silkworms and by August we stopped because the weather started to get cold and the mulberry trees gradually withered ... Some farmers depended on silkworms as their main source of livelihood, others depended on growing crops. We had different kinds of vegetables in the village. Each month the kind of vegetables we ate was different ... beans, yams, potatoes, sweet potatoes ... They were plenty and varied.

Those farmers not in crop cultivation depended on raising fish as a source of livelihood. They used silkworm waste as feed for the fish. That was why the fish were big ... There are people in our village who did not cultivate at all because of their small family size. They did some business or some seasonal work to get by. In my family, my brothers and sisters were in their early teens, how could they manage heavy physical work? So, we went out to work at anything we could manage. There was no clear economic activity. Sometimes I raised a few chickens and took them to the market to sell. Some vegetables we grew were too much for us so we took them to the market to sell in exchange for money to buy oil, salt and salted fish. Sometimes we did not have enough rice so we sold vegetables in return for some rice.

In a month, between my grandmother and myself, we could earn $3 or $4. If we were frugal, we could manage to survive. If we did not work, where could we get the money? ... and it wasn't every day that we had work. By the time I came to Singapore, no one was raising silkworms and I had no skill to do anything else. The silk industry collapsed because business was so bad that farmers replaced mulberry trees with sugar cane. That's how the silk industry ended ... Villagers were unable to market silk textiles overseas and there was no capital accumulated for further production. In one month we had to work so hard, after we covered the cost of the raw materials, the money we made was not enough for our food. That's why villagers had no incentive or motivation to continue with silk cultivation.

Male Bias

In China when you gave birth to a son you had to contribute a barrel of wine to the ancestral temple. If a village produced eight or 10 sons there would be eight or 10 barrels of wine in the temple. During cold winters, they were heated up and the men sat there drinking wine all night. The wine could not be brought home, it had to be consumed at the ancestral temple. The barrel of wine was only contributed to the temple when one produced a son. In return the family received a portion of meat contributed by other villagers. If they had no money to buy a barrel of wine then no meat would be given and the son that was produced would be looked down upon as a girl. That was the custom in the village. Those who did not have money were sad. By the time they were in their teens their fathers were still too poor to contribute a barrel of wine.

Sisterhood Learnt in the Village

In China the Seven Sisters ceremony was a happy occasion.[9] By mid-June the women in the group started to prepare their prayer items for the ritual: flowers of different colours were used to make the clothes for the seven sisters. On the 29th and 30th nights all the things for the ceremony were ready and arranged for prayers: incense, light, candles, decorative clothes. The ceremony lasted seven days. Womenfolk delighted in this occasion. There was no need to work. In our village there were many girls so if you had money, interest and the time away from helping mother with household chores, you could join the seven sisters' socio-religious group. I did not join it because I was too young and my family situation was miserable. My grandmother and myself both had to earn a livelihood, where would we find the time to be involved in activities like this?

Motivations for Leaving: Breaking Out

In the period before I came to Singapore, Guangdong and Guangxi were engaged in civil war. The villages were in chaos and starvation was common. The soldiers robbed, plundering chickens and pigs, even pots and pans, anything they could lay their hands on. Soon afterwards the Japanese invaded China ... it was a chaotic situation. We were always on the run to escape from soldiers ... When the soldiers came to any village and needed labour to help them carry the cannons, bullets and foodstuff, they captured the male villagers to do the job. Some mothers and wives even accompanied their sons and husbands carrying the load. Some husbands never returned: they were either killed or starved along the way ...

I had seen parents who were poor like beggars. I am telling the truth, I had seen all kinds of situations ... for myself it was miserable enough but I could still manage two meals ... For others they could not even manage to secure for themselves porridge ... how did they overcome their hunger, it was really sad for the villagers.

Life was miserable. A household without a father was poor but without a mother it was miserable. No one to take care of our meals and our clothing. It was just miserable. That was why I came to Singapore to seek my own livelihood. As long as there was work and food, even if I had to bear more hardship, I was satisfied. It was still better this way than to be a vagabond in the village having nothing to eat and no work. I also wanted to earn some money that I could send back to my father.

So before I came to Singapore, I already knew that we had to work to earn our meals. When there was no work there was no food to eat (no livelihood). I understood all that, just as my father had said to me that it could be miserable working abroad. But he said too that if I could endure the suffering, there would be no difficulty getting my two meals on the table; if I could not endure the hard work, there was just no way out ... one could not depend on borrowing money from friends.

The Passage: First Test of Self-Determination

I came to Singapore at 18 years old [in 1935], accompanied by a village 'sister' from Shan-shui. We did not seek the service of a migration broker but on our own we took the boat to Hong Kong and from there came directly to Singapore. We were not afraid. Upon arrival, we were admitted to the Po Leung Kuk, because no one *tanggung* (guaranteed) us. The immigration officers were afraid of our being abused or misled, that was why we had to stay at the Po Leung Kuk. The officer asked me, 'Why did you come to Singapore?' I replied, 'I came here to earn money to return home one day to look after my father who is too old and can no longer work.' He said, 'Many women are kidnapped to come here, do you know that?' I said, 'Not me, I came here voluntarily to look for work.' I knew he was afraid that I came here to prostitute myself or that I would be made to become a prostitute. But after I explained myself clearly, I was let out with the rest of my sisters [people from the same village who were travelling with her].

Coolie Rooms: The Sisterhood Nexus

Upon arrival, I went straight to the coolie room at Selegie Road with my 'adoptive sister' ... I changed coolie rooms several times. Whenever our sisters found a place more comfortable with bigger kitchens or toilets for example, they would consider moving and invite me to join them. These sisters were adoptive sisters. The one who came with me was accompanied by her mother and brother. I then stayed with another sister whom I had asked to come to Singapore ... I helped to pay her fare to come here. She subsequently got married and went to stay in Malaysia, so I was alone again.

Before the war the rent of a coolie room was 80 cents a month. Thirty or 40 of us altogether, sleeping on rolled-out mats arranged by rows. After I found work, I returned to my coolie room only once a month, usually around 4 or 5 o'clock in the evening, after the lunch was prepared and I had finished with the chores in my employers' house. Then I stayed over one night at the coolie room. Whenever there were festive occasions or friends and relatives whom I wanted to meet, I would visit the coolie room.

Those were the happy times ... after work we gathered together to chat and exchange stories of the day's events ... Coolie rooms were rarely vacant. There was always someone who was unemployed. Some women worked for the whites as nannies and some worked for Chinese employers. Those who could speak English or Malay could find jobs with Eurasian employers. Those who could not learn this foreign language had to work with Chinese employers. There were all sorts of dialect groups in our coolie rooms ... as long as you were introduced by someone who knew you well, you could share shelter with the group. I was brought in by my adoptive sister.

When I first started working I did not stay with my employer. His rented house had no space, not even enough for himself. If you worked with Indians or whites, they were likely to let you sleep comfortably in your own private room. They preferred that you did not sleep in the living room or the kitchen. So you chose a place close by to work and travelled to work by taking the tram costing only two cents. If one was frugal, one walked to work early in the morning and in the evening walked back to the coolie room to rest. Most employers did not pay for travelling expenses. Wages were only a few dollars a month. Some *sin-ke* (newcomers) were paid only $3 a month. But I was paid $6 a month.

To maintain occupation of a coolie room, each of us contributed a dollar or two a month to pay for the rent. After the rent was paid the remaining money was saved to pay for food during Chinese New Year. In bigger coolie rooms there would be a leader to collect a few dollars from anyone who visited the place.

During the year we gathered together in the coolie room a few times to celebrate certain festive occasions, like the Ghost Month or the Mooncake Festival. If you had money to spare, you would buy some food, for example mooncakes to celebrate with your sisters. On those occasions, we ate, shopped and were merry. We did that more often when we were younger. Now that we are older we have less interest in visiting the coolie room.

Terms of Employment: Low Skill, Long Hours, Low Pay

About a month after my arrival, I found a job. Someone came to our coolie room and announced the kind of jobs that were available. Most of the employers preferred new migrants, because we were cheap, only a few dollars for wages. My first job paid me $6 a month, doing all the household work, serving more than 10 people ... washing, ironing, cooking, everything and anything in the household ... There was no time to rest and I worked late, it seemed like I was always working. I woke up at five in the morning every day. After a year, I quit this job and looked for one that paid a little better.

My second job was with a doctor. There were nine persons in this household, but there were six workers: two cooks, one to do the marketing, one to prepare the dinner tables and serve the meals as well as to prepare children's food, one to keep the premises clean on the ground floor and I was in charge of cleaning, ironing and making the beds upstairs. I still woke up at six in the morning and worked until seven at night. There were a lot of clothes to wash and iron and in the evenings I had to arrange them in the cupboards, then prepare the beds, pull down the mosquito nets, bring two flasks of hot and cold water to my boss's room so that he could drink them in the night ... Then I went down to have my dinner ... After dinner, I went to bed. I had plenty to eat and the living environment was good, I was happy. I only worked there a year. There was an old servant there who had looked after my boss since he was young. She had a daughter who was jobless, so she persuaded my boss to get rid of me and to give my job to her daughter. I left and went back to work for my first boss. But the work was hard and the money was too little, so I quit after a few months.

'Careering' in a Family: Dedication and Commitment

Then I found a Serani [Eurasian] family. My wage was $6 and working hours were from six in the morning to eight at night. I did not live in. I went back to the coolie room to sleep. Although the money was little, the job was a little more *senang* (light) – I did not need to cook, I only washed and ironed, cleaned the house and washed the plates after dinner. I had to learn some English and Malay since they did not speak dialects. Time passed, I have worked for them for 50 years now ...

My employer increased my wages after some years of service. When his daughter married and the household expanded with one more member, he added one more dollar to my wage. At that time, a $1 increase was considered a lot. When his second daughter got married, he added another dollar and when his son got married, he again added another dollar. After the Japanese Occupation, he paid me about $20.

During the Japanese Occupation, I was still working with the Serani family. We went to hide in the market at Rochor ... my boss had a friend there. At Telok Kurau where we were hiding, there were bombings and fire ... houses were totally destroyed ... I carried one bundle of belongings to Rochor and returned the next day to our house after the bombings quietened down … I saw so many bodies on the road, they were awful …

I went about my duties as usual, washing, cleaning, ironing … I was not afraid. My boss was too old to work, but his daughter, sons and in-laws worked for the Japanese, so we had rice and vegetables to eat every day, plenty of fresh vegetables to eat … but there was no meat, only salted fish … If you wanted fresh meat and fish, you had to go to register to get some from the Japanese or go to Siglap to buy them straight from the fishermen at eight in the morning. I sometimes did that with my boss.

I never ate with my boss at the same table. He ate first and we ate the leftovers … I was a servant, I was used to my status, I didn't feel as if he looked down on me. My boss was considerate, he knew that I didn't take chilli, so he bought me extra meat and vegetables and allowed me to cook my food separately … My friends could visit me any time and he would not get angry. After 20 years of my service, when I got older and sick, he supported me by employing a younger person, about 13 years old, to help me in the heavier duties such as washing, ironing clothes and sweeping the floor. She worked for the family until she was 30 years old. The neighbours all thought that she was my daughter because we were together all the time. She got married and moved to Hong Kong. She came to visit me once after an absence of 14 years. Ever since she returned to Hong Kong, she has sent me a few hundred dollars every year. She often invited me to go to Hong Kong and her husband too had invited me. Two of them, plus one old person like me and their daughter – four of us could go for picnics, have morning breakfasts in the restaurants – life would be so happy, she said in her letters.

I worked for three generations in this family … now I am getting older, physically weaker and less agile; in comparison, Filipino maids are younger, healthier, stronger and cheaper to employ – there was no more need for my service. I decided to leave and let them employ younger maids. My employer now (the grandson of my first boss) did ask me to stay on even though I was no longer in his employment. I declined and decided to leave.

Some employers were kind and generous enough to give retiring maids a few thousands dollars as an old-age pension. My employer was not that generous, moreover, he was not wealthy … not that he could not afford the money, but he was not willing … I did not care to have his money, I have my provident fund to live on … day by day until I find an alternative arrangement.

Remittances: Women as Earners and Providers

I sent money back to my brother and sister every year for them to buy food. We kept in touch this way through our letters and remittances – just my way of giving them news about myself and being remembered by them … I know of families who pestered their relatives for money all the time, thinking it was so easy to earn money out here. My family never did that to me … In all these years my brother never asked me for any money … even when I sent back some money, he told me not to … 'It was not the money I cared about, I just wanted some news from you, that's all,' he said.

Work Ethic: Pragmatism and Endurance

We had no illusions about working abroad, believing that we would get rich here … My family knew that life was hard here … especially when one fell sick and was left alone in the coolie room. In the morning everyone had left to go to work. A sister could help out by placing a flask of boiled water beside you but once you finished that and needed more, there was no one to help you to get it if you were yourself too weak to go to the kitchen … that was why my father told me before, that going abroad to earn a living was a very tough experience. But what could we do, my father said he had no ability to take care of us and now as grown adults, it was better to look for an alternative livelihood than to stay at home to starve.

Each time I sent back letters to my family I simply informed them that I had a job, my health was good and told them not to worry. I never talked about how hard life was here …

I never thought of doing any other kind of work. I was used to domestic work … I had work and I had enough to eat, I was happy inside. When I had free time I could come out to walk about. The pay was little, but at least there was a job and my living conditions were generally comfortable. I must say I felt very contented with the households that I worked with.

I did not feel insulted by being called *amah jie*. As a domestic servant, what you were called did not matter. It was only words. I don't think anyone looked down on domestic servants. In life if you meet a good friend you are happy. And if you have enough to eat and life is comfortable and free, it is a good life.

Attitudes to Marriage

Shu ti was a tradition against marriage. After a woman had decided not to marry she would invite her sisters to a meal. That day she had to go to the temple to pray. If she had the money she would give a big feast. If she did not have enough she would just invite a few friends. It was just like acquiring a daughter-in-law or carrying out a marriage ceremony. The reason for not marrying was a woman's fear of suffering ill-treatment by her parents-in-law. As for husbands … if she was lucky and married someone good she would be happy. If husbands returned home and battered their wives, like most Chinese men would do … sometimes battering them until their heads bled … When women heard these stories, they decided not to marry. Even when their mothers prohibited them from leaving, they were still determined to leave. In my village I was the only one coming out to work. I had an older brother and sister who were not married. I was number four in the family, it was not my turn to marry first.

I had never clearly decided not to marry. I simply led a working life and it was satisfactory. I never met anyone suitable. All the time I was bent on work, how could I have thought of marriage? As long as my meals were provided and at the end of the month I received my salary, I was contented. Yes I am now old and feeling lonely but I do not find life to be difficult. I have my own money to do as I like, to visit friends, relatives or my sisters … So for myself, I never thought of *shu ti*, nor of marriage, I was only concerned about having work to do each day; that was enough to be happy.

My parents would not have been happy at my decisions [her indifference to *shu ti* and marriage and the decision to leave China], of course. But I did not have parents controlling me at that time. I had to decide for myself, I was totally free. I did not receive any pressure from my other sisters. It was totally according to my own wishes. Only those sisters who were more conservative and feudal in their outlook were not pleased at my decisions.

Some women carried out this *shu ti* ceremony in their villages before they came abroad. But after they came to Singapore they met up with suitable partners and I knew of a few who eventually got married here. No one despised them for changing their minds. In a realistic society like Singapore, as long as you have money there will be followers deferring to you.

Clan Associations

I did pay my membership fee to the Shan-shui Association. I am a member but I did not visit the place. I was told that you could go there to listen to talks and participate in their activities, like ancestor worship. I had no time to visit the Association when I was working. But now when I am not working my legs are not that agile so I still do not go there.

Those people in the Association will not look for us. If I were to join its mutual aid society I would have to pay a monthly fee; if we want to make it simpler we pay only $20 a year. We received letters from the Association inviting us to attend their activities. We declined to go … I heard from others that it is useful to join the Association, especially when one gets older.

Costs of Migration: Isolation and Loneliness

I went back to China when I was 40 and since then, about 30 years ago now, I have not gone back. My father passed away and my relationships with relatives back home have grown distant. My father died during the Japanese invasion, during which my family and I lost communication and by the time peace was approaching, I received a letter from them telling me that my father had died.

When I was younger I hoped to return to China to reunite with my family and sisters but now I am gradually ageing I somehow feel that we have grown apart from one another so I no longer feel like going back to reunite with my family … I do not think about going back to China to retire. The last visit I made to the village, I stayed for two weeks. In that meeting, we understood one another in our hearts … I knew their lives in China and they too learnt about my situation abroad … It was not that meaningful to me … My brother bought some food and invited friends and relatives to a feast at home … The older persons who knew me had died, the younger ones did not know me, so it was really not meaningful … Of course those who knew me were happy to see me … they were sad to see me go

... It was quite fun visiting interesting places around my village ... but I felt that since I was already earning a livelihood in Singapore, it was still better that I returned here to live ... I did not want to stay on in the village, there was nothing I could do in that farming environment.

Now that I am old, I am feeling lonely. I have to find a place to settle in permanently as it is not easy to depend on friends and relatives. I take each day as it comes, it is difficult to say where I will eventually end up.

Companionship in Old Age

I am now living with three or four other sisters. We share all our expenses: rent and utilities. If we want to eat together, we share, buying a little of different kinds of food. Sometimes we cook our own meals according to what we like to eat. We have separate stoves and we take turns to cook our meals. We have our own plates, dishes and cooking utensils ... If we get along we will stay, if not we will separate. We don't quarrel, coming out to work means learning to tolerate one another. The younger ones do not live with us. In this place we are all 70 or 80 years old, not totally mobile and agile in our movements.

When I am free I go to the temple to pray. I believe that once you believe in one religion you should stick to it. That means if you are a Buddhist you cannot believe in Christianity. I used to know a priest who invited me to a church but I was not influenced ... my friends are not Christians and I don't know how to recite Christian prayers.

Shan-shui Women as Earth-carriers

The literature on Shan-shui women is limited and sketchy but I have culled together data from various sources to reconstruct the salient characteristics of these women (Tang C.H. 1961; Boey 1974). A study of a group of 50 in Singapore reported that they were all of peasant background, relying on rice cultivation, poultry rearing and fruit growing for sustenance (Boey 1974 p. 27), exploiting the hills for wood and charcoal to use for fuel or for sale in the village market. Floods, famines, banditry and starvation had forced them to seek alternative means of livelihood in Singapore.

Of the 50 women interviewed 45 became earth-carriers. These women were uneducated. As the minimum qualifications of a factory worker was at least primary six level, they could not work in factories. Working as an earth-carrier was not an activity learnt in the village, but once this group was established in this trade, the gradual process of ethnic occupational induction led members to concentrate in the industry, and subcontractors needing workers in construction sites naturally 'selected out' the Shan-shui women and offered them employment.[10] The regular gatherings of Shan-shui women at Upper Chin Chew Street in the evenings made it convenient for subcontractors to approach them for work. The harsh environment they had been exposed to helped predispose them to this tough work.[11]

Of the 50 women, 36 were widows, and five were separated from their husbands at the time of the interviews, making them the principal earners and providers for their families. Hence there was a strong determination to work and send money back to their children in China. All 50 had had their marriages arranged by their parents as blind marriages. There was no evidence linking unhappiness in marriage with their motivation to leave China. Economic survival seems to have been the propelling factor.

Only three of the 50 women did not send money back to China, because all their relatives had died. In general, their remittances were needed and were expected by their relatives on festive occasions. Not only did the remittances meet basic material needs, a portion was sent back for spiritual purposes, for example for veneration of the ancestors or the fulfilment of ritual vows. Thus in more ways than one these women were the prime agents in perpetuating family traditions and continuity.

Their work ethic was fundamentally pragmatic: to earn a livelihood for their families and themselves. Strongly aware of what they were and had, proud of being called 'the working heroes' by others, they expressed a sense of accomplishment in being independent. Realistic about their own educational limitations, they made the best of what their labour could fetch. Of the 50 women in the study, 45 became earth-carriers on arrival, three became washerwomen, one worked in a factory and one became a domestic servant. Most remained in the same industry for about 40 years and only stopped work to retire. It appeared that they preferred the freedom their kind of work offered. Being daily rated, their work commitments were flexible. If they did not want to work they just took the day off. There was no need to apply for leave. Limited by lack of English, they could not work for foreign employers. They 'preferred to face the weather to taking orders from people,' said a Shan-shui interviewee. Such attitudes became so prevalent among the Shan-shui women that they dominated the construction field between the 1930s and 1950s.

Although they cherished the flexible work schedule, these women was noted for their work commitment. They all believed in work and self-sufficiency. Most were recruited by a foreman through a headwoman. They could get a new job two or three days after leaving their former one. This was attributed to their co-operation: whenever one was unemployed, friends would look for a job for her. In the construction field, their skills in concrete mixing were valued. Being industrious and robust, disciplined and committed, they had a reputation for completing their tasks within the time specified. As concrete mixing could not be done by machine in some cases, their skills and services were considered important in the industry. Most of these women had been in the construction line for most of their working lives.

None belonged to a labour or trade union. Most of them did not meet their employers directly. Before being employed, they had only to fix their wages, working time and transport allowances with the headwoman before they agreed to start work. There was no need to form any relationship with the male contractors except when building materials were short. They deliberately avoided making friends with contractors in order not to create problems with sister fellow workers. Social relationships were established primarily at work and loyally guarded among female fellow workers from the same village. They congregated at lunch time in a corner to gossip. They kept to themselves, not mixing, or mixing only superficially, with other female workers not of Shan-shui origin. But friendship networks were fluid. Once a project was completed friendships also terminated unless workers lived close to one another. Hence social relations at work with fellow workers were determined by the seasonal and temporary nature of their jobs, by village affinity and the propinquity of the residents.

Shan-shui women wore distinctive red headgear, oblong in shape, measuring about 14 by 18 inches. Other Shan-shui groups, like the Sun Yap workers, sometimes wore a different-coloured square scarf, blue instead of red. For all of them, the red headgear was used to frighten off evil spirits, protecting them from hazards at work such as falling off scaffolds. Although the women were advised to wear safety helmets at work, most of them refused to do so.

Known for their frugality and physical endurance, their daily diet consisted of simple food like boiled rice, salted beans, salted fish, vegetables and pig skin. Everyday routine began at 5am and ended at 5pm. A few more enterprising women would then hunt for cement paper to sell in Chinatown, at 10 cents per catty, or collect wooden planks from the streets for firewood. Their only luxury was a little 'red cigarette' they rolled for themselves. Their main leisure was the evenings spent with other Shan-shui workers at Upper Chin Swee Street. Their quarters were poorly ventilated, poorly lit cubicles without windows or external openings, which encouraged them to spend the long evenings in the streets in fresher air, at the same time saving costs by minimising the use of oil lamps. Gossiping among themselves was their only distraction after a hard day's work. Their only holidays were during the Chinese New Year festival. The study concluded that for such a woman 'work is an integral part of her until she is either too old to work or dies' (Boey 1974 p. 55).

On retirement, most admitted to having cash savings to fall back on. Of the 50 women, 20 decided to go back to China because they still considered it the 'land of their ancestors'; two considered China the only place for their souls to rest in peace and not drift aimlessly in the other world, and the rest wanted to go back because their children and grandchildren were there. The other 28 decided to stay because their children and grandchildren were all in Singapore; they had adapted to Singapore society and felt distant from China. Superstitious and a follower of many deities, such as the Kitchen God (for assurance of food), Heaven and Shen (for safety, health and prosperity), Ta Pe Gong (for protection) and Kuan Yin (for benevolence), a Shan-shui woman religiously carried out her terrestrial duties to propitiate the gods for protection against all evil things that might befall herself, her children and grandchildren in this life.

In sum, these women, as wives, mothers, daughters, sisters and aunts, fulfilled multiple functions to facilitate the productive and reproductive roles of the other members of their families.

Three Case Studies

Sin Tai Mui, 84 years old at the time of the interview (1986), came to Singapore when she was 24. She was betrothed at the age of nine but was permitted to remain in her parents' home until she was 15 when she went to live with her husband's family. She had no children from this arranged marriage. After the marriage her husband left the home and went to Guangzhou to work, and died when she was only 20 years old. She came from a farming village which subsisted on potatoes, peanuts and yams – an economy that was barely adequate to support a big family. She told an anecdote showing why women 'ran away' from their villages to come to *Nanyang*: sometimes a mother-in-law ill-treated her daughter-in-law by dragging her by her long hair across the room. Escape from fierce mothers-in-law and violent husbands were common reasons for immigration. What was more interesting, however, was the independence women in her village had in making their decisions to migrate and about marriage.

'When your husband was no longer around, even your mother-in-law could not control you any more. So you decided as you liked. Some husbands tracked down their wives and "captured" them halfway through their journey to *Nanyang*. If a woman had run away to earn a decent livelihood in *Nanyang*, she was pardoned; if she had run away with another man, she would be brought home, tied outside the door post, shamed and made to apologise by serving tea to her husband and mother-in-law.'

In travelling to Singapore, she said, 'I was not afraid, there were other sisters coming here so I followed.' Before she left, she knew that she was going to be an earth-carrier. This implies that women were already sought after for specific types of work before their departure from their villages. She chose to work as an earth-carrier because the pay of 65 cents a day was better than the 45 cents a day for other jobs like domestic service.

Lock Fong Khen, 80-plus at the time of the interview (1986), was married to a Shan-shui man at the age of 12 but was allowed to stay with her own family and study until she was 18. Protesting against her husband's ill-treatment of her, she decided to leave home to come to Singapore, leaving behind three daughters, the eldest eight years old. She came to Singapore with her 'sisters' without the aid of a passage broker. She was 30 when she arrived. She started work as an earth-carrier at a construction site earning 55–70 cents a day, adding up to $12–$14 a month. She had to carry big stones up six storeys.

Wong Sau Eng, 75 years old at the time of the interview (1984), came from an upland Shan-shui village where drought was so persistent that poor crop yields, famine and hunger were common. In reminiscing about poor village days, she highlighted the comforts and benefits elderly people received in Singapore. It was as though she was reminding herself of how comfortable she was now, and conversely, how miserable life had been before. Her village was unusual in that the men did not do the hard farmwork. The women were in control of the entire rice cultivation process, while the men spent their time 'drinking tea'. If a man was to help his wife, he would be laughed at or scoffed at. This pattern was so prevalent that upland Shan-shui men were known to be lazy and useless. They did not migrate to *Nanyang*. The upland Shan-shui women were noted for hard work and robustness. They were used to tough farmwork: 'We had no money to hire extra hands, we did everything on the farm ourselves – how difficult it was to obtain that one grain of rice!' Wong Sau Eng sighed.

She was married at 10 years old but, being the only daughter, her mother allowed her to stay on in the home until she was older. By the time she moved to her husband's village her in-laws were already dead, so 'nobody controlled me', she said. She initially planned to work in Singapore for only three years, earning a few hundred dollars and returning home to have children. She was motivated by a relative who returned with gold and fine clothes. Still young and able, she thought this might be an opportunity for her to make money and return in 'just as grand a manner' as her relative. She was sure her husband would object, so she planned her departure without his knowledge. She paid $30 for her passage, borrowing the money from her mother, who was glad to see her daughter seeking a better livelihood abroad. Leaving a daughter to be raised by her mother, Sau Eng embarked on her journey.

She cleared the immigration interrogations by lying to officers at every immigration point, telling them she was unmarried and had lost all her family members. Talking about her fears, she said with pragmatism, 'I did not think twice about whether or not I had a relative in Singapore; the more you deliberated, the more you were afraid to decide, the more you vacillated. So I abandoned all thoughts and simply decided to come and see what awaited me.' She was, however, fortunate in having an uncle already in Singapore to offer her shelter on her arrival.

Inner Resilience

These three women were married very young and were unhappy in their marriages. Determined to break out of traditional norms and maximise youth and opportunity, they took the decision to step out of their marriages, households and villages and start new lives abroad. They were motivated by only one ambition: to earn more money for their families.

The three women shared similar work experiences as earth-carriers. Work was seasonal, depending on weather conditions, job availability, friends' recommendations and whether or not one was on good terms with male and female contractors (*kapala*). Their wages, 60 cents a day, were 20 cents higher than those earned by rubber tappers and factory workers, but the Shan-shui earth-carriers worked fewer days because of the cyclical nature of the job and weather variability. 'We were lucky to have a month of work,' one said. Most of them earned about $10 for a month's work, averaging out at $6 or $7 a month. There were idle days when they sat at home waiting for the rain to stop or to be called up for new work assignments. Sometimes they were cheated of their wages by subcontractors who ran away with their money or gave them less than the chief contractor had agreed to. The early days of adapting to their working conditions were a test of endurance: Lock Fong Kheng recalled how she cried every night for at least a year, suffering from painful blisters and fatigue because her work consisted of carrying big stones up several flights of stairs.

Wong Sau Eng gave an account of her work: 'In this industry, it is your own people cheating your own kind; we knew we were cheated and that our contractors manipulated our wages, but none of us dared breathe a word for fear of the dreaded words "Tomorrow you don't have to report for work." So we kept quiet, making sure that we followed every rule and worked hard. We tried not to let our contractor see us taking breaks to drink. Sometimes we would befriend our female *kapala* so that we could count on her calling us up for work the next time. She was more skilled than we were, having to tidy up our handiwork at the end of the day … It was really not easy for *sin-ke* like us … getting jobs was not that easy … it was through a lot of endurance that we lasted until today … I don't know how we lived to such long lives when what we had as meals in our working days was so unnourishing – only vegetables and beans …

'In the beginning, I got up at four in the morning to get ready to go to work. Sometimes I dared not sleep for fear of not being able to wake up in time to report to work at seven. Being frugal, I wanted to save on transport costs, so I walked to work. After the Japanese Occupation, economic opportunities were better and jobs were easier to get. By that time, we already had established regular contract networks with male contractors who came to us directly to recruit us for work. We helped them by bringing in other Shan-shui friends whom we found reliable … Different dialect groups concentrated in different streets in Chinatown, each group having its own contractors to turn to for work assignments … So there was no competition really.'

All three women received support from other 'sisters' in the evenings when they gathered in the streets to exchange work news and stories from their families back home. The 'sisters' helped one another during depressed moments, drumming up tolerance thresholds and telling each other again and again 'to work on and get used to the routine and hard work'. There was no time for regret since returning to China could be a worse alternative, particularly for those who had 'escaped' from home. There was also the loss of face and pride to think about. Even on bad days when there was no work, they endured their hardships, simply eating rice with salt, Wong Sau Eng recalled.

Determined to eke out a livelihood in Singapore, these Shan-shui earth-carriers laboured on, switching from work site to work site, always on the lookout for available jobs and keeping their 'sisters' and contractors informed of their employment status and whereabouts. Because of the transitory nature of their work, Shan-shui women had no labour unions to fight for their rights. Hence, they did not have any experience of strikes. Neither did they receive compensation for work-related injuries. Accidents were not uncommon. Lock Fong Kheng stopped work when she was 74 because of an old leg injury caused by work.

In each of the women there was a fierce pride attached to their work. 'Why should anyone look down on us? Down here, we are all workers coming out to earn a livelihood – what makes you able to look down on other workers?' Only Wong Sau Eng joined the Shan-shui Association, to gain a sense of belonging to a larger entity. However, like the other two, she declined to participate in Association activities. Lack of time for and interest in organisation life were two primary reasons for their low involvement with the Shan-shui Association. If a crisis arose, they preferred to seek help from their own relatives, friends and fellow workers.

Originally they had all had the ambition to earn enough money to return home. All of them had returned home at least once and none desired to resettle in their farms and villages. All three expressed their loneliness at the time of the interviews, and one was getting increasingly immobile because of a leg injury.

Sin Tai Mui said: 'I had thought earlier that I would one day return to China. After my husband died, I had not thought of remarrying. Work was on top of my mind. Now I am getting older and my legs weaker yet I cannot die off so easily, even in my 80s … I do think it might be quite nice to have a daughter whom I could live with … I am suffering now … I did not know that I would get ill … my leg treatment cost me close to $10,000, but it is no use … '

But they quickly rationalised that marriage and children did not necessarily bring happiness.

'It is still unquestionably more rewarding to be on your own, making your own money which you can then send home to raise your family … There was no need to depend on anyone or pander to someone else's whims … Instead you are free to do as you wish … Is that not a good thing?' concluded Wong Sau Eng.

Conclusion

I have extensively used the verbatim data of one interview transcript to reconstruct the developmental experiences of the individual before and after her decision to leave her village. My main aim in doing this was to highlight aspects of her socialisation in the village and her early adaptation to work in Singapore as being formative influences on her development as a self-determining individual.[12] The second aim was a methodological one: my belief in the narrative role of sociology and in presenting data in an organised chronological flow so that the woman's history is recorded in her own words.[13]

I interpret her decision to leave her village as a move to 'break out' and 'step out of' a crumbling socio-economic order and not acquiesce in its constraints. Within her own framework of action, she had 'taken over'[14] and structured her life by this one single, determined decision to break out of conventions.[15] Leaving behind one reality that held no promise, she now had an alternative field of action to play out new roles and develop new competencies that made her an autonomous being. An eminent sociologist said, 'In the dialectic between nature and the socially constructed world, man produces reality and thereby produces himself.'[16]

By taking on a productive economic role at home and abroad, in a limited labour situation, she learnt lessons in pragmatism and acceptance, not helplessness and resignation. These were significant cognitive tools developed in response to the knowledge of her own market value.[17] Labouring with its hard work and long hours was an accepted 'immigrant way of life'.

By establishing sisterhood networks in coolie houses, 'seven-month sisters' and vegetarian halls in Singapore, immigrant women learnt on the one hand to be independent from men, and on the other hand they 'collectivised', at least at the emotional level, along both class and gender lines.

In practically all aspects of everyday living, the men did not matter in their lives. They got their emotional and material sustenance from the 'sisters' around them, organising themselves in various social institutions based on friendship, mutual aid and support. From the data I read and heard, the spirit of 'self-empowerment' and 'collective empowerment' in the ways these women had arranged their lives were clear. These social patterns were not new to them in Singapore as these women already had experience in China of girls' houses, unmarried women's festival associations and spinsters' houses (Gaw 1988 pp. 25–37; see also Watson).

An 84-year-old Cantonese interviewee recollected her village days in a 'girls' house' as follows:

> Girls' houses consisted of a group of young girls. Some were in their teens, some were married but did not consummate their marriages (*buluojia*) and others were spinsters who combed up their hair and decided not to marry (*shu ti*). They all lived together in a big house. Usually the girls were all very young. If you had the physical strength, you could earn your livelihood as a coolie, helping to carry cargo from the village market to homes.
>
> There were more than 10 girls in a girls' house; there was no need to pay rent because these houses were abandoned, left vacant by women who married and left or widows who passed away. Most of the girls were from the same village. When you were older and still unmarried, it was embarrassing still to stay with your parents. So grownup daughters had to seek alternative places to sleep.
>
> I joined the girls' house at the age of 13. All that I brought with me was a blanket and a mosquito net. Every day, I went back to my parents' home to eat dinner, after which I washed my face, took a bath and went back to the girls' house to sleep. In the evenings, we worked on our embroidery handiwork to earn some money. Such piecework was contracted and assigned to the villages by merchants in Canton city [Guangzhou]. We embroidered flowers on skirts and shoes which upon completion were exported to the West. We earned about $10 a month; if we were diligent we embroidered more and earned more. If we were not, we earned less. I used these savings to pay my expenses, as I no longer depended on my parents. When there was a show in town, I would go to spend my money or sometimes I bought clothes for myself. By the age of 13, I was totally independent, living on my own earnings.
>
> The girls' house was located in the neighbourhood, two or three paths away from my own house. It was a common social arrangement, nobody found that strange or incorrect. If we were not doing embroidery, we spent our time gathering wood and grass for use as fuel to cook our food ... [18]

By comparing the data two theoretical leads surfaced. One was the relevance of socio-economic environment and socialisation experiences in shaping self-determination and work attitudes. Leong Ah Hou came from the lowlands of Shan-shui, close to the Pearl River delta silk-producing region. Her early years of exposure to productive work reinforced a fundamental belief in human effort – that to work is to live. Sin Tai Mui, Lock Fong Kheng and Wong Sau Eng came from upland Shan-shui, a rugged and difficult terrain but suitable for crop cultivation. It has been argued that Shan-shui villagers were more able than other migrant women to endure hard physical work as earth-carriers in construction work in Singapore because they had long been exposed to harsh physical conditions in their home villages. Other Chinese women, like the Hakka, known for their hard work and determination, had also been exposed to harsh work environments. Being a special group of women with unbound feet, the Hakka were able to work in fields and the mountains, making them hardy workers abroad. It was not a coincidence that they were the ones who later replaced the Shan-shui women in construction work (Boey 1974 p. 33).[19]

Marjorie Topley in her study of the anti-marriage movement in the silk-producing delta region cites as one of the reasons for its origins the fact that economic opportunity allowed women to work in paid jobs. Their economic power was strengthened by the absence of the many men who had gone abroad. Other scholars have portrayed the delta culture giving rise to so much diversity socially and economically that women had opportunities to explore different economic and social roles (Watson above; Stockard 1989). Such economic independence and the degree of autonomy that came with it ran into direct conflict with a gender order that deprived women of their social status and family estates, in favour of their husbands and brothers. Feelings of relative deprivation emerging among working women possibly enabled them to choose different life patterns to challenge the structure of male authority. I would argue that the experience of doing productive work – handling and spending money earned by their own efforts – gave women a direct sense of competence, a cognitive experience that was indispensable for self-empowerment.[20]

Although those who were raised in this environment might be exploited to perform 'subordinate' roles as prostitutes, for those who broke out of their traditions, their paid work experience was a necessary, if not a sufficient, factor in fostering self-determination. As Wong Sau Eng said, 'The only way to protect yourself from being bullied and cheated by men was to be strong and determined.' This argument is more convincing if we compare their experiences with those of *mui tsai* and prostitutes. Those sold as *mui tsai* as children or kidnapped in their teens to become prostitutes did not have the work experience to foster self-determination. Age, work socialisation and the social circumstances leading to immigration, whether voluntary or forced, were cogent factors explaining the differences in women's work abroad.

That said, I am not negating the 'subordination' thesis, or the structural gender division of labour which confined women to low-skilled, poorly paid jobs with no security. The macro-structural features of women's work perpetuating unjust and exploitative working conditions for them are not overlooked. It is indeed their very pervasiveness that made these uneducated womenfolk all the more interesting in the ways they managed the brutalisation of work. But I would argue that even while the individual woman was limited by social structures and exploited by their abuse, she was not totally brutalised under the machinery of capitalism. Even if women did not express protest through organised labour unions, their autonomy was still apparent in their consciousness and in their lifestyles, in their perceptions and in their interpretations of their reality. One level of analysis says people do something because they have no choice; there is another level, one more attentive to the inner meanings of social actions and respectful of actors' own 'stock of knowledge' – their intentions, histories, hopes and fears – that says people do things because they choose to.[21] Indeed there is a need to exercise choice among a range of behavioural pathways in deciding whether to be a domestic servant, an earth-carrier, a factory worker or a prostitute. It is through exercising this choice that a female migrant 'makes' or 'achieves' her life.[22] By focusing on the micro-person level of social reality, I am placing these migrant women's coping strategies and self-agency foremost, disputing the 'tyranny of social structures' and elevating, hence celebrating, 'the personal will' which enabled them to transcend this tyranny.

This brings me to the second theoretical lead: a need to establish socio-psychological linkages between the individual and the system.[23] When restrictions were imposed on the entry of male migrants to Singapore in 1933 because of unemployment, female migrants became for some families in China the principal wage earners and providers. For the first time, their status was changed from a dependent to an independent one, from recipients of to contributors to family welfare. This said a lot about their efficacy, a competence slowly shaping an emerging selfhood capable of mobilising inner resources to control aspects of their lives.

As argued by the distinguished socialisation theorist Brewster Smith, when individuals solve a problem and achieve something on their own, this experience deepens their intrinsic motivation, which only emerges from having effectively and satisfactorily dealt with their world.[24] This suggests that the individual's resources of inner resilience are significant in adaptation. What seems necessary is a conceptual and empirical elaboration of the linkages between the processes of the self and the external reality, an area of research lacking in colonial immigration literature.

In everyday organisation of life, there are bridging linkages which make the transaction between the individual and the social structure less tyrannical.[25] Indeed, structural barriers are all-pervasive, limiting and confining individuals to specific work types and social norms. But it is important to understand how individuals cope with these constraints. Psychological coping processes of resignation, insulation, rationalisation and legitimation are means by which individuals interpret and accept an unfortunate destiny. For these women I have written about I suggest other concepts such as pragmatism, acceptance, resilience and psychological hardiness as additional coping mechanisms by which they faced up to difficulties, exercised personal control over imponderables, and mobilised resources around them to break out of isolation and reach out for sisterhood support. They did not have families in Singapore so they created surrogate family ties, either with their employers' families or with their sister-workers.

In all four women, their personal attributes of self-reliance, motivation and discipline were important internal resistance resources that enabled them to stay in work and endure their sufferings.[26] I looked inwards into the 'cognitive states' of the individual and saw how they used their skills, resources and values to cope with stresses in everyday living. They did not resist domination or exploitation, or negotiate for more autonomy in the work order; instead they used all their resources to exploit their environment with the experience and learning accumulated over the years.

Associated with their fundamental belief in personal control was their commitment to work – an ethic suggesting a certain degree of mental and emotional toughness, a readiness to 'tough it out', 'wait out the sufferings', 'plod on with life' and 'take life as it presents itself'.[27] In this embracing work ethic, every responsible person must strive to support herself and her family in China. Working to live and living to work were inextricable compelling motivations present in these women, shaping their pragmatic acceptance and perseverance, their frugality and diligence, their work commitment and dignity.

What made it easier for any discouraged individual to face even the most difficult times was the way sister-workers normalised each other's pains, repeatedly reminding one another that everyone was struggling in this 'migrant way of life', and would get used to it. Even more powerful a motivation to remain steadfast was the rationalisation that life in China might be worse. In return for their long years of loneliness without their families, they had more freedom, as singles and workers, to choose their own friends, their leisure patterns, their residences and the way they spent their money than their village sisters in China. Compared to the latter their independence was worth savouring.

Their freedom might be circumscribed, but so was their subordination. Though limited by inadequate skills and education, they adapted to their work situations by seeking out the work that suited them. They were free to take and leave jobs, leading a work life characterised by flexibility, purposefulness and personal autonomy. 'Life in Singapore is what I am used to,' they all said, showing little nostalgia for their villages and families in China, reflecting a pragmatic approach that put the past behind them in order to accept the present loneliness without regrets. Life is the way anyone perceives it to be, as social reality has both an objective and a subjective dimension to it; if a domestic helper or an earth-carrier earning her own livelihood cognitively perceives her work as having given her 'freedom' – she is free.

Notes

1. See Alfred H.Y. Lin, 'Paddy Production and the Question of Rice Shortage in Guangdong in the 1930s'. Paper contributed to the 12th Conference of the International Association of Historians of Asia, Hong Kong, 24–8 June 1991.

2. See Chin Y.F., 'Chinese Immigration to Malaya in the 19th and 20th Centuries'. Paper presented at the 8th Conference of the International Association of Historians of Asia, Kuala Lumpur, Malaysia, August 1980.

3. In 1984, the Oral History Department of the Ministry of Community Development of Singapore (now under the new Ministry of Information and the Arts) completed a four-year project on 51 Singapore business pioneers. Several transcripts highlighted the ways mothers paid for the passages of their sons and husbands to Nanyang, borrowing, hawking, saving, doing handiwork and extra farmwork. See Ho Yeow Koon, OHIT 1981, pp. 4–5, interview conducted in Mandarin by Lim How Seng, Reference No. A 000034/06; and Chew Choo Keng, 1980, p. 43, interview conducted in Hokkien by Lim Choo Hoon, Reference No. A 000045/24.

4. Such an orientation is still apparent in contemporary migration literature. See Paralikar Kalpana R., 'Women in Migration: Theoretical, Moral, Practical and Legal Issues Concerning Plans and Policies for Their Development' (paper contributed to the International Conference on Migration organised by the Centre for Advanced Studies, Faculty of Arts and Social Sciences, National University of Singapore, 7–9 February 1991). She appealed for a more 'practical' and 'moral' approach in promoting plans and policies pertaining to migration of women as 'dependants' as well as 'independents' (pp. 5–8).

5. See Evelyn Hong, 'Problems and Potential of Rural Women in Development,' in *Rural Development and Human Rights in South East Asia: Report of the Seminar on Appropriate Technology, Culture and Lifestyle in Development*, held on 3–7 November 1981 in Penang, organised by the Consumers' Association of Penang and the Institute Masyarakat. She particularly highlighted discrimination against women in statistical data and argued against the marginalisation of women in development projects (pp. 104–12).

6. Leong Ah Hou, OHIT 1986. Interview conducted in Cantonese by Chong Soon Yew. Reference No. A 000635/06.

   Sin Tai Mui and Lock Fong Kheng, OHIT 1986. Interview conducted with both of them in the same session in Cantonese by Chong Soon Yew and Tan Beng Luan. Reference No. A 000743/03.

   Wong Sau Eng, Oral History Interview Transcript, Oral History Department, Ministry of Information and the Arts, Singapore, 1984. Interview conducted in Cantonese by Tan Beng Luan. Reference No. A 000805/05.

7. The Oral History Department of the Ministry of Information and the Arts of Singapore recorded a number of interviewees under the Vanishing Trades Project as well as the Dialect Groups Project. These interviews were recorded on reels of tape and then transcribed, and in some cases, translated, for public use.

8. For elaboration on oral history as a method as well as an interpretative approach, see A. Seldon & J. Pappworth, *By Word of Mouth: Elite Oral History* (Methuen, London and New York, 1983); N. Denzin, *Interpretive Biography*, Qualitative

Research Methods Series 17 (Sage Publications, Newbury Park, 1989); C. Oblinger, *Interviewing the People of Pennsylvania: A Conceptual Guide to Oral History* (Pennsylvania Historical and Museum Commission, Harrisburg, 1978); P. Thompson, *The Voice of the Past: Oral History* (Oxford University Press, New York, 1978).

9. See Leong Yin Yoke, OHIT 1984, pp. 23–5. Interview conducted in Cantonese by Claire Chiang. Reference No. A 000505/08. The Seven Sisters' ceremony is an elaborate religious and social gathering held once a year in Chinese temples during the seventh lunar month for the purpose of venerating the legendary 'Seventh Sister', a beautiful celestial woman who on this date each year will meet up with her lover from Earth. The 'Seven Sisters' group is normally formed by 30 women from all classes, each person contributing one or two dollars each month to the group fund, which is used as expenses for organising this religious ceremony. Flowers, gifts, crafts and food of a great variety are contributed and displayed in abundance on this festive occasion. At the end of the ceremony, each person takes home something to remember this day by, to bless their fortunes and good looks, and maybe bring them good husbands.

10. I. Light & E. Bonacich, in *Immigrant Entrepreneurs: Koreans in Los Angeles 1965–1982* (University of California Press, California, 1988), employ the concept 'chained migration' to describe the chain effect of job recruitment among relatives, giving rise to ethnic occupational enclaves in specific trades. Building contractors selected Shan-shui women because they were robust and hardy but more particularly because they were paid less than men (see Boey 1974 p. 33).

11. The kind of work Shan-shui women had to perform on construction sites under the hot sun was rough: loading and unloading cement powder, mixing cement and preparing concrete, digging trenches and clearing the ground for piling. Such work requires physical toughness as well as specific skills.

12. See O.G. Brim & S. Wheeler, *Socialisation After Childhood: Two Essays* (New York, John Wiley & Sons, 1966).

13. See J.S. Reed, *On Narrative and Sociology* (Presidential Address to the Southern Sociological Society, Norfolk, Virginia, 1989).

14. See P. Berger & T. Luckmann, *The Social Construction of Reality* (Penguin Books Ltd., Harmondsworth, 1966), p.150.

15. See A. Schutz, *Reflections on the Problem of Relevance* (Tale University Press, New Haven and London, 1970). The term is used to denote a conscious attempt by an actor to demarcate his life world into segments of relevance and reachability (pp. 3–5).

16. See P. Berger & T. Luckmann, *The Social Construction of Reality* (Penguin Books Ltd., Harmondsworth, 1966), p. 204.

17. See D.H.J. Morgan, 'Autonomy and Negotiation in an Industrial Setting', in *Sociology of Work and Occupation,* Vol. 2, No. 3, August 1975, pp. 203–27.

18. Leong Yin Yoke, OHIT 1984, interview conducted in Cantonese by Claire Chiang, Reference No. A 000505/08, pp. 15–22. For a colourful description of a *shu ti* (spinsterhood vow) ceremony and the stress of reciprocity among 'sisters', listen to Leong Sau Heng, Oral History Interview Cassette, Singapore, Oral History Department, Ministry of Information and the Arts, 1984, Reel 1.

Interview conducted in Cantonese by Claire Chiang. In Singapore the vegetarian halls serve the same social functions (Topley 1958).

19. With industrialisation, most of the younger workers preferred to work in industry instead of on construction sites because of better pay and working conditions. The Hakka and Hokkien girls who later replaced the Shan-shui workers were mostly uneducated and unable to get factory work.

20. M. Gordon, *The Scope of Sociology* (Oxford University Press, New York, 1988), emphasises the ego factor in any social action and advocates broadening the scope of sociology to include psychology to understand the complexities of human interaction and social reality (p. 84).

21. P. Berger & T. Luckmann, *The Social Construction of Reality* (Penguin Books Ltd., Harmondsworth, 1966), p. 27, say that stock of knowledge, based on common sense rather than ideas, 'constitutes the fabric of meanings which allow societies to function'. See also A. Schutz, *Reflections on the Problem of Relevance* (Tale University Press, New Haven and London, 1970), where he asserts that 'knowledge has to be conceived in the broadest possible sense ... referring to the possible, conceivable, imaginable, to what is feasible or practical, workable or achievable, accessible or obtainable, what can be hoped for and what has to be dreaded' (p. 153).

22. P. Berger & H. Kellner, *Sociology Reinterpreted: An Essay on Method and Vocation* (Anchor Books, Garden City, New York, 1981), p. 7. The concept of 'makeability' is central to the writers: in everyday living, any person must construct his social reality and take it over; once taken over, he can modify and recreate his social world. Therefore, man can 'achieve' himself, despite and in view of social structures – 'this capacity for freedom is an inherent and universal human trait' (p. 95).

23. See J.A. Clausen, *Socialisation and Society* (Little, Brown and Company, Boston, 1968).

24. See M. Brewster Smith, 'Socialisation for Competence', in *Social Science Research Council Items*, Vol. 19, No. 2, June 1965, pp. 17–23.

25. See A. Giddens, 'Power, the Dialectic of Control and Class Structuration', in A. Giddens & G. Mackenzie, *Social Class and the Division of Labour* (Cambridge University Press, Cambridge, 1982), pp. 29–45.

26. See A. Antonovsky, 'Conceptual and Methodological Problems in the Study of Resistance Resources and Stressful Life Events', in B.S. & B.P. Dohrenwend (eds.), *Stressful Life Events: Their Nature and Effects* (John Wiley and Sons, New York, 1974), pp. 245–58. He conceptualises the term 'internal resistance resources' as personal power within individuals to accept alternatives in difficult situations, a capacity for 'rolling with the punches and coming to liveable terms with suffering' (p. 251).

27. See M. Pines, 'Psychological Hardiness: The Role of Challenge in Health', in *Psychology Today*, December 1980, pp. 34–44.

Part IV: Epilogue

12. Traditionalism, Continuity and Change

By Maria Jaschok and Suzanne Miers

The Resurgence of the Trade in Women and Children in China

It seems from many articles appearing in the press inside and outside the country that there has been a resurgence of customary and early marriages in China, and even of the transfer of *san po tsai* (see e.g. Tang H. 1988). Worse still, nearly 30 years after the practice was believed to have ended, women and girls are once more being sold. In fact, in 1989 the government found it necessary to launch an 'Anti-Six Evils Campaign' against trading in women, prostitution, gambling, drugs, feudal superstition and pornography.

The press articles stress an increasingly lucrative traffic in females for childbearing and prostitution – a traffic run by organised crime on a huge scale. One article may be quoted:

> One ... slave trader is Ho Lai Wen, a farmer in central Hunan province and boss of a notorious 'One Hundred People Gang', whose nationwide Kidnap Inc. has been compared by police to an assembly line. Police said Ho employed teams of surveyors to select young female victims, kidnappers to abduct them, a network of transport crews to ferry them across the nation, receivers to hide them and, finally, a unit of super salesmen to market his stock. Gang members invariably brutalised the young women, and customers were allowed to inspect and handle the merchandise, police said. The salesmen promised prices would be adjusted to the quality of the goods ... In Hunan and neighbouring Jiangxi, rich agricultural centres where single farmers traditionally have paid for a wife, police said last year alone they rescued 10,000 women who had been abducted for sale in slavery (*South China Morning Post*, Hong Kong, 31 August 1991).

The traffic is said recently to have increased to an alarming degree. It began to surface in the 1970s and since 1985 cases have increased dramatically in spite of active police efforts to suppress it. The scale is extraordinary both in numbers of victims and of criminals. Thus 4,000 abductors are reported to have been arrested in Anhui province alone within several months of the start of the Anti-Six Evils Campaign (*Fazhi Ribao*, 6 February 1990). Police are said to have uncovered nearly 40,000 cases of women and children being abducted and sold in 1989 and

1990 and to have freed some 30,000 (*South China Morning Post*, Hong Kong, 1 July 1991). Although some traffickers have been executed (*Observer*, London, 9 June 1991; *Sunday Morning Post*, 4 November 1980), the police complain that most receive only sentences of five years or less – the same as if they had stolen an ox (*South China Morning Post*, Hong Kong, 1 July 1991; *International Herald Tribune*, 5 August 1991). Moreover, officials are often involved in the traffic.

The reasons given for this resurgence of an ancient traffic include greater affluence in rural communities and enduring patriarchal values, which push up the value of women as childbearers while at the same time perpetuating the low esteem in which they continue to be held. Police trying to free victims of the traffic have met with violent resistance. According to Li Zhongxiu of the All-China Women's Federation: 'People still believe that, as long as they have the money, buying a wife or child is their own affair.' Moreover, it is not considered disgraceful to sell one's own child as long as he or she 'can obtain an adequate life' (*The Christian Science Monitor*, 29 March 1990). On the economic side, bride prices have become too steep to be affordable and rather than spending up to 10,000 yuan (US$2,200), men are tempted by the market price of about 2,000 yuan (US$425) for an abducted woman (Song H.B. 1991 p. 15). Not only does it make economic sense to buy a wife, but girls from some areas, Sichuan for instance, are considered to be especially hardworking (*ibid.*). However, not all are bought for marriage, many are sold into prostitution or to rural sweatshops (*ibid.*).

The victims come, as in the past, largely from the poorer regions, such as Yunnan and Sichuan, and are sold in the richer ones, such as Shandong and Fujian. Some are seized in their homes, some are hijacked from trains, buses, hotels, labour markets or dance halls, sometimes at knifepoint. Others are enticed into the net by promises of jobs or money. They seem to come from all walks of life, including peasants, university students, teachers and foreigners (*ibid.*). Children, of course, are the easiest to abduct. Once bought, some women are retained by force, sometimes until they have borne children and thus become less anxious to leave. Others do not attempt to escape. With little education, without money, in a strange place, they may be unaware that their plight is illegal. Many are afraid even to help the police free them.

It is also possible that the 'one child' per family policy instituted in 1981 to control the population explosion may have encouraged trafficking in infant girls, so that families may sell their daughters and try a second time to produce a son. Statistics show female births to be below the world average, perhaps because of amniocentesis or because families are again resorting to infanticide, although the authorities deny this, or perhaps because they are trading girls away so that they do not show up in the official figures (*Times*, London, 25 June 1991). It must be noted that boys are also abducted and sold but girls seem to be the main victims.

China also seems to be importing foreign women, mostly Vietnamese, for prostitution. They are lured into the country by the promise of lucrative jobs (*International Herald Tribune*, 7 September 1991).

The International Exploitation of Women

This volume deals only with Chinese women but it raises issues that are now the subject of international attention. Thus the sale of women and children in China today is simply part of a worldwide traffic in women, and of a continuing pattern of exploitation.

We have in fact a strange dichotomy. On the one hand women's rights are being promoted and discussed as never before. Since World War I long battles have been fought and largely won for equal rights, and for such benefits as free child care and maternity leave. Men are under pressure to share in domestic chores and child rearing. More women than ever are in the labour force and many are opting out of marriage in favour of an ever extending and more rewarding range of career options. The advances have been spectacular. In the Second or former Communist world of eastern Europe, as in China, legal equality was part of Communist doctrine from the start. While complete equality has not been achieved anywhere, important strides have been made.

In other areas, however, patriarchy and polygyny still persist. In those parts of Africa where there is a semblance of democracy, women are being wooed by politicians and many hold good jobs, but overall they still do most of the menial agricultural work as well as the domestic work, and in many countries they do not even have equal rights to property or in marriage, or rights to children in cases of divorce. Moreover, wife beating is common. Often the laws protect women, but the courts are operated by men, and local traditions or fear of a parental curse prevent women from seeking their legal rights. In much of the Muslim world women are still secluded and completely under male domination, and have no political rights. However, some elite women in Muslim countries take an active part in politics and in practice seem to have achieved much the same position as Western women. Thus the picture is mixed in much of the Third World.

Third World feminists are fighting indigenous patriarchal institutions as well as claims by Western women to represent women in other cultures. Thus, for instance, they have denounced the efforts of Western activists to end female circumcision. Muslim women, back in purdah with the rise of fundamentalism, have sometimes made it very clear that they accept their position as part of Koranic teaching.

The basic fact remains, however, that not only do old forms of exploitation persist, but they have taken new turns. Space precludes that we do more than simply highlight some of these. The United Nations has provided a forum for the discussion of many forms of exploitation of women and children, both new and old. Of particular interest have been the proceedings since 1975 of the Working Group on Slavery, which each year hears evidence of new types of exploitation, some of it sadly the result of the growing network of trade, communications and free enterprise, which offers new opportunities for enrichment at the expense of the poor and vulnerable.

Perhaps the clearest example of a pernicious new twist is 'sex tourism'. This is particularly rife in Sri Lanka, the Philippines and Thailand. Western males pay travel agents to provide them with women and children for sexual exploitation as part of a package deal. Asian feminists have rightly denounced this as a result of the unequal nature of First-Third World relations. Thus tourism, which has given rise to the commercial use of women and children for the gratification of the sexual desires of tourists from the First World, including Japan, is seen as economic imperialism practised by rich countries against poor ones – an imperialism which commercialises sacred sites and religious rituals, degrades the environment with hotels and a Western lifestyle. It thus contributes to a shift in local morals, leading to the acceptance of the selling of women and children for sexual exploitation (Srisang 1991 p. 46).

There is also an international traffic in women flowing from poorer areas, such as the Philippines or Vietnam, to richer ones such as Japan, and even, as we have seen, parts of China, for brothels, for marriage, for domestic service or for entertainment. Laws against illegal aliens have led to the exploitation of women in such countries as Britain, the U.S.A. and Japan. They are enticed with offers of well-paid jobs and then find themselves exploited, but they dare not appeal to the authorities for fear of being sent back to their poverty-stricken homelands.

The exploitation of prostitutes, often minors, who may enter the profession voluntarily but are then kept in it by threats from pimps who are often backed by organised crime, is rife in developed nations as well as poor ones. Evidence has been presented, for instance, of forced prostitution in the U.S.A. and France, both countries where prostitution is illegal, as well as in Germany, where it is legal and supposedly controlled.

There is a modern equivalent of the *mui tsai* system in the sale of children for domestic service and to sweat shops in the Third World. Attention has been called to it in Thailand, Sri Lanka and India, among other countries.

If we are to understand these developments we must see them in the light of the history of the women involved and through their eyes. We will hope, therefore, that this volume will spur scholars to produce more studies of the kind we have brought together. Only thus will we be able to compare the experience of women in various areas of the world and to comprehend their historic role. Even more important, only thus can we provide information for the many activists in the First and Third World who are struggling to end patriarchal forms of exploitation.

Bibliography

Abbreviations

APDC	Asian and Pacific Development Centre
CDO	Contagious Diseases Ordinance
CETWCE	League of Nations Reports
CO	Colonial Office Records
HKPRO	Hong Kong Public Records Office
HKSP	Hong Kong Sessional Papers
HMSO	His/Her Majesty's Stationery Office
JHKBRAS	Journal of the Hong Kong Branch of the Royal Asiatic Society
JSEAS	Journal of Southeast Asian Studies
OHIT	Oral History Interview Transcript, Oral History Department, Ministry of Information and the Arts, Singapore
PLK	Records of the Po Leung Kuk
PRO	Public Record Office, London
SCII	Singapore Coroners Inquest and Inquiry
SFTS	San Francisco Theological Seminary
SSAR	Straits Settlements Annual Report
SSLC	Straits Settlements Legislative Council Proceedings
WOBFM	Women's Occidental Board of Foreign Missions

Select Bibliography

References to interviews, to newspapers and other periodicals are cited in the text and endnotes only.

Unpublished conference papers are cited only in the endnotes.

References in the text showing the surname of the author and no date refer to chapters in the book (e.g. Jaschok).

Unpublished Primary Sources

Long documentary references are only in the endnotes of each chapter. Short documentary references are in the text. Only documentary sources referred to in more than one chapter or of particular general interest are included here.

Colonial Office Records in the Public Record Office, London (CO in text)
Colonial Office Records Public Records Office Hong Kong
Hong Kong Public Records Office Archives (HKPRO in text).
Oral History Interview Transcripts, Oral History Department, Ministry of Community Development (now the Ministry of Information and the Arts), Singapore.
Po Leung Kuk Archives, Hong Kong (PLK in text)

Government and League of Nations Publications

Only publications actually cited in the text have been included.

British Parliamentary Papers, China 1882–1899. Irish University Press 1971, Shannon.

Correspondence respecting Child Adoption and Domestic Service among Chinese. Hong Kong Legislative Council Sessional Paper, 1 of 1887. Irish University Press, 1971–) Vol. 26. (*HKSP* 1/87 in text).

Correspondence respecting the Alleged Existence of Chinese Slavery in Hong Kong (March 1882) [C.-3185]. British Parliamentary Papers: China. Irish University Press, Shannon 1971–. Vol. 26.

Eitel, E.J. (1879) Report on Domestic Servitude in Relation to Slavery, 25 October 1879. Correspondence Respecting the Alleged Existence of Chinese Slavery in Hongkong, Presented to Both Houses of Parliament by Command of Her Majesty [C.-3185], London, HMSO, 1882. Also in *HKSP*.

First Report of the Advisory Committee on Social Hygiene, 1925. Colonial Office, HMSO, London.

Further correspondence relating to measures adopted for checking the spread of venereal disease in continuation of [c. 9253]. Straits Settlements; Hong Kong; Gibraltar. HMSO, 1906.

Hong Kong Legislative Council Sessional Papers. Papers laid before the Legislative Council of Hong Kong. Government Printer, Hong Kong. (*HKSP* in text).

Loseby, F.H. (1935) *Mui Tsai* in Hong Kong. Hong Kong Legislative Council Sessional Papers pp. 195-282.

Nanyo no Gojunen Shingaporu o Chusin ni Doho Kotsuyaku, 1937, Nanyo oyobi Nippon jinsha, Tokyo.

Orme, G.N. (1912) Report on the New Territories for the Years 1899 to 1912. Hong Kong Legislative Council Sessional Papers.

Report on the Commission of Enquiry into the Traffic in Women and Children in the East. League of Nations, New York, 1933 (*CETWCE* 1933 in text).

Report by Commissioners appointed to inquire into the working of the Contagious Diseases Ordinance, 1867 (1880) [C-118] XLIX, British Parliamentary Papers: China. Irish University Press, 1971. Vol. 25. (Report on CDO 1880 in text).

Report of the Committee appointed to enquire into the working of Ordinance XXIII of 1870, commonly called the Contagious Diseases Ordinance. Straits Settlements Legislative Council Proceedings 1877, Appendix 7. (CDOSSLC in text).

Report of the Special Committee to Investigate and Report on the Bill for the Incorporation of Po Leung Kuk. Hong Kong Legislative Council Sessional Paper, 1 of 1887.

Report of the Venereal Diseases Committee. Council Paper No. 86, Straits Settlements Legislative Council Proceedings 1923, December 17, 1923, CO 275/109.

Woods, W.W. (1937) *Mui Tsai* in Hong Kong and Malaya: Report of Commission, His Majesty's Stationery Office, Colonial 125. London.

General Bibliography

Only published works and unpublished secondary sources (Ph.D. dissertations, etc.) cited in the text and directly relevant to the subjects discussed in this volume are listed. Works of general interest (e.g. introductions to sociology) are in endnotes.

Aijmer, G. (1967) 'Expansion and Extension in Hakka Society'. *Journal of the Hong Kong Branch of the Royal Asiatic Society (JHKBRAS)* 7.

Airlie, S. (1990) *Thistle and Bamboo. The Life and Times of Sir James Stewart Lockhart.* Oxford University Press, Hong Kong.

Albrecht-Heide, A. (1988) 'Women and War: Victims and Collaborators'. *Women and the Military System.* Edited by Eva Isaksson. Harvester-Wheatsheaf, London.

Andors, P. (1983) *The Unfinished Liberation of Chinese Women 1949-1980.* Indiana University Press, Bloomington, Indiana.

Asian and Pacific Development Centre (1987) Proceedings of the APDC-ACWF International Seminar on 'Agricultural Change and Rural Women'. APDC, Kuala Lumpur.

Atwell, P. (1985) *British Mandarins and Chinese Reformers: The British Administration of Weihaiwei, 1898-1930 and the Territory's Return to Chinese Rule.* Oxford University Press, Hong Kong.

Baker, H.D.R. (1968) *A Chinese Lineage Village: Sheung Shui.* Stanford University Press, Stanford. Frank Cass, London.

Barnett, K.M.A. (1974) 'Do Words From Extinct Pre-Chinese Languages Survive in Hong Kong Place-Names?' *Journal of the Hong Kong Branch of the Royal Asiatic Society (JHKBRAS)* 14.

Barrett, D.B. (ed.) (1982) *World Christian Encyclopedia: A Comparative Study of Churches and Religions in the Modern World AD 1900–2000.* Oxford University Press, Nairobi.

Beaver, R.P. (1980) *American Protestant Women in World Mission: A History of the First Feminist Movement in North America.* William B. Eerdsman Publishing Co., Grand Rapids, Michigan.

Bendelack, G.L. (1921) *The City of Rams*, London, Church Missionary Society, 1921.

Berry, M.L. (1893) 'San Francisco Homes'. WOBFM, *Annual Report*, SFTS.

Bevans, S. (1991) 'Seeing Mission Through Images'. *Missiology*, No. 1, January.

Blake, F. (1978) 'Death and Abuse in Marriage Laments: The Curse of the Chinese Bride'. *Asian Folklore Studies*, No. 37.

Boulding, E. (1988) 'Warriors and Saints: Dilemmas in the History of Men, Women and War', *Women and the Military System.* Edited by Eva Isaksson. Harvester-Wheatsheaf, London.

Boey C.K. (1974) 'A Sociological Study of the Shan Shui Women Construction Workers'. University of Singapore, Academic Exercise for the B. A. Degree.

Boulais, G. (1966) *Manuel du Code Chinois (Varietes Sinologiques No. 55)*. Shanghai, 1924, reprinted in Taipei, Ch'eng-wen Publishing Co.

Buck, J.L. (1937) *Land Utilization in China*. University of Nanking, Nanking.

Bulbeck, C. (1991) 'Hearing the Difference: First and Third World Feminisms'. *Asian Studies Review*, Asian Studies Association of Australia, Vol. 15, No. 1, July.

Bushnell, J.E. (1938) *The History of Westminster Presbyterian Church of Minneapolis, Minnesota*. The Lund Press, Minnesota.

Buxbaum, D. (1978) 'A Case Study of the Dynamics of Family Law and Social Change in Rural China'. *Chinese Family Law and Social Change*. Edited by D. Buxbaum. University of Washington Press, Seattle.

Campbell, P.C. (1923) *Chinese Coolie Emigration to Countries Within the British Empire*. London. Reprinted 1969, Negro Universities Press, New York.

Cameron, D. (1908–9) 'Report of the Mission Home Superintendent'. WOBFM, *Annual Report*, SFTS.

— (1919) 'Annual Report for Nineteen Nineteen'. WOBFM, *Annual Report*, SFTS.

— (1920) 'The Mission Home'. WOBFM, *Annual Report*, SFTS.

Chan, S.C. (1986) *This Bitter-Sweet Soil: The Chinese in California, 1860-1910*. University of California Press, Berkeley CA.

Chang C.C. (1960) *Enquiry into Hakka Creeds and Customs*. I-Ch'ing Publishing House, Taipei (Chinese text).

Chang, C.P. (1969) *K'u Ko Tzu Tz'u*. Yu Hua Publishing Society, Hong Kong.

Chen, H.S. (1936) *Landlord and Peasant in China: A Study of the Agrarian Crisis in South China*. International, New York.

Chen, K.Y. (1972) 'A Century of Chinese Christian Education: An Analysis of the True Light Seminary and its Successors in Canton and Hong Kong'. PhD. dissertation, University of Connecticut.

Chen, T. (1939) *Emigrant Communities in South China*. Kelly and Walsh, Shanghai.

— (1940) *Emigrant Communities in South China: A Study of Overseas Migration and its Influence on Standards of Living and Social Change*. Secretariat, Institute of Pacific Relations, New York.

Cheng, I. (1976) *Clara Ho Tung: A Hong Kong Lady, Her Family and Her Times*. The Chinese University of Hong Kong, Hong Kong.

Cheng L.K. (1985) *Social Change and the Chinese in Singapore*. Singapore University Press, Singapore.

Cheng, T.K. (1980) *The World of the Chinese: A Struggle for Human Unity*. Chinese University Press, Hong Kong.

— (1983) *Chinatown: An Album of a Singapore Community*. (1983) Times Books, Singapore.

Chinn, T. (1989) *Bridging the Pacific: San Francisco Chinatown and its People*. Chinese Historical Society of America, San Francisco.

Ch'u, T.T. (1961) *Law and Society in Traditional China*. Mouton, Paris.

Chun Fah (1888) 'Report of the Chinese Girls. Light House Mission Band'. WOBFM, *Annual Report*, SFTS.

Cohen, M.L. (1968) 'The Hakka or "Guest People": Dialect as a Sociocultural Variable in Southeastern China'. *Ethnohistory*, Vol. 15, No. 3.

— (1976) *House United, House Divided: The Chinese Family in Taiwan*. Columbia University Press, New York.

— (1992) 'Family Management and Family Division in Contemporary Rural China'. *China Quarterly*, June 1992.

Condit, I.M. (1874) 'Secretary's Report'. WOBFM, *First Annual Report*, SFTS.

— (1893) 'The Occidental Board: An Historic Board, 1873–1893'. WOBFM, *Statistical Report*, SFTS.

Connor, J.H. (1991) 'When Culture Leaves Contextualized Christianity Behind'. *Missiology*, No. 1, January.

Coolidge, M.R. (1909) *Chinese Immigration*. Henry Holt, New York.

Croll, E. (1974) *The Women's Movement in China: A Selection of Readings, 1949-1973*. Anglo-Chinese Educational Institute, London.

— (1981) *The Politics of Marriage in Contemporary China*. Cambridge University Press, Cambridge.

Crown, J.G. (1911–2) 'The Year's Work of the Occidental Board'. WOBFM, *Annual Report*, SFTS.

Culbertson, M. (1881) 'Missionary's Report'. WOBFM, *Annual Report*, SFTS.

— (1888) 'Report of Mission Home'. WOBFM, *Annual Report*, SFTS.

— (1890) 'Report of Chinese Mission Home'. WOBFM, *Annual Report*, SFTS.

Cummings, S. (1876) 'Missionary's Report'. WOBFM, *Annual Report*, SFTS.

— (1877) 'Missionary's Report'. WOBFM, *Annual Report*, SFTS.

Davin, D. (1975) 'Women in the Countryside in China'. *Women in Chinese Society*. Edited by M. Wolf & R. Witke. Stanford University Press, Stanford, California.

— (1976) *Woman-Work*. Clarendon Press, Oxford.

Davis, S.G. (ed.) (1964) *Land Use Problems in Hong Kong*. Hong Kong University Press, Hong Kong.

Dietrich, J. (1989) *Erinnerungen eines China-Missionars*. Ugarit Verlag, Muenster.

Dillon, R. (1962) *The Hatchet Men: The Story of the Tong Wars in San Francisco's Chinatown*. Coward-McCann, New York.

Dymond, M.M. (1928) *Yunnan*. Marshall Brothers Ltd, London.

Eberhard, W. (1972) *Cantonese Ballads*. Oriental Cultural Service, Taipei.

Ee, J. (1955) 'Chinese Migration to Singapore, 1896-1941.' Academic Exercise, University of Malaya, Singapore.

— (1961) 'Chinese Migration to Singapore, 1896–1941'. *Journal of Southeast Asian History*, 2.

Eitel, E.J. (1895) *Europe in China*. Kelly and Walsh, Hong Kong.

Endacott, G.B. (1958) *A History of Hong Kong*. Oxford University Press. Hong Kong.

Eng, R.Y. (1986) *Economic Imperialism in China: Silk Production and Exports, 1861-1932*. University of California Press, Berkeley.

— (1990) 'Luddism and Labor Protest among Silk Artisans and Workers in Jiangnan and Guangdong, 1860–1930'. *Late Imperial China*, Vol. 11, No. 2.

Evans, D.M. Emrys (1973) 'The New Law of Succession in Hong Kong'. *Hong Kong Law Review*, No. 3.

Fagg, M. (n.d.) *Two Golden Lilies from the Empire of the Rising Sun*. Church of England Zenana Missionary Society, Marshall Brothers, Ltd. London.

Fairbank, J.K. (ed.) (1974) *The Missionary Enterprise in China and America*. Harvard University Press, Cambridge.

Faure, D. (1986) *The Structure of Chinese Rural Society: Lineage and Village in the Eastern New Territories, Hong Kong*. Oxford University Press, Hong Kong.

Faure, D., J. Hayes & A. Birch (eds) (1984) *From Village to City, Studies in the Traditional Roots of Hong Kong Society*. Centre of Asian Studies, University of Hong Kong.

Fei H.T. (1949) *Peasant Life in China, A Field Study of Country Life*. London, Kegan Paul, Trench, Trubner, 1939.

— & C.I. Chang (1939) *Earthbound China, A Study of Rural Economy in Yunnan*. Routledge and Kegan Paul. London.

Fielde, A.L. (1884) *Pagoda Shadows, Studies from Life in China*. W.G. Corthell. Boston.

Flemming, L.A. (1989) 'Introduction: Studying Women Missionaries in Asia'. *Women's Work for Women: Missionaries and Social Change in Asia*. Edited by L.A. Flemming. Westview Press, Boulder.

Freedman, M. (1958) *Lineage Organization in Southeastern China*. Athlone, London.

— (1966) *Chinese Lineage and Society: Fukien and Kwangtung*. Athlone, London.

Gallin, B. & R. Gallin (1982) 'The Chinese Joint Family in Changing Rural Taiwan', *Social Interaction in Chinese Society*. Edited by S.L. Greenblatt, R.W. Wilson and A.A. Wilson. Pergamon Press, New York.

Gallin, R. (1984) 'Rural Industrialization and Chinese Women: A Case Study from Taiwan'. *Journal of Peasant Studies*, Vol. 12, No. 1.

Gamble, S. (1943) 'The Disappearance of Foot-Binding in Tinghsien'. *American Journal of Sociology*, Vol. 49, No. 2.

Garth, A. (1973) *Silent Invasion: the Chinese in South East Asia*. McDonald, London.

Gates, H. (1989) 'The Commoditization of Chinese Women'. *Signs*, Vol. 14, No. 4.

Gaw, K. (1988) *Superior Servants: The Legendary Cantonese Amahs of the Far East*. Oxford University Press, Singapore.

Gibson, O. (1877) *The Chinese in America*. Hitchcock & Walden, Cincinnati.

Giles, H.A. (1911) *The Civilization of China*, Thornton, Butterworth, Ltd. London.

Ginsberg, N. & C. Roberts (1958) *Malaya*. Washington Press.

Gittins, J. (Hotung) (1969) *Eastern Windows – Western Skies*. South China Morning Post, Hong Kong.

Gordon, D. (1988) 'Introduction: Feminism and the Critique of Colonial Discourse'. *Inscriptions*, UCSC, Santa Cruz, Nos. 3/4.

Gordon-Cumming, C.F. (1900) *Wanderings in China*. William Blackwood & Sons, Ltd. Edinburgh.

Gray, J.H. (1878) *China, A History of the Laws, Manners and Customs of the People*. 2 vols. Macmillan and Co. London.

Grimshaw, P. (1983) '"Christian Woman, Pious Wife, Faithful Mother, Devoted Missionary": Conflicts in Roles of American Missionary Women in Nineteenth-Century Hawaii'. *Feminist Studies*, Vol. 9, No. 3, Fall.

Gronewold, S. (1982) *Beautiful Merchandise: Prostitution in China 1860-1936*. The Institute for Research in History and the Haworth Press, New York.

Guangdong Funu Jiefang Xiehui (1926) 'The Association's Mission Hereafter'. *The Women's Liberation Association of Guangdong*. A Special Commemorative Issue, Guangzhou.

Guinness, M.G. (1894) *The Story of the China Inland Mission*. 2 vols. Morgan and Scott, London.

Hane, M. (1982) *Peasants, Rebels and Outcastes*. Pantheon Books, New York.

Hayes, J. (1967) 'The Japanese Occupation and the New Territories'. *South China Morning Post*, Hong Kong, 15 December 1967.

— (1977) *The Hong Kong Region 1850–1911, Institutions and Leadership in Town and Countryside*. Archon Books, Hamden.

— (1983) *The Rural Communities of Hong Kong, Studies and Themes*. Oxford University Press, Hong Kong.

— (1985) 'Specialists and Written Materials in the Village World'. *Popular Culture in Imperial China*. Edited by D. Johnson, A. Nathan & E. Rawski. University of California Press, Berkeley.

— (1990) 'Women and Female Children in Hong Kong and South China to 1949'. *Collected Essays on Various Historical Materials for Hong Kong Studies*. Urban Council, Hong Kong.

— (1991) 'Chinese Customary Law in the New Territories of Hong Kong: The Background to the Operation of the New Territories Ordinance, 1899–1987'. *Asian Profile*, 19, No. 2, April 1991.

Headland, I.T. (1912) *China's New Day, A Study of Events that have Led to its Coming*. The Central Committee on the United Study of Missions, West Medford, Mass.

Hensman, B. (1971) (compiler) *More Hong Kong Tale-Spinners, Twenty-five*

Traditional Chinese Tales Collected by Tape-Recorder and translated into English. The Chinese University Press, Hong Kong.

Hershatter, G. (1986) *The workers of Tianjin, 1900-1949*. Stanford California Press, Stanford.

— (1991) 'The Prostitutes of Shanghai'. *Marriage and Inequality in Chinese Society*. Edited by R. Watson & P. Buckley Ebrey. University of California Press, Berkeley.

Hirata, L.C. (1979) 'Free, Indentured, Enslaved: Chinese Prostitutes in Nineteenth Century America'. *Signs* 5 (1).

Ho, E.P. (1990) *The Welfare League: The Sixty Years 1930-1990*. Privately Printed, Hong Kong.

Hoe, S. (1991) *The Private Life of Old Hong Kong*. Oxford University Press, Hong Kong.

— (n.d.) '"It Made Their Blood Boil": The British Feminists' Campaign Against Licensed Prostitution in Hong Kong 1931.' Unpublished Manuscript.

Holder, C.F. (1897) 'Chinese Slavery in North America'. *North American Review*, 165 (490).

Honig, E. (1986) *Sisters and Strangers: Women in the Shanghai Cotton Mills, 1919-1949*. Stanford University Press, Stanford.

Honig, E. & G. Hershatter (1988) *Personal Voices*. Chinese Women in the 1980s. Stanford University Press, Stanford.

Houseworth, A.M. (1894) 'Report of Assistant'. WOBFM, *Annual Report*, SFTS.

Howard, C.W. (1923) *The Sericulture Industry of South China*. Canton Christian College, Canton.

Howard, C.W. & K.P. Buswell (1925) *A Study of the Silk Industry of South China*. Ling Nan Agricultural College, Agricultural Bulletin No. 12. The Commercial Press, Hong Kong.

Hsieh K. (1962) *K'ang Lu San Wen Chi*. Commercial Press, Taiwan.

Hsieh P.Y. (1943) *Autobiography of a Chinese Girl, A genuine autobiography*. George Allen and Unwin, London.

Hsieh, W. (1974) 'Peasant Insurrection and the Marketing Hierarchy in the Canton Delta, 1911'. *The Chinese City Between Two Worlds*. Edited by M. Elvin & G.W. Skinner. Stanford University Press, Stanford.

Hu, H.C. (1948) *The Common Descent Group in China and its Functions*. Viking Fund Publications in Anthropology, No. 10. Viking Fund, New York.

Huang, P. (1985) *The Peasant Economy and Social Change in North China*. Stanford University Press, Stanford.

— (1990) *The Peasant Family and Rural Development in the Yangzi Delta, 1350-1988*. Stanford University Press, Stanford.

Irick, R.L. (1982) *Ch'ing Policy Towards the Coolie Trade 1847-1878*. Chinese Materials Centre, Taipei.

Jackson, L. (1983) 'Prostitution'. *Chinese Women in Southeast Asia*. Edited by J. Lebra & J. Paulson. Times Books International, Singapore. Orig. published in 1980.

Jackson, R.N. (1961) *Immigrant Labour and the Development of Malaya, 1786-1920*. Government Press, Kuala Lumpur.

— (1965) *Pickering, Protector of Chinese*. Oxford University Press, Kuala Lumpur.

Jamieson, G. (1921) *Chinese Family and Commercial Law*. Kelly and Walsh, Shanghai.

Jaschok, M. (1981) 'A Social History of the Mooi Jai Institution in Hong Kong, 1843-1938'. Unpublished Ph.D. thesis, London University, S.O.A.S.

— (1984) 'On the Lives of Women Unwed by Choice in Pre-Communist China'. *Republican China*, Vol. 10, No. 1a., November.

— (1988) *Concubines and Bondservants*. Zed Books, London.

Johnson, E.L. (1976) 'Households and Lineages in a Chinese Urban Village'. Unpublished Ph.D. thesis, Cornell University. No. 77–18, University Microfilms, Ann Arbor.

— (1984) 'Great-Aunt Yeung: A Hakka Wage Laborer'. *Lives, Chinese Working Women*. Edited by M. Sheridan & J. Salaff. Bloomington, Indiana University Press, 1984.

— (1988) 'Grieving for the Dead, Grieving for the Living: Funeral Laments of Hakka Women'. *Death Ritual in Late Imperial and Modern China*. Edited by J.L. Watson & E.S. Rawski. University of California Press, Berkeley.

Johnson, K.A. (1983) *Women, the Family, and Peasant Revolution in China*. University of Chicago Press, Chicago.

Johnston, L.E. (1922) *(Peeps at Many Lands) China*. A. & C. Black, Third edition, London.

Johnston, R.F. (1910) *Lion and Dragon in Northern China*. John Murray, London.

Judd, E. (1989) 'Niangjia: Chinese Women and Their Natal Families'. *Journal of Asian Studies*, Vol. 48, No. 3.

Kani H. (1979) *Kindai Chugoku no kuri to choka (The Coolies and 'Slave Girls' of Modern China)*. Tokyo. Chinese translation: Sun G.Q. and Chao C.P. (1990) *Juhua – bei fanmai haiwai di funu*. Henan Renmin Chuban She.

Keller, R.S. (1981) 'Lay Women in the Protestant Tradition'. *Women and Religion in America*. Edited by R.R. Reuther & R.S. Keller. Vol. I. Harper & Row, San Francisco.

Kidd, S. (1841) *China, Or Illustrations of the Symbols, Philosophy, Antiquities, Customs, Superstitions, Laws, Government, Education and Literature of the Chinese*. Taylor and Walton, London.

Ko, D. (1989) 'Toward a Social History of Women in Seventeenth Century China'. Unpublished Ph.D. thesis, Stanford University.

Kopytoff, I. & S. Miers (1977) 'African Slavery as an Institution of Marginality'. *Slavery in Africa: Historical and Anthropological Perspectives*. Edited by S. Miers & I. Kopytoff. University of Wisconsin Press, Madison WI.

Kulp, D.H. (1925) *Country life in South China, The Sociology of Familism*.

Vol. 1, Phenix Village, Kwantung, China. Teachers' College, Columbia University, New York.

Lai A.E. (1986) *Peasants, Proletarians and Prostitutes. A Preliminary Investigation into the Work of Chinese Women in Colonial Malaya*. Institute of Southeast Asian Studies, Singapore.

Lang, O. (1946) *Chinese Family and Society*. Yale University Press, New Haven.

Lau S.K. (1990) *Decolonization Without Independence and the Poverty of Political Leaders in Hong Kong*. Hong Kong Institute of Asia-Pacific Studies, Hong Kong, Occasional Papers No. 1, November.

Lebra, J. (1983) 'Immigration to Southeast Asia'. *Chinese Women in Southeast Asia*. Edited by J. Lebra & J. Paulson. Times Books International, Singapore. Orig. published in 1980.

Lee, F. (1986) 'The Careers of Village Women: Some Case Studies'. *Proceedings of the Eighth International Symposium on Asian Studies 1986*. Vol. 1, China. Hong Kong, Asian Research Service.

Lee L.T. (1988) *Early Chinese Immigrant Societies: Case Studies from North America and British Southeast Asia*. Heinemann Asia, Singapore.

Lee P.P. (1978) *Chinese Society in Nineteenth Century Singapore*. Oxford University Press, Kuala Lumpur.

Lethbridge, J.H. (1978) 'Prostitution in Hong Kong: A Legal and Moral Dilemma'. *Hong Kong Law Journal*.

— (1978a) 'The Evolution of a Chinese Voluntary Association in Hong Kong'. *Hong Kong: Stability and Change*. Edited by J.H. Lethbridge. Oxford University Press, Hong Kong.

— (1978b) 'Sir James Stewart Lockhart: Colonial Civil Servant and Scholar'. *Hong Kong: Stability and Change*. Edited by J.H. Lethbridge. Oxford University Press, Hong Kong.

Leung, P.C. (1978) *Wooden-fish Books: Critical Essays and an Annotated Catalogue Based on the Collections in the University of Hong Kong*. Hong Kong University Press, Hong Kong.

Levy, M.J. Jr (1968) *The Family Revolution in Modern China*, Atheneum Paperback, New York.

Lewis, J. (1986) *Women in England 1870–1950*. Wheatsheaf Books, Sussex. First published in 1984.

Li C.C. (1975) 'A Description of Singapore in 1887'. *China Society Twenty Fifth Anniversary Journal*.

Li, L.M. (1981) *China's Silk Trade: Traditional Industry in the Modern World, 1842-1937*. Harvard University Press, Cambridge.

Lim, J. (1958) *Sold For Silver: An Autobiography by Janet Lim*, William Collins & Sons, London, reprinted 1985 Oxford University Press, Singapore, Oxford and New York.

Lim J.H. (1967) 'Female Immigration into the Straits Settlements, 1860–1901'. *Journal of South Seas Society* Vol. xxii.

Lim S.H. (1983) 'Chinese Women in Early Twentieth Century Singapore'.

Department of Chinese Studies, National University of Singapore, Academic Exercise.

Lin, S.T. (1975) 'Chinese Women on the Road to Complete Emancipation'. *Women in the World: A Comparative Study.* Edited by L.B. Iglitzin & R. Ross. Clio Press, Santa Barbara, California.

Lin Y.H. (1947) *The Golden Wing, A Sociological Study of Chinese Familism.* Kegan Paul, Trench, Trubner, London.

Little, Mrs A. (1912) *In the Land of the Blue Gown.* London.

Liu, H.C. (1959) *The Traditional Chinese Clan Rules.* J.J. Augustin, Locust Valley, N.Y.

Livingston, D. (1977) 'The Chinese as Sojourners: A study in the Sociology of Migration'. The City University of New York, unpublished Ph. D. Dissertation.

Logan, L.E. (1976) *Ventures in Mission: The Cameron House Story.* Privately printed.

Lou T.K. (1968) *Chieh-hun Chih.* Commercial Press, Taiwan.

Lum, R.D. (1985) 'Philanthropy and Public Welfare in Late Imperial China'. Ph.D. Thesis in History, Harvard University.

Ma, L.E.A. (1990) *Revolutionaries, Monarchists, and Chinatowns: Chinese Politics in the Americas and the 1911 Revolution.* University of Hawaii Press, Honolulu.

Maclay, R.S. (1861) *Life Among the Chinese: With Characteristic Sketches and Incidents.* Carlton and Porter, New York.

McCutcheon, J.M. (1991) 'Protestant Missionaries in Asia and the Pacific: Agents of Change for What Purpose?'. A Paper Presented at the 12th Conference of Asian Historians, Hong Kong.

McLeod, A. (1947) *Pigtails and Gold Dust.* The Caxton Publishers, Caldwell, Idaho.

Mallory, W.H. (1926) *China: Land of Famine.* American Geographical Society, New York.

Mani, L. (1990) 'Multiple Mediations: Feminist Scholarship in the Age of Multinational Reception'. *Feminist Review,* No. 35, Summer.

Martin, M.C. (1977) *Chinatown's Angry Angel: The Story of Donaldina Cameron.* Pacific Books, Palo Alto, California.

Martin, W.A.P. (1896) *A Cycle of Cathay, or China South and North.* Fleming H. Revell Company, New York.

Mason, S.R. (1981) 'The Chinese'. *They Chose Minnesota: A Survey of the State's Ethnic Groups.* Edited by J.D. Holmquist. Minnesota Historical Society, St Paul, Minnesota.

Meijer, M.J. (1979) 'Slavery at the end of the Ch'ing dynasty'. *China's Legal Tradition.* Edited by J.A. Cohen, F.M. Ch'en and R. Edwards. Princeton University Press, Princeton.

Meillassoux, C. (1983) 'Female Slavery'. *Women and Slavery in Africa.* Edited by C. Robertson & M. Klein. University of Wisconsin Press, Madison.

Miners, N. (1987) *Hong Kong Under Imperial Rule, 1912-1941.* Oxford University Press, Hong Kong.

— (1990) 'The Attempts to Abolish the Muitsai System in Hong Kong 1917-1941'. *Between East and West. Aspects of Social and Political Development in Hong Kong.* Edited by E. Sinn. Centre of Asian Studies, Hong Kong University, Hong Kong.

Mohanty, C. (1988) 'Under Western Eyes: Feminist Scholarship and Colonial Discourses'. *Feminist Review*, No. 30, Autumn.

Neill, S.C. (1966) *Colonialism and Christian Missions.* McGraw-Hill, New York.

Nevius, J.L. (1882) *China and the Chinese.* Presbyterian Board of Publication, Philadelphia.

Niccol-Jones, S.E. (1941) 'Report on the Problem of Prostitution in Singapore.' Mss. Ind. Ocn. S203, Rhodes House Library, Oxford.

Ng, V.W. (1987) 'Ideology and Sexuality: Rape Laws in Qing China'. *Journal of Asian Studies*, No. 46.

Noble, D.W. (1981) *The Progressive Mind: 1890-1917.* Burgess Publishing, Minneapolis, Minnesota.

Norton-Kyshe, J.W. (1971) *The History of the Laws and Courts of Hong Kong.* 2 vols. Vetch and Lee, Hong Kong. First published 1898.

Ocko, J. (1991) 'Women, Property, and Law in the People's Republic of China'. *Marriage and Inequality in Chinese Society.* Edited by R. Watson & P. Ebrey. University of California Press, Berkeley.

Ong, A. (1987) *Spirits of Resistance and Capitalist Discipline.* State University of New York Press, New York.

— (1988) 'Colonialism and Modernity: Feminist Re-Presentations of Women in Non-Western Societies'. *Inscriptions*, Nos. 3/4. UCSC, Santa Cruz.

Pagel, A. (ed.) (1979) *So War's In China.* Francke Buchhandlung GmbH, Marburg a.d. Lahn.

Palmer, M.J. (1991) 'Lineage and Urban Development in a New Territories Market Town'. *An Old State in New Settings, Studies in the Social Anthropology of China in Memory of Maurice Freedman.* Edited by H.D.R. Baker & S. Feuchtwang. Journal of the Anthropological Society of Oxford, Oxford.

Parish, W.L. & M.K. Whyte (1978) *Village and Family in Contemporary China.* University of Chicago Press, Chicago.

Pascoe, P. (1990) *Relations of Rescue: The Search for Moral Authority in the American West, 1874-1939.* Oxford University Press, New York.

Pasternak, B. (1983) *Guests in the Dragon: Social Demography of a Chinese District, 1895-1946.* Columbia University Press, New York.

Phillips, F.C.N. (1876) 'Report of Missionary and Matron'. WOBFM, *Annual Report*, STFS.

— (1878) 'Journal'. In report by Robbins, P. (no title), WOBFM, *Annual Report*, SFTS.

Pinney, H.B. (1894) 'Twenty-first Annual Meeting'. WOBFM, *Annual Report*, SFTS.

Pitt, K.W. (1978) 'Chinese Coolie Immigrants in Nineteenth Century Singapore'. *Review of Southeast Asian Studies*, Volume XIV.

Po Leung Kuk (PLK in text) (1978) *Centenary History of the Po Leung Kuk 1878–1978*. Board of Directors, Hong Kong.

Potter, J. (1974) 'Cantonese Shamanism'. *Religion and Ritual in Chinese Society*. Edited by A. Wolf. Stanford University Press, Stanford.

Potter, S.H. & J.M. Potter (1990) *China's Peasants, The Anthropology of a Revolution*. Cambridge University Press, Cambridge.

Pruitt, I. (1979) *Old Madam Yin: A Memoir of Peking Life 1926–1938*. Stanford University Press,

Quahe, Y. (1986) *We Remember Cameos of Pioneer Life*. Landmark Books, Singapore.

Rankin, M.B. (1975) 'The Emergence of Women at the End of the Ch'ing: The Case of Ch'iu Chin'. *Women in Chinese Society*. Edited by M. Wolf & R. Witke. Stanford University Press, Stanford.

Renmin Ribao (1990) 'Many Abducted Women, Children Rescued'. Beijing, 30 December.

Renmin Gongan Bao (1991) 'Resolutely Crack Down on Underworld Criminal Gangs'. Beijing, 6 August.

Reynaud, C.M. (1897) *Another China, Notes on the Celestial Empire as Viewed by a Catholic Bishop*. Dublin.

Robbins, P. (1874) 'An Appeal in Behalf of Woman's Work for Woman, Made at the Recent Annual Meeting'. WOBFM, *Annual Report*, SFTS.

— (1878) 'Secretary's Report'. WOBFM, *Annual Report*, SFTS.

Robertson, C. & M. Klein (1983) 'Women's Importance in African Slave Systems'. *Women and Slavery in Africa*. Edited by C. Robertson & M. Klein. University of Wisconsin Press, Madison.

Rosen, R. (1982) *The Lost Sisterhood: Prostitution in America, 1900–1918*. The Johns Hopkins University Press, Baltimore.

Said, E.W. (1979) *Orientalism*. Vintage Books, New York. Orig. published in 1978.

— (1985) 'Orientalism Reconsidered'. *Race & Class*, Vol. 27, No. 2.

Sankar, A. (1978) 'Female Domestic Service in Hong Kong'. *Female Servants and Economic Development*. Edited by L. Tilly *et al*. Michigan Occasional Papers in Women's Studies, Ann Arbor, No. 1.

— (1984) 'Spinster Sisterhoods: Jing Yih Sifu, Spinster-Domestic Nun'. *Lives: Chinese Working Women*. Edited by M. Sheridan & J. Salaff. Indiana University Press, Bloomington, Indiana.

Sayer, G.R. (1937) *Hong Kong 1841–1862. Birth. Adolescence and Coming of Age*. Oxford University Press, Hong Kong.

Schumsky, N.L. (1986) 'Tacit Acceptance: Respectable Americans and Segregated Prostitutes, 1870–1910'. *Journal of Social History*, Vol. 19, No. 4.

Seagrave, S. (1985) *The Soong Dynasty*. Harper & Row, New York.

Sheridan, J. (1975) *China in Disintegration: The Republican Era in Chinese History 1912-1949.* The Free Press, New York.

Sheridan, M. & J.W. Salaff (eds) (1984) *Lives. Chinese Working Women.* Indiana University Press, Bloomington, Indiana.

Silber, C. (1992) 'From Daughter to Daughter-in-law in the Women's Script (Nushu) of Southern Hunan'. Paper presented at Conference 'Engendering China: Women, Culture, and the State'. Harvard University and Wellesley College, February 7–9.

Sinn, E. (1984) 'Materials for Historical Research: Source Materials on the Tung Wah Hospital 1869-1941'. *Research Materials for Hong Kong Studies.* Edited by A. Birch, Y.C. Jao & E. Sinn, Centre of Asian Studies, Hong Kong University, Hong Kong.

— (1989) *Power and Charity: The Early History of the Tung Wah Hospital, Hong Kong.* Oxford University Press, Hong Kong.

— (1990) (ed.) *Between East and West: Aspects of Social and Political Development in Hong Kong.* Centre of Asian Studies, Hong Kong University, Hong Kong.

Siu, B. (1982) *Women of China: Imperialism and Women's Resistance 1900-1949.* Zed Press, London.

Siu, H. (1989) *Agents and Victims in South China: Accomplices in Rural Revolution.* Stanford University Press, Stanford.

— (1990) 'Where Were the Women? Rethinking Marriage Resistance and Regional Culture in South China'. *Late Imperial China,* Vol. 11, No. 2.

Smith, C.T. (1981) 'The Chinese Church, Labour and Elites and the Mui Tsai Question in the 1920s'. *Journal of the Hong Kong Branch of the Royal Asiatic Society (JHKBRAS)* 21.

So, A.Y. (1986) *The South China Silk District: Local Historical Transformation and World-System Theory.* State University of New York Press, Albany.

Song H.B. (1991) 'Fanzuide falu wenti; daji guaimai funu ertong' (Legal Issues pertaining to Criminality; cracking down on the Abduction and Selling of Women and Children). *Fazhi Ribao,* Beijing, April.

Song O.S. (1923) *One Hundred Years' History of the Chinese in Singapore.* Methuen, London. Reprinted University of Malaya Press, Kuala Lumpur, 1967, and Oxford University Press, Singapore, 1987.

Spence, J.D. (1981) *The Gate of Heavenly Peace: the Chinese and their Revolution, 1895–1980.* Viking Press, New York.

Srisang, K. *et al.* (eds) (1991) *Caught in Modern Slavery: Tourism and Child Prostitution in Asia.* The Ecumenical Coalition on Third World Tourism, Bangkok.

Srisang, S.S. (1991) 'Tourism and Child Prostitution in Thailand'. *Caught in Modern Slavery: Tourism and Child Prostitution in Asia.* Edited by K. Srisang *et al.* The Ecumenical Coalition on Third World Tourism, Bangkok.

Stacey, J. (1983) *Patriarchy and Socialist Revolution in China.* University of California Press, Berkeley.

Stockard, J. (1989) *Daughters of the Canton Delta: Marriage Patterns and Economic Strategies in South China, 1860–1930*. Stanford University Press, Stanford.

Strauch, J. (1983) 'Community and Kinship in Southeastern China: The View from the Multilineage Villages of Hong Kong'. *Journal of Asian Studies*, Vol. 43, No. 1.

Sun, G.Q. (1988) *Jiu Shanghai Changji Mishi* (The Inside Story of Prostitutes in Old Shanghai). Henan Renmin Chubanshe.

Tang C.H. (1961) 'The Cantonese Women Building Labourers: A Study of a Group of Samsui Women in the Building Trade'. University of Singapore, Academic Exercise for B.A. Degree.

Tang H. (1989) 'Nongcun funude ruogan wenti fenxi' (An Analysis of certain Issues pertaining to Peasant Women). *Nongcun Jingji Yu Shehui*, June.

Terrill, R. (1984) *The white-boned demon: a biography of Madame Mao Zedong*. Heinemann, London.

Tomoko, Y. (1975) 'Sandakan No. 8 Brothel'. *Bulletin of Concerned Asian Scholars*.

Topley, M. (1952) 'Chinese Rites for the Repose of the Soul with Special Reference to Cantonese Custom'. *Journal of the Malayan Branch of the Royal Asiatic Society*, Part 1, No. 25.

— (1954) 'Chinese Women's Vegetarian Houses in Singapore'. *Journal of the Malayan Branch of the Royal Asiatic Society*, Vol. 27, No. 1.

— (1958) 'The Organisation and Social Functions of Chinese Women's Chaitang in Singapore'. University of London, Ph. D. Dissertation.

— (1959) 'Immigrant Chinese Female Servants and their Hostels in Singapore'. *Man*, No. 59.

— (1975) 'Marriage Resistance in Rural Kwangtung'. *Women in Chinese Society*. Edited by M. Wolf & R. Witke. Stanford University Press, Stanford.

Tremewan, C. (ed.) (1985) *Faith in Modernization*. CCA Youth, Christian Conference of Asia, Singapore.

Trinh, T.M.H. (1988) 'Not You/Like You: Post-Colonial Women and the Interlocking Questions of Identity and Difference'. *Inscriptions*, UCSC, Santa Cruz, Nos.3/4.

Trocki, C. (1979) *Prince of Pirates: The Temenggongs and the Development of Johore and Singapore 1784–1885*. Singapore University Press, Singapore.

Tseng, P.S. (1931) 'The Chinese Woman Past and Present'. *Symposium on Chinese Culture*. Edited by S.H. Chen Zen. China Institute of Pacific Relations, Shanghai.

Turnbull, C.M. (1972)*The Straits Settlements 1826-67: Indian Presidency to Crown Colony*. Oxford University Press, Singapore.

— (1977) *A History of Singapore 1819–1975*. Oxford University Press, Singapore.

Van Der Valk, M.H. (1939) *An Outline of Modern Chinese Family Law*. Henri Vetch, Peking.

— (1949) *Interpretations of the Supreme Court at Peking, Years 1915 and 1916*. Originally published at Batavia 1949, reprinted Paragon Book Company, n.d., New York.

Vaughan, J.D. (1974) *The Manners and Customs of the Chinese of the Straits Settlements*. Oxford University Press, Kuala Lumpur.

Visweswaran, K. (1988) 'Defining Feminist Ethnography'. *Inscriptions*, UCSC, Santa Cruz, Nos. 3/4.

Wakeman, F. (1966) *Strangers at the Gate: Social Disorder in South China, 1839–1861*. University of California Press, Berkeley.

— (1975) *The Fall of Imperial China*. The Free Press, New York.

Walby, S. (1990) *Theorizing Patriarchy*. Basil Blackwell, Oxford.

Wang Y. (1989) *The Child Bride*. Foreign Languages Press, Beijing.

Warner, M. (1972) *The Dragon Empress: The Life and Times of Tz'u-hsi, Empress Dowager of China, 1835–1908*. MacMillan, New York.

Warren, J.F. (1986) *Rickshaw Coolie. A People's History of Singapore (1880–1940)*. Oxford University Press, Singapore.

— (1987) *At the Edge of South East Asian History*. New Day Press, Quezon City.

Watson, J.L. (1975a) 'Agnates and Outsiders: Adoption in a Chinese Lineage'. *Man*, No. 10.

— (1975b) *Emigration and the Chinese Lineage: The Mans in Hong Kong and London*. University of California Press, Berkeley.

— (1976) 'Chattel Slavery in Chinese Peasant Society: A Comparative Analysis'. *Ethnology*, No. 15.

— (1977) 'Hereditary Tenancy and Corporate Landlordism in Traditional China: A Case Study'. *Modern Asian Studies*, No. 11.

— (1980) 'Transactions in People: The Chinese Market in Slaves, Servants, and Heirs'. *Asian and African Systems of Slavery*. Edited by J.L. Watson. Basil Blackwell, Oxford.

— (1991) 'Waking the Dragon: Visions of the Chinese Imperial State in Village Myth'. *An Old State in a New Setting: Studies in the Social Anthropology of China in Memory of Maurice Freedman*. Edited by H. Baker & S. Feuchtwang. *Journal of Anthropological Society of Oxford*, Occasional Papers, No. 8.

— (1993) *Ah Ku and Karayuki-san Prostitution in Singapore 1870–1940*. Oxford University Press, Singapore.

Watson, R. (1981) 'Class Differences and Affinal Relations in South China'. *Man*, No. 16.

— (1985) *Inequality among Brothers: Class and Kinship in South China*. Cambridge University Press, Cambridge.

— (1990a) 'Confucian Daughters? China and Korea'. Paper presented at Sixth International Conference on Korean Studies, The Academy of Korean Studies.

— (1990b) 'Corporate Property and Local Leadership in the Pearl River Delta,

1898–1941'. *Chinese Local Elites and Patterns of Dominance*. University of California Press, Berkeley.

— (1991a) 'Afterword: Marriage and Gender Inequality'. *Marriage and Inequality in Chinese Society*. Edited by R. Watson & P. Buckley Ebrey. University of California Press, Berkeley.

— (1991b) 'Wives, Concubines, and Maids: Servitude and Kinship in the Hong Kong Region, 1900–1940'. *Marriage and Inequality in Chinese Society*. Edited by R. Watson & P. Buckley Ebrey. University of California Press, Berkeley.

— (n.d.) 'Dutiful Daughters and Loyal Wives: Women and Community in South China'. Manuscript.

Wehle, F. (1950) *Lien-min. Die Geschichte einer erbarmungswuerdigen kleinen Chinesin*. Marburg a.d. Lahn.

— (1974) *Darum Gehe Hin*. Haenssler Verlag, Stuttgart-Neuhausen.

Wilson, C.G. (1974) *Chinatown Quest: 100 Years of Donaldina Cameron House 1874–1974*. California Historical Society, San Francisco.

Wing, M. (1903) *'Report of Native House to House Visitor'*. WOBFM, Annual Report, SFTS.

Witke, R. (1977) *Comrade Chiang Ching*. Weidenfield and Nicolson, London.

Wolf, A. (1975) 'The Women of Hai-shan: A Demographic Portrait'. *Women in Chinese Society*. Edited by M. Wolf & R. Witke. Stanford University Press, Stanford.

— & Huang C.S. (1980) *Marriage and Adoption in China, 1845–1945*. Stanford University Press, Stanford.

Wolf, M. (1968) *The House of Lin, A Study of a Chinese Farm Family*. Appleton-Century-Crofts, New York.

— (1972) *Women and the Family in Rural Taiwan*. Stanford University Press, Stanford.

— (1975) 'Women and Suicide in China'. *Women in Chinese Society*. Edited by M. Wolf & R. Witke. Stanford University Press, Stanford.

— (1985) *Revolution Postponed: Women in Contemporary China*. Stanford University Press, Stanford.

Wright, M. (1983) 'Bwanika: Consciousness and Protest among Slave Women in Central Africa, 1886-1911'. *Women and Slavery in Africa*. Edited by C. Robinson & M. Klein. University of Wisconsin Press, Madison.

Wu Z.X. (1989) *Green Bamboo Hermitage*. Panda Books, Chinese Literature Press, Beijing.

Xiang H. (translated by H. Goldblatt) (1988) *Tales of Hulan River*. Hong Kong, Joint Publishing (HK) Ltd.

Yang, C.K. (1965) *Chinese Communist Society: The Family and the Village*. M.I.T. Press, Cambridge, Massachusetts.

Yen C.H. (1981) 'Early Chinese Clan Organisations in Singapore and Malaya 1819–1911'. *Journal of Southeast Asian Studies (JSEAS)*, Vol. 12, No. 1.

— (1985) *Coolies and Mandarins: China's Protection of Overseas Chinese*

During the Late Ch'ing Period (1851–1911). Singapore University Press, Singapore.

— (1986) *A Social History of the Chinese in Singapore and Malaya 1800–1911*. Oxford University Press, Singapore.

Yeo S.N. (1986) *Pre-War Literature in Singapore and Malaysia: Reflections about the Lives of Chinese Workers*. Singapore Employees' Association, Singapore.

Yeung, P. (1985) 'Bibliography of New Territories Historical Literature'. *Journal of the Hong Kong Branch of the Royal Asiatic Society (JHKBRAS)* 25.

Yong C.F. (1977) 'Leadership and Power in the Chinese Community of Singapore During the 1930s'. *Journal of Southeast Asian Studies (JSEAS)*, Vol. VIII, No. 2.

Yung, S.S. (1987) 'Mu-yu Shu and the Cantonese Popular Singing Arts'. *The Giest Library Journal*, Vol. 2, No. 1.

Zunz, O. (1985) *Reliving the Past: The Worlds of Social History*. University of North Carolina Press, Chapel Hill.

Index